REFLECTIONS AND NEW PERSPECTIVES ON VIRGIL'S *GEORGICS*

REFLECTIONS AND NEW PERSPECTIVES ON VIRGIL'S *GEORGICS*

Edited by

Bobby Xinyue & Nicholas Freer

BLOOMSBURY ACADEMIC

LONDON • NEW YORK • OXFORD • NEW DELHI • SYDNEY

BLOOMSBURY ACADEMIC
Bloomsbury Publishing Plc
50 Bedford Square, London, WC1B 3DP, UK
1385 Broadway, New York, NY 10018, USA

BLOOMSBURY, BLOOMSBURY ACADEMIC and the Diana logo are trademarks of
Bloomsbury Publishing Plc

First published in Great Britain 2019
Paperback edition first published 2020

Library of Congress Cataloging-in-Publication Data
Names: Xinyue, Bobby, editor. | Freer, Nicholas, editor.
Title: Reflections and new perspectives on Virgil's Georgics / edited by
Bobby Xinyue & Nicholas Freer.
Description: London : Bloomsbury Academic, 2019. | Includes bibliographical
references and index.
Identifiers: LCCN 2018040922| ISBN 9781350070516 (hardback) | ISBN 9781350070530 (epub)
Subjects: LCSH: Virgil. Georgica. | Virgil—Influence.
Classification: LCC PA6804.G4 R44 2019 | DDC 871/.01—dc23 LC record
available at https://lccn.loc.gov/2018040922

ISBN: HB: 978-1-3500-7051-6
PB: 978-1-3501-7748-2
ePDF: 978-1-3500-7052-3
eBook: 978-1-3500-7053-0

Typeset by RefineCatch Ltd, Bungay, Suffolk

To find out more about our authors and books visit www.bloomsbury.com
and sign up for our newsletters.

CONTENTS

CONTRIBUTORS

William M. Barton is a key researcher at the Ludwig Boltzmann Institute for Neo-Latin Studies, Innsbruck, Austria. His research has focused on engagements with the natural environment and landscape in Neo-Latin literature, in particular the shifting attitudes towards the mountain as an extreme locus of nature in the early modern period and the creation of literary concepts of 'landscape' from the Renaissance to the present day. Barton's more recently published work in these fields includes the monograph *Mountain Aesthetics in Early Modern Latin Literature* (2017).

Susanna Braund moved to the University of British Columbia in 2007 to take up a Canada Research Chair in Latin Poetry and its Reception after teaching previously at Stanford University, Yale University and the Universities of London, Bristol and Exeter. She has published extensively on Roman satire and Latin epic poetry among other aspects of Latin literature. She has translated Lucan for the Oxford World's Classics series and Persius and Juvenal for the Loeb Classical Library. She held a Killam Research Fellowship in 2016–18 for her major project 'Virgil Translated'.

Robert Cowan is Senior Lecturer in Classics at the University of Sydney, having previously held posts in Exeter, Bristol and Oxford. His research interests range over much of Greek and Latin poetry, and he has published on Sophocles, Aristophanes, Plautus, Lucretius, Catullus, Cicero, Cinna, Ticida, Virgil, Horace, Ovid, Columella, Martial, Suetonius and Juvenal, as well as ancient graffiti and the operatic reception of Greek tragedy. However, his main specialisms are imperial epic and republican tragedy.

Katharine M. Earnshaw is a lecturer in Classics at the University of Exeter. She works on Latin hexameter poetry (Virgil, Lucretius, Lucan) and is especially interested in conceptions of time, space and landscape. She co-manages the 'Cognitive Classics' website, and is currently co-editing a volume on mental imagery and classical poetry, which draws on neuroscientific and philosophical understandings of the mind and the imagination. Her work on the *Georgics* has led to collaborative activities with farmers in Devon, and, related to this, she is about to begin a funded project on digital approaches to imagined (didactic) spaces.

Nicholas Freer teaches at the University of Iceland, having previously held positions as Lecturer in Classics and Postdoctoral Research Fellow at the University of Durham. He has published on a range of topics relating to Latin literature and its reception, and he is currently writing a book on Virgil's engagement with the works of Philodemus.

Elena Giusti is currently Assistant Professor in Latin Literature and Language at the University of Warwick. She is the author of *Carthage in Virgil's* Aeneid: *Staging the Enemy under Augustus* (2018) and is currently writing a book for I.B.Tauris Bloomsbury on Dido of Carthage and her reception.

S. J. Heyworth has been Bowra Fellow and Tutor in Classics at Wadham College, Oxford since 1988; he is Professor of Latin in the University. In 2007 he issued a new Oxford Classical Text of Propertius together with a detailed textual commentary entitled *Cynthia*. With James Morwood he has produced literary and grammatical commentaries on Propertius 3 (2011) and *Aeneid* 3 (2017). His main focus is now on Ovid's *Fasti*: in 2019 a commentary on book 3 will appear in the Cambridge Greek and Latin Classics series, to be followed by an Oxford Classical Text of the whole poem.

Ailsa Hunt is a lecturer in Ancient History at the University of Birmingham. Her research interests include Roman religion and the history of its scholarship, and Roman attitudes to nature. Her first monograph was published in 2016: *Reviving Roman Religion: Sacred Trees in the Roman World*.

Tom Mackenzie is the A. G. Leventis Research Fellow in Ancient Greek Culture at University College London. His research focuses on the intersection between ancient philosophy and literature, with particular interests in the Presocratics and didactic poetry. He has published articles on Parmenides and Empedocles.

Sara Myers is Professor of Classics at the University of Virginia. She is the author of *Ovid's Causes: Cosmogony and Aetiology in the Metamorphoses* (1994), a commentary on Ovid's *Metamorphoses* 14 (2009) and articles on Ovid, Catullus, Roman Elegy, Roman gardens and Statius. Her current research interests include ancient garden literature, gender and genre, and the poetics of commencement.

Martin Stöckinger is a lecturer ('Wissenschaftlicher Assistent') in Classics at the University of Cologne. Before that he taught at the University of Heidelberg and the Humboldt University Berlin. He is a co-editor of *Horace and Seneca: Interactions, Intertexts, Interpretations* (2017) and the author of *Vergils Gaben: Materialität, Reziprozität und Poetik in den* Eklogen *und der* Aeneis (2016) as well as articles on republican and early imperial Latin literature. His new project is concerned with the depiction of writing in Roman historiography.

Richard F. Thomas is George Martin Lane Professor of the Classics at Harvard University. He teaches and writes on Hellenistic Greek and Roman literature, intertextuality, aesthetics, reception and Bob Dylan. Publications include more than 100 articles and reviews and the following books: *Lands and Peoples in Roman Poetry* (1982), *Reading Virgil and his Texts* (1999), *Virgil and the Augustan Reception* (2001) and *Why Bob Dylan Matters* (2017); and commentaries on Virgil, *Georgics* (1988) and Horace, *Odes* 4 and *Carmen Saeculare* (2011). He has co-edited and contributed to *Classics and the Uses of Reception* (2006), *Bob Dylan's Performance Artistry* (2007) and the *Virgil Encyclopedia* (2014).

Bobby Xinyue is British Academy Postdoctoral Fellow at the University of Warwick. He works on Latin literature of the Augustan age and its reception in the early modern period. He has published articles on Virgil, Cicero and Propertius, as well as a number of Neo-Latin poets. He is currently writing a book on poetic representations of the divinisation of Augustus.

PREFACE

This volume began its life as an international conference held at University College London in April 2014; most of the chapters are based on papers presented at the conference. Some papers did not make it into the present volume, but we would like to offer our heartfelt thanks to the participants for their contribution and stimulating discussion.

We would also like to thank the following, without whose support, generosity and enthusiasm the present volume would not have been possible: Fiachra Mac Góráin, Tom Geue, Stephen Harrison, Damien Nelis, Maria Wyke, and Alice Wright and Emma Payne at Bloomsbury. Of course, we would also like to thank the contributors and the anonymous readers for their hard work and encouragement.

In addition, Bobby Xinyue would like to thank the British Academy for the award of a Postdoctoral Fellowship, which enabled him to undertake much of the editorial work for this book.

NOTES ON THE TEXT

The text of Virgil used in this volume is the Oxford Classical Text by R. A. B. Mynors (ed.), *P. Vergili Maronis Opera* (Oxford, 1969). Abbreviations of ancient authors and texts follow the conventions of *OCD*⁴ and *OLD*. All translations are our own, unless otherwise stated.

INTRODUCTION
Bobby Xinyue and Nicholas Freer

To borrow a few words from Seneca's famous line about Virgil's *Georgics*, the present volume has no grand ambitions 'to instruct', though it does aim to achieve more than just 'to delight readers'.[1] As its title suggests, this collection has two central objectives: first, to generate thoughtful new readings of the *Georgics* which *reflect* the major scholarly concerns and activities of Virgilian studies since the turn of the twenty-first century; and second, to present innovative and heretofore underutilized *perspectives* – approaches, interpretive methods, and ways of reading the *Georgics* – which we hope will promote further explorations of the poem.

In the years following the publication of Katharina Volk's *Vergil's Georgics: Oxford Readings in Classical Studies* (2008) – itself a very reflective work gathering ten classic essays written between 1970 and 1999 – there has been no shortage of provocative and worthwhile studies of the *Georgics*, many of which have significantly advanced our understanding of the poem. The aim of this introduction is to show that the recent developments and emergent trends in *Georgics* criticism have not only helped to crystallize the content, organization and aspirations of the present volume, but also fundamentally underpin our vision of how Virgil's poem might be read and continuously renewed. For us, what is most absorbing and impressive about the *Georgics* is the breadth of its intellectual activity, the richness and depth of the poem's engagement with its creative environment, and the myriad ways in which the poem is reflected in the works of others. This collection of essays strives to capture this image of Virgil's poem, and in doing so seeks to expand on scholarly understanding of what the *Georgics* says about its subject matter, its medium and its time.

As we hope to show throughout this introduction and the rest of the book, the *Georgics* actively invites reflections on the relationship between reader and addressee, content and meaning, message and medium, idealism and reality. Indeed, we take the view that the poem's exploration of these relationships lies at the heart of its inexhaustible interpretive possibilities. In what follows, we will make a case for seeing recent developments in scholarship on the *Georgics* as a direct result of critics' increasing sensitivity to the poem's frequent and multifarious self-reflections. The proliferation of metapoetic and allegorical readings of Virgil's agricultural *didaxis*; the expansion of the corpus of intertexts with which the *Georgics* is thought to interact; the understanding that Virgil's 'middle poem' encapsulates and negotiates with contemporary socio-political changes; and the growing recognition that throughout the history of its reception the *Georgics* has acted as a prism through which later authors, critics and translators have engaged in self-representation and self-definition: these major shifts in the scholarly landscape are not only representative of more nuanced, less historicizing and better theorized approaches to the poem, but they have also indelibly left their imprint on the methodological contours of the present volume.

Scholarly approaches to the *Georgics* in the twentieth and twenty-first century

At the risk of repeating what has been said well and extensively by others, we begin with a brief overview of the scholarship on the *Georgics* in order to draw out the major shifts in the study of the poem which have shaped our thinking.[2] Modern scholarship on Virgil's *Georgics* was injected with fresh energy in the 1970s, which saw the publication of a number of still-influential studies; and this verve for diversifying the interpretation of the *Georgics* has not only sustained itself but even intensified in subsequent decades. The methodologies adopted by the so-called 'Harvard School' of Virgilian critics in conceiving their pessimistic readings of the *Aeneid*, which emerged in the 1950s and came into their own in the mid-1960s, began to be applied to the study of the *Georgics* in the 1970s – a delay that testifies to the poem's secondary status within the Virgilian oeuvre in the eyes of critics.[3] The deeply melancholic and even despondent tenor of 1970s American scholarship on the *Georgics*, exemplified by Michael Putnam's *Virgil's Poem of the Earth* (1979), stands in sharp contrast to the earlier, more optimistic views of the poem emanating mainly from the works of two German scholars: *Virgils Georgica* (1963 = 1967: 175–363) by Friedrich Klingner; and *Der Anspruch des Dichters in Vergils Georgika* (1972) by Vinzenz Buchheit.[4] Broadly speaking, early optimistic readings maintain that Virgil's poem celebrates the dignity of the agricultural life and professes a hope for the arrival of an Italian Golden Age under Octavian; whereas later pessimistic readings, which ostensibly took hold of Anglophone scholarship on the *Georgics* in the 1980s and 1990s, tend to stress the harsh realities of life in the Iron Age, the futility of human toil, and the problems and uncertainties surrounding the rise of Octavian.[5] This divergence between (American or Anglophone) pessimism and (European) optimism is arguably less pronounced, but still detectable in two of the major commentaries on Virgil's *Georgics*, both of which were conceived in the 1980s: the two-volume English commentary by Richard Thomas (1988), and the two-part German study by Manfred Erren, completed over the course of eighteen years (*Band* 1, 1985; *Band* 2, 2003).[6] The commentary of Roger Mynors, which appeared in 1990, judiciously sidesteps the question throughout.

Emerging from the shadow of this 'optimistic versus pessimistic' debate, a number of critics, such as Christine Perkell (*The Poet's Truth*, 1989) and Monica Gale (*Virgil on the Nature of Things*, 2000), have attempted to steer clear of both sets of readings by arguing that the *Georgics* is fixated on life's inherent complexities and unsolvable ambiguities; but their conclusions in the end often appear more pessimistic than not.[7] On the other hand, revisionist optimistic readings have also begun to materialize: the study by Llewelyn Morgan (*Patterns of Redemption in Virgil's Georgics*, 1999), for instance, as its title implies, sought to frame the poem's troubling images of destruction as having a 'constructive potential', which offered hope for the rebirth of Rome following its political collapse.[8] The works of Morgan and Gale, moreover, also exemplify the hegemony of intertextual reading as a critical tool in Latin literary scholarship of the 1990s and early 2000s.[9] Gale's book maintains that Virgil complicates the worldview of his poem by staging a dialogue between the *Georgics* and a diverse range of (often conflicting) intertexts, above all Lucretius; while Morgan's thoroughgoing allegorical reading of the Aristaeus episode as a symbol of Rome's rebirth under Octavian derives from a detailed analysis of Virgil's interactions with Homer and the tradition of Stoic allegoresis. Seen together, the studies of Gale and Morgan underline the intertextualist's conviction that Virgil's *Georgics* communicates its message through the poem's dialogism. In the present volume, the contributions by Mackenzie (Chapter 4) and Freer (Chapter 5) continue this tradition of reading the *Georgics* by identifying further relevant intertexts, such as the theogonical poetry attributed to Orpheus and the philosophical treatises of Virgil's teacher Philodemus, and in doing so shed new light on the poem's generic self-reflexivity.

'[In] the past few decades', however, as Volk observes in the introduction to her 2008 collected volume on the *Georgics*, 'there has been a kind of metapoetic turn, a shift away from reading Vergil for his message and toward studying him for his poetics'.[10] This metapoetic approach to the *Georgics* was partly stimulated by Volk herself, who in *The Poetics of Latin Didactic* (2002) argued that Latin didactic poetry was defined by four central features: explicit didactic intent, the teacher–student constellation, poetic self-consciousness and poetic simultaneity (that is, the creation of the dramatic illusion of a lesson in progress as the poem proceeds).[11] It is worth noting that two of the four features identified by Volk – namely the teacher–student constellation and poetic simultaneity – are concerned with the narratology of didactic poetry, while the other two features – explicit didactic intent and poetic self-consciousness – characterize didactic poetry as a literary discourse that is interested in the relationship between didactic content and poetic form, *res* and *carmen*, message and medium. Volk's goal of 'uncover[ing] the *poetics*' of didactic poetry,[12] combined with narratologically informed reading, leads her to make two important claims about the *Georgics*: first, since Virgil's poem names not only farmers but also Maecenas among its internal audiences, the *Georgics* can be seen as consisting of two parallel discourses – one addressed to the farmers and meant to teach agriculture, and the other directed at Maecenas and largely taken up with reflections about poetry and the artificiality of the poem's own construction; and second, that the parallel discourses of the *Georgics* are fundamentally inseparable.[13] Virgil's narratological innovation of having two internal addressees, with one (Maecenas) performing the role of the learned reader, demonstrates in Volk's view that the *Georgics* is not (or, at least, not only) about agriculture, but rather about the acts of poetic composition and reading poetry.[14]

Yet despite its emphasis on poetics, Volk's reading does not openly claim that the agricultural discourse of the *Georgics* functions as a vehicle for the poem's self-reflections on poetry. However, a number of subsequent readings treat the poem's agricultural language and content precisely as allegories for poetic composition. One of the most recent examples of this approach is John Henkel's essay, 'Virgil Talks Techniques: Metapoetic Arboriculture in *Georgics* 2'.[15] Henkel's close reading of *Georgics* 2.9–82 suggestively argues that while this passage purports to teach farmers how to domesticate different types (*genera*) of trees, it simultaneously shows poets how to cultivate and refine literary genres.[16] By thus treating the *Georgics'* discourse on farming as metapoetic allegory, Henkel's approach demonstrates the vitality of the poetics-centred way of reading the *Georgics* in today's scholarship, and lends further support to Volk's argument that Virgil's poem contains parallel discourses on agriculture and poetic composition. The contributions by Cowan (Chapter 1) and Heyworth (Chapter 2) in this volume continue to build on the works of Volk and Henkel respectively. Cowan's chapter draws out the vast potential of the narratological strand of Volk's discussion, and probes, specifically, what second-person narration in the *Georgics* tells us about the relationship between the poem's narrator and its various internal and external addressees, as well as, more broadly, how narrative patterns in ancient didactic poetry can expand the study of narratological theory. Heyworth's chapter, on the other hand, eradicates crucial misunderstandings that have long clogged interpretations of the poem's teachings on irrigation and ploughing, and in doing so demonstrates that *correct* understandings of Virgil's agricultural instructions are central to the detection of metapoetic statements embedded in previously overlooked passages of the *Georgics*.

Despite the flourish of metapoetic allegorical readings of the *Georgics*, however, critics are no less interested in what Virgil's poem can tell readers about life. This search for the poem's 'message' has a long history in the interpretative tradition of the *Georgics* beginning with Servius, and its practitioners typically rely on treating the poem's agricultural teaching as moral or political allegory. The debate about the poem's meaning, as we alluded to earlier, has gained particular stimulus from studies (such as those of Gale and Morgan) engaging in thorough explorations of the poem's intertextual relationships. In more recent years, with critics generally moving away from (the critical vocabulary associated with) the binary opposition of 'optimism' and 'pessimism', those who take the meaning-finding approach to the *Georgics* have been more inclined to see the poem as acting out different modes of life and exploring their merits, dangers or deficiencies. Three scholarly works, in our view, best represent this shift in *Georgics* criticism: *Reading After Actium* (2005) by Christopher Nappa; *Allegories of Farming from Greece to Rome* (2009) by Leah Kronenberg; and *Playing the Farmer* (2011) by Philip Thibodeau. Whilst this is not the place to offer a detailed 'literature review', it will be helpful to provide below a synthesizing account of these studies, not only to justify our claim that they exemplify the key characteristics of new directions in the study of the *Georgics*, but also to highlight the ways in which the present volume is stimulated by and builds on the works of these critics.

Nappa's monograph argues that Virgil, as the protreptic teacher, offers in the *Georgics* a series of challenging lessons to his contemporary readers in order to provoke them to develop their own views of the world and man's place within it.[17] Amongst the many contemporary readers of the *Georgics*, Nappa sees Octavian as the poem's most important student, and emphasizes throughout the value of the *Georgics* as political didactic for the new ruler of the Roman world.[18] Nappa's argument builds on ambivalent interpretations of the *Georgics*;[19] but rather than seeing the poem's chaotic vision of the world as potentially troubling or deeply ambiguous, Nappa reads it as an act that reflects man's need to find reliable meaning in the world and the world's resistance to such attempts to fix meaning.[20] Nappa's work thus moves *Georgics* criticism on from merely asking 'what the poem means' to 'what the poem can tell us about meaning'; and in this respect, it offers a valuable counterpoint to Batstone's assessment of the *Georgics* as an uninterpretable poem overloaded with problematic models, doctrines and allegories.[21] Nappa is, however, less persuasive in suggesting that Virgil took upon himself the serious task of advising Octavian on how to govern the Roman world following the civil wars: for even if there were such an ancient tradition of poets writing in the capacity of special political advisors (which there was not), the notion that Octavian soberly reflected on images of himself in the *Georgics* and, heeding the advice of the protreptic Virgil, looked for solutions to the world's problems by soaking up four books of poetry about farming, seems rather fanciful.[22] In the present book, two contributions can be seen as a direct response to Nappa's work and subsequent *Georgics* scholarship: Thomas in Chapter 3 extends the enquiry into 'what the poem can tell us about meaning' by arguing that the pleasure of reading the *Georgics* – its aesthetic quality – is itself meaningful, while Xinyue in Chapter 6 reconsiders the issue of whether Virgil presents the *Georgics* as a political lesson for Octavian, by examining the poem's discourse on its own didactic effectiveness with regard to the divinization of Octavian.

Kronenberg's book, as its title suggests, also treats the *Georgics*' instruction on farming as an extended allegory for various approaches to life; but where her work differs significantly from that of Nappa – in addition to not sharing his view that the *Georgics* was a political protreptic aimed primarily at Octavian – is that Kronenberg thinks that Virgil's poem parodies and satirizes the human need to create order and construct systems of meaning.[23] Examining the *Georgics* alongside Xenophon's *Oeconomicus* and Varro's *De Re Rustica* as texts that exhibit characteristics of philosophical satire (a topic to which we will return later), the main difference between this approach and most previous ones is that Kronenberg sees the agricultural allegory in these works as 'embodying *negative* ethical and political behavior, and not as the models of wise and virtuous activities they are traditionally set up to be'.[24] Kronenberg suggests that the *Georgics* puts forward several different ways of understanding the world – for example, in the opposition between *religio* (book 1) and *ratio* (book 2); but the ultimate failure of each of these systems, she argues, conveys to the reader the futility of finding meaning and imposing order in life.

The strength of Kronenberg's argument lies not only in the attractive idea that the *Georgics* challenges contemporary ways of thinking by problematizing farming and its construction as a cultural ideal in Roman society,[25] but also in the notion that the poem acts out in the course of its four books the deficiencies of various beliefs and organizing principles – an entirely plausible function for a didactic text.[26] By treating the *Georgics* as engaging with the satirical strand of the tradition of philosophical dialogue, Kronenberg reinforces our understanding of the *Georgics* as a poem informed by a range of philosophical traditions. Indeed, her point that Virgil's poem embodies and questions the utility of different modes of thinking should usefully provoke critics to broaden their search for texts and systems of thought (beyond those of Hesiod, Aratus and Lucretius) with which the *Georgics* is engaging.[27] Here in this volume the essay by Freer (Chapter 5) takes on the task of locating such intertexts and philosophical substrata in the *Georgics* by investigating the influence of Epicurean poetic theory on Virgil's poem.

On the other hand, Kronenberg's reading of the *Georgics* is, in our view, overly nihilist, and privileges too much the Batstonian view that Virgil's poem ultimately only teaches us about the impossibility of obtaining meaning. It seems to the editors of this book counterproductive to argue that the sole purpose of a didactic text is to teach its readers paradoxically the futility of attempting to understand anything. Furthermore, whilst there may well be a satirical tenor of this kind in Xenophon's *Oeconomicus* and Varro's *De Re Rustica*, the *Georgics* does not fall squarely within this tradition, since it is written and meant to be consumed as *poetry*. The notion that in composing a poem Virgil simultaneously questions *poetry*'s didactic force is explored by Myers (Chapter 9) through the lens of Virgilian reception in the work of Columella, as well as by Freer in his study (Chapter 5). Finally, Kronenberg's reading of the *Georgics* stops short of establishing broader connections between Virgil's satirizing of agricultural allegory and contemporary Roman thought: could the poem's treatment of farming as an embodiment of ethical and political behaviour be a response to social change? This question requires further consideration (even if one does not take the view that the *Georgics* is a countercultural satire) and is addressed in this volume by Stöckinger in Chapter 8, which examines the poem's presentation of agricultural economics as a nexus of reciprocal processes reflecting the increasing complexity of social relationships during Rome's transitional period.

Arriving soon after Kronenberg's *Allegories of Farming in Greece and Rome*, Thibodeau's book took a more socio-historical approach, seeking to 'situate the *Georgics* within the discourse of agrarianism in ancient Rome'.[28] The major argument presented by *Playing the Farmer* is that the *Georgics* deliberately diverges from the conventions of agrarian discourse and practice, which Thibodeau refers to as 'systematic distortions' of 'useful truth',[29] in order to achieve various poetic and rhetorical ends. Specifically, Thibodeau claims that the *Georgics* provides its original readers with an imaginary experience of being a farmer that is so far removed from the daily realities of contemporary Roman agricultural life that it essentially amounts to a 'fantasy', within which the reader 'plays the farmer' and is shown by Virgil the value of the *uita rustica*.[30] The poem's agricultural fiction is, however, constructed with the principle of *decorum* in mind – a notion referred to by Seneca the Younger in his critique of the *Georgics*,[31] and defined by Thibodeau as rhetorically or stylistically appropriate and relating to the virtue of moderation;[32] thus the *Georgics*' presentation of its agronomic fantasy appeals to both the aesthetic and social judgement of the reader.

The most attractive aspect of Thibodeau's work lies in his assertion that the *Georgics*' unrealistically positive representation of the *uita rustica* might have been an attempt to console and ennoble the rustication of the elite readers of the poem, a large number of whom withdrew from public life to their country estates as a result of the civil wars of the 40s and 30s.[33] Whilst this line of inquiry eventually leads Thibodeau to the familiar conclusion that the text 'reinterprets . . . loss as a gain',[34] his characterization of the *Georgics* as a poem that encapsulates and seeks to reconcile profound socio-political changes should be pursued further, as it usefully adumbrates an aspect of Virgil's poetry which critics in recent years have begun to emphasize. Of course, the notion that the *Georgics* is concerned with change is nothing new: scholars have long recognized the poem's 'transitional' nature, for it marks not only an intermediate period in Virgil's career but also a juncture in Rome's political transition from republic to principate.[35] But more recently, a number of studies have explored the ways in which Virgil's poetry can simultaneously embody and naturalize political shift. For example, Nelis has suggested that by offering both pre-Actium and post-Actium visions of the Roman world, the *Georgics* reanimates the fluctuations of the civil war period, while also synchronizing itself with political time and looking ahead to the future (along with Caesar himself).[36] In a more recent study, Geue has argued that the *Georgics* can be understood as Virgil's exploration of the relationship between slavery and imperialism in the years between 31 and 29 BCE, and that the poem's representation of the bee-community in book 4 implements the new dominant logic of compelling others to produce and give up the fruits of their labour for the ruling elite.[37] The current scholarly understanding of the *Georgics* as a text that seeks to negotiate socio-political changes in the Roman world receives substantial coverage in the present book, especially in Part III (Chapters 6 to 8). The contribution by Giusti (Chapter 7), in particular, addresses how the so-called 'proem in the middle' of *Georgics* 3 constructs a space within which Virgil highlights, and reconciles himself and his readers with, the changing political and cultural climate in the aftermath of the civil wars.[38]

Another useful aspect of Thibodeau's book is its sustained focus on how the *Georgics* was read in antiquity and how the poem's reception might inform our own interpretation of it. Throughout his work, Thibodeau uses Seneca's assessment of the *Georgics* as a hermeneutic anchor, basing his readings around the Senecan view of Virgil as an agronomist 'who considered not what to say most truthfully but most elegantly, not wanting to instruct farmers but to delight his readers' (Sen. *Ep.* 86.15).[39] Indeed, substantial parts of Thibodeau's book are devoted to examining the rhetorical flourish of the *Georgics* and the poem's 'psychagogical elements', which according to Thibodeau are narrative methods used by Virgil to represent and evoke passion for the *uita rustica* with a view to enchanting his readers.[40] While Thibodeau's reception-informed approach is circumscribed by his lack of discussion of the context, subjectivity and moralizing thrust of Seneca's assessment of Virgil, an enquiry into why within a hundred years of its publication the *Georgics* was already thought of as a text that 'delighted' (*delectare*) rather than taught its readers is clearly worthwhile, as it will allow us to understand better how the *Georgics* contributed to Roman aesthetic and literary criticism. In this book, Thomas (Chapter 3) and Myers (Chapter 9) offer a pair of studies which explore precisely this topic; the latter achieves this by offering a new reading of book 10 of Columella's *De Re Rustica*, which explicitly engages with Virgil's garden in *Georgics* 4. On the other hand, not all ancient readers of the *Georgics* thought of it as mere poetic delight: Servius's commentary strongly suggests that he saw the poem as capable of offering epistemological insight; the often undetected but significant influence of Servius's commentary in our understanding of the *Georgics* is not touched upon by Thibodeau, but is addressed here extensively by Hunt in Chapter 10.

Compared to the poem's reception in Greco-Roman antiquity, the post-Classical and modern receptions of Virgil's *Georgics* have been well covered by a number of studies.[41] Since the publication of Domenico Comparetti's *Virgilio nel medio evo* (1872; latest repr. 1997, *Vergil in the Middle Ages*), the reception of the *Georgics* in the Western literary and artistic traditions has been traced comprehensively by Patrick Wilkinson, Richard Jenkyns, and the contributors to Jan Ziolkowski and Michael Putnam's anthology *The Virgilian Tradition*.[42] Meanwhile, David Scott Wilson-Okamura, Yasmin Haskell and Theodore Ziolkowski, amongst others, have focused on the intellectual impact of the *Georgics* on Renaissance humanist culture, Latin didactic poetry produced by members of the Society of Jesus in the early modern period, and the literature of the twentieth-century, respectively.[43] Collectively, their work has shown, firstly, that throughout its post-Classical reception the *Georgics* has provoked serious contemplation among later authors and thinkers on issues such as the relationship between humankind and the land, the values of rural life, and the nature and merits of pedagogy; and secondly, that Virgil's exploration of the poet-teacher figure (through, for example, his representation of Orpheus in book 4 or passages such as the *laudes Italiae* and *laus ruris* in book 2) proved especially influential for later writers and philosophers.[44] The final part of the present volume ('Modern Responses') synthesizes both these aspects of the *Georgics'* reception history. Barton takes on the Neo-Latin and vernacular traditions of georgic writing in Chapter 11, while Earnshaw in Chapter 12 considers the British Romantic poets' engagement with the *Georgics*.[45] In the twentieth century, the *Georgics* became a canvas onto which writers and translators projected their own aspirations and anxieties, memories and losses;[46] this phenomenon is addressed by Braund in Chapter 13, where she explores how female scholars have responded to Virgil's poem in the modern age.

The thirteen studies that constitute this book seek to address the central issues which, as the above discussion shows, lie at the heart of *Georgics* scholarship today. This volume can of course be consulted piecemeal according to each reader's individual interests; however, its structure has been planned for sequential reading. The next section of this introduction outlines the argument of each chapter, and explains the rationale behind grouping the thirteen studies into five interrelated parts.

Our contributions

Part I of the book offers three very different approaches to the fundamental question of how to read the *Georgics*. Investigating, in turn, the relationships between the poem's narrator and narratees/addressees, the metapoetic significance of the *Georgics'* agricultural *didaxis*, and the notion that meaning can also be found in the poem's artistic and aesthetic qualities, these discussions exemplify the diversity of current methodological approaches to the Virgilian text, and the vitality of the debate surrounding issues of form and function, message and medium in the *Georgics*.

We begin with Cowan's groundbreaking treatment of second-person narration in the *Georgics*. Virgil's varying modes of narration within the poem, often combining second- and third-person narration in a single passage, has important implications for our understanding of the poem's message on the dynamic between (natural) determinism and (individual) agency. By focusing on issues such as the relationship between narrator and narratees within and outside the 'fiction' of the poem, the indeterminacy of the internal and external narratees/addressees, and the function of apostrophe, Cowan's chapter offers a refreshing reassessment of the *Georgics*' narratology. Through sustained engagement with recent narratological theory and productive comparisons with narratological modes deployed in modern texts, Cowan sheds new light on not only what narratology can do for a literary critic's interpretation of the *Georgics*, but also, more crucially, what the *Georgics* can do for narratological studies.

The second chapter, by Heyworth, is explicitly concerned with the interpretation of technical didactic in the *Georgics* and subsequent scholarly (mis)interpretations of the poem's agricultural *didaxis*. Yet despite this seemingly uncomplicated understanding of the *Georgics* as a poem about farming techniques, Heyworth hardly takes the view that the reader of Virgil's poem can only be a farmer; rather, his central argument, that Virgil in the passages on agricultural 'beginnings' teaches the notion that to begin one needs already to have begun, builds on the now increasingly prevalent metapoetic reading of the *Georgics*' technical didactic, treating the poem's instructions on agricultural technology as capable of conveying literary ideals to an audience attuned to them as much as to the correct methods of farming. This chapter offers more than a series of new, agriculturally meaningful readings of specific verses and phrases: it demonstrates in detail that giving practical instructions on farming and offering literary-compositional reflections are not mutually exclusive but mutually reinforcing, and that an *accurate* understanding of Virgil's agricultural instructions helps the reader to fully grasp their broader literary implications, even when language charged with metapoetic connotations (e.g. *genus*) is absent from Virgil's text.

With Thomas, in Chapter 3, we consider the interpretive possibilities opened up by an aesthetic reading of the *Georgics*. As Thomas himself points out, although his way of reading the poem falls firmly within the framework of New Criticism, it nevertheless presents fresh perspectives in that a robust aesthetic reading of the *Georgics* not only has the potential to unearth which aspects of Virgil's language contribute to the poem's being regarded as pleasurable and delightful (e.g. by Seneca), but it can also open up the question of whether *style* can communicate, add to or reinforce the poem's powerful sense of empathy. By identifying numerous passages which deserve further formal analysis, this chapter demonstrates how an aesthetic reading of the *Georgics* can be utilized to reinvigorate the discussion of the poem's literary force. Together with the preceding two chapters, Thomas's study completes the first part of this book, which presents three different ways of catalysing new readings of the *Georgics*.

Focusing on two important and interrelated topics that underpin the religious and philosophical aspects of the *Georgics* – Orphism and Epicureanism – Part II offers fresh insights derived from close intertextual readings of Virgil's poem. While expanding our knowledge of the range of possible sources exploited by Virgil, the two studies in this section address the book's larger concern with the poem's generic positioning – in particular, its status as a didactic text – and the relationship between poetic form and function in the *Georgics*.

Mackenzie's essay (Chapter 4) argues that, if the figure of Orpheus in *Georgics* 4 can be seen as evoking Orphic religion and the kind of literature that was attributed to Orpheus's authorship in antiquity – which survives mainly in fragmentary form today – then Virgil's poem (or at least the fourth book) can be regarded as a kind of mystic literature that teaches the student how to expiate an original sin and gain access to a privileged afterlife. Mackenzie identifies parallels between specific episodes in the *Georgics* and in the so-called Orphic theogonies, and makes the attractive suggestion that the Virgilian *Orpheuserzählung* shares with Orphic texts a pragmatic function that facilitates not only a generic repositioning of the *Georgics* but also further, previously unexplored allegorical readings of Virgil's reflections on the immortality of Octavian.

Freer's essay (Chapter 5) picks up where Mackenzie left off: the *sphragis* of the *Georgics*. Drawing on recent developments in the study of Epicurean poetic theory, Freer argues that Virgil's conception of the nature and function of poetry in the *Georgics* was shaped by the Athenian tradition of the Epicurean school – including Virgil's own teacher Philodemus – which viewed poetry as a source of mental disturbance unsuited to the goal of instruction. Moreover, by foregrounding the irrational and potentially harmful effects of poetry, Virgil can be seen as offering a direct riposte to the unorthodox position of the Epicurean poet Lucretius, who claimed that the psychagogic power of poetry can be harnessed effectively in the service of *ratio*. Weighing up two competing positions in an Epicurean intra-school debate, Virgil comes down firmly on the side of Epicurus and Philodemus, and in the process hints at profound reservations about the efficacy of his own poetic *didaxis*.

The studies in Part III of the book broaden the scope of the debate to consider the contemporary relevance and impact of the *Georgics*. The discussions in this section are united by the conviction that the *Georgics* can tell us a great deal about how the social and political dynamics of the Roman world were being changed by the emergence of the *princeps*. Building on the well-recognized notion that the *Georgics* is a 'transitional' text that synchronizes itself with recent Roman history, these essays provide new insights on the poem's participation in political discourse by highlighting its varied and sustained attempts at the negotiation of power, especially the poem's striking reconfigurations of the relationship between ruler and poet.

The issue of Octavian's divinization comes into focus in Chapter 6 (Xinyue), where the topic is conceived as one of the ways in which Virgil reflects on the political future of Rome and the poet's place within it. Continuing the book's interrogation of the didactic element of the *Georgics* in Parts I and II, Xinyue's main contention is that the unravelling and eventual ineffectiveness of Virgil's *didaxis* on deification could be seen to anticipate the diminishing relevance and even inevitable failure of political intervention in the forthcoming age of Augustus, who asserts himself as a kind of god amongst men. By portraying the apotheosis of Octavian as a predetermined event pursuing a course of its own, the language of divinization in the *Georgics*, as Xinyue argues, necessitates a meditation on Rome's constitutional shift towards autocracy as much as a re-evaluation of the power of poetry in the post-Actian world.

The next chapter, by Giusti (Chapter 7), marks the halfway point of the volume, an appropriate place for discussion of the monumental centrepiece of the *Georgics*, the 'proem in the middle' at the beginning of book 3. Giusti argues that this passage places the *Georgics* in an artificially created continuum between the age of republican triumph (envisaged in the poet's procession) and the future triumphal expansionism of Augustus's empire (conveyed by the ekphrasis of the theatre-temple). In doing so, this chapter establishes important new connections between theatrical representation and the language of Roman foreign policy during Rome's transition from republic to principate.

In Chapter 8, Stöckinger offers a study of the language of reciprocity in the *Georgics* to facilitate a reading of the poem that underlines Virgil's concern for the rapidly-changing social relationships amongst the elite precipitated by the growing status of the *princeps*. Stöckinger argues that ideas of exchange are conveyed metaphorically by Virgil in scenes of gift-giving and social reciprocity, through which relationships between 'unequals' – such as the one between man and nature, or the one between the poet/ farmer and Octavian (also a central issue in Xinyue's discussion in this section) – are established. These reciprocal relations, as Stöckinger illustrates, function both at a social and poetic level, thereby acting out cohesion between conflicting or asymmetrically-matched elements in the complex and uncertain world of the *Georgics* as well as in the increasingly stratified Roman society under the *princeps*.

The discussions in the first three parts of this book amply illustrate the polyvalence of Virgil's *Georgics*, encompassing almost every aspect of Roman life; and the poem's vast hermeneutic potential is reflected in the diversity of approaches and interpretations offered in the preceding chapters. With this in mind, it is perhaps no surprise that the question of how to read the *Georgics*, and very different views of what the poem is about, surfaced early on in the history of the poem's reception. In Part IV of the book, we explore this aspect of the *Georgics'* ancient reception by focusing on a pair of texts that present two contrasting ways of reading the *Georgics*: Columella's *De Re Rustica* and Servius's commentary on Virgil's poem.

As Myers demonstrates in Chapter 9, the tenth book of Columella's *De Re Rustica* – the only hexameter book on gardening in an otherwise prose treatise on agriculture – is not merely an expansive imitation of Virgil's garden at *Georgics* 4.116–48, but also a creative, aesthetically-informed engagement with and supplementation to the *poetic* horticultural didactic tradition. By insinuating that verse is the medium of fictionality and pleasure (in contrast to the pragmatism of prose), Columella's poetry draws attention to its decorative function, and implicitly enshrines itself, as well as Virgil's *Georgics*, in the non-utilitarian mode of horticultural teaching. Columella's composition of a verse book on horticulture is thus revealed as a metaliterary nod to the aesthetic principles of didactic poetry, highlighting the tension within the genre between message and medium – the same tension explored from the perspective of ancient philosophy in Freer's contribution in Part II – while reinforcing the idea of the *Georgics* as a poem that privileges style and pleasure over *praxis*.

By contrast, Servius's commentary on the *Georgics* construes Virgil's poem as a text of epistemological insight and an opportunity for the commentator to display his own antiquarian expertise and erudition. As Hunt shows in Chapter 10, Servius defends Virgil against any suggestion of error in religious matters and even amplifies the poem's religious content by supplying mythologizing commentary. Using his note on *G.* 1.21 as a case study, Hunt illustrates Servius's propensity for academic one-upmanship, and considers the impact of his approach on subsequent scholarship on the *Georgics*, as well as on Roman religion more broadly. Hunt's study demonstrates the importance of separating out Servius's thinking about Roman religion from Virgil's, and it urges us to become self-aware readers of Servius. The two studies in this section reveal strikingly different ancient responses to the *Georgics,* and highlight how a reader's intellectual interests and priorities have determined what kind of poem the *Georgics* was thought to be in the first 400 years of its reception.

The fifth and final part of this book turns to early modern and modern receptions of the *Georgics.* Our focus is on what readers and translators of the *Georgics* made of the 'textuality' of Virgil's landscape, and in particular how the relationship between man/woman and land, poet and poetic landscape, is transfigured in subsequent reworkings and translations of the *Georgics.* Each of the three studies in this section demonstrates powerfully how translators of Virgil and later poets engaging with the *Georgics* have sought not only to replicate, but also to add their own voices to, the evocative and (meta) poetic qualities of the Virgilian landscape.

The first chapter in this section, by Barton (Chapter 11), examines Marc Lescarbot's poem *A-dieu à la Nouvelle-France* (1609), written during his return from the French settlement of Port-Royal. Offering a close reading of the *A-dieu* in the context of early modern receptions of the *Georgics,* this study advances our understanding of how Virgil's poem and the georgic tradition – especially their representations of landscape and man's place within it – were interpreted and exploited in early modern literature beyond the prominent Neo-Latin tradition of georgic writing. Barton traces a thoroughgoing programme of engagement with the *Georgics* in the *A-dieu,* from the imitation or emulation of individual passages, to the transplantation of familiar Virgilian themes – such as the virtues of (agricultural) *labor* – to the still largely unexplored territory of the New World. At the same time, Lescarbot locates his text firmly within the tradition of *didactic* georgic poetry, aiming both to delight and instruct his readership back in France with his vivid descriptions of the landscape and wildlife around Port-Royal.

The next chapter focuses on Shelley's neglected translation of *Georgics* 4.360–73, the descent of Aristaeus into Cyrene's underwater realm. Shelley's text, as Earnshaw argues in Chapter 12, engages in a creative dialogue with an already intertextually significant space within the *Georgics,* and contemplatively re-performs the act of intertextual reading by itself evoking Orpheus's descent to Hades and the descent to Hell in Dante. Shelley situates himself as the inheritor of the Virgilian polyphonic and metatextual voice by infusing into his translation the motif of poetic landscape (originating in Homer) along with Dante's reception of Virgil. Furthermore, as Earnshaw points out, Shelley reads metatextuality back into the landscape of *Georgics* 4.360–73 as he characterizes the 'underworld' as a geocritical space where different texts – Homeric, Virgilian, Dantean and Shelleyan – are brought into dialogue with each other.

The final chapter of the volume, by Braund (Chapter 13), brings us into the twentieth and twenty-first centuries. Braund's essay focuses on the representation of land and landscape in adaptations and translations of the *Georgics* by two female poets and scholars: the English poet, novelist and garden designer Vita Sackville-West (*The Land*, 1926), and the American essayist, naturalist and translator Janet Lembke (translation published in 2005). Concentrating on the authors' choice of language and the actual landscapes evoked in their response to or representation of Virgil's Italy, Braund's study examines where these adaptations and translations can be located on the spectrum of domestication and foreignization. In the process, it considers why women are significantly overrepresented among the ranks of translators of the *Georgics* (compared with the rest of Virgil's oeuvre) and whether female responses to the *Georgics* offer something unavailable in versions by male translators. Braund's original discussion underscores the continuing relevance and significance of Virgil's poem of the earth, and its status as fertile ground for future generations of poets and scholars.

PART I
READING THE *GEORGICS*

CHAPTER 1
THE STORY OF YOU: SECOND-PERSON NARRATIVE AND THE NARRATOLOGY OF THE *GEORGICS*
Robert Cowan

The way I tell 'em: narratology, classical literature and didactic poetry

Narratology is among the most important and widely-deployed tools for the analysis of Classical literature.[1] Following the trailblazing work of de Jong on Homer and Winkler on Apuleius, the (for want of a better term) 'fictional' narrative genres of epic and the novel have offered particularly fertile ground for narratologists to plough.[2] Other narrative genres, such as historiography, and even those which are not conventionally 'narrative', such as lyric, drama and elegy, have also proven susceptible to narratological analysis. In contrast, didactic poetry has remained largely untouched by narratologists. In many ways this is unsurprising, since 'didactic poetry is a genre of discourse, not narrative.'[3] When narrative technique is discussed, it tends to focus on the more conventionally narrative sections of the poems, such as Lucretius's plague or Virgil's *Aristaeus*, in short the parts of the poems which are least characteristic of the didactic genre.[4] There are a handful of very distinguished exceptions to this tendency.[5] Gale on Lucretius, Trépanier on Lucretius and Empedocles, and Fowler on didactic poetry more broadly have all shown how both the Aristotelian antithesis between Homer and Empedocles, and Benveniste's between narrative and discursive modes can be deconstructed and how Classical didactic poetry can not only be illuminated by modern narratological theory but even at times self-consciously exploit some of its preoccupations.[6] All three, though they glance briefly at narrators, narratees and related issues of focalization, concentrate overwhelmingly on plot and its narratological aspects of closure, order, rhythm and repetition. In doing so, they pass over what is, if we take seriously the proposition that didactic can be approached as narrative, its most prominent, distinctive and problematic feature: the identification of narratee and protagonist which makes didactic correspond to the rare and largely postmodern mode of second-person narrative.

Stories of you: second-person narration, didactic poetry and their scholarship

Although the case has been made for earlier instances, and although it is debated whether closely-related narrative phenomena such as epistolary fiction should be included under its heading, second-person narration is generally accepted as having developed in the second half of the twentieth century, taking as its foundational text Michel Butor's 1957 novel *La Modification* (English translation retitled *Second Thoughts*). Notable examples include Edna O'Brien's *A Pagan Place* (1970), John Updike's 'How to Love America and Leave It at the Same Time' (1972), Italo Calvino's *Se una notte d'inverno un viaggiatore* (*If on a Winter's Night a Traveller*, 1979), Jay McInerney's *Bright Lights, Big City* (1984), and several stories in Lorrie Moore's *Self Help* (1985), as well as the children's literature genre of 'Choose-your-own-adventure' books.[7] Narratological scholarship on second-person narration had its own foundational text in Morrissette's 1965 article 'Narrative "You" in Contemporary Literature', but only really underwent significant development in the early 1990s in articles by Richardson, Fludernik and Wiest and above all an agenda-setting special issue of the journal *Style* edited by Fludernik.[8] In the subsequent twenty-five years, there has continued to be a steady stream of research, expanding into areas such as conversational storytelling and above all the new narrative forms of digital and interactive fiction and computer games.[9] Except for a brief but stimulating section near the end of Akujärvi's article on Pausanias and an equally brief entry in de Jong's comprehensive introduction, the narratology of second-person narrative has not been applied to Classical texts.[10]

The affinity between didactic poetry and second-person narration is a close one. As Richardson, discussing the 'literary' nature of second-person narration with no reference to Classical literature, notes, its 'non-fictional analogues [are] the pseudo-narrative forms of the cookbook, the travel guide, and the self-help manual'.[11] Yet it is not merely on the grounds of distant family resemblance that I propose using the techniques developed to interpret second-person narrative to explore didactic poetry and the *Georgics* in particular. There are striking parallels, though largely without explicit mutual reference, in the scholarly preoccupations about and approaches to both genres, notably the positionality and authority of the narrator, the indeterminacy of the addressee/narratee and the role of apostrophe.[12] It is on the second of these that this chapter will focus, adding also a significant sub-strand in second-person narrative studies: the way in which the narrative mode constructs a dialogue between determinism and individual autonomy.

Much of the scholarship is devoted to establishing precise definitions of what constitutes genuine second-person narrative, but there is a general consensus as to the broad outlines. The key factor is that the narratee is identical to the protagonist (or at least a major actant) of the narrative.[13] Second-person narratives do not merely include the occasional aside to a heterodiegetic addressee of the 'dear reader' kind, as when Trollope self-referentially invokes the title of his own novel by asking 'But can you forgive her, delicate reader?'[14] As we shall see, the reader *qua* reader can be a protagonist, in Virgil as in Calvino, but not when she takes no other role in the narrative. DelConte offers probably the most comprehensive, if cumbersome, definition: 'second-person narration is a narrative mode in which a narrator tells a story to a (sometimes undefined, shifting, and/or hypothetical) narratee – delineated by *you* – who is also the (sometimes undefined, shifting, and/or hypothetical) principal actant in that story'.[15]

Of course the equivalence between the *Georgics*' farmer-protagonist(s) and the implied reader(s), be he Maecenas, the Young Caesar or a hypothetical educated urban Roman, is by no means unproblematic, any more than are the identities of the subcategories of different types of farmer and of reader.[16] Yet, so far from being an issue which sets the poem apart from modern second-person narratives and their narratology, it is one of those in which both the texts themselves and their scholarship show striking similarities and immense potential for mutual illumination. Phelan writes that 'most writers who employ this technique take advantage of the opportunity to move readers between the positions of observer and addressee and, indeed, to blur the boundaries between these positions'.[17] This moving of readers and blurring of boundaries is precisely the sort of move which many readers of the *Georgics* have detected and which some have challenged. Horsfall writes about a 'sharp separation between intended reader and imagined addressee' and admittedly the teacher does often make it explicit, by means of vocatives and the nominative subjects of jussives and other third-person imperativals, when he is addressing farmers.[18] Nevertheless, even here the wide range of types and status of agricultural workers so signalled in itself blurs boundaries and discourages a sharp demarcation of the 'imagined addressee'.[19] At one end of the scale, direct addresses to Maecenas overwhelmingly imply a discrete, literary reader, though even here the possibility of Virgil's patron pruning a vine is not *explicitly* ruled out. At the other end, direct addresses to farmers overwhelmingly imply a practical, uneducated audience, but do not explicitly rule out the possibility of their familiarity with Alexandrian aesthetics. The range of vague second-persons which occupies the spectrum between blurs further any clear sense of demarcated audiences, especially when practical instruction has simultaneous metapoetic significance, as with the intertextual grafting of book 2.[20] I would by no means wish to reject the 'two audiences' model of the *Georgics*' implied readership, especially with Volk's ingenious refinement that 'both exist *inside the poem*', though even here I would prefer a model of a spectrum of multiple audiences.[21] Yet insights from the study of second-person narration can show just how far – and in what ways – the positions can be blurred, sharpened and blurred again, especially with the vague and shifting 'you' of the *Georgics*: 'what second-person narration shows is that the more fully the narratee is characterized, the greater the distance between narratee and narrative audience; similarly, the less the narratee is characterized, the greater the coincidence between the two'.[22]

Particularly useful for the *Georgics* is Herman's application of the pragmatic concept of deixis (of which Classicists have begun to make some use, especially in the study of lyric) to the narratology of second-person narration to produce the notion of 'double deixis'.[23] As Herman himself puts it, '[f]unctionally speaking *you* superimposes the deictic role of the audience or overhearer (in this instance the reader) onto the deictic role(s) spatiotemporally anchored in the fictional world elaborated over the course of the narrative'.[24] This perfectly describes the effect produced in the *Georgics* when the urbane, urban reader in his townhouse finds himself addressed as the 'you' who must snatch down strainers and colanders from 'your' smoky rafters (*tu* spisso uimine qualos | colaque prelorum fumosis deripe tectis*, 2.241–2) or smear the hive with mud and cover it with leaves (*tu tamen et leui rimosa cubilia limo | ungue fouens circum et raras superinice frondes*, 4.45–6), his spatiotemporal location thus blurred with a rustic cottage or apiary. Yet, as always with narratology, it is not sufficient to stop at identifying the mechanism; it is the effect which is important. Herman makes important observations about the wide-ranging implications of double deixis, which 'compel[s] us to reflect on the conditions and limits of participation in discourse generally' and 'highlights narrative meanings that derive from the nonrigidity, the permeability, of the border between texts and contexts'.[25] So with the *Georgics*, the reader not only shifts between being herself and a farmer (not to mention Maecenas, the young Caesar and a range of other farmers), but in parallel motion shifts in her interpretation of what is being taught, agriculture to a farmer or the nature of the universe to a reader.[26] Yet it also reflects more broadly still, beyond its own specific concerns, about the nature of poetry, *didaxis* and the relationships between text, author, reader and world.[27]

Naming of parts: standard, autotelic and hypothetical narratives

In his influential 1991 article (lightly revised in his 2006 book), Richardson proposed a useful, but not unproblematic, taxonomy of three main types of second-person narration.[28] The first, which he rather tendentiously labels 'standard', is superficially similar to more conventional first- and third-person narratives, using the past or present tense, and differing primarily in the use of second-person verbs and pronouns. *La Modification*, *Bright Lights, Big City* and many other examples belong to this, the largest category. This is not to say that there is nothing distinctive about such narratives nor, *pace* some sceptics,[29] that the second-person pronouns and verbs could simply be converted into the third-person without substantial impact. The point is rather that 'standard' second-person narratives do not possess the other, even more distinctive features which set apart Richardson's other two categories, the autotelic and hypothetical. Nevertheless, they still produce the complex effects of double deixis, blurring positions, creating a contingent storyworld, and others which are shared by all second-person narratives.

'Standard' second-person narration, which can formally be defined as second-person verbs in indicative present or past tenses, is not a feature of the *Georgics* or of Latin didactic poetry in general. This is a significant absence. Gibson has carefully taxonomized and analysed the range of imperatival expressions used in Latin didactic poetry and although all three persons, both numbers, both voices, three moods and two tenses feature, including the third-person present indicative, the second-person equivalent does not.[30] It is by no means alien to the didactic mode, as this example from a modern gardening manual shows, giving instructions on mineralizing the soil using second-person narration: 'First, you find out what the actual chemical nature of your soil is. Then you add nutrients.'[31] Of course, the force and implication of these indicatives are imperatival, but their *form* is indistinguishable from, for example, a similar pair in the narrative of *Bright Lights, Big City*: 'You read it over. Then you tear the sheet out of the typewriter and insert a new one.'[32] Because of this formal similarity, there is inevitable slippage between discursive and narrative modes. Indeed, Gibson himself identifies a similar slippage in the striking prevalence of the third-person indicative (the so-called *dant* imperatival) in the *Georgics*, where 'the reader [may] choose between recognising it as prescriptive or descriptive.'[33] Unlike 'standard' second-person narrations and modern gardening manuals, the *Georgics* does not blur the boundary between the prescriptive and descriptive using the second-person present or past indicative. Instead, Virgil makes a sharper divide between second-person future indicative, subjunctive and imperative forms, representing instruction and the efficacy of following that instruction, and third-person present indicatives representing narrative and the determinism of its course. The tension between these modes and the worldviews they represent will be the main focus of the next section.

Richardson's second category is the 'autotelic'. By this he means texts in which the narratee is explicitly identified with the reader of the text but, unlike incidental apostrophes of the 'dear reader', the addressee's act of reading the story in itself constitutes a narrative.[34] The identity of 'you' thus oscillates – or blurs the boundary – between extradiegetic and intradiegetic narratee. This is the rarest of the three types and one best exemplified by Calvino's *If on a Winter's Night a Traveller*. Such a form of narrative has something in common with 'poetic simultaneity', one of Volk's four defining characteristics of didactic poetry, of which the *Georgics* 'presents a textbook case', and a phenomenon to which we shall return in a different context.[35] Poetic simultaneity is the conceit or illusion that the poem is being composed in real time simultaneously as it is being read. Admittedly Volk's emphasis – and indeed Virgil's – is on the simultaneity of the act of composition rather than that of reading or reception. There is nothing in the *Georgics* quite as explicit as the famous opening sentence of Calvino's novel: 'You are about to begin reading Italo Calvino's new novel, *If on a winter's night a traveller*.' Yet there is a pervasive implicit dramatization – or perhaps better narrativization – of the act of reading the *Georgics*.

Sometimes the act of reading is inextricably entwined with the poetic simultaneity of composition, as in the almost jarring juxtaposition of (second-person) imperative and first-person future indicative at 4.149–50: *nunc age, naturas apibus quas Iuppiter ipse | addidit, expediam* ('Now come, I shall set out the natures which Jupiter himself has added to bees'). The vague, Lucretian *age* grabs the addressee's attention and sets up the expectation of a further imperative specifying what he is to 'come on' and do. This is what happens at 1.35 (*agite . . . discite*) and 1.63–5 (*ergo age, terrae | pingue solum . . . | fortes inuertant tauri*), as well as in seven of the fifteen instances of *age*, always preceded by *nunc*, in Lucretius.[36] Virgil even plays with the didactic function of the formula by using it twice in the *Aristaeus*, as Aristaeus himself gives (ironic, apostrophic) instructions to Cyrene (*quin age . . . erue . . . fer . . . ure . . . molire*, 4.329–32), and in Cyrene's more straightforward commands to her fellow nymphs (*duc, age, duc*, 4.358). Yet at 4.149–50, instead of a more specific instruction for the reader, the poet follows *age* with a statement about what he himself is about to do. Virgil blurs the second-person agency of the reader (*nunc age*) with a first-person emphasis on that of the author (*expediam*), expressing the complementary and even symbiotic functions of composing and receiving in the (simultaneous) generation of the text. This too is a Lucretian technique, deployed on seven occasions in the *De Rerum Natura*.[37] However, while Lucretius too blurs the roles of poet and reader, his reader is only a reader and his narrative only that of reading the *De Rerum Natura*. Virgil's reader is also a farmer, actant as well as narratee. The blurring of distinctions between reading and farming, between being a reader and being a farmer, combine with the multiplicity of possible referents for 'you' to encourage a complex of identification and distance.

The type of second-person narrative which corresponds most closely to the formal features of the *Georgics* is what Richardson initially called 'subjunctive', but later retitled 'hypothetical'.[38] I shall use the latter term, if only to avoid the potential for ambiguity and confusion of the word 'subjunctive' in the context of discussing a Latin poem. 'Hypothetical' narratives tend to have verbs in the imperative, subjunctive or future, and a non-specific narratee-protagonist, though all of these features are often played with.[39] Their primary formal model is the manual, cookbook, self-help guide or similar instructional text; in short, didactic literature. Often the relationship is a very close one, as when Lorrie Moore, Pam Houston and others mimic and even parody self-help and self-improvement guides, especially those targeted at women. The formal mimesis has a thematic significance, as when, for example, a 'scene [from Moore's 'How to be an Other Woman'], in the form of standard advice-book instructions, stands as another example of how the narrator, like so many other women, has her identity inscribed by external expectations and cultural narratives, instead of creating it on her own'.[40] The parallelism with the *Georgics* and other didactic poems is obvious, and it will be on the insights which narratological studies of these hypothetical narratives offer that the rest of this chapter will focus. The non-specificity of the narratee-protagonist facilitates the reader's identification with her or him even more than in other second-person narratives.[41] Moreover, the use of the moods and tenses expressing the potential for the narratee-protagonist (and hence by implication the reader) to influence the course of events combines with the second-person address to produce a distinctive view of the world, or at least of the storyworld.

Hypothetical second-person narrative and the determinism of the third-person

As Schofield notes in his discussion of Bill Manhire's 1988 novella, *The Brain of Katherine Mansfield*, part of the 'work being done' by the second-person pronoun is 'to facilitate the reader's conceit in thinking that she or he does choose the path of the adventure, the illusion – the role-play illusion – that he or she is the person upon whose wisdom and fortune rests the final outcome'.[42] An extreme version of this scenario is to be found in 'Choose your own adventure' books, in which the reader, identified with the second-person narratee, can indeed actually choose the path of the adventure by selecting one action from a range of options, turning to the corresponding page and continuing the narrative in a way that is determined by that choice.[43] The more technologically-advanced successor of such books is the genre of Interactive Fiction (IF), which gives an even stronger illusion of readerly control by occluding the mechanism of choosing between alternative but still pre-written and hence predetermined narrative paths. As Ryan puts it, '[r]ather than imaginatively pre-existing to the act of narration, the events of the fictional world are made to happen at the very moment of their description through the performative force of the discourse that appears on the screen.'[44] Of course, the *Georgics* is not a digital narrative being generated as the reader progresses through it, but Ryan's description does bear striking resemblances to Volk's 'poetic simultaneity'.[45] Both the act of composition (*nunc quo quamque modo possis cognoscere dicam*, 2.226) and agricultural activity (*iam uinctae uites, iam falcem arbusta reponunt, | iam canit effectos extremus uinitor antes*, 2.416–17), and often, in addition, the nexus of the two (*rursus cura patrum cadere et succedere matrum | incipit*, 3.138–9), as in IF, 'are made to happen at the very moment of their description through the performative force of the discourse'.[46]

Yet we need not go to this extreme of simultaneity to feel the connection of second-person narration and of the *Georgics* with notions of contingency and autonomy. It is worth noting that even 'standard' second-person narratives such as *La Modification* and *Bright Lights, Big City* have a tendency to create storyworlds where contingency and the power of the protagonist to change the course of the events is foregrounded. Indeed, *La Modification*, as its title indicates, is centred on the protagonist's change of mind, not to abandon his family and move in with his mistress in Rome. At one point in *Bright Lights, Big City*, McInerney vividly reifies the narrative ramifications of his narratee's decisions: 'Downstairs, you semi-revolve, through the doors and think about how nice it would be not to have to return at all, ever.'[47] Yet it is in hypothetical narratives that the association of second-person narration and alternative scenarios – whether contingencies beyond the narratee's control or the results of autonomous decisions – is most prominent. Updike's 'How to Love America …' neatly illustrates both types of alternative scenario: the autonomous decision ('Walk, family man, with the kids, out from the parking lot and down the main street … Or, alternatively, get into the car at the motel and drive around the back streets') and the contingencies ('The kids want a quick clean hamburgery place … Perhaps the kids win … Or perhaps you talk the kids into the Mexican restaurant'), the forking paths thematically relating to competing views of the nature of America ('This is America, a hamburger kingdom, one cuisine, under God, indivisible, with pickles and potato chips for all … This is America, where we take everything in, tacos and chow mein and pizza and sauerkraut, because we are only what we eat, we are whatever we say we are').[48]

While the reader-narratee, outside IF and adventure gamebooks, cannot actually change the course of the narrative, she is frequently given choices and alternatives which give the illusion of control over the narrative and the world it represents, a feature shared by second-person narratives and the *Georgics*. Sometimes there is not even the illusion of choice and only one option is offered for each of a set of alternative scenarios. Thus, different types of soil (rich or sloping and uneven) will lead to the narratee planting his vines in different ways (densely or more widely spaced), suggesting not choice, but still the variety of narrative paths which denies linear determinism.[49] Sometimes the alternative narrative paths are dependent on the narratee, who can choose his own adventure, whether to sow wheat or spelt (note the further ramifications within each option), which will lead to planting at the setting of the Pleiades, or vetch, beans or lentils, leading to a planting at the setting of Bootes (1.219–30). The illusion of contingency and autonomy is produced by the second-person narration.[50]

Of course, it *is* an illusion of autonomy, but there remains the key question as to whether the mode of second-person narration goes so far in acknowledging this illusory quality as actually to deny autonomy and self-determination, and conversely assert a model of determinism. This is, of course, a central debate in the interpretation of the *Georgics*. Few would deny that the Iron Age world of the poem is a harsh one, unforgiving of lapses in *labor* and *cura*, as illustrated by the image of the oarsman rowing unceasingly against the current (1.201–3). It is more controversial whether only such lapses cause calamities and, as Nappa writes of the fire at 2.303–14, the poem 'allows for the possibility of both failure and success and ... puts the choice between the two squarely in human hands'.[51] Or are there times when disaster strikes, regardless of the efforts and precautions of human or animal *labor* and *cura*, as seems to be the case with the plough-ox killed by the plague?[52] If the narrative mode of the *Georgics* is to contribute to this debate, we must look at the issue in modern second-person narratives.

Scholars of second-person narrative have tended to see an ethos of determinism in the mode. Certainly passages such as the following from Moore's 'How' tend to reinforce such a notion: 'MAKE ATTEMPTS AT a less restrictive arrangement. Watch them sputter and deflate like balloons.'[53] For DelConte, it is the very non-specificity of the narratee that produces the feeling of determinism, as 'the hypothetical and shifting nature of the narratee-protagonist suggests a sense of inevitability of events', whereas for Richardson, it is the illusory range of alternative scenarios, as 'ironically, this very wealth of possibility gradually gives way to a strange kind of necessity'.[54] The key word here is 'ironically', for it reveals that, though many 'how-to' second-person narratives construct a sense of inevitability, they do so by perversely, polemically and ironically deconstructing the underlying tendency of the mode to construct a sense of empowerment and autonomy. Indeed, in the case of the stories in Moore's *Self-Help*, this formal move reinforces the thematic thrust, which is to parody and deflate the empowering discourse of real self-help manuals.[55] It is quite possible that such second-person narrations have a further tendency to set up the deconstruction of their own construction of a worldview of autonomy and empowerment, but the key point is that they do fundamentally construct such a worldview.

If second-person narrative, and especially its 'hypothetical' mode, does indeed tend to conjure a storyworld – and a vision of a world beyond the narrative – which is contingent and non-determinist, and which a more-or-less autonomous 'you' has the potential to shape and change, then it does so most clearly when set in antithesis with the determinist tendencies of third-person narrative. The close relationship between narrative – and it is surely not too tendentious to gloss this as more specifically first- or third-person past-tense narrative – and a determinist worldview was most vigorously asserted by Barthes, writing of 'Destiny, of which narrative all things considered is no more than the "language"'.[56] These ideological associations have been more specifically linked with a single narrative genre, 'epic with its linear teleology'.[57] This adds a further layer of complexity to the interplay, since the *Georgics* famously plays with its relationship to epic, turning epic simile into narrative and vice versa, depicting the farmer's struggle against nature as an epic battle.[58] Scholars of nineteenth- and twentieth-century novels have explored the ways in which techniques such as sideshadowing and the evocation of counterfactual narrative paths serve to challenge and destabilize such a determinist and often triumphalist view of both literature and history, and similar approaches have been adopted towards Classical epic.[59] Yet the existence of such moves towards subversion and destabilization is in itself clearer proof of the dominant determinist tendency against which they are reacting.

This tension between the determinism of third-person narrative and the (ostensible) autonomy of second-person narrative is most sharply shown when the two narrative modes are juxtaposed. It is a common feature of modern second-person, especially 'hypothetical', narratives which are frequently 'playing on the boundaries of other narrative voices'.[60] In Houston's 1990 short story, 'How to Talk to a Hunter', there is constant oscillation between second-person instructions urging the narratee to assert her personal autonomy and emotional integrity, and third-person narrative of what her faithless and manipulative male lover 'will' inevitably do. The following passage is characteristic:

> Plan to be breezy and aloof and full of interesting anecdotes about all the other men you've ever known. Plan to be hotter than ever before in bed, and a little cold out of it. Remember that necessity is the mother of invention. Be flexible.
>
> First, he will find the faulty bulb that's been keeping all the others from lighting. He will explain in great detail the most elementary electrical principles. You will take turns placing the ornaments you and other men, he and other women, have spent years carefully choosing. Under the circumstances, try to let this be a comforting thought.[61]

Of course, the inevitability in Houston's short story is not that of cosmic determinism, but rather a pessimistic view of the unalterable nature of the Western male in sexual relationships and indeed of the Western female's passive victimhood. Nevertheless, the same tension between the action of ineluctable forces and the attempt to overcome them lies at its heart and is in large part dramatized by the formal tension between narrative modes. In this case, the competition is overwhelmingly weighted in favour of third-person inevitability, and the narrator's instructions to the narratee have a particularly despairing quality. Indeed, most of the imperatives are not even direct calls to assert agency, but stand at one step removed, exhortations to 'plan' or 'try' to do something effective, at one point even abrogating the narrator's authority as advisor and the value of advice by advising improvisation, falling back on the platitude 'Remember that necessity is the mother of invention.' This despairing *didaxis* encodes its own inevitable failure and throws into question the very possibility of autonomy which its second-person form tends to assert. Undeniably there is a tendency for second-person narrative to deconstruct and ironize its own anti-determinist worldview, but such deconstruction and irony only work because of the narrative form's more fundamental tendency to *assert* that worldview. Houston's despairing imperatives to 'plan' and 'try' are in overt dialogue with her third-person narrative of what 'will' happen, but they are also in a more implicit dialogue with more effective exhortations to 'do' things and demonstrate an agency that will make a difference.

Both the ironized and 'straight' versions can be found in the *Georgics*, and I shall now re-examine two very familiar passages from the perspective of the ideologically-charged interplay between second- and third-person narrative. The first is the gadfly (3.146–56):

> est lucos Silari circa ilicibusque uirentem
> plurimus Alburnum uolitans, cui nomen asilo
> Romanum est, oestrum Grai uertere uocantes,
> asper, acerba sonans, quo tota exterrita siluis
> diffugiunt armenta; furit mugitibus aether
> concussus siluaeque et sicci ripa Tanagri.
> hoc quondam monstro horribilis exercuit iras
> Inachiae Iuno pestem meditata iuuencae.
> hunc quoque (nam mediis feruoribus acrior instat)
> arcebis grauido pecori, armentaque pasces
> sole recens orto aut noctem ducentibus astris.

Around the groves of Silarus and the green holm oaks of Alburnus swarms a fly, whose Roman name is *asilus*, but the Greeks have called it in their speech *oestrus*. Fierce it is, and sharp of note; before it whole herds scatter in terror through the woods: with their bellowings the air is stunned and maddened, the groves, too, and the banks of parched Tanager. With this monster Juno once wreaked her awful wrath, when she devised a pest for the heifer maid of Inachus. This, too – for in midday heat more fierce is its attack – you will keep from the pregnant herd, and will feed the flock when the sun is new-risen, or the stars usher in the night.

The passage opens with an existential, third-person present indicative *est*. Of course this is the conventional mode of introducing an ekphrasis, going back to Homer, brought to Rome by Ennius and oft-used by Virgil elsewhere. Yet even this marks it as a distinctively epic phrase, even more so if we detect an anagrammatic wordplay on the common *est locus* ...[62] The word is thus aligned with narrative, the language of Destiny, but more specifically with epic and its linear teleology. The gadfly exists, and exists as a threat to the pregnant cows of the narratee's herd. That existence is indisputable and unalterable, as the emphatic and unqualified indicative proclaims, but the threat is not unavoidable, as the second-person verbs to come will show. Yet for now, further indicatives present a picture of herds scattering (*diffugiunt*) before it and all of nature, spanning air, forest and bank, raging (*furit*) with the resultant mooing. The characteristic transformation of Homeric simile into *Georgic* narrative further assimilates these lines to epic with its linear teleology.[63] We seem to be in the world of the most pessimistic readings of the *Georgics*, where no amount of *labor* and *cura* can overcome the malign forces of the Iron Age.[64]

Then comes the shift into past-tense third-person narrative of myth, with complex and paradoxical effect. The brief narrative of Juno and Io has the generalizing, paradigmatic force of a mythical exemplum, the more so as the erotic connotations of Io's frenzy and the polyvalence of the word *pestis* forge links with book 3's other threats, love, snakes and plague.[65] Yet it also has a particularity, involving as it does specific individuals (*Inachia, Iuno*) and occurring at a specific time in the past (*quondam . . . exercuit*), which offers greater hope than the totalizing presents which precede it. And indeed the transition from this specific attack of the gadfly is into the second-person narrative of how you will (successfully) keep this pest from your herd.[66] The use of future indicatives as imperativals (*arcebis, pasces*) is common in the *Georgics* but still retains a marked quality of confidence in the narratee's capacity to follow the instruction and for that instruction to be efficacious. Far from Houston's despairing imperatives in the second degree urging the narratee to 'try' to do something, Virgil's future indicatives simultaneously function as instructions and self-fulfilling predictions of those instructions' efficacy: do this as part of the autonomous agency that is yours within your second-person narrative and you *will* succeed, as surely as Houston's third-person 'hunter' *will* snuff out her second-person narratee's attempts to do anything. For Virgil, as for Yoda, there is no 'try'. Even the parenthetic intrusion of a further third-person present indicative (*nam . . . instat*) only serves to reinforce the dominance of the second-person narrative here and the power of the narratee to overcome any reversion to the determinism of third-person narrative. Second-person narrative defeats third-person, and efficacious autonomy overcomes determinism, in this case, at least, and provided, of course, that you follow the instructions.

Yet this is not always the balance of power between narrative modes and their corresponding worldviews. The storm in book 1 is another much-studied passage, but one which can be further illuminated by looking at the interplay of second- and third-person narrative (1.299, 305–6, 311–21, 335–8):

nudus ara, sere nudus . . .

. . .

sed tamen et quernas glandes tum stringere tempus   305
et lauri bacas oleamque cruentaque myrta,

. . .

quid tempestates autumni et sidera dicam,
atque, ubi iam breuiorque dies et mollior aestas,
quae uigilanda uiris? uel cum ruit imbriferum uer,
spicea iam campis cum messis inhorruit et cum

frumenta in uiridi stipula lactentia turgent?   315
saepe ego, cum flauis messorem induceret aruis
agricola et fragili iam stringeret hordea culmo,
omnia uentorum concurrere proelia uidi,
quae grauidam late segetem ab radicibus imis
sublimem expulsam eruerent: ita turbine nigro   320
ferret hiems culmumque leuem stipulasque uolantis.

. . .

hoc metuens caeli mensis et sidera serua,   335
frigida Saturni sese quo stella receptet,
quos ignis caelo Cyllenius erret in orbis.
in primis uenerare deos . . .

Strip to plough, strip to sow . . .

. . .

Still, then is the time to strip the acorns and laurel berries, the olive and blood-red
   myrtle,

. . .

Why should I speak of autumn's changes and stars, and for what our workers must
watch, as the day now grows shorter and summer softer, or when spring pours
down in showers, as the bearded harvest now bristles in the fields, and the corn on
its green stem swells with milk? Often, when the farmer was bringing the reaper
into his golden fields and was just beginning to strip the barley from the frail stalk,
I have seen all the winds close in conflict, tearing up the heavy corn far and wide
from its deepest roots and tossing it on high; so in a black whirlwind did the storm
sweep away the light straw and flying stubble.

. . .

In fear of this, mark the months and signs of heaven; whither Saturn's cold star
withdraws itself and into what circles of the sky strays the Cyllenian fire. Above all,
worship the gods . . .

Here the shift is not from third- to second-person narrative, but rather in the opposite
direction, only returning retrospectively to a very qualified form of the latter. The
confident Hesiodic imperatives *ara* and *sere* (299) unambiguously put the narratee in
control of his own second-person narrative. There is a slight shift in 305–6 as the narratee
is still the primary actant, but his agency and even his identity is occluded by the ellipse
of the *tibi*, so that his quasi-autonomous action is even more subject than usual to the
restrictive rules of the world of the *Georgics*.

More radical is the shift into the description of the storm proper. The superficially
conventional *praeteritio* (*quid . . . dicam*) takes on a troubling quality in the mouth of a
didactic *praeceptor*. The obvious answer to the question 'Why should I speak of . . .?' is
'Because it is an integral part of the material you are teaching.' Defamiliarized thus, it
becomes not a topos but an expression of futility: 'What is the point in my speaking of . . .

since it is going to happen anyway whatever precautions you take?'[67] This undermining of the efficacy of *didaxis*, and with it of the autonomy of the narratee against the forces of determinist third-person narrative, is made overt by the way in which the storm strikes *just as* the farmer is starting to reap and *already* (*iam*, 317) stripping the grain from the pathetically fragile stalks (316–17). It is not made explicit whether or not the farmer has taken precautionary measures, which in any case the narrator's *praeteritio* has reneged on teaching him. The resumptive instruction to watch the skies in fear of this (*hoc metuens caeli mensis et sidera serua*, 1.335) might suggest that '[i]t can be predicted, and it can be survived',[68] though the privileging of the dubious recourse to honouring the gods (*in primis uenerare deos*, 1.338) tends to undermine the sense that unmediated human agency can have any effect.[69] However, the question as to whether or not the destructive effects of the storm can be anticipated, limited and managed is separate from the narratological issue here, whereby the third-person mode (313–21) reflects the (uncontroversial) inevitability of the storm.

This inevitability is evoked, not only by the shift from second- to third-person narration, but by the further shift to a deeper level of intradiegetic narration. The storm and the farmer's failure to avoid it are focalized through the narrator and his claim to autopsy. This shift is doubly emphasized by the combination in the poem of *ego* and *uidi*, each of which appears only once elsewhere in the poem (2.101, 1.93) and nowhere else together. Of course, the assertion of autopsy is a claim to authority and reliability,[70] but it also separates and distances the narratee from the protagonist by setting her alongside the narrator as spectators of events which play out without any prospect of being controlled by 'you'. The farmer has moved from autonomous narratee-protagonist to passive object of the narrator's gaze.[71] The contrast is marked still further by the way in which the storm-episode is not merely third-person narration but aligns itself with epic narrative. Both the futile actions of the farmer in sending his reaper into the fray (*messorem induceret*, 1.316; cf. *Aen.* 11.620) and the battles of the winds (*uentorum … proelia*, 1.318) evoke epic warfare, while the whole episode constitutes one of the poem's characteristic transformations of epic simile (here Hom. *Il.* 16.384–92) into didactic narrative.[72] The fact that 'you', the narratee-protagonist of the *Georgics*' second-person narration, cannot influence the inevitable, calamitous storm is reinforced, not only by its being depicted in the language of Destiny that is third-person narrative, but more particularly in the language of epic, with its linear teleology. Whether the return to second-person verbs urging vigilance (*serua*, 1.335) and piety (*uenerare*, 1.338) reasserts a sense of empowered autonomy or, by their very impotence and desperation, ironically undercut it remains one of those questions which the poem is so good at raising and so reluctant to answer.

Epilogue

This chapter aims at only a sketch of the ways in which the narratology of second-person narration might contribute to the interpretation of the *Georgics* in particular, but also of didactic poetry in general and even a wider range of Classical texts, in particular hymns, lyric, oratory and epistolography. One other important aspect, which I shall explore elsewhere, is the interrelationship of apostrophe, didactic address and second-person narrative.[73] A further hope is that the flow of influence might not only be in one direction. All too often Classics stands as a passive and sometimes belated receiver of theoretical approaches from other disciplines, though it has much to offer in return. I hope that the story of 'you' may not only be one of what second-person narration can do for the *Georgics*, but also what the *Georgics* can do for second-person narration.[74]

CHAPTER 2
CLEARING THE GROUND IN *GEORGICS* 1
S. J. Heyworth

New beginnings

How to begin is a problem shared by farmer and writer. Virgil himself seeks a new beginning midway through the *Georgics* when (as he presents it) he realizes that uncultivated trees provide as much benefit to mankind as the vine – and wine is destructive too (2.454–6). He therefore seeks a new course. First of all he wishes to write natural philosophy in the Lucretian mode (2.475–82), but he does not have the capacity for this, whereas he does gain pleasure from the innocent life of the idyllic countryside far from the city, the world familiar from the *Eclogues* (2.483–9: n.b. *siluas*, 486; *umbra*, 489). Both are commendable; the urban and the rustic are compared at length (2.495–540), but no clear choice is determined before the book ends.[1] Book 3 begins announcing pastoral as its subject (*Te quoque, magna Pales, . . . canemus*, 'You too we shall sing, mighty Pales', 3.1), and rejecting mythological narrative; but then the poet seeks a way to raise himself from the earth (3.8–9) and promises to build a temple for Caesar (3.13–39). Even when he returns to *siluae*, and the animal husbandry that will form the topic of the third book, he describes the work as *haud mollia iussa*, and emphasizes the way he has delayed embarking on this material, and is continuing to defer the epic to come (3.40–3, 46–8):[2]

> interea Dryadum siluas saltusque sequamur
> intactos, tua, Maecenas, haud mollia iussa:
> te sine nil altum mens incohat. en age segnis
> rumpe moras.
>
> . . .
>
> mox tamen ardentis accingar dicere pugnas
> Caesaris et nomen fama tot ferre per annos,
> Tithoni prima quot abest ab origine Caesar.

> In the meantime let us head for the woods and virgin glades of the Dryads – your ungentle commands, Maecenas: without you my mind begins nothing lofty. Come then, away with idle delay. . . . In time to come, however, I shall gird myself to speak of the blazing battles of Caesar, and to maintain his name in glory through as many years as Caesar is distant from the first beginning of Tithonus.

Delay in starting his epic will continue through book 4, but by treating the bees, his tiny topic, as epic warriors in miniature (4.3–6, 67–87), and by constructing the story of

Aristaeus as a combination of *Iliad* and *Odyssey*,[3] he ensures that when he begins the *Aeneid* he has already prepared himself.

Farmers similarly need to clear the ground before they begin; the difficulty and the destructive effects of this are another intermittent but major theme of the *Georgics*. Both aspects are present in the narrative that dominates the closing of the poem, for example where Aristaeus undergoes frightening adventures in his quest to discover how to acquire a new stock of bees, and then sacrifices four bulls, four heifers, a calf and a sheep in order to gain what he seeks (4.360–553).[4] Destruction is the striking accompaniment of instructions on how to get the richest farmland at 2.203–11:

> nigra fere et presso pinguis sub uomere terra
> et cui putre solum (namque hoc imitamur arando),
> optima frumentis: non ullo ex aequore cernes
> plura domum tardis decedere plaustra iuuencis;
> aut unde iratus[5] siluam deuexit arator
> et nemora euertit multos ignaua per annos,
> antiquasque domos auium cum stirpibus imis
> eruit; illae altum nidis petiere relictis,
> at rudis enituit impulso uomere campus.

Earth that is nearly black and rich beneath the pressure of the plough and that has crumbling soil (for this is what we imitate when ploughing) is best for corn – from no plain will you see more wagons head off home behind slow oxen; or land from where the angry ploughman has carted off the wood and overturned the groves that have been idle through many years, and uprooted the ancient homes of birds, root and trunk; they have abandoned their nests and sought the sky, while the fresh field has begun to gleam where the plough has been driven over it.

This chapter is an attempt to apply Virgil's teaching to the interpretation of the opening paragraphs of the didactic.

Georgics 1.104–10

Georgics 1.104–10 famously imitate Homer's simile comparing Achilles' fight with the Scamander to a man irrigating a garden (*Il.* 21.257–62), and thus turn epic embellishment into didactic reality:[6]

> quid dicam, iacto qui semine comminus arua
> insequitur cumulosque ruit male pinguis harenae,   105
> deinde satis fluuium inducit riuosque sequentis,
> et, cum exustus ager morientibus aestuat herbis,

ecce supercilio cliuosi tramitis undam
elicit? illa cadens raucum per leuia murmur
saxa ciet, scatebrisque arentia temperat arua.   110

What am I to say of the man who when he has scattered the seed gets to grips with the fields and rakes out piles of barren sand, then guides a river and streams to follow him to the crops, and then, when the field is burned out by the heat and the blades of grass are dying, **look, he decoys the wave from the brow of the channelled slope?**[7] Descending over the smooth rocks it produces a loud purling and softens the dry fields with its bubbling water.

My first topic is nothing so grand, but simply the grammar of verse 108. Modern commentators take *supercilio* to be a separative ablative: hence Wilkins' translation (in bold, above), or Shipham's 'lo! from the brow of its hillside bed, lures forth the stream'. But Servius shows some uncertainty about the meaning:

ECCE SVPERCILIO id est ex improuiso. 'supercilio' autem altitudine, summitate terrarum. alii 'supercilia' loca in obliquum delimata quae superne habeant alia fastigia ex accidenti dicunt. tramites autem sunt conualles, quae de lateribus utrimque peruiae limitant montes, quae solent etiam saltus nuncupari. sed hic tramitem nunc pro ualle ac saltu accipere debemus et pro supercilio simpliciter edito loco, ut Ἴλιος ὀφρυόεσσα; nam ideo ait 'cliuosi'.

ECCE SVPERCILIO i.e. unexpectedly. However, *supercilio* is 'from a height, the top of an area of land'. Others say on the basis of similarity that *supercilia* are places cut off at an angle that have further tops above. *tramites* are enclosed valleys which are passable from either side and which bound mountains; these are also called *saltus* ['ravines' or perhaps 'saddles']. But here we ought now to take *trames* as standing for 'valley' or 'ravine' and for *supercilio* simply 'from a raised area', as in 'high-browed Troy' [*Iliad* 22.411]; that is why he says *cliuosi* ['hilly' or 'on a slope'].

This is an accumulation of comments rather than a single thought-out view. It is hard to see what the commentator who writes on *trames* and *supercilio* supposes the sense to be: 'he elicits water from the raised area of a hilly valley' – what sort of water collects in the raised area of a valley? One commentator who explicitly follows Servius is Sargeaunt:[8] 'Servius is here right in taking the word to mean a small valley, chine or ravine. At the top of it is a pond or stream held up by a gate. When the gate is lifted, the water flows down the *trames* and is conducted by ditches through the fields below.' This gives a text that ignores the prior efforts of the farmer, however, as Virgil says nothing about the ditches; nor does Sargeaunt explain *supercilio*, which does not mean 'gate'. Most other modern commentators seem to follow Servius's interpretation, at least of *supercilio*, though they do little to clarify what he might mean. Thus Richter too finds a Homeric model for the use of *supercilium*, namely ὀφρύς for the top of a hill at *Iliad* 20.151, and for the use in

Latin he compares Livy 27.18.10, *ipse expeditos . . . ad leuem armaturam infimo stantem supercilio ducit* ('he himself led the unencumbered troops . . . to meet the lightly armed force standing on the lowest brow of the hill [*or* the bottom of the brow]'); clearer is 34.29.11, *supercilio haud procul distantis tumuli* ('on the brow of a hill not far distant'). Thomas merely paraphrases: 'look, over the slope comes a channel of water'. Neither explains how the word works in context, but the fact that they both claim *cliuosi tramitis* renders Homer's χώρωι ἔνι προαλεῖ⁹ suggests 'from the brow of a sloping area', so that the *trames* is the slope down which the water will run. There is a passage where we might without damaging the sense give *trames* the meaning 'slope': Ovid, *Fasti* 3.13: *uentum erat ad molli decliuem tramite ripam*.¹⁰ However, among the many instances of *trames* with its regular meaning 'path' are a group where the context shows that a sloping path is visualized, for example *Aeneid* 5.610: *cito decurrit tramite* (Iris 'descends by a swift path', i.e. the rainbow); Ovid, *Met.* 10.53: *carpitur accliuis per muta silentia trames* ('a sloping path is taken through the quiet silence'); Seneca, *Ep.* 84.13: *per difficiles . . . et arduos tramites adeuntur* ('they are approached by steep and difficult paths'); and Silius 6.120: *cliuoso tramite uitae* ('on the steep path of life', cited by Mynors); and this gives an appropriate sense at *Fasti* 3.13: Silvia 'had come to the bank that descended with a gently sloping path' (*uentum erat ad molli decliuem tramite ripam*). I can find no other warrant for the sense 'slope', and in combination with *cliuosus* the reader looks for a more specific force in *trames* than simply 'area'.

Helpful, though very muddled, is the account in Mynors. He first suggests that *supercilio* is to be taken as 'brim' rather than 'brow', a point to which we shall return; next he says *cliuosi* (first found here) means 'downhill', unlike at 2.212 where *ieiuna . . . cliuosi glarea ruris* is the 'barren gravel of steep [*or* hilly] country', before glossing *tramitis* as 'cross-path' (which seems to conflict with 'downhill'). Finally, he concludes that we should 'think of the water as flowing in its irrigation channel across the upper edge of the field' – which conflicts with both the previous glosses. It is true, as we have seen, that *trames* means 'path'; but paths are irrelevant to this account of managed irrigation, and Mynors' final thought is better: *tramitis* must rather mean 'channel' here, as it does in Columella's passage about horticultural irrigation, at 10.48: *ueniant decliui tramite riui* ('let streams flow from [*or* in] a downhill channel'); at Apuleius, *Met.* 6.14.3; and in Porphyrio's commentary on Horace's poem to his bailiff, *Epist.* 1.14.29–30:

> addit opus pigro riuus, si decidit imber,
> multa mole docendus aprico parcere prato.

If rain has fallen, the brook adds labour for you in an idle moment: it needs educating with considerable effort¹¹ to spare the meadow that has caught the sun.

Porphyrio comments (on *multa mole docendus*) 'Hoc est praefossis tramitibus. sic alibi ipse de fluuio: *doctus iter melius*' ('i.e. with pre-dug channels. So elsewhere Horace himself says of a river, "taught a better route"').¹²

Similar is Erren's view in his commentary.[13] However, he explains that the whole phrase is a 'dreiteiliger Ringtausch von *e tramite cliuoso supercilii*, "aus dem abschüssigen Kanal am First"' ('A triple transference from *e tramite cliuoso supercilii*, out of the sloping channel on the ridge'). No parallels are given for this improbable series of transferences; and in any case what does *supercilio* contribute?[14] Rather we should, with Wagner (and Sheridan), put *cliuosi tramitis* with *undam* ('he elicits the water of a channel on a slope'): this enables the reader to envisage the plausible picture in which Mynors' note culminates. How then should we take *supercilio*? If Mynors were right to render it 'brim', we could read the form as an ablative of the route, 'over the brim'.[15] Instances in Apuleius confirm that *supercilium* was used for 'the top of a bank': *Met.* 5.25.3: *tunc forte Pan deus rusticus iuxta supercilium*[16] *amnis sedebat complexus Echo* ('by chance the rustic god Pan was sitting embracing Echo near the brow overlooking the stream') and 7.18.2. But the top of a bank is not the same thing as a 'brim', and I have found no evidence for such a usage. It is possible that it simply means 'from the top',[17] as when Pliny describes the construction of reservoirs to produce sudden waterfalls designed to clear hillsides undermined by goldmines: *Nat. Hist.* 33.75: *ad capita deiectus in superciliis montium piscinae cauantur* ('at the head of the waterfall pools are dug out at the tops of mountain slopes'). But elsewhere this geographical metaphor is expressed, as in the Pliny and the Apuleius passages, with greater clarity,[18] or else *supercilium* means a 'hillock' or a ridge of earth used as a boundary marker, as repeatedly in the Agrimensores.[19] Here, as we have seen, to take *supercilio* with the following genitive leads only to confusion.

Instead we should try the sense 'eyebrow', the meaning *supercilium* has in Virgil's only other usage, at *Ecl.* 8.33–4 (where the persona adopted by Damon for his song is playing the part of a Polyphemus):

dumque tibi est odio mea fistula dumque capellae
hirsutumque supercilium promissaque barba

And while you loathe my pipe and my goats, my shaggy eyebrow and my uncut beard . . .

Throughout Augustan poetry, the noun only ever has the basic sense 'eyebrow' or 'brow'. 'With an eyebrow' means 'with an easy command'. This sense perhaps lies behind Servius's *ex improuiso* at the start of his note; but that may simply render *ecce*.[20] Erren, after his fantasy about *supercilio cliuosi tramitis*, ends his main note with a rather different reading, seeing the metaphorical *supercilium* as allowing a shift to the eyebrow of the farmer, whose facial gesture instigates the irrigation.[21] He cites one key parallel, Horace, *Odes* 3.1.8: *Iouis cuncta supercilio mouentis* ('Jupiter moving everything with his brow'), which helpfully shows the availability of the instrumental ablative in Virgil's day. The analogy is a significant one too: the master of the universe controls things with a flicker of his eyebrow; so does the farmer who has prepared his irrigation channels in advance – for once in the *Georgics* we get a hint of the slaves who will do the work at their master's command.[22] One should acknowledge that Horace might have invented the expression on the basis of *Iliad* 1.528: κυανέῃσιν ἐπ' ὀφρύσι νεῦσε Κρονίων ('Zeus the son of Cronus nodded with his dark brows'), also imitated by Apuleius at *Met.* 6.7.2: *nec rennuit Iouis caerulum supercilium* ('nor did the dark brow of Jupiter refuse to nod'). But eyebrows regularly play a speaking role in Roman culture: see especially Pliny, *Nat. Hist.* 11.138 on their wide use to convey emotion and will:[23]

> frons et aliis, sed homini tantum tristitiae, hilaritatis, clementiae, seueritatis index. in assensu eius supercilia homini et pariter et alterna mobilia. et in his pars animi: <his> negamus, annuimus. haec maxime indicant fastum. superbia aliubi conceptaculum, sed hic sedem habet: in corde nascitur, huc subit, hic pendet.

> Other creatures have a brow too, but only in man does it signify sadness and happiness, clemency and sternness. In conformity with it human eyebrows are mobile, either together or one at a time. An element of the mind lies in them: <with them> we refuse and we assent. In particular they indicate contempt. Arrogance is conceived elsewhere, but has its home here: it is born in the heart, but comes to the brow and lingers there.

Eyebrows frown and imply arrogance, sternness or disapproval; but they are also used by lovers to communicate, as repeatedly in Ovid, for example at *Amores* 1.4.19: *uerba superciliis sine uoce loquentia dicam* ('with my eyebrows I shall say words that communicate without voice');[24] and they are used by masters to address their slaves with simple authority: note how *supercilium* is the mark of the *dominus* in Petronius, *Sat.* 113.10: *nec domini supercilium induebat, sed amici quaerebat obsequium* ('he did not put on the frown of the master, but sought the subservience of a friend'); and Martial 1.4.1–2: *Contigeris nostros, Caesar, si forte libellos,* | *terrarum dominum pone supercilium* ('Caesar, if you happen to touch my little books, drop the brow that rules the world').[25] Thus the use of *supercilium* to connote something that gives commands is not an isolated one, nor is the use of the adverbial ablative.

What confirms the interpretation is the imitation in Columella, *De Re Rustica* 10.47–9 (of *tellus*):

> at si cruda manet caelo durata sereno,
> tum iussi ueniant decliui tramite riui;
> terra bibat fontis et hiantia compleat ora.

> But if it remains untouched and hardened by clear weather, then give the command and let streams come from the sloping channel; let the earth drink the springs and fill its gaping mouths.

In time of drought the gardener is told to order streams of water to come 'from the sloping channel': 'by a sloping channel' would have less point – the streams are drawn from the channel to irrigate the soil. As *riui* corresponds to *undam*, and *decliui tramite* to *cliuosi tramitis*, so *iussi ueniant* interprets *supercilio elicit*. Because it is the eyebrow that elicits the water, we may more easily now give weight to the sound play between *supercilio* and *elicit*:[26] it is as if the *supercilium* is designed for eliciting. The soundplay draws attention to the verb, and thus evokes the ceremony known as *aquaelicium*, referred to with that name by Festus (p. 2.24–6, Lindsay): *aquaelicium dicitur cum aqua pluuialis remediis quibusdam elicitur, ut quondam, si creditur, manali lapide in urbem ducto* ('it is called Aquaelicium when rainwater is conjured up by certain remedies, as in the past, if you believe it, through the bringing of the *lapis manalis* into the city'), through a brief description of the rite by Varro (*de Vita Populi Romani* fr. 52.7–9, Riposati), and another Festus entry (p. 115.8–12, Lindsay):[27]

> Manalem lapidem uocabant etiam petram quandam, quae erat extra portam Capenam iuxta aedem Martis, quam cum propter nimiam siccitatem in urbem pertraherent, insequebatur pluuia statim.

> They also called a certain rock the *lapis manalis* ['the flowing stone']: this was outside the *porta Capena* near the temple of Mars, and when they dragged it into the city because of a drought, rainfall immediately followed.

Virgil's hard-working farmer has no need of such a ritual nor such effort. This is the key point: already the farmer has sown (cf. *seres*, 73), and worked the ground, following the advice previously given (45–9, 63–70, 84–99); already he has stored water and prepared channels for irrigation. So, when there is a period of hot drought and his plants are in danger of dying, he simply raises an eyebrow, and they are quickly irrigated – thanks to the preparation he has done in advance.

So ends my first act of ground clearing, a demonstration of the weeds that still clog the interpretation of Virgil's poem, and of the need always already to have begun.

Georgics 1.43–83

> Vere nouo, gelidus canis cum montibus umor
> liquitur et Zephyro putris se glaeba resoluit,
> depresso incipiat iam tum mihi taurus aratro   45
> ingemere et sulco attritus splendescere uomer.

> At the start of spring, when the chill moisture melts on the white mountains and the loosened soil has relaxed beneath the west wind, already then I'd want the ox to begin to groan over the plough as it is forced down and the blade to shine as it is rubbed smooth in the furrow.

Vere nouo: after the 42-line proem the didactic starts with a decisive and obvious first phrase.[28] The remainder of 43–4 glosses early spring as the time when snow melts and the soil relaxes under the warming breath of Zephyr: this is the time for beginning (*incipiat*, 45). 'Already then' (*iam tum*) Virgil wants to see oxen groaning with the effort of pulling the plough, and the blade to start gleaming again as it is polished by the soil. Already then the work should have begun. But verses 47–9 are less clear:

> illa seges demum uotis respondet auari
> agricolae, bis quae solem, bis frigora sensit;
> illius immensae ruperunt horrea messes.

That crop (?) at last matches the prayers of the greedy farmer, which has twice felt the sun, twice the cold; the immeasurable harvest from that source has burst the barns.

The word *seges*, which makes good sense as 'crop' in 47, shifts to the less common meaning 'field' or 'ground' as it gets redefined by the relative clause in 48 and when *illius* is attached to *messes* in 49.[29] The shift is significant: the reader may think we are concerned already with the crops that are going to be harvested, but that is merely our greedy hopes talking, and the focus is first on the bare earth.

But the controversial issue here is the meaning of the relative clause. Servius comments *ad loc.*:

> BIS QVAE SOLEM BIS FRIGORA SENSIT: quae bis et dierum calorem et noctium senserit frigora: per quod duplicem ostendit arationem, uernalem et autumnalem. nec enim ad tempora aestatis uel hiemis referre possumus, quod ait 'bis solem, bis frigora', quia non sunt in Italia in uno anno duae aestates et duae hiemes, sicut geometrae dicunt esse in quadam parte Indiae, in insula Taprobane. aut sicut quidam dicunt ideo 'bis', ut semel cum fructibus, semel uacua solem et frigus perpessa accipiamus.

> BIS QVAE SOLEM BIS FRIGORA SENSIT: which has twice experienced the warmth of days and the chill of nights: by this he points to the double ploughing, in spring and autumn. We cannot refer to the periods of summer or winter the fact that he says *bis solem, bis frigora*, because there are not two summers and two winters in a single year in Italy, as the geographers say there are in part of India, on the island of Sri Lanka. Or else, as some say, 'twice' on the following basis, that we take it as enduring sun and cold once with crops, once empty.

Though some modern commentators follow Servius, this looks like nonsense. On the one hand, it is pointless to say that the ploughland must twice be exposed to the diurnal cycle: what could it possibly mean? Two days are to pass before what? And how does the text point to spring and autumn? The objection is feeble too: of course Italy only has one summer and one winter each year, but the reference can simply be to two years. Mynors begins his commentary on 43–9 (and 63–70) with a clear account of the basic practices of cultivation that Virgil assumes:

> The normal ancient practice, here taken for granted by V., as by Hesiod (see West on *op*. 462–3), was to take a crop off the ground in alternate years; every other year the field lay fallow to recover its fertility, and save up its scanty moisture. After harvest in early summer, the land is let alone, except perhaps for burning the stubble (84f.) ... Next spring this fallow ... is broken up by the first ploughing (*proscindere*) and again left; a second and a third ploughing follow in that same summer (*iterare* and *tertiare*); and the ground is then ready for the sowing, which is normally accompanied by another ploughing to cover the seed ...[30]

Though not corresponding in every detail, this gives a structure against which to understand 47–9. The reader has just been told to plough in early spring. The heat of the summer sun will follow spring, and the cold of winter will follow that: for a huge crop the farmer is to expose the field through two summers and two winters before hoping for a harvest. Though the context concerns ploughing, the more important message is about leaving the land fallow. Of course in normal practice a crop would be taken off in the summer before the land is left fallow. But for the farmer, Virgil's reader, who is just starting out, there can be no hope of a big harvest until two years of work have prepared the way.

Sargeaunt comments on *sensit* in 48 that 'Unless loosened by the plough the land would be little aware of either sun or frost.' That may be right, but it is possible that Virgil thinks of the soil as first exposed by the harvest (and the burning of stubble); it will then need repeated ploughing so that the effects of winter frost and summer sun can be felt. The notion that the fourth ploughing should precede the sowing is drawn out as Virgil's lesson by the Elder Pliny, at *Nat. Hist.* 18.181:

> quarto seri sulco Vergilius existimatur uoluisse, cum dixit optimam esse segetem, quae bis soles, bis frigora sensisset. spissius solum, sicut plerumque in Italia, quinto sulco seri melius est, in Tuscis uero nono. at fabam et uiciam non proscisso serere sine damno compendium operae est.

> When Virgil said that the best ground was what had twice felt the sun, twice the cold, he is thought to have wanted the sowing to happen in the fourth furrow [i.e. the one made by the fourth ploughing]. It is better that denser soil, such as is common in Italy, be sown in the fifth furrow, but in Tuscany actually in the ninth. However, it is possible without any loss to save labour by sowing beans and vetch in soil that has not been ploughed in advance.

As scholars have observed, *existimatur* here implies that the interpretation of the Virgilian passage was already controversial by Pliny's time. But his references to five ploughings, and in the richer soil of Tuscany nine, show that it is repetition that matters.

However, what Virgil stresses with his numbers is the desirability of leaving land fallow. Hence my outline of the sequence Virgil here implies:

Year 1:	*Vere nouo* (43):		plough [and so repeatedly]
	summer:	heat 1 (*solem*, 48)	
	winter:	cold 1 (*frigora*, 48)	
Year 2:	summer:	heat 2 (*solem*, 48)	
	winter:	cold 2 (*frigora*, 48)	[sow, 208–30]
[?Year 3:	spring:		plough and sow]

The process takes time; and yet, he goes on, even before that the farmer has to learn about his land, currently 'unknown' (*ignotum*, 50), and about the local climate and practices: he needs to find out what will grow there, and whether it is fertile or dry – for that will (it transpires) affect how he treats the land and how often he ploughs (1.50–4).

> at[31] prius ignotum ferro quam scindimus aequor,
> uentos et uarium caeli praediscere morem
> cura sit ac patrios cultusque habitusque locorum,
> et quid quaeque ferat regio et quid quaeque recuset.
> hic segetes, illic ueniunt felicius uuae . . .

> But first, before we plough the unfamiliar plain, it should be a concern to learn in advance about the winds, the varying character of the climate, and the customary cultivation and conditions of the place, what each area bears and each refuses. Here corn, there grapes are produced more successfully . . .

The practice of leaving land fallow is clearly present in the diction of two Greek passages regularly cited on *Georgics* 1.47–9: de la Cerda already mentions Theophrastus, *de Causis Plantarum* 3.20.7: ἡ κατεργασία δὲ ἐν τῶι νεᾶν κατ' ἀμφοτέρας τὰς ὥρας, καὶ θέρους καὶ χειμῶνος, ὅπως χειμασθῆι καὶ ἡλιωθῆι ἡ γῆ ('Working the land through ploughing up of fallow happens in both seasons, summer and winter, so that the earth may feel the effects of cold and heat'),[32] which is obviously close to Virgil's phrasing in pairing winter and summer, bad weather and sun; and it helps underpin the interpretation by explaining the reasons for working fallow land repeatedly. The form from which νεᾶν stems appears also in an Idyll included in the Theocritean collection, at 25.25–6: τριπόλοις σπόρον ἐν νειοῖσιν | ἔσθ' ὅτε βάλλοντες καὶ τετραπόλοισιν ὁμοίως ('casting the seed on fallow three times ploughed, and sometimes actually four times ploughed'); this again shows that it is the repetition of ploughing that matters, not the precise number. This interpretation was that preferred already by de la Cerda and some of his predecessors, and it is found too, most recently, in Erren. But many commentators have failed to see the relevance of the implied fallow period, and so 47–9 have remained controversial. Wagner found them so disruptive of the argument that he wished to delete them (despite the specific reference already in Pliny), and others such as Forbiger have sympathized with this. In his note on 47–8, Mynors, working from Pliny and Theophrastus, sees some of the truth ('four cultivations, starting early in the winter after harvest, and giving a four-times ploughed fallow … as in Theocr. 25.25f.'), but he fails to link this with his earlier account of the cultivation Virgil assumes, and he gets waylaid by false objections. Firstly, 'V. has told us emphatically in 43 to start in the spring, when we shall get no *frigora*', but this is of no weight if *frigora* means 'winter', as at *Ecl.* 2.22: *lac mihi non aestate nouum, non frigore defit* ('I do not lack fresh milk in summer, nor in winter'), and 5.70: *ante focum, si frigus erit; si messis, in umbra* ('before the hearth, if it is winter; if harvest time, in the shade').[33] Moreover, as Mynors himself saw, the sequence manifestly complicates the simple notion of beginning in spring: 'We return after an enthusiastic start to a topic which logically should come first', he comments on 50–3. Despite the clarity of the opening, the ongoing instructions do not simply detail what is to be done at the start of the plant year. Secondly, he claims, 'Repeated *bis* in G. 2.410, A. 6.32 and 134 indicates the repetition of one process divided into two stages or seen from two aspects': this is true, but utterly irrelevant, for in those instances *bis* is accompanied by different verbs (*bis conatus erat … bis patriae cecidere manus*, 6.32), whereas here the verb remains the same and the emphasis is on the opposed objects, *solem* and *frigora*. If (alternatively) we combine the two into a single cycle, the reference is clearly to two years.

Again Erren gets it right, but in a rather unsatisfactory way, for he hardly acknowledges the controversy.[34] Whereas at 108 he allows thorns to keep growing amid his crops, here he acts as if there were no need to clear the ground at all. However, he, like others, usefully cites Cato, *Agr.* 61: *Quid est agrum bene colere? bene arare; quid secundum? arare; tertio? stercorare* ('What is it to be a good farmer? To plough well. What comes second? Ploughing. Third? Spreading dung'). One might think that sowing is the key aspect of a farmer's activities; but before the farmer sows for the first time, he needs already to have ploughed (45–6) and waited, just as he needs to have learnt in advance about his land (50–6), and in Virgil's account, about the world (56–63). Verses 63–72 then reprise the pattern:

> ergo age, terrae
> pingue solum primis extemplo a mensibus anni
> fortes inuertant tauri, glaebasque iacentis   65
> puluerulenta coquat maturis solibus aestas;
> at si non fuerit tellus fecunda, sub ipsum
> Arcturum tenui sat erit suspendere sulco:
> illic, officiant laetis ne frugibus herbae,
> hic, sterilem exiguus ne deserat umor harenam.   70
> alternis idem tonsas cessare noualis
> et segnem patiere situ durescere campum;

Come then, immediately from the first months of the year, where the soil of the earth is rich, the powerful oxen should overturn it, and dusty heat roast the exposed clods when the sun is at its prime; but if the ground has not proved to be fertile, it will be enough to lift it up with a shallow furrow, just before the rising of Arcturus [mid-September]: in the former case so that weeds do not interfere with the successful growth of the crops, in the latter so that the little moisture does not abandon the sandy soil and leave it unfertile. In alternate years you will also allow the field that has been cut to lie fallow and the idle ground to harden with disuse.

Once more we begin at the start of the season of plant growth (*primis extemplo a mensibus anni*), but we are to plough then only if the land is heavy (*pingue*, 64).[35] If the soil is not *fecunda* (67), we delay to the autumn. Thus 63–70 repeats 43–6, with more complexity and qualification to take account of the farmer's newly gained knowledge of his land. Verses 71–2 then revisit the substance of 47–9, this time more explicitly (*alternis . . . tonsas cessare noualis*). In 73–8 comes the added qualification that one may rotate crops instead:

aut ibi flaua seres mutato sidere farra,
unde prius laetum siliqua quassante legumen
aut tenuis fetus uiciae tristisque lupini   75
sustuleris fragilis calamos siluamque sonantem.
urit enim lini campum seges, urit auenae,
urunt Lethaeo perfusa papauera somno;
sed tamen alternis facilis labor, arida tantum
ne saturare fimo pingui pudeat sola neue   80
effetos cinerem immundum iactare per agros.
sic quoque mutatis requiescunt fetibus arua,
nec nulla interea est inaratae gratia terrae.

Or in the new season you will plant yellow spelt where you have previously harvested a successful crop of beans, with their quivering pods, or the produce of slender vetch and the fragile stems and rustling foliage of bitter lupin. A crop of flax dries out the field, so does a crop of oats, so do poppies drenched in forgetful sleep. But the labour is easy if you alternate – as long as you are not ashamed to cover the dry soil with rich dung or to toss dirty ash over the exhausted field. So too fields rest when crops are changed and in the meantime there is gratitude in unploughed land.

After the double instruction to plough (43–6, 63–6), those who remember Cato's *sententia* will not be surprised by the introduction of dung in line 80. But the text then provides a Virgilian surprise by pointing out that there can be benefit to not ploughing too (83).[36] The sequence allows us to construct a modified timeline; my version is designed to bring out some of the disorderliness of what Virgil has constructed here (63–8 before 43). Others are possible, but all I think would acknowledge the play with time.

Geo. 1.43–83:

Year – 2:	midsummer:		harvest (+ fertilize 79ff)
	late summer:	heat 1 (*solem*, 48)	
	winter:	cold 1 (*frigora*, 48)	
Year – 1:	spring (63–6):		plough heavy soil
	mid summer:	fallow/rotate (71ff)	no harvest/different crop
	late summer:	heat 2 (*solem*, 48)	
	autumn (67–8):		plough dry soil
	winter:	cold 2 (*frigora*, 48)	[sow, 208–30]
Year 1:	*Vere nouo* (43):		plough [+ sow]

The tenses of 47–9 already suggest the need to have begun in the past:[37] the present *seges . . . respondet* depends on the perfect *sensit*; a good harvest now is due to a fallow past. And the point is compounded when 49 returns to the successful *seges* with *ruperunt horrea messes*; though we may analyse this as a gnomic usage of the perfect, the change of tense from *respondet* has the effect of taking us into the past: the farmer needs this experience in advance, hence *prius . . . praediscere . . . cura sit* ('It should be a concern to learn in advance', 50–2).

The word *uotis* in 47, on the other hand, looks ahead to the importance of prayer, especially prominent in the passage at 338–50 that begins *in primis uenerare deos atque annua magnae | sacra refer Cereri* ('in first place honour the gods and bring the due annual offerings to mighty Ceres'). Mention of Ceres takes us back to verses 95–6 (on the man who works hard at following Virgil's instructions): *neque illum | flaua Ceres alto nequiquam spectat Olympo* ('and golden–haired Ceres does not look down on him to no good effect from lofty Olympus'). But more significantly for my case, the opening phrase *in primis* (338) seems designed to bring out the need already to have begun with something else.

These observations should have an effect on the text. All the editions I have consulted put a paragraph break at 71 before *alternis*. If there is to be a break at all, it should come before *ergo age* in 63: this would mark the resumption of the opening sequence, whereas one at 71 only obscures the way that Virgil is continuing to repeat himself and revise his material. To understand that we need to understand the true point of 47–9; and then we can see that the poet, like the farmer, needs already to have started before he can properly begin.

CHAPTER 3
AESTHETICS, FORM AND MEANING IN THE *GEORGICS*
Richard F. Thomas

Virgil ... aimed not to teach the farmer, but to please the reader.

Seneca, *Epistles* 86.15

It has always seemed to me that in poetry Virgil, Lucretius, Catullus, and Horace hold the first rank by very far, and especially Virgil in his *Georgics*, which I consider the most accomplished work in poetry.

Montaigne, *Of books*

The best poem by the best poet.

John Dryden

One of the reviewers of the abstract for the current chapter predicted, not with approval on my reading, that in terms of methodology my contribution will look 'rather like a re-invention of New Criticism'.[1] There was a day, thirty or more years ago, when that would have been a sufficient basis for dismissal, back in 1980 when Lentricchia suggested that the New Criticism was 'dead in the way an imposing and repressive father-figure is dead'.[2] Since those heady days the death of literature and literary studies may seem more to the point, for which the various successors to the New Criticism, particularly deconstruction and new historicism, are among the contributors. It is not my purpose here to refight battles from the last century, but the fact is reports of the demise of that repressive father-figure may be premature. As Mark Jancovich puts it at the beginning of *The Cultural Politics of New Criticism*, '[c]ontemporary critics have often misrepresented the positions of the New Criticism, and the extent to which it defines their own activities. They have often failed to acknowledge its specific strengths, while reproducing many of its problems'.[3] It was convenient to characterize the New Criticism as unconcerned with social or historical contexts, with a focus only on the 'work itself' and preoccupied only with form, but those charges are now seen to be in good part caricature, or simply false.

The work of Jancovich (1993, reissued by Cambridge University Press in 2006) was joined by others, particularly the edited volume by Hickman and McIntyre, *Rereading the New Criticism* (2012). Their Preface is unambiguous on the project:

One of the clear objectives of this volume is to revisit and interrogate the many myths that the concept of the New Criticism has accrued over the years – in order to shed new light on the origins, complicate them, and sometimes to overturn them.[4]

In particular, New Criticism was always concerned with close reading, and it is true to say that close reading survived the rejection of the New Critics. Indeed, in 2003 Lentricchia himself came to co-edit the volume *Close Reading: The Reader*, with essays by John Crowe Ransom, the founder of New Criticism, and Cleanth Brooks, Ransom's student and best known of the New Critics. In recent years, there has also been a revival of the notion that form and aesthetics provide a worthwhile point of focus, that meaning may be sought, for that is the job of the critic. Charles Martindale among classicists has led the way here. It is at first sight curious that Martindale, whose *Redeeming the Text* (1993) is among the better treatments of deconstruction and the Classics, should in 2005 produce *Latin Poetry and the Judgement of Taste: An Essay in Aesthetics*. But on reflection the defamiliarizing of texts through close reading that is at the heart of deconstruction, is not a wholly different process from reading for ambiguity and irony that were part of the task of New Criticism.

As for aesthetics, in 1996 the poet and critic Lisa Samuels put it this way:

The problem is compounded by some of the critical correctives of the last couple of decades. As we pursue historical, cultural, and gender-based critical modes, theories of beauty are often labeled hegemonic models bequeathed by white males, in part because they often are (Shelley's, for example). Taking beauty seriously, developing theories of beauty, is out of fashion.[5]

How can a New Critical reading of the *Georgics* be a new reading of the *Georgics*? It can be such, I would argue, because there exists no New Critical reading of the *Georgics*, in part because the poem itself was read as a straight didactic poem until fairly recently, that is before the 1970s and 1980s when the sense of it as a poem celebrating the ethos of *labor*, largely unexamined against the realities of the poem, began to be dismantled.[6] I have been teaching the *Georgics* for over thirty years, most recently in the autumn of 2018. What attracts students, what gives them pleasure and what therefore makes the poem live and breathe, is its music in the broadest sense: its rhythms, its structures, its intertexts, the word order and wordplay, its frames and rings, the way it builds meaning through intratextuality and intertextuality.

One of the central critiques of New Criticism focused on its insistence that what matters is the significant form and aesthetic response it evokes, that historical context, for instance, should play little or no part in the critic's approach.[7] In the case of the *Georgics*, a poem framed by the presence of Octavian Caesar, addressed to Octavian's political advisor Maecenas, and demonstrably written in the tumultuous years before and more hopeful years after the Battles of Actium and Alexandria, that would be a hard act to carry off. But in the case of this chapter, since my views of the political meanings of the poem have been available for some time, a focus on aesthetics and form will presuppose historicist approaches.

I am interested in the fact that Seneca, Dryden and Montaigne thought Virgil's *Georgics* was the greatest poem – poem, not didactic poem. Seneca is clear that it is about pleasure not instruction. I have said what I think the poem is about. It is about the struggles of all the creatures of the post-lapsarian Iron Age of Jupiter, and it is a poem which has an endless empathy for those creatures caught in the failures of effort that Virgil brings to life in this poem. My goal here is to look at the mechanics of how the *Georgics* communicates its powerful aesthetic sense of empathy for those caught up in the world of Jupiter. This in fact becomes useful as art helps us to deal with the realities of the world.

William Batstone has enquired in effective ways into the meaning of the poem in relation to its didactic function. In tune with scholarship that looks to the failures of the *Georgics* as much as to its successes, he suggests that the '"failure of message" can enrich our lives even as it exceeds our grasp',[8] implying that this enrichment is where the *didaxis* of the poem lies. That may be true, and if so, Batstone points the way to a sort of *didaxis* of aesthetics, a spiritual *didaxis* (for him such emerges from contemplation of the failure of Orpheus and Eurydice) that does not directly help us to get along in a world that is deeply problematic, but that impresses us and compensates us through its artistic and aesthetic qualities. Whether this is precisely a form of *didaxis* at all is debatable. It seems to me not distinct from contemplation of Meliboeus's loss in *Eclogue* 1, or the failure of Daedalus to depict his son's fall at the outset of *Aeneid* 6, or the Augustan settlement compromised by the death of Marcellus at the end of the same book. If all of these constitute lessons, then all great poetry becomes potentially didactic, but such an outcome is generically unhelpful.

Empathy and melancholy

Although I generally avoid the term 'pessimism' in discussing the *Georgics*, T. E. Page reasonably uses the word to describe 3.66–8:

> optima quaeque dies miseris mortalibus aeui
> prima fugit; subeunt morbi tristisque senectus
> et labor, et durae rapit inclementia mortis.

> Life's fairest days are ever the first to flee for hapless mortals;
> on creep diseases, and gloomy age, and suffering:
> and stern death's ruthlessness sweeps us away.

That the sentiment is expressed exquisitely helps the three lines to participate in a sort of sublime melancholy. The inexorable expansion and progression from *morbi* to *tristisque senectus* to *durae inclementia mortis* is interrupted by the emphatically positioned *et labor*. The *mortales* in question are oxen, here fully humanized. When at the end of the book we encounter them dying of the *morbus* that will soon overtake their handlers, Virgil focalizes the voice of the oxen, whose words evoke empathy and humanity in the midst of the plague's horrors (3.525): 'What use their hard work and good deeds?' (*quid labor aut benefacta iuuant?*).

The pleasure that comes to readers along with the melancholic, is something that recurs throughout the poem, and it may be evoked by the plight of humans: those taking shelter from the storm at 1.330–1, or overwhelmed by the bloodshed of civil war at 1.501–14; Hero and Leander at 3.258–63; Orpheus and Eurydice at 4.490–510. But a fundamental part of the empathy of Virgil's poem is to be located in the extension of empathy to the animal world, as with the oxen in the example just given; to birds driven from their nests (2.207–11, 4.511–15); to aging horses (3.95–100); to a bull, defeated and exiled – though soon to return (3.214–41); to the dying horse (3.498–514). But Virgil goes further: at 2.80–2 a tree can marvel at/be surprised at new leaves and fruits that are not its own, a brilliant glimpse into the psychological condition of metamorphosis.

Stylized archaizing

Here I begin on a small scale, with some examples from Thomas (1995) that show Virgil at pains in the reworking of technical material to produce aesthetically pleasing effects. This process, which can be considered 'modernizing archaism', is one of the ways in which technical material is transformed, and indeed inverted. What in Varro provides *utilitas* with little *delectatio*, now gives delight, with utility only part of the generic appearance or fiction. At the beginning of the *Georgics* (1.1–9), Virgil's prayer turns to Liber and Ceres, and their products, vital to human existence, grape and grain. The debt to Varro is evident, but so too is Virgil's artistic transformation of the mundane:

Liber et alma **Ceres**, uestro si munere tellus Chaoniam pingui glandem *mutauit* **arista**, poculaque inuentis Acheloia *miscuit* **uuis**	tertio Cererem et Liberum, quod horum fructus maxime necessari ad uictum; ab his enim cibus et potio uenit e fundo.
Liber and nourishing Ceres, if through your gift the earth exchanged Chaonian acorn for rich ear of corn, and mixed Acheloan cups of water with newly discovered grapes. Virgil, *G.* 1.7–9	Thirdly, Ceres and Liber because their products are particularly vital for sustenance; from them food and drink come from the farm. Varro, *De Re Rustica* 1.1.5

The elegant and intricate ordering of nouns and adjectives, patterns of chiasmus and general perfection, suggest a further intertext, on precisely the same essential agricultural products. Calvert Watkins has well brought out how the following passage may be visualized as the third strophe of a four-strophe, essentially poetic, format of the *suouetaurilia*, or purification of the fields:[9]

utique tu

fruges **fru**menta	ụịnẹta ụịrgultaque
grand*ire*	(du)eneque **euen**ire siris
pastores **p**ecuaque	salụa serụassis

and that you

let grow tall	and turn out well
grains (and) corn	and vineyards (and) shrubwork
and keep safe	shepherds and cattle

Cato, *Agr. 141*

Virgil modernizes the style, creating an even more visually pleasing patterning and removing all of the alliterative doublets that are inherent in the archaic oral style of Cato's old hymn. This process of trading juxtaposition of doublets, with or without alliteration, is one that can be seen at work elsewhere in the *Georgics*, even with the scanty remnants we have of the old *carmina* and their archaic literary counterpoints, as in these two passages:

Umida solstitia atque hiemes orate serenas,

agricolae; **hiberno** *laetissima* **puluere** *farra*,

laetus ager

Pray for moist summers and warm winters, farmers;
With winter's dust most fruitful is the wheat, fruitful
The field

G. 1.100–2

hiberno puluere, *uerno luto*, <u>grandia farra,</u>

camille, metes.

With winter's dust, springs's mud you'll reap great harvests of wheat, lad

Macrobius, *Sat.* 5.20.18

---

nụnc **facilis** *rubea* texatur **fiscina** *uirga*,

nụnc torr**ete** igni frụges, nụnc frạngite saxo.

Now let the pliant basket be woven from bramble twigs,

now roast grain with fire, now crush it with a stone

G. 1.266–67

nocturna saxo **fruges franges [frendas** *Nonius*] torridas?

By night grind dried grain with a stone

Accius, fr. 478 Ribb.

fruges frendo *solidas* <u>saxi</u> <u>robore</u>

I grind hard grains with the strength of a rock

Pacuvius, fr. 11 Ribb.

In this matter especially, we are victims of the fragmentary nature of what survives from instructional *carmina*. At the same time, even where no surviving archaic models are available, it is possible to suggest that Virgil is modernizing and stylizing such material, as for instance in this case of how to deal with the threat that snakes pose to your livestock:

> **cape** <u>saxa</u> manu, **cape** <u>robora</u>, pastor,
> *tollentem*que minas et sibilạ collạ **tumentem**
> **deice**!

Grab a rock, grab a club, shepherd,
and he rises up in threat and its hissing neck swells,
knock him down!

G. 3.420–1

To turn to a more literary intertext of Virgil, Hesiod's *Works and Days*, Virgil engages aesthetically engaging material with his own emulative poetics, the reality of which belongs in the mundane world of the farmer. Hesiod elevated that material, and Virgil followed suit, showing that Latin could respond:

---

at rubicunda *fruges* **medio** succiditur **aestu**
et **medio** tostas **aestu** terit area *fruges*.
nudus ara, sere *nudus*. hiems ignaua colono:
frigoribus parto agricolae plerumque fruuntur
mutuaque inter se laeti conuiuia curant.

And in the heat of midday the threshing-floor rubs the grain. Plough naked, sow naked, winter is the tiller's idle time: in the cold season farmers generally enjoy their gains and enjoy parties in groups together.

G. 1.297–301

γυμνὸν σπείρειν, γυμνὸν δὲ βοωτεῖν, γυμνὸν δ' ἀμάειν

plough naked and sow naked and harvest naked.

Hesiod, *Op.* 391–2

---

nocte leues melius stipulae, **nocte** arida prata tondentur, **noctes** lentus non deficit umor.

At night it's best to mow the light stubble, at night the dry meadow, softening moisture fails not the night.

G. 1.289–90

ἠὼς γὰρ τ' ἔργοιο τρίτην ἀπομείρεται αἶσαν,
ἠώς τοι **προφέρει μὲν** ὁδοῦ, **προφέρει δὲ** καὶ ἔργου,
ἠώς, ἥ τε φανεῖσα πολέας ἐπέβησε κελεύθου
ἀνθρώπους πολλοῖσί τ' ἐπὶ ζυγὰ βουσὶ τίθησιν.

Dawn claims a third part of the work, dawn gets you started on your way, started on your work, dawn, whose appearance sets many men on their path, and puts the yoke on many oxen.

Hesiod, *Op.* 578–81

---

tum pingues agni et *tum* mollissima uina
tum somni dulces densaeque in montibus umbrae

Then are the lambs fat, then the wine most mellow, then is sleep sweet and the shadows dense on the mountains.

G. 1.341–2

τῆμος πιόταταί τ' αἶγες, καὶ οἶνος ἄριστος,
μαχλόταται δὲ γυναῖκες, ἀφαυρότατοι δέ τοι ἄνδρες

Then are goats fattest, then wine is best, women most lascivious and men at their feeblest.

Hesiod, *Op.* 585–7

In each of these instances it is clear that aesthetic criteria are at the heart of Virgil's enterprise as he uses interlocking word order, the tricolon, assonance and alliteration in engaging with the Hesiodic model to further his poetic enterprise: to sing his Ascraean song of the earth but through the stylistic medium of Callimachus and the poets.

In a similar move at 2.408–13, in a section on when to do various tasks, Virgil instructs in highly archaizing style, with a concatenation of archaic imperatives ending in *-to*:

primus humum **fodito**, primus deuecta cremato
sarmenta, et uallos primus sub tecta **referto**;
postremus **metito**. bis uitibus ingruit umbra,
bis segetem densis obducunt sentibus herbae;
durus uterque labor: **laudato** ingentia rura,
exiguum **colito**.

Be the first to dig the ground, first to bear away and fire the prunings, first to carry the poles under cover: be the last to reap. Twice the shade thickens on the vines; twice weeds cover the vineyard with thronging briars. Heavy is either toil: 'Give praise to large estates, farm a small one.'

As I noted in my commentary, this takes us back to some of the earliest agricultural language, where the formula has the same sacral ring as others in Cato, who here quotes Minius Percennius of Nola on gathering and planting of cypress seeds and on the propagation that follows (Cato, *Agr.* 151):

Semen cupressi quando legi, seri propagarique oporteat et quo pacto cupresseta seri oporteat, Minius Percennius Nolanus ad hunc modum monstrauit:

'semen cupressi tarentinae per uer legi oportet; materiem, ubi hordeum flauescit. id, ubi legeris, in sole **ponito**, semen **purgato**; id aridum **condito**, uti aridum expostum siet. per uer **serito** in loco, ubi terra tenerrima erit (quam 'pullam' uocant), ubi aqua propter siet: eum locum **stercorato** primum bene stercore caprino aut ouillo, tum **uortito** bipalio; terram cum stercore bene **permisceto**, **depurgato** ab herba graminibusque, bene terram **comminuito**. areas **facito** pedes latas quaternos: subcauas **facito**, uti aquam continere possint: inter eas sulcos **facito**, qua herbas de areis purgare possis; ubi areae factae erunt, semen **serito** crebrum, ita uti linum seri solet. eo cribro terram **incernito**, dimidiatum digitum terram altam **succernito**: id bene tabula aut manibus aut pedibus **complanato**. si quando non pluet, uti terra sitiat, aquam **inrigato** leniter in areas; si non habebis unde inriges, **gerito inditoque** leniter …'

As to cypress seed, the best method for its gathering, planting, and propagation, and for the planting of the cypress bed has been given as follows by Minius Percennius of Nola:

'The seed of the Tarentine cypress should be gathered in the spring, and the wood when the barley turns yellow; when you gather the seed, expose it to the sun, clean it, and store it dry so that it may be set out dry. Plant the seed in the spring, in soil which is very mellow, the so-called *pulla*, close to water. First cover the ground thick with goat or sheep dung, then turn it with the trenching spade and mix it well with the dung, cleaning out grass and weeds; break the ground fine. Form the seed-beds four feet wide, with the surface concave, so that they will hold water, leaving a footway between the beds so that you may clean out the weeds. After the beds are formed, sow the seed as thickly as flax is usually sowed, sift dirt over it with a sieve to the depth of a half-finger, and smooth carefully with a board, or the hands or feet. In case the weather is dry so that the ground becomes thirsty, irrigate by letting a stream gently into the beds; or, failing a stream, have the water brought and poured gently; see that you add water whenever it is needed. If weeds spring up, see that you free the beds of them …' (Loeb trans.)

There can be no doubt about the general flavour of this style in the time of the *Georgics*. At *De Re Rustica* 1.2.25–7, Scrofa shows himself to be a modern in response to Stolo's suggestion that Varro is jealous of the two Sasernae, whose agricultural writings were thought to be second only in antiquity to those of Cato. Scrofa knew the works of the Sasernae and despised them (*non ignorabat libros et despiciebat*). Agrasius asks Stolo to give a quote on the usefulness of their writings, even when not directly on agriculture proper. Stolo shows his familiarity on how to kill bed-bugs (Varro, *RR* 1.2.25):

cucumerem anguinum condito in aquam eamque infundito quo uoles, nulli accedent; uel fel bubulum cum aceto mixtum, unguito lectum.

Soak a wild cucumber in water and sprinkle it wherever you want, no bugs will come; or mix ox gall with vinegar, smear it on your bed.

Fundanius notes the advice is good, even if it did not belong in a book on agriculture, to which Scrofa replies (*RR* 1.2.26):

Ille, 'Tam hercle quam hoc, siquem glabrum facere uelis, quod iubet ranam luridam coicere in aquam, usque qua ad tertiam partem decoxeris, eoque unguere corpus.'

Just as good, by god, as this one if you want to depilate someone where he tells you to throw a yellow frog in a pot of water, boil it down to a third, and smear it on your body.

While Stolo is happy to quote Saserna directly (*condito, infundito, unguito*, 1.2.25), Scrofa, whose tastes coincide with those of Varro (both being moderns), and Varro himself throughout, will do no such thing. He like Varro throughout avoids these imperatives 'preferring *oportet*, the passive periphrastic, or a jussive subjunctive' (Thomas 1995: 2.408–13).

What does that make Virgil? Again, I would say (as in the prayer to Liber and Ceres, *G*. 1.7–9) that he promotes a stylized archaizing; his lines are as far from the archaism – or more likely archaizing – of Saserna as they are from the prosaic modernism of Varro and his interlocutor (*G*. 2.408–13):

> *primus* humum **fodito**, *primus* deuecta **cremato**
> sarmenta, et uallos *primus* sub tecta **referto**;
> postremus **metito**. bis uitibus ingruit umbra,
> bis segetem *densis* **obducunt** *sentibus* herbae;
> durus uterque labor: **laudato** ingentia rura,
> exiguum **colito**.

> Be first to dig the ground, first to carry off and burn the prunings, first to carry off the stakes and store them away; be last to harvest. Twice the shade falls down on the vines, twice weeds cover over the harvest with thick brambles; heavy is either toil: praise large estates, cultivate a small one.

The gently ascending tricolon (7>10>11 syllables in lines 408–9) with one *-to* imperative form in each limb and the anaphora of *primus* is a stylistic hybrid, imparting agricultural authenticity in the archaizing of the imperatives, and Ciceronian elegance in the rhetoric of the tricolon. *Postremus* (410) responds emphatically to the three *primus*-units, and *postremus metito* is followed by another rhetorically elegant phenomenon, an unusual dicolon with anaphora of *bis* drawing attention to the doublet (410–11). Vine pruning and weeding were never so elegantly put. As John Clare puts it in 'The Progress of Rhyme':

> For everything I felt a love
> The weeds below, the birds above,
> And weeds that bloomed in summer's hours,
> I thought they should be reckoned flowers;
> They made a garden free for all
> And so I loved them great and small
> And sung of some that pleased my eye,
> Nor could I pass the thistle by
> But paused and thought it could not be
> A weed in nature's poesy.

The final elegance is to be found in the closing injunction (*G*. 2.412–13): *laudato ingentia rura*, | *exiguum colito*. Exquisite as they are, the words would have left any actual farmer scratching his head. Why praise a large estate if cultivating a small one is desirable?

Servius tried to make sense by turning *rura* into *siluas* ('woods'): *laudato ingentes siluas, colito agrum minorem.*

As commentators have noted, the *sententia* is also a witty reversal of Hesiod (*Op.* 643): νῆ᾽ ὀλίγην αἰνεῖν, μεγάλη δ᾽ ἐνὶ φορτία θέσθαι ('Praise a small ship, put your cargo in a large one'). But as above, invocation of Hesiod includes invocation of the elevated style of Hesiod (as opposed to the archaism of a Cato or Saserna on the one hand, or the mundanity of Varro on the other). For Hesiod's gnomic line is followed by an artful couplet, characterized by a double anaphora justifying the thought of the *sententia* (*Op.* 643–5):

> νῆ᾽ ὀλίγην αἰνεῖν, μεγάλη δ᾽ ἐνὶ φορτία θέσθαι·
> **μείζων** μὲν φόρτος, **μεῖζον** δ᾽ ἐπὶ **κέρδεϊ κέρδος**
> ἔσσεται, εἴ κ᾽ ἄνεμοί γε κακὰς ἀπέχωσιν ἀήτας.

> Praise a small ship, put your cargo in a big one;
> The bigger the cargo, the bigger will be the profit
> upon profit, if the winds hold off their evil blasts.

Form made visible: patterning in the *Georgics*

I now proceed to set out a variety of patterns that contribute to the aesthetic appeal of the poem. Because of constraints of space, I set out the evidence with only brief commentary in the belief that the distinctiveness of the play with form in each example is palpably clear.

Golden lines

In this system of patterning the verb (V) occupies a central place and is surrounded by two nouns (N/n) on one side, two adjectives (A/a) on the other, the agreement of nouns and adjectives being in chiastic or interlocking order (i.e. NnVaA, NnVAa) – 'two substantives and two adjectives, with a verb betwixt them to keep the peace', as John Dryden put it in the Introduction to his *Silvae*. The pattern is visual more than anything, presenting the eye of the reader with a syntactical picture. The high incidence of such lines in higher register in *Eclogue* 4 – six times in sixty-three lines (2, 4, 14, 22, 23, 29) – is part of the elegance of that poem. The same may be said of the more restrained use of the pattern in the *Georgics*:

1.117   unde cauae tepido **sudant** umore lacunae

1.190   magnaque cum magno **ueniet** tritura calore

1.251   illic sera rubens **accendit** lumina Vesper

1.266   nunc facilis rubea **texatur** fiscina uirga

1.468	impiaque aeternam **timuerunt** saecula noctem
1.497	grandiaque effossis **mirabitur** ossa sepulcris
2.198	et qualem infelix **amisit** Mantua campum
2.362	Ac dum prima nouis **adolescit** frondibus aetas,
2.387	oraque corticibus **sumunt** horrenda cauatis
2.390	hinc omnis largo **pubescit** uinea fetu
2.465	alba neque Assyrio **fucatur** lana ueneno
2.522	mitis in apricis **coquitur** uindemia saxis
2.540	impositos duris **crepitare** incudibus ensis
3.25	purpurea intexti **tollant** aulaea Britanni
3.178	sed tota in dulcis **consument** ubera natos
3.330	currentem ilignis **potare** canalibus undam
3.399	primaque ferratis **praefigunt** ora capistris
3.448	ut tonsum tristi **contingunt** corpus amurca
3.469	dira per incautum **serpant** contagia uulgus
3.487	lanea dum niuea **circumdatur** infula uitta
4.302	tunsa per integram **soluuntur** uiscera pellem
4.366	omnia sub magna **labentia** flumina terra
4.417	dulcis compositis **spirauit** crinibus aura
4.506	Illa quidem Stygia **nabat** iam frigida cumba.

The so-called silver line, with non-agreeing nouns and adjectives arranged on either side of the verb (NaVnA, NaVAn), has an aesthetic effect that is indistinguishable from the golden line:

2.389	oscilla ex alta **suspendunt** mollia pinu
2.396	pinguiaque in ueribus **torrebimus** exta colurnis
2.512	atque alio patriam **quaerunt** sub sole iacentem
2.531	corporaque agresti **nudant** praedura palaestra
4.24	obuiaque hospitiis **teneat** frondentibus arbos

A structural oddity

As Mynors noted at 3.486–93, 'we are given what is virtually one sentence of eight lines, all end-stopped and seven of them ending with a noun relating to the ritual':[10]

saepe in honore deum medio stans hostia ad ***aram***,
lanea dum niuea circumdatur infula ***uitta***,

inter cunctantis cecidit moribunda ***ministros***;
aut si quam ferro mactauerat ante ***sacerdos***,
inde neque impositis ardent altaria ***fibris***,
nec responsa potest consultus reddere ***uates***,
ac uix suppositi tinguntur sanguine ***cultri***
summaque ieiuna sanie infuscatur ***harena***.

Often in the middle of sacrifice to the gods, the victim, standing at the **altar**
while around its brow is bound the woolen fillet's snowy **headband**,
has fallen dead in the midst of the hesitating **officiants**;
or, if beforehand one had been slaughtered by the **priest**,
the altars fail to blaze up when he sets on the fire the **entrails**
and when consulted, no response can come from the **seer**,
but hardly any stain of blood touches the applied **knife**
and with thin gore is stained the surface of the **sand**.

There must be a reason for this remarkable piece of writing, perhaps, with emphasis in the reading of the lines, a suggestion of liturgical regularity that is disturbingly at odds with the irregularity of what is taking place – the failure of ritual as the pestilence wipes out the livestock that is the subject of *Georgics* 3.

Another oddity

Maecenas appears in the poem four times:

Quid faciat laetas segetes, quo sidere terram
uertere, **Maecenas**   1.2

What makes plentiful harvests, at what season to turn
the soil, **Maecenas**

o decus, o famae merito pars maxima nostrae,
Maecenas.   2.41

O my splendour, o rightly the greatest part of our fame,
Maecenas.

interea Dryadum siluas saltusque sequamur
intactos, tua, **Maecenas**, haud mollia iussa   3.41

Meanwhile let us pursue the Dryads' woods and untouched
glades, no easy order from you, **Maecenas**

Protinus aërii mellis caelestia dona
exsequar: hanc etiam, **Maecenas**, aspice partem   4.2

Onward I go to describe the gods' gifts of honey from the sky:
Look also to this section, **Maecenas**

Why verses 2 and 41 I know not. Maecenas was two years older than Virgil, and turned forty-one around the time the *Georgics* was published. Octavian, on the other hand, is to be found in line 42 (*iuuenem*) of *Eclogue* 1. Coincidences or not, these patterns, when noted, bring pleasure, the same sort of aesthetic satisfaction that comes with hearing musical structures or observing poetic ring composition.

The same may be said of the following numerical arrangements:

2.1–8	**8** lines:	**Invocation of Bacchus**	2.346–53	**8** lines:	Manuring
2.9–34	**26** lines:	Methods of propagation I	2.354–61	**8** lines:	Hoeing
2.35–46	**12** lines:	**Delayed proem**	2.362–70	**9** lines:	Pruning
2.47–72	**26** lines:	Methods of propagation II			
2.73–82	**10** lines:	**Grafting**	3.384–93	**10** lines:	Wool
2.83–108	**26** lines:	Variety of species	3.394–403	**10** lines:	Milk
2.109–135	**26** lines [129]:	Variety of lands	3.404–13	**10** lines:	Hounds

Again, why Virgil produces these patterns is a matter of speculation. We may see the twenty-six lines as representing 'a page' on each of the technical topics (twenty-six lines notionally even being the length of a papyrus column). The shorter sections could represent 'a page' on these three minor topics. Indeed, Virgil even comments on such aesthetic ordering when at 2.277–87 he advises setting out trees according to the *quincunx*, describing the arrangement by the avenues so formed:

The arrangement is practical, giving the trees the optimum amount of space and light, not just aesthetic (2.285): *non animum modo uti pascat prospectus inanem* ('not only so the viewing may feed an idle mind'). Not only, but that is one reason, otherwise why mention it? Train travellers in northern Italy who suddenly see the avenues at 10:30 o'clock to the left and quickly look over their left shoulders to see the intersecting avenues at 7:30, can experience that same idle nourishment. What once was a mass of trees, raw nature, momentarily becomes culture and art. We can be sure that Virgil fed his idle mind as he had this experience, at a slower speed! Finally, this line from the *Georgics* resonates with *Aeneid* 1.464 (*atque animum pictura pascit inani*, 'and he feeds his mind with the empty painting'), where it is reworked to describe the aesthetic effect on the memory of Aeneas as his gazes at the pictures of his city's fall with all the ultimate emptiness of nostalgia.

Stylistic catalogue uariatio

The catalogues of nymphs and of rivers in *Georgics* 4 are each one long sentence, The nymphs appear in organized groups of two and fours (4.336–44):

Drymoque Xanthoque Ligeaque Phyllodoceque,
caesariem effusae nitidam per candida colla, **(4)**

Cydippe et flaua **Lycorias**, altera uirgo,
altera tum primos Lucinae experta labores, **(2)**

Clioque et **Beroe** soror, Oceanitides ambae,
ambae auro, pictis incinctae pellibus ambae, **(2)**

atque **Ephyre** atque **Opis** et Asia **Deiopea**
et tandem positis uelox **Arethusa** sagittis **(4)**

Drymo and Xantho and Ligea and Phylodoce, their hair tumbling about their white necks, Cydippe and blonde Lycorias, one a virgin, the other right after her first experience of Lucina's birth pangs, and Clio and her sister Beroe, both Oceanids, both dressed in gold and both in dappled hides, and Ephyre and Opis and Asian Deiopea, and swift Arethusa, her arrows put aside at last.

The list of rivers, on the other hand, is one long syntactically exquisite period (4.363–73):

And now, marvelling at his mother's home, a realm of waters, at the lakes locked in caverns, and the echoing groves, he went on his way, and, dazed by the mighty rush of waters, he gazed on all the rivers, as, each in his own place, they glide under the great earth – Phasis and Lycus, the fount whence deep Enipeus first breaks forth, whence Father Tiber, whence the streams of Anio and rocky, roaring Hypanis, and Mysian Caïcus, and Eridanus, on whose bull's brow are two gilded horns: no other stream of mightier force flows through the fertile fields to join the violet sea.

Its 'syntactic colometry' is exquisite:[11] two main verbs, Aristaeus 'was going' (*ibat*, 4.365) and 'was watching' (*spectabat*, 4.367), each with complex subordination, and with the mighty Po holding the final climactic place (4.363–73):

iamque
    domum mirans genetricis
    et umida regna |
        speluncis

-que lacus

     clausos

lucosque

     sonantis |

ibat, et

  ingenti motu stupefactus aquarum |

omnia

  sub magna labentia

flumina

  terra |

spectabat

     diuersa locis,

  Phasimque Lycumque, |

  et caput

     unde altus primum se erumpit Enipeus, |

     unde pater Tiberinus

     et unde Aniena fluenta |

     saxosusque

       sonans

     Hypanis Mysusque Caicus |

     et

       gemina auratus taurino cornua uultu |

     Eridanus,

       quo non alius per pinguia culta | in mare purpureum uiolentior

                effluit amnis. |

Periodic elegance

Virgil attained similar periodic and intratextually figured complexity in similar places across the poem, describing the springtime emergence of the ploughing ox in book 1,[12] and the bee in book 4:

Vere nouo,

  gelidus canis cum montibus umor | liquitur

  et Zephyro putris se glaeba resoluit, |

  depresso

incipiat iam tum mihi taurus

    aratro |

    ingemere

et

       sulco attritus

    splendescere

uomer.

1.43–6

In the dawning spring, when icy streams trickle from snowy mountains, and the crumbling clod breaks at the Zephyr's touch, even then would I have my bull groan over the deep-driven plough, and the share glisten when rubbed by the furrow.

    Quod superest,

    ubi pulsam hiemem sol aureus egit |

    sub terras caelumque aestiua luce reclusit, |

illae continuo saltus siluasque peragrant |

purpureosque metunt flores

et flumina libant | summa

    leues.

4.51–5

For the rest, when the golden Sun has driven winter in rout beneath the earth, and with summer light unlocked the sky, straightway they range through glades and groves, cull bright flowers, and lightly sip the stream's brink.

Iconic periodic elegance

At 3.322–38, just before the plague brings destruction to the world of flocks and herds and so ends the third book in grim destruction, Virgil invokes the idyllic world of pastoral, in four equal sentences, with the morning and evening stars framing the vignette:

At uero

       Zephyris

    cum laeta

       uocantibus

    aestas | in saltus utrumque gregem atque in pascua mittet, |

Luciferi primo cum sidere frigida rura | carpamus,

    dum mane nouum,

    dum gramina canent, |

    et ros in tenera pecori gratissimus herba.||

Inde

    ubi quarta sitim caeli collegerit hora |

    et cantu querulae rumpent arbusta cicadae, |

    ad puteos aut alta greges ad stagna

iubebo |

       currentem ilignis

    potare

       canalibus

    undam; ||

    aestibus at

at

    mediis umbrosam exquirere uallem, |

       sicubi magna Iouis antiquo robore quercus | ingentis tendat ramos,

       aut sicubi nigrum | ilicibus crebris sacra nemus accubet umbra; ||

tum

    tenuis dare rursus aquas

    et pascere rursus | solis ad occasum,

       cum frigidus aëra Vesper | temperat,

       et saltus reficit iam roscida luna, |

       litoraque alcyonen resonant, acalanthida dumi. ||

But when, at the Zephyrs' call, joyous Summer sends both sheep and goats to the glades and pastures, let us haste to the cool fields, as the morning star begins to rise, while the day is young, while the grass is hoar, and the dew on the tender blade most sweet to the cattle. **Then, when heaven's fourth hour has brought thirst to all, and the plaintive cicadas thrill the thickets with song, I will bid the flocks at the side of wells or deep pools drink of the water that runs in oaken channels.** But in midday heat let them seek out a shady dell, anywhere that Jove's mighty oak with its ancient trunk stretches out giant branches, or where some grove, black with many holms, lies brooding with hallowed shade. **Then give them once more the trickling stream, and once more feed them till sunset, when the cool star**

of eve freshens the air, and the moon, now dropping dew, gives strength to the glades, when the shores ring with the halcyon, and the copses with the finch.

When Virgil closely encounters the intertexts of the technical tradition, his formalistic concerns come most to the surface, and he is at his most aesthetically and musically sublime. In 1.351–462/3 this occurs at a high level, as he moves from the storm and its aftermath to the treatment of *signa*, a treatment that will engage Aratus, Varro of Atax, and Theophrastus.[13] The closing line of that previous section is virtually unique in its metrical clumsiness (1.350: *det motus incompositos et carmina dicat*, 'do artless dances and chant hymns'), well capturing the clumsy dancing of the Italian rustic.

What follows enters a new world, replacing Hesiod and archaic Italian rustic piety with Hellenistic science, with Aratus in particular and with the Roman Aratean reception tradition of Cicero and Varro of Atax. For the next 100 lines, Virgil gives a virtuoso display of consummate artistic signs, the word *signum* itself appearing six times and framing the lines. The opening is an elegant period, with two increasing tricola (marked below with numbers 1 to 3) shaping the two subordinate clauses (1.351–5):

Atque
> haec ut certis possemus discere **signis**, |
> aestusque(1) pluuiasque(2) et
>> agentis frigora
>
> uentos(3), |
ipse pater statuit
> quid menstrua luna moneret(1), |
> quo signo caderent Austri(2),
> *quid*
>> saepe uidentes |
> agricolae propius stabulis armenta tenerent(3).

The effect of the whole is to put the reader on notice that a higher register is at hand.

Skipping reels of rhyme

Almost thirty years ago an undergraduate at Yale University wrote to me, pointing to a remarkable stretch of lines at *Georgics* 1.393–423, where Virgil created extensive rhyming patterns, assembled around lines 406–9, themselves unique in the *Georgics* for their virtuosity:

Nec minus ex imbri soles et aperta serena
prospicere et **certis** poteris cognoscere **signis**:
nam neque tum stellis acies obtunsa uidetur,   395

nec fratris radiis obnoxia surgere Luna,
tenuia nec lanae per caelum uellera ferri;
non tepidum ad solem pennas in litore pan**dunt**
dilectae Thetidi alcyones, non ore solu*tos*
immundi meminere sues iactare manipl*os*.   400
at nebulae magis ima petunt campoque recum**bunt**,
solis et occasum seruans de culmine summ**o**
nequiquam seros exercet noctua cant*us*.
apparet liquido sublimis in aëre Nis*us*,
et pro purpureo poenas dat Scylla capill**o**:   405
quacumque illa leuem fugiens secat aethera pennis,
ecce inimicus atrox magno stridore *per auras*
insequitur Nisus; qua *se fert Nisus ad auras*,
illa leuem fugiens raptim secat aethera pennis.
tum liquidas corui presso ter gutture uoces   410
aut quater ingeminant, et saepe cubilibus **altis**
nescio qua praeter solitum dulcedine laeti
inter se in foliis strepitant; iuuat imbribus **actis**
progeniem paruam dulcisque reuisere nidos.
haud equidem credo, quia sit diuinitus il**lis**   415
ingenium aut rerum fato prudentia mai*or*;
uerum ubi tempestas et caeli mobilis um*or*
mutauere uias et Iuppiter uuidus Aust**ris**
denset erant quae rara modo, et quae densa relaxat,
uertuntur species animorum, et pectora motus.   420
nunc alios, alios dum nubila uentus agebat,
concipiunt: hinc ille auium concentus in agris
et laetae pecudes et ouantes gutture corui.[14]

G. *1.493–23*

Acrostic

Finally, there is the famous acrostic at *Georgics* 1.429–33, with Virgil's backwards initials
(**MA**ro **VE**rgilius **PV**blius) responding to the ΛΕΠΤΗ acrostic in the very lines of Aratus
that Virgil was translating:

MAximus agricolis pelagoque parabitur imber;	ΛΕΠΤΗ μὲν καθαρή τε περὶ τρίτον ἦμαρ ἐοῦσα
at si **uirgineum** suffuderit ore ruborem, 430	Εὔδιός κ' εἴη, λεπτὴ δὲ καὶ εὖ μάλ' ἐρευθὴς
VEntus erit: uento semper rubet aurea Phoebe.	Πνευματίη· παχίων δὲ καὶ ἀμβλείῃσι κεραίαις
sin ortu quarto (namque **is certissimus auctor**)	Τέτρατον ἐκ τριτάτοιο φόως ἀμενηνὸν ἔχουσα
PVra neque obtunsis per caelum cornibus ibit,	Ἠὲ νότου ἀμβλύνετ' ἢ ὕδατος ἐγγὺς ἐόντος.
G. 1.429–33	Aratus, *Phaen.* 783–87

Lines 430 and 432, sandwiched between the three lines bearing Virgil's signature (*MA*, 429; *VE*, 431; *PV*, 433), have their own points of reference: *uirgineum* alludes to Virgil's nickname conferred because of his shyness (*Parthenias*, 'maidenlike', cf. Suet. *Vita Verg.* 11); and the multivalent pronoun *is* in 432 ('it/he is the trustiest authority') continues the ludic extravagance: 'it' (the moon), 'he' (Aratus, the translated author), 'he' (Publius Vergilius Maro).[15]

I started working on this poem more than forty years ago, and I still teach it every two or three years. The pleasure of reading, teaching and writing about it is hard to quantify and explain, but these are some of the ways in which Virgil laboured in order to create what Dryden justly described, as noted at the beginning of the chapter, as the best poem of the best poet.

PART II
RELIGION AND PHILOSOPHY

CHAPTER 4
GEORGICA AND *ORPHICA*: THE *GEORGICS* IN THE CONTEXT OF ORPHIC POETRY AND RELIGION[1]

Tom Mackenzie

The aim of the present chapter is to open new perspectives on the *Georgics* by contextualizing the poem alongside surviving fragments of Orphic poetry. The perspectives are newly available because our knowledge of Orphic poetry has been substantially increased in recent decades by the discovery and publication of new evidence,[2] and because the fragments are now readily accessible in the monumental collection of Alberto Bernabé.[3] The hypothesis to be tested here, then, is that this body of evidence should be added to the rich web of intertexts that can inform our reading of the poem. Such an investigation is warranted primarily by the prominence of Orpheus at the end of the poem, but it also seems a natural step in light of the recent surge of scholarly interest in the subject of Bacchus in Augustan poetry and culture in general, and the *Georgics* in particular.[4] Orpheus is closely associated with Bacchus/Dionysus from at least the mid-fifth century BCE onwards, and 'Orphic' and Bacchic mystery cults are not easily distinguishable.[5] An evocation of Orphic poems can be regarded as part of the poem's wider engagement with mystery cults and initiation.

Indeed, the ritual function of Orphic texts gives them a specific pragmatic force. Whilst most intertextual studies of the *Georgics* explore, broadly speaking, the semantics of Virgil's allusions to his predecessors, it shall be argued here that the Orphic material can highlight the pragmatics of the poem. That is to say, the Orphic material has implications not merely for what the *Georgics* means, but for what it does to its readers. The pragmatic aspect of poetry is salient in the genre of didactic, which typically dramatizes a particular (i.e., teacher–pupil) relationship between narrator and reader, and purports, at least fictionally, to have a particular effect (i.e. that of education) upon the latter, issues that are explored in detail in Robert Cowan's contribution to this book. It shall be suggested here that the Orphic material serves to inscribe the *Georgics* into a tradition of texts that have a distinctive pragmatic function: they explain the current mortal condition as resulting from an original sin; as a result, a correct understanding of the text enables the interpreter to expiate that sin and surpass mortal limitations. First, it will be necessary to provide a brief overview of the Orphic material under consideration. I shall then present some evidence in support of the view that the *Georgics* could be seen to evoke the Orphic texts. Finally, I shall suggest some implications of these parallels for our understanding of the function of the poem.

The *Orphica*

The 'Orphic poems' form a notoriously fragmentary and complex corpus. The complete texts which survive under Orpheus's name – the Orphic *Argonautica* and the eighty-seven hymns that survive in the manuscript tradition alongside the hymns of Homer, Callimachus and Proclus – are almost certainly later than the Augustan period.[6] Of the various poems attributed to Orpheus, the most ostensibly relevant text to the *Georgics* might *prima facie* seem to be *Georgia* mentioned by Tzetzes (*OF* 768–76), but this is the same poem as the extant *Katarchai* that comes down to us under the authorship of 'Maximus'; it is dated to the second century CE, and Orpheus's authorship only seems to have been ascribed to it sometime in the Byzantine period.[7] A more promising candidate for a Virgilian source is the *Katabasis* of Orpheus (*OF* 707–13). Norden argued that this poem was a model for the *katabasis* in *Aeneid* 6.[8] This view has more recently been endorsed by Nicholas Horsfall and Jan Bremmer, with particular reference to the detail of the sinners who appear in Virgil's Tartarus (*Aen.* 6.548–636).[9] This description of the sinners bears certain similarities with the Bologna papyrus (*OF* 717 = *P. Bonon.* 4, *c.* 2–4 CE), a hexameter text thought to date from the early empire, which also describes the punishment of certain sinners in the underworld.[10] Horsfall and Bremmer argue that an earlier Orphic *Katabasis* was a common source for both texts. If we accept this view, it is of course possible that such a poem was in some sense a model for Orpheus' descent to the underworld in *Georgics* 4, but it should be noted that the description at *Georgics* 4.474–84 does not feature the extended description of punished sinners that seems to be the key point of similarity between the *Aeneid* and Bologna papyrus. Unfortunately, no verbatim fragment for the Orphic *Katabasis*, or summary of its contents, survives, and so it can be of limited explanatory value for the *Georgics*.

More can be said, however, about two further types of Orphic text which could, at least on purely chronological grounds, have been available to Virgil and his earliest readers. The first are the so-called 'Orphic' gold tablets (*OF* 474–96), which have been found throughout the Greek world but most copiously in southern Italy (one has even been found in Rome, *OF* 491), and which date from the end of the fifth century BCE to second or third centuries CE. They contain hexameters (or attempted hexameters) ostensibly offering instructions which are to be followed in order to reach the path of the blessed and, in some cases, describe the addressee's divinization (*OF* 484, 487 and 491).[11]

The second relevant type are the fragments of theogonical poetry attributed to Orpheus. The transmission and interrelation of the various Orphic theogonies is a highly complex topic, of which only the most rudimentary overview can be offered here.[12] We know of at least four such theogonies. The earliest attested is that quoted by the author of the Derveni papyrus, a poem which must be at least as early as the fifth century BCE. Additionally, Damascius, writing in the sixth century CE, summarizes some of the contents of three separate Orphic theogonies (*Princ.* 123–4). The earliest of these is the 'Eudemian' theogony (*OF* 19–27), so called because it was summarized by the Peripatetic Eudemus, and seems to be the source of the Orphic fragments quoted by Plato and

Aristotle. Damascius knew of a second theogony from a summary by 'Hieronymus and Hellanicus if he is not the same person', neither of whom can be securely identified. This poem (*OF* 69–89) seems to post-date the mid-third century BCE, given the author's apparent familiarity with Stoicism and Alexandrian poetry. Finally, Damascius had access to the *Rhapsodic Theogony* in twenty-four books, an amalgam of theogonical material found in the earlier poems, and well known among the Neoplatonists.[13]

All four poems are, like Hesiod's *Theogony*, succession myths that describe Zeus's accession to the throne by means of his overthrow of Kronos. They differ in the names they use for certain gods, and in some of the genealogies they draw, but they are united by their purportedly Orphic authorship, by their theogonical form and by certain distinctive plot details. In particular, they all feature a primordial god named Phanes or Protogonos (*OF* 12, 81, 121–6), who contains the seeds of the rest of the cosmos. Zeus, after overthrowing Kronos (who is sometimes allegorized as Chronos, *OF* 76, 78, 79, 96, 97, 99, 111, 114) swallows Phanes/Protogonos to encompass the whole universe (*OF* 14, 31, 241). A further distinctive story, which shall be of relevance to the *Georgics*, occurred in the *Rhapsodic Theogony*, and perhaps also the Eudemian: the myth of Dionysus Zagreus (*OF* 301–31). In this myth, Dionysus is the son of Zeus and Persephone. As a boy, the Titans murder him by slashing him into seven pieces, which they then cook and eat. Zeus, in turn, destroys them with the thunderbolt, and from the resulting ashes humans are created. According to Olympiodorus, as a result, humans have both a divine element (from the swallowed chunks of Dionysus) and a Titanic one, and the point of certain Orphic practices – such as vegetarianism – is explained as an attempt to cultivate the divine and reject the Titanic.[14] It is unclear whether this myth occurred in the other Orphic theogonies, but it is attested at least as early as Euphorion.[15] It may be alluded to by Pindar (fr. 133) and, according to some scholars, is presupposed by the gold tablets.[16]

Whilst the precise nature of the relationship between these different theogonies is hard to determine, it shall be assumed here that Orphic theogony in a general sense, with its key features of Zeus's swallowing of Phanes/Protogonos, and the myth of Dionysus Zagreus, was familiar to at least some readers in Augustan Rome. Indeed, Orphic theogony was known to Cicero and Nigidius.[17] Apuleius quotes an extensive Orphic fragment, which seems to come from a theogony (*de Mund.* 401a25 = *OF* 31, with Bernabé's introduction to the fragment). Philodemus also demonstrates awareness of Orphic theogony, making Virgil's acquaintance with it most likely.[18]

Orphica in the *Eclogues*

Where Orpheus's name occurs in *Eclogues* 4 and 6, it is associated with the composition of theogonical poetry. In *Eclogue* 4, the narrator is compared with Orpheus (55–6):

non me carminibus uincet nec Thracius Orpheus
nec Linus, huic mater quamuis atque huic pater adsit

Then shall neither Thracian Orpheus nor Linus defeat me in song,
though mother give aid to the one and father to the other.

Servius comments *ad loc.*: *genere stili se Orpheo vel Lino meliorem fore commemorat* ('he relates that he will be better at this type of writing than Orpheus or Linus'). 'This type of writing' surely refers to theogonical poetry, as the surviving fragments of Linus, like the majority of the Orphic fragments, are theogonical in nature.[19] In the *Eclogue*, the golden age imagery and the return of the *Virgo* (6) align the poem with Hesiod, the poet who, above all, sang of the origins of man and the gods.[20] Yet there is also here the pattern of an ancient guilt (*si qua manent sceleris vestigia nostri*, 13) to be atoned for, in order to realize a pre-fall state, expressed in terms of the golden age, a pattern which finds closer parallels in the *Rhapsodic Theogony* (in the crimes of the Titans) than Hesiod. This association, then, may be activated by the occurrence of Orpheus' name.

In *Eclogue* 6, Silenus's song is asserted to be more effective than that of Orpheus (30, *nec tantum Rhodope miratur et Ismarus Orphea*, 'nor did Rhodope and Ismarus admire Orpheus so much'). The song is a cosmogony which is usually understood to be modelled on that of Orpheus in Apollonius's *Argonautica* (1.496–511).[21] But there are good reasons for thinking that Virgil was aware of Orphic theogony beyond Apollonius's depiction. The details of intoxicating and binding a god to make him speak are paralleled in an episode of the Orphic succession myth in which Zeus gets Kronos drunk with honey, then binds him and castrates him, after which Kronos graciously tells him how he is subsequently to gain control of the universe (*OF* 219–25). These binding episodes also bear comparison with the binding of Proteus by Menelaus in *Odyssey* 4 and by Aristaeus in *Georgics* 4: in the *Georgics* passage too, the binding may evoke Orphic theogony as well as the *Odyssey* and *Eclogue* passages. The evidence for the circulation of Orphic theogony in first-century BCE Rome and the possible connections between *Aeneid* 6 and an Orphic *Katabasis* render this view plausible. Whilst Orpheus's theogony in the *Argonautica* is significant, it also makes sense to think of the theogonical poems attributed independently to Orpheus in antiquity when his name occurs in Virgil.

Orphic religion and *Orphica* in the *Georgics*

The prominence of Orpheus in the *Georgics* can be seen as part of its wider evocation of mystery cults, specifically the Eleusinian cult of Demeter and Persephone, and Dionysiac/Bacchic mysteries which developed especially in Italy.[22] Eleusis is mentioned at 1.160–8:

Dicendum et quae sint duris agrestibus arma,   160
quis sine nec potuere seri nec surgere messes:
uomis et inflexi primum graue robur aratri,
tardaque Eleusinae matris uoluentia plaustra,
tribulaque traheaeque et iniquo pondere rastri;
uirgea praeterea Celei uilisque supellex,   165

arbuteae crates et mystica uannus Iacchi;
omnia quae multo ante memor prouisa repones,
si te digna manet diuini gloria ruris.

I must tell, too, of the hardy farmers' weapons,
without which the crops could be neither sown nor raised.
First the share and the curved plough's heavy frame,
the slow-rolling wains of the Mother of Eleusis,
sledges and drags, and hoes of cruel weight;
further, the common wicker ware of Celeus,
arbute hurdles and the mystic winnowing-basket of Iacchus.
All of these you will remember to provide and store away long beforehand,
if the glory the divine country is to be yours in worthy measure.

The reference to Demeter as the 'Mother of Eleusis' (*Eleusinae matris*, 163) clearly alludes to the Eleusinian mysteries. The 'winnowing-basket' (*uannus*, 166) is 'mystic' (*mystica*, 166) and belongs to Iacchus (*Iacchi*, 166) as the tool was carried by λικνοφόροι in the Eleusinian procession, and Iacchus, although at times identified with Bacchus, was originally a personification of the cultic cry of the participants in the Eleusinian mysteries.[23] The reference to Eleusis here may be related to the anticipation of the apotheosis of Octavian mentioned earlier (1.20–42), given the initiation of Octavian into the Eleusinian mysteries in 31 BCE (Dio 51.4.1), two years before the publication of the poem, and the eschatological benefits conferred upon initiates.[24]

Bacchism comes into book 4 where Orpheus's death is likened to a Bacchic *sparagmos*, in which a sacrificial victim is torn to pieces (4.519–22).[25] By the Hellenistic period, Orpheus is mentioned as the founder of mystery cults in general, including those at Eleusis (Diodorus 1.96.4–6), and moreover, Orphism is always closely associated with – and arguably indistinguishable from – Bacchism/Dionysism.[26] Orpheus is said to have introduced the mystery cults from Egypt (Diod. Sic. 1.96.4–6 = *OF* 48T II), where the *bugonia* episode is set. The prominence of mystery cults in the poem suggests that we are to regard Virgil's Orpheus as the founder of religious institutions; this may identify him as the Orpheus to whom the theogonies were attributed.[27]

Indeed, the emphasis on the southern Italian context in the *sphragis* (4.563–4), which indicates that the poem was written at Naples, may serve to hint at an association with Orphic mystery cult. *Magna Graecia* was a hotbed for Orphic religion and mystery cult more generally: the area has yielded more gold tablets than any other region, and a fifth-century BCE burial ground at Cumae, in close proximity to Naples, seems to have been reserved for those initiated into a Bacchic mystery cult.[28] In *Aeneid* 6 – a book which, as we have seen, has been regarded as evocative of Orphism – Aeneas enters the underworld at Cumae. The mystic associations of the general area, then, that are so memorably evoked in the *Aeneid*, may already be implicit in the *Georgics*.

These general connections with Orphic religion should alert us to the possibility of more specific parallels with Orphic literature. The similarity between the binding of

Proteus and the binding of Kronos has already been mentioned. In both cases the protagonist (Orpheus's Zeus / Virgil's Aristaeus) must go to a cave and ask a goddess (Night, in the Derveni and Rhapsodic theogonies, *OF*6, 220) for help, who tells him to bind a god. Another parallel comes earlier in book 4 in the mention of Jupiter's childhood in the Dictaean cave, where he is fed honey and guarded by the noisy Curetes (4.149–52, cf. 2.536):

> Nunc age, naturas apibus quas Iuppiter ipse
> addidit expediam, pro qua mercede canoros
> Curetum sonitus crepitantiaque aera secutae
> Dictaeo caeli regem pauere sub antro.

> Come now, the qualities which Jove himself has given bees,
> I will unfold – even the reward for which they followed
> the tuneful sounds and clashing bronzes of the Curetes,
> and fed the king of heaven within the cave of Dicte.

Now, the tradition that Zeus was nursed in the Dictaean cave and guarded by the Curetes is well attested in Hellenistic sources, but no earlier. It crops up in Aratus (at line 35) and features prominently in Callimachus's *Hymn to Zeus* (lines 46–54) where, as in Virgil, there is an emphasis on honey. It also seems to have featured in Nicander's *Georgics* (or *Melissurgica* – depending on whether that is a separate poem, Nicander fr. 94 = Columella *De Re Rustica* 9.2.4.5). But the story seems to have been particularly associated with Orphism. It appears in the song of Orpheus in Apollonius's *Argonautica* (1.508–9), and features prominently in the *Rhapsodic theogony* (*OF* 205–15), where honey is especially important, for feeding Zeus (*OF* 209) and for getting Kronos drunk (*OF* 220, 221). West tentatively suggests that an Orphic theogony could ultimately have been the source for all Hellenistic versions of this myth.[29] Be that as it may, Philodemus appears to allude to the story in an Orphic context, in referring to the 'drum of an Orpheotelest' (*On Poets* fr. 181, Janko). As Janko points out, an explanation for this image can be supplied by the third-century BCE Gurôb papyrus (P.Gurôb 1 = *OF* 578), from Ptolemaic Egypt, which indicates that participants in Orphic initiation rituals imitated the Corybantes/Couretes with such drums.[30] On the basis of this evidence, then, I suggest that the occurrence of the myth in the *Georgics*, in a book where Orpheus will feature so prominently, could activate associations with Orphic poetry and religion, as well as with the better-known Hellenistic poems.

A further example is book 4.219–27, describing a kind of pantheism where the divine pervades everything:

> His quidam signis atque haec exempla secuti
> esse apibus partem diuinae mentis et haustus   220
> aetherios dixere; deum namque ire per omnis
> terrasque tractusque maris caelumque profundum;

hinc pecudes, armenta, uiros, genus omne ferarum,
quemque sibi tenuis nascentem arcessere uitas:
scilicet huc reddi deinde ac resoluta referri   225
omnia, nec morti esse locum, sed uiua uolare
sideris in numerum atque alto succedere caelo.

Led by such tokens and such instances,
Some have thought that the bees have received a share of the divine intelligence,
    and a draught
of heavenly ether; for God, they say, pervades all things,
earth and sea's expanse and heaven's depth;
from him the flocks and herds, men and beasts of every sort
draw, each at birth, the slender stream of life;
to him all beings thereafter return, and when unmade, are restored;
no place is there for death, but still quick, they fly
unto the ranks of the stars, and mount to the heavens aloft.

Thomas comments that this view 'is in essence a combination of Stoic and Pythagorean theory, but [Virgil] may also have in mind the famous opening of Aratus' *Phaenomena*'.[31] Yet Pantheism also evokes Orphism, in particular the episode where Zeus swallows Phanes/Protogonos to encompass the entire universe. This episode is alluded to in the Orphic fragment quoted by Apuleius.[32] The anonymous people who, in the *Georgics*, hold this theory, have inferred it from the nature of bees (219–21). Bees seem to have been particularly important in the *Rhapsodic Theogony* for getting Kronos drunk. The 'divine draughts' (*haustus aetherios*, 220–1) that belong to Virgil's bees could recall the draughts of honey drunk by the gods in the *Rhapsodic Theogony*. This is not to deny the Pythagorean or Stoic associations of the passage: Pythagoreanism is, from its earliest stages, closely associated with Orphism and Orphic texts,[33] and Orphic poems seem to have been particularly susceptible to Stoic allegorical interpretations.[34] The placement of this description shortly before the Orpheus episode may activate the Orphic associations of the theory in particular.

Finally, when Aristaeus arrives in the cave of the nymphs, as Philip Hardie has argued, the nymph Clymene seems to be singing a theogony at 4.345–7:[35]

inter quas curam Clymene narrabat inanem
Volcani, Martisque dolos et dulcia furta,
aque Chao densos diuum numerabat amores.

Among these Clymene was telling of Vulcan's baffled care,
of the wiles and stolen joys of Mars,
and from Chaos on was rehearsing the countless loves of the gods.

She tells of the loves of the gods *a Chao* (347). Although the most ostensible topic of her song is the adultery of Aphrodite with Ares (as sung by Demodocus at *Odyssey* 8.266ff.), the phrase *a Chao* recalls theogonical poetry above all, and *densi divum amores* (347) could refer not only to the story of Aphrodite's adultery, but also to the sexual reproduction which, in theogonies, leads to the creation of the recognizable world. The fact that this occurs shortly before the story of Orpheus makes a connection with Orphic theogony most likely. Creation myth is evoked more generally in the *Georgics* by the mention of anthropogony at 1.60–6 and the recurring theme of the golden age, which features in Hesiod, Empedocles and in the theogonies attributed to Orpheus.[36] So the importance of Orpheus, known in antiquity as the author of theogonies, at the end of the poem could further associate it with that genre.

Orphica and expiation

To summarize the case made so far, certain images in book 4 (the birth of Dictaean Zeus at 149–52; the pantheism at 219–27; the theogony at 345–50) evoke Orphic theogony, given that Orpheus occurs prominently in the *bugonia* episode and is associated with theogony elsewhere in Virgil's oeuvre. I want to suggest that this affects our understanding of the function this book is presented as performing. Both the *Georgics* and the Orphic theogonies conform to a more widely attested pattern in the function of certain hexameter texts: the poem explains aetiologically an original sin, so that a correct interpretation enables the interpreter to expiate that sin and overcome the negative aspects of death. This reward takes the form of access to a privileged afterlife reserved for the initiates, or possibly of divinization.[37] A further characteristic feature is that the sin is part of a general decline from a historical golden age, but the golden age can again be realized if the correct instructions are followed. Both the prospect of realizing the golden age and the possibility of eschatological benefits are relevant to the *Georgics*.

Traces of this pattern of decline are already evident in the *Works and Days*, which explains the current mortal condition aetiologically as resulting from both the myth of the races and the story of Prometheus and Pandora. Although the golden age is set in the past, one is able to realize a quasi-divine golden age by being just and following the instructions – hence the language of the land of the just city echoes that of the golden race, suggesting that they too enjoy the supernatural benefits of the golden race.[38] A past golden age also occurs in Empedocles (B128) and in the *Rhapsodic Theogony* (*OF* 216, 320). In both cases, the golden age appears as something to aspire to for the present, if we follow certain instructions correctly. This synchronic use of golden age imagery occurs notably in the *laudes Italiae* of the *Georgics* (2.136–76). The inconsistencies between that episode and the rest of the poem have been problematic for some, but they are perhaps less problematic if we regard the golden age imagery not as a literal description of the actual present, but as something to aspire to provided that we follow the correct instructions, as seems to be the case in Hesiod, Empedocles and 'Orpheus'.[39]

In Hesiod, there is original sin in the form of Prometheus's deception of Zeus (*Op.* 47–9), and there is the prospect of realizing a quasi-divine golden age, and even of becoming a *theios anēr* (*Op.* 731), but there are no clear eschatological benefits to following the instructions, and no particular sense that we must atone for Prometheus's crime. This aspect of the pattern becomes conspicuous in Empedocles: his narrator is an exile from the immortals because of a sin committed (B115), but if the correct instructions are followed, immortal powers and superior reincarnation await (B111). In the case of Orphism, the external evidence from Plato (and others) suggests that *Orpheotelestai* used books according to which they conducted rituals and were able to persuade individuals and entire cities that they could expiate their sins and so earn a blessed afterlife.[40] It is likely that these kinds of texts were the sorts of theogony attested in the Derveni papyrus, as the commentator offers instructions for certain rituals (Col.II). The underlying assumption is that a correct understanding of the theogony enables one to perform the correct rituals to earn a blessed afterlife. The Philodemus testimonium (*On Poems* 181, Janko) attests to the familiarity of this stereotype in the Roman world of the first century BCE. An explanation of how an Orphic theogony was used aetiologically to justify certain rituals is provided by the myth of Dionysus Zagreus: if we accept Olympiodorus's interpretation, the function of Orphic rituals is to expiate our sinful Titanic component, and cultivate the divine, Dionysian element. Indeed, the myth appears to be reflected in two of the gold tablets where the initiate is described as having been struck down by lightning, as well as being the 'child of Heaven and Earth', a formula which reflects humanity's Titanic origins.[41] In Orphism, then, the text is used to explain an original sin, which must be expiated, just as Aristaeus must expiate his sin against Orpheus and Eurydice.

The kinds of Orphic texts mentioned by Plato (which may include the Derveni theogony), the poetry of Empedocles and the Orphic gold tablets (which seem to draw upon theogonical myth) are all supposed to enable their addressees to conquer death, either by promising them a happy and exclusive afterlife, or by granting them immortality. The *Georgics*, too, conforms to this pattern in its explanation of how to resurrect the bees, and in the prospective divinization of the new Caesar,[42] who himself seems to be a resurrection of the previous, dead Caesar (*exstincto … Caesare*, 1.466). Aristaeus's sin of raping Eurydice must be atoned for to achieve the resurrection of the bees (4.453–6). If I am correct, by evoking Orphism and Orphic texts, Virgil, at least in book 4, aligns the poem with this kind of mystic literature.

Implications

There are, I suggest, some respects in which this alignment might affect an interpretation of the poem. I have mentioned that Orphic texts seem especially to have invited allegorical interpretations. The Derveni commentator identifies the hidden meanings of theogony he quotes. The reasons for the association between allegoresis and mystery cults are readily available: mystery cults offer the prospect of distinguishing their initiates from the masses; one means by which to do this is to claim that the myths and texts involved have a hidden meaning that is only accessible to the initiated.[43] Orphic theogony would then become a common subject for Stoic allegorical interpretation (Cic. *DND*

1.40–1; Plut. *De defectu orac.* 415ff.). The evocation of Orphic texts and mystery cults in the fourth *Georgic*, then, may support the allegorical interpretation of the Aristaeus narrative:[44] Aristaeus, as the guardian of the bees/*quirites* (4.201) is Octavian, whilst Orpheus, as the *Ur*-poet, is Virgil.

A further consequence of this alignment is that it implies that the *Georgics* have a similar function to the texts of 'Orpheus' and Empedocles, in enabling their addressee to conquer death. Formally didactic texts[45] inherently draw attention to their pragmatic force: they are presented as teaching a specific body of knowledge, and thereby modifying the attitudes and behaviour of their addressee, in a more specific manner than, say, narrative epic. The texts of the gold tablets in particular seem to have been thought to have a specific pragmatic function, given that they were inscribed on gold and buried with the deceased. They thus seem to be instrumental in enabling their addressees to enjoy a blessed afterlife, and, in some cases, in effecting a transition from mortal to immortal. The pragmatic function of poetry was, as Freer's chapter in the present book shows, a topic of debate in Epicurean poetics, which Virgil explores throughout the *Georgics*. Perhaps the most explicit example of this theme, however, occurs in the Orpheus narrative: Orpheus is initially the poet whose song, above all others, moves its hearers (4.464–84); but, once he fails to follow the instructions, his song no longer moves the spirits and divine laws of the underworld (4.505, *quo fletu Manis, quae numina uoce moueret?*). His song ceases to have its pragmatic force, yet it still resonates even after its author has been dismembered (523–7).

This invites us to reflect on the pragmatic force of the poem itself, especially if the Orphic parallels do indeed support the allegorical interpretation. The *Georgics* has a number of addressees (Octavian, Maecenas, farmers, Romans in general), but if Aristaeus is Octavian, Octavian is clearly brought to the fore at this point, especially given his mention in the *sphragis* which immediately follows the episode (4.559–66). Octavian is given the prospect of apotheosis (1.24–42), but as Damien Nelis has recently stressed,[46] this has not yet been achieved: it is still uncertain which council of the gods will claim him (1.24–5), and there seems a real risk that Tartarus will choose him as its king (1.36–9). Octavian, then, has not yet achieved immortality. Whilst Virgil's poetry could hardly determine whether or not Octavian would be deified, it could prove instrumental in conferring a kind of poetic immortality. This seems to be encapsulated by the temple to Caesar that Virgil intends to construct in book 3 (3.13ff.), which clearly functions as a metapoetic metaphor, perhaps referring to the *Aeneid*, or to the *Georgics* itself.[47] The temple marks Octavian's divine status, given the number of sacrifices he will receive (3.22–3). In that case, his immortality, in a sense, depends upon Virgil's divinization of him through song: to achieve this kind of poetic immortality, he must rely on Virgil, just as initiates into Orphic mystery cult rely upon the songs of Orpheus to conquer death.[48] Virgil is like Orpheus, as his song will be instrumental in the divinization of his addressee, Octavian.

As in the case of the Orphic material, there is a crime that must be atoned for. In the Aristaeus narrative, this is the rape of Eurydice; in the wider narrative of the poem, this is the horrifying civil war description at the end of book 1 (461ff.), where right and wrong are inverted (505). This was itself a punishment for an earlier crime, the perjury of Laomedon (501–2).[49] It may seem that this cycle of punishment is never-ending, but Virgil's exclamation that, for too long, Heaven has grudged Caesar's presence on earth (1.503–4) implies that Octavian may bring an end to it. Indeed, a similar dynamic is operative in Horace at *Odes* 1.2, a probable adaptation of the Virgilian passage, where the civil war is also depicted as a crime to be expiated: the impassioned narrator asks, 'Who will Jupiter give the task of expiating our crime?' (29–30, *cui dabit partis scelus expiandi* | *Iuppiter?*), before we find out that the most promising candidate in response to the question will be Octavian (41–52).[50] The *Georgics* raises a similar prospect, partly by means of its Orphic imagery: Octavian may expiate Rome's crime, just as the addressees of the Orphic tablets may bring an end to their lengthy cycle of reincarnations by purifying themselves of their ancestral fault.[51] If we press the analogy with the Orphic model further, Octavian must achieve the 'purification' of the sins of Rome in order to attain divinization.

The poem, then, presents the prospect of Octavian's divinization, but that prospect is contingent upon his successful 'purification' of Rome from the crimes of civil war. To return to the Orpheus narrative, Aristaeus/Octavian has a choice whether or not to follow the instructions of Proteus, and, 'seeking peace' (*petens pacem*, 535), revitalize his hive of bees/ Roman citizens. In other words, he has a choice, whether or not to allow the complaints and lamentations of Orpheus/Virgil to have an effect on him. If he ignores them, Virgil's *carmen*, with its now empty praise of Octavian, will sound as hollow and haunting as the lamentations of Orpheus that have failed to persuade the *manis* and *numina* of the underworld (4.505), but remain to be heard long after his death (4.523–7).

CHAPTER 5
VIRGIL'S *GEORGICS* AND THE EPICUREAN SIRENS OF POETRY

Nicholas Freer

Scholars have long identified a broad Epicurean undercurrent in the *Georgics*, citing its notion of human progress, the poet's intense appreciation of nature, and the contrast between rural *otium* and the *negotia* of public life.[1] Several studies have also examined Virgil's extensive interactions with Lucretius's *De Rerum Natura* and the Epicurean worldview it espouses.[2] Monica Gale, in particular, has shown how Virgil interrogates, and problematizes, Lucretius's conception of poetry as an appropriate vehicle for Epicurean *didaxis*.[3] Building on Gale's thesis, this chapter proposes that Virgil's discussion of the nature and function of poetry in the *Georgics* contains an even richer and more persistent Epicurean strand than previously thought.

Focusing on the *sphragis* to book 4 and a series of programmatic passages in books 2 and 3, I will argue that Virgil stages a confrontation between Lucretius's unorthodox Epicurean poetic programme and the theory of poetry advanced within the Athenian tradition of the Garden, represented by the founder, Epicurus, and Virgil's own teacher, Philodemus.[4] In the process, I suggest, Virgil challenges the position adopted by Lucretius while foregrounding Epicurus's conception of poetry as a seductive but dangerously irrational medium unsuited to the goal of instruction, a view encapsulated by Epicurus's allusion to the 'Sirens' of poetry in his famous *Letter to Pythocles*. Finally, I consider the implications of this reading for the interpretation of the *Georgics* as a whole, and attempt to explain Virgil's seemingly paradoxical emphasis on the limitations of poetry as a mode of *didaxis* within a poem that itself purports to teach.[5]

The *sphragis*

The *Georgics* concludes with a *sphragis* ('seal' or 'signature') – a common vehicle for reflexive discussions of poetry and the poet's literary achievement[6] – portraying Virgil as a young poet at leisure while Octavian campaigns in the East (4.559–66):

> Haec super aruorum cultu pecorumque canebam
> et super arboribus, Caesar dum magnus ad altum   560
> fulminat Euphraten bello uictorque uolentis
> per populos dat iura uiamque adfectat Olympo.
> illo Vergilium me tempore dulcis alebat
> Parthenope studiis florentem ignobilis oti,

carmina qui lusi pastorum audaxque iuuenta,   565
Tityre, te patulae cecini sub tegmine fagi.

Thus I sang on the care of fields, flocks, and trees, while great Caesar thundered in war by the deep Euphrates, and gave laws as victor to willing peoples, and tried a path to Olympus. At that time sweet Parthenope nourished me, Virgil, as I flourished in the pursuits of inglorious leisure, I who played with shepherds' songs and in the boldness of youth sang of you, Tityrus, in the shade of a spreading beech.

We are invited to read the *sphragis* not simply as the conclusion to the present poem, but as the culmination of the period of the poet's life devoted to the composition of the *Eclogues* and the *Georgics*.[7] Thus the final line echoes the first line of the *Eclogues* (*Tityre, tu patulae recubans sub tegmine fagi*), and lines 559–60 summarize the first three books of the *Georgics*, the tending of fields, flocks and trees. Moreover, *carmina . . . pastorum* (565) could be seen to encompass the subject matter of the *Eclogues* as well as of the *Georgics*.[8]

The setting within which Virgil composes these works is saturated with possible allusions to his life at the Epicurean school in Naples. The poet's *otium* suggests the Epicurean ideal of *ataraxia*, while its epithet *ignobile* recalls the central Epicurean precept 'live unknown' (λάθε βιώσας), recommending withdrawal from public life;[9] the significance of the concept of *otium* for the interpretation of the *sphragis* is reinforced by the terminal acrostic spelling *o t i a* in lines 562–5.[10] Virgil's philosophical education is further suggested by *studia* in 564 (which can be translated either as 'pursuits' or 'studies'), and by the image of the poet as a flower (*florentem*), evoking the Garden of Epicurus.[11] Additionally, Parthenope (564) was a poetic pseudonym for Naples,[12] where the poet spent a portion of his youth (cf. 565: *iuuenta*), while its epithet *dulcis* recalls the Epicurean goal of pleasure.[13]

However, I would argue that the image of the poet 'nourished' (*alebat*) by Parthenope points to a further Epicurean intertext. Servius *ad G.* 4.563 recalls the tradition that Naples was named Parthenope after one of the Sirens, who was said to have been buried there.[14] This has led Gale to interpret Virgil's reference to Parthenope in the *sphragis* as 'an assertion of the Siren-like power of song inspired by this "Muse" . . . and [Virgil's] poetry as the product of an unpredictable and perhaps dangerous *furor poeticus*'.[15] Interestingly, Epicurus appears to have interpreted the myth of the Sirens in a very similar manner in his *Letter to Pythocles*, where he urges his disciple to 'flee all education at full sail' (παιδείαν δὲ πᾶσαν, μακάριε, φεῦγε τἀκάτιον ἀράμενος).[16] Epicurus's injunction recalls Odysseus's account of his adventures at the court of Alcinous in Homer's *Odyssey*, where Odysseus tells of how he escaped the Sirens' deadly allure by tying himself to the mast of his ship while his companions filled their ears with wax (12.39–54, 158–200). For Epicurus, the traditional Greek education was a harmful distraction from philosophy, the only true path to happiness,[17] and poetry was a central element of the curriculum shunned by Epicurus – the privileged status of poetry within Greek *paideia* is recognized by his allusion to the Sirens in particular, who exploited the power of song to lure and destroy their victims.[18]

In fact, as far as we can glean from the extant sources, the myth of the Sirens perfectly encapsulates Epicurus's views on poetry. While Epicurus recognized that poetry can impart pleasure,[19] like many ancient critics he rejected its mythic content,[20] which he regarded as a source of mental disturbance inimical to the pursuit of *ataraxia*. Thus in his *Letter to Pythocles* (87) Epicurus associates myth with 'irrationality' (ἀλογία) and 'empty opinion' (κενὴ δόξα), while Plutarch reports Epicurus's condemnation of 'poetic confusion' (ποιτικῆς τύρβης) and 'Homer's absurdities' (τῶν Ὁμήρου μωρολογημάτων).[21] Heraclitus also asserts that Epicurus purified himself from poetry as 'a destructive lure of myth' (ὀλέθριον μύθων δέλεαρ, *Quaest. Hom.* 4). A similar ambivalence can be found in the works of Philodemus, our most extensive surviving source on Epicurean poetic theory. Philodemus writes of the pleasure of poetry,[22] and its power to fascinate and attract,[23] and he was himself a keen epigrammatist.[24] However, Philodemus also emphasized poetry's potentially harmful effects; he warns, for example, that dirges and love songs tend to inflame the emotions,[25] and that poems, in general, cause a great deal of harm (βλάβη μεγίστη).[26] Both Epicurus and Philodemus appear to have assumed that the wise man, fortified by Epicurean philosophy, may enjoy poetry without succumbing to its disturbing influence.[27] Nonetheless, Epicurus (followed by Philodemus) clearly indicated that poetry should not be used to teach,[28] and he placed severe restrictions on poetic composition in general (if he allowed it at all).[29]

Epicurus's injunction to Pythocles was well known in antiquity,[30] and its Siren allusion was clearly recognized by his readers. Plutarch, for example, responds to Socrates' exile of poetry from his ideal city by asking whether the ears of the young should be filled with wax as they hoist sail in their Epicurean ship and evade the Siren song of poetry (*Mor.* 15d), and the same Siren imagery lies behind Heraclitus's assertion that Epicurus condemned poetry as 'a destructive lure of myth'. Returning to the *sphragis*, therefore, it is not unreasonable to think – given the dense cluster of Epicurean associations in these lines – that Virgil's *dulcis Parthenope* may signal an allusion to Epicurus's conception of the Siren-like qualities of poetry.

This reading may be supported by the fifth poem of the *Catalepton*, a collection of short poems that purports to be Virgil's juvenilia.[31] Like the *sphragis*, *Catalepton* 5 presents an autobiographical account of the poet's early life. After announcing his departure from the schools of rhetoric (1–7), the speaker bids farewell to the *Camenae*, or Roman Muses, as he hoists sail for the blessed harbours of Naples, seeking to liberate himself from cares through the teachings of the Epicurean philosopher Siro (8–14):[32]

> nos ad beatos uela mittimus portus
> magni petentes docta dicta Sironis,
> uitamque ab omni uindicabimus cura.   10
> ite hinc, Camenae, uos quoque ite iam sane,
> dulces Camenae (nam fatebimur uerum,
> dulces fuistis); et tamen meas chartas
> reuisitote, sed pudenter et raro.

We set sail for happy harbours, seeking great Siro's learned teachings, and shall free our life from every care. Away with you, Muses, away even with you, sweet Muses (for we must profess the truth – you have been sweet). Even so, revisit my pages, though modestly and rarely.

The poem displays striking parallels with the *sphragis* to Virgil's *Georgics*. Both portray the poet as a young man (*Cat.* 5.5: *ite hinc . . . cymbalon iuuentutis*; *G.* 4.565: *audax . . . iuuenta*), while the speaker's carefree existence at Siro's school resembles Virgil's distinctly Epicurean *otia* at Parthenope/Naples.[33] Of particular interest for the present discussion are the *dulces Camenae*, which correspond to Virgil's 'Muse' in the *sphragis*, *dulcis Parthenope*. As Clay has pointed out, *Cat.* 5.8–12 is informed by Epicurus's allusion to the myth of the Sirens in his *Letter to Pythocles*: lines 8–9 echo Epicurus's image of setting sail to escape the Sirens of *paideia* (the genitive *Sironis* may even be a pun on *Sirenum*, 'Siren'), while the poet's rejection of the sweet Roman Muses in lines 11–12 recognizes Epicurus's specific objection to the poetic element of traditional education.[34] If *Catalepton* 5 is indeed an early Virgilian composition, then Virgil may have expected his audience to recall the *dulces Camenae* and the allusion to Epicurus's harmful Sirens of poetry when confronted with *dulcis Parthenope* in the *sphragis* to the *Georgics*. But even if the poem is not authentic, the image of an 'Epicurean' Virgil inspired by a Siren in the *sphragis* may well have prompted recognition of an allusion to Epicurus's advice to Pythocles, such was its notoriety in antiquity. Indeed, Virgil's reference to Parthenope may have encouraged the Virgilian imitator to incorporate Epicurus's injunction into his own reworking of the *sphragis*.

Georgics 2 and 3

In book 1 of *De Rerum Natura* (1.921–50, lines 926–50 repeated at 4.1–25), Lucretius famously defends his use of poetry as a vehicle for Epicurean philosophical instruction, arguing that poetry is necessary to attract his audience to the otherwise 'cheerless' (*tristior*, 944) teachings of Epicurus. He emphasizes poetry's seductive charm and sweetness (924–5: *suauem . . . amorem* | *musarum*, 'sweet love of the Muses'; 934: *musaeo . . . lepore*, 'the Muses' charm'; 945–6: *suauiloquenti* | *carmine Pierio*, 'sweet-spoken Pierian song'; 947: *musaeo dulci . . . melle*, 'sweet honey of the Muses'), and likens himself to a doctor spreading 'sweet honey' (*mellis dulci*, 938) around the rim of a cup in order to trick children into drinking bitter medicine. But in composing his work, Lucretius tells us, he too experiences the ecstasy of poetry (1.922–30); here he combines the conventional imagery of Dionysiac possession (*sed acri* | *percussit thyrso laudis spes magna meum cor*, 'but a great hope of glory has struck my heart with a sharp thyrsus') with the language of passion (*et simul incussit suauem mi in pectus amorem* | *musarum*, 'and at the same time [a great hope of glory] has injected into my breast a sweet love of the Muses') to convey the overwhelming force and pleasure of poetic inspiration as it drives him across uncharted terrain.

However, Lucretius's decision to deploy the psychagogic power of poetry in the service of *ratio* (1.948–9) sets him at odds with Epicurus, who – as I have noted above – rejected poetry precisely because of its irrational qualities and its attendant capacity to beguile. As Gale argues, Lucretius's use of poetry as a mode of *didaxis*, and the description of his own poetic inspiration as a kind of *furor*, sits uncomfortably with the goal of promoting Epicurean rationality: '[Lucretius] leaves himself open to the accusation that his medium is in its very nature detrimental to the ataraxic calm which he seeks to recommend to his reader.'[35]

Virgil draws out this tension between Lucretius's Epicurean message and his medium in a series of programmatic passages in *Georgics* 2 and 3, where the narrator offers extended reflections on the nature and function of his own poetic activity. As I aim to demonstrate, in these passages Virgil highlights poetry's potentially disturbing influence by appropriating and intensifying the language of *amor* and Dionysiac possession that Lucretius had used to convey the power and pleasure of his medium in his apology for poetry in book 1. In the process, he casts doubt on Lucretius's claim that poetry may complement the pursuit of reason, and reasserts the dangerous, Siren-like qualities of poetry emphasized by Epicurus and his successors within the Athenian Epicurean tradition.

At the beginning of book 2 the narrator presents himself as a civilizing influence, teaching the farmer to create order from the chaos of nature (35–8):

quare agite o proprios generatim discite cultus,
agricolae, fructusque feros mollite colendo,
neu segnes iaceant terrae. iuuat Ismara Baccho
conserere atque olea magnum uestire Taburnum.

So come now, farmers, learn the methods of cultivation appropriate to each species, and tame wild fruits with your care, and don't let your fields lie idle. It is a pleasure to plant vines in Thrace and to cover great Taburnum with the olive.

The image of the poet as teacher and public benefactor is reinforced in the following lines (47–52), where the narrator maintains that trees can be disciplined to 'follow' (*sequentur*) the farmer's directions; here perhaps we are to think of Orpheus, whose power over nature was interpreted allegorically as a symbol for poetry's capacity to subdue man's irrational impulses and to create order in society.[36] In fact Orpheus himself was widely regarded as the archetypal poet-teacher in antiquity, and he was even counted among the first philosophers.[37] At the same time, the passage quoted above resonates with Lucretius's discussion of his own poetic ambitions in his apology. Virgil's *iuuat* (37) echoes the language applied to the pleasure of poetic composition at *DRN* 1.927–8 (*iuuat integros accedere fontis | atque haurire, iuuatque nouos decerpere flores*, 'It pleases me to visit untouched springs and draw from them, and it pleases me to pluck unfamiliar flowers'), while the narrator's twofold emphasis on his poetry's usefulness (35–7) and its adherence to Callimachean ideals of brevity and refinement (42–6) recalls (while subtly modifying) the central concerns of Lucretius's poetic programme: the didactic efficacy of poetry and the originality of his work (in turn cast in distinctly Callimachean terms).[38]

Like Orpheus and Lucretius, Virgil suggests, he is performing a valuable public service by promoting order and reason. However, the narrator's faith in the civilizing power of his poetry is problematized towards the end of book 2 (475–94), when he interrupts his praise of country life to consider the alternatives, broadly defined, of natural-philosophical and pastoral poetry. The passage begins with an invocation to the Muses as the narrator announces his desire to treat natural-philosophical themes (475–7):

> me uero primum dulces ante omnia Musae,
> quarum sacra fero ingenti percussus amore,
> accipiant caelique uias et sidera monstrent

> As for me, first may the Muses, sweeter than all else, whose sacred emblems I carry struck by a great love, receive me and reveal to me the courses of the stars through heaven . . .

These lines are partly modelled on Lucretius's discussion of his poetic inspiration in the apology: Virgil's *dulces Musae* (*G.* 2.475) recalls Lucretius's 'sweet love of the Muses' (*suauem . . . amorem | musarum*, *DRN* 1.924–5) and his 'sweet honey of the Muses' (*musaeo dulci . . . melle*, *DRN* 1.947), while *percussus* (*G.* 2.476) echoes Lucretius's language of overwhelming inspiration (*DRN* 1.923–4: *percussit . . . incussit*, 'struck . . . injected').[39] Although, unlike Lucretius (cf. *DRN* 1.923: *percussit thyrso*, ' struck with a thyrsus'), the Virgilian narrator does not explicitly indicate Dionysiac possession, our awareness of the Lucretian model may in turn remind us of his own appeal to Bacchus as inspiring deity at the beginning of book 2 (2: *nunc te, Bacche, canam*, 'Now I shall sing of you, Bacchus'; 7: *huc, pater o Lenaee, ueni*, 'Come now, Father of the vine').

There is, however, a significant development in the narrator's discussion of his own poetic inspiration in the finale to *Georgic* 2. Whereas Lucretius only briefly exploited the language of irrational inspiration to illustrate the pleasurable and attractive aspects of poetry – and hence its suitability as a vehicle for Epicurean *didaxis* – this element now dominates the Virgilian narrator's discussion of his poetic options.[40] Thus *amor* reappears in the following lines, where his passion for natural-philosophical poetry gives way to love of pastoral themes (486: *flumina amem siluasque*, 'may I love the streams and woods'). Meanwhile, Dionysiac possession is confirmed by the ecstatic outburst in lines 486–9:

> o ubi campi
> Spercheosque et uirginibus bacchata Lacaenis
> Taygeta! o qui me gelidis conuallibus Haemi
> sistat, et ingenti ramorum protegat umbra!

Oh, for the plains, and the waters of the Spercheus, and the mountains of Taygetus where Spartan maidens hold bacchanals! Oh, set me down in the cool valleys of Haemus, and shelter me with the shade of great branches!

Haemus and the River Spercheus are both associated with Bacchus, who came to Greece via Thrace and Thessaly, while the Bacchanalia on Taygetus are here explicitly invoked.[41]

In this context, however, the narrator's connection with Bacchus has disturbing implications. Whilst book 2 began with praise of Bacchus as a creative god who nourishes the vine and fills the wine vats (4–6), Virgil's discussion of poetry at the end of the book appears soon after an illustration of Bacchus's destructive power: as god of the vine, Bacchus was blamed for inciting the drunken battle between the Centaurs and the Lapiths (454–7).[42] Bacchus's association with violence, madness and death in this passage introduces the possibility that the irrational aspect of poetry – indicated by the narrator's Dionysiac inspiration in the following lines – itself has destructive potential.[43]

By appropriating the language and imagery employed by Lucretius to emphasize the irrational and potentially harmful qualities of poetry, Virgil may be challenging Lucretius's view of poetry as a suitable vehicle for the transmission of Epicurean *ratio*, and suggesting that poetry itself may be detrimental to this aim. Indeed, the suggestion that poetry is the product of *furor* can be seen to call into question the narrator's role in society, highlighting a possible conflict between his medium and his own efforts to recommend order and control.[44] At the same time, Virgil's representation of the *dulces Musae* is consistent with the conception of poetry advanced by Epicurus and his successors within the Athenian tradition of the Garden. As we have seen, in his *Letter to Pythocles* Epicurus likened poetry's dangerous allure to the song of the Sirens, and this in turn may have inspired Virgil's reference to his sweet Siren-'Muse' (*dulcis Parthenope*) in the *sphragis* to the *Georgics*. Virgil's emphasis on the seductive but dangerously irrational qualities of his *dulces Musae* at the end of book 2 might therefore be interpreted as a rejection of Lucretius's poetic programme, with its honey-sweet Muses (*musaeo dulci . . . melle, DRN* 1.947), in favour of the canonical teachings of Epicurus.

Book 3 begins with another extended self-referential discussion of poetry, occupying a position of programmatic significance at the centre of the work.[45] Erecting a metaphorical temple in celebration of Octavian's victories over foreign enemies (26–33), the narrator promises to immortalize the *princeps* by enshrining his achievements in verse (46–8). He appears alongside Octavian, presiding over his own poetic triumph (16–25), and proposes to win fame as the first to import the Muses from Mt Helicon into Mantua (8–12):

> temptanda uia est, qua me quoque possim
> tollere humo uictorque uirum uolitare per ora.
> primus ego in patriam mecum, modo uita supersit,   10
> Aonio rediens deducam uertice Musas;
> primus Idumeas referam tibi, Mantua, palmas

I must try a path by which I too may rise from the earth and fly, victorious, on the lips of men. I'll be the first, if my life lasts, to return to my homeland leading the Muses with me from the heights of Helicon. I'll be the first, Mantua, to bring you the palms of Idumaea . . .

The narrator signals his desire to emulate Ennius by echoing his famous claim to poetic immortality as well as Lucretius's praise of Ennius for importing the Muses from Greece into Italy.[46] Significantly for our purposes, however, these lines also echo Lucretius's discussion of Epicurus's achievement in liberating mankind from the destructive irrationality of religion in *DRN* 1;[47] as we saw above, the narrator had assumed the didactic posture of Lucretius early in book 2 (35–8), but he now goes one step further by emulating Lucretius's Epicurus, the ultimate source of truth. Furthermore, as at the beginning of book 2 (47–52), there is also a suggestion of Orphic powers: his dream of leading the Muses down from Mt Helicon (*Aonio rediens deducam uertice Musas*, 11) recalls the language and imagery applied to Gallus's initiation into the tradition of Orphic poets in *Eclogue* 6, where one of the Muses led the poet onto Mt Helicon (64–5: *Gallum | Aonas in montis ut duxerit una sororum*) and Gallus received the pipe which Hesiod used to draw trees down from the mountains in the manner of Orpheus (70–1: *quibus ille solebat | cantando rigidas deducere montibus ornos*). In the programmatic opening to book 3, therefore, the narrator signals not only his future mastery of the poetic tradition, but also his desire to become an Epicurus-like/Orpheus-like teacher and civilizing influence, complementing Octavian's efforts to extend Roman *imperium* throughout the world.

However, the narrator's aspirations are once again called into question by the suggestion that he is subject to a violent and disturbing poetic *furor*, and here too Virgil can be seen to respond to Lucretius's poetic programme. In lines 40–5 he sets aside his proposed epic on the achievements of Octavian and returns to the task at hand:

> interea Dryadum siluas saltusque sequamur   40
> intactos, tua, Maecenas, haud mollia iussa:
> te sine nil altum mens incohat. en age segnis
> rumpe moras; uocat ingenti clamore Cithaeron
> Taygetique canes domitrixque Epidaurus equorum,
> et uox adsensu nemorum ingeminata remugit.   45

Meanwhile let's make for the Dryads' woods and untouched glades, no easy task you have set, Maecenas: without you my mind attempts no great enterprise. Come then, break with idle delay; Cithaeron resounds with loud cries, Taygetus with its hounds and Epidaurus, mistress of horses, and the call echoes back, doubled by the approving groves.

The passage begins with an allusion that signals Virgil's engagement with Lucretius's apology, the *saltus intactos* of the *Georgics* recalling Lucretius's Callimachean *integros fontis* (*DRN* 1.927).[48] The narrator then marks the continuation of the present poetic enterprise with a hunting metaphor (*rumpe moras*) accompanied by references to three Greek mountains; while Epidaurus (*domitrix ... equorum*) seems to anticipate the discussion of horse-training later in book 3, Cithaeron and Taygetus both have strong associations with Bacchus.[49] The narrator has already invoked the Bacchanalia on Taygetus in the context of his poetic ecstasy towards the end book 2 (487–8), while Cithaeron (along with Parnassus) was one of the sites of Bacchus's trieteric *oreibasia*, gruesome rites which involved the dismemberment of wild animals.[50] As in the finale to book 2, therefore, Virgil may be hinting at the irrational and potentially destructive character of the Dionysiac element of his poetic inspiration. Indeed, Virgil would later allude to the destructive aspect of the trieteric festival in Dido's famous simile in *Aeneid* 4 (300–3):

> saeuit inops animi totamque incensa per urbem
> bacchatur, qualis commotis excita sacris
> Thyias, ubi audito stimulant trieterica Baccho
> orgia nocturnusque uocat clamore Cithaeron.

> Out of her mind, and all aflame, she raved throughout the city in a frenzy, like a Thyiad driven to madness by the shaken emblems, when the trieteric festival rouses her with the cry of Bacchus and Cithaeron roars in the night.

Although Dido's frenzy is inspired by *amor* in the immediate context, her maenad-like frenzy sets the stage for her own death and ultimately the destruction of her people. Significantly, Virgil here explicitly invokes the *trieterica orgia* of Bacchus on Cithaeron while employing an exact verbal echo of the narrator's description of his poetic experience in the third Georgic (*uocat clamore Cithaeron* = *G.* 3.43: *uocat ... clamore Cithaeron*).

In the context of Virgil's hunting metaphor, the reference to Cithaeron may also signal an allusion to the Bacchic violence of Euripides' *Bacchae*. Hunting has been described as the 'key metaphor' of the *Bacchae*,[51] and the play ends with Dionysus and his maenads hunting down and dismembering Pentheus on Cithaeron.[52] Just as Euripides portrayed his maenads as 'hounds' (731, 872, 977), the Virgilian *canes* of Taygetus (44) might also be construed as maenads; we have in fact already encountered the maenads of Taygetus, during the narrator's Dionysiac ecstasy at *G.* 2.487–8. The Euripidean connection is also suggested by the cry of Cithaeron (43: *uocat ingenti clamore Cithaeron*), which evokes Dionysus's call to his maenads to hunt down Pentheus on Cithaeron (*Bacch.* 1078–9: φωνή τις ... ἀνεβόησεν, 'a voice ... cried out'), while the voice redoubled by the groves (45: *uox adsensu nemorum ingeminata remugit*) recalls the voice of Dionysus ringing out a second time in the woods of Cithaeron (*Bacch.* 1084–8).[53] By presenting himself as a maenad in the grip of a destructive Bacchic frenzy, I would suggest, the poet continues his engagement with the Dionysiac imagery applied to the allure of poetry in Lucretius's apology, highlighting the dangerously irrational qualities of the medium that Lucretius had overlooked. Moreover, the connection between Virgil's discussion of his poetic inspiration in lines 42–5 and Lucretius's apology is strengthened by an allusion to the irrational force of *amor*, which Lucretius had also associated with the seductive power of poetry. Thus the word *amor* is embedded in the very language with which the poet announces his metaphorical call to the hunt in line 43 (*rumpe moras; uocat ingenti clamore Cithaeron*), *ingenti clamore* recalls the narrator's ecstatic love of the Muses in book 2 (476: *ingenti . . . amore*). This in turn may gesture towards the common metaphor of love as hunting, also found in Euripides' *Bacchae*,[54] while the description of Epidaurus as a *domitrix* (44) calls to mind the *dominae* of Latin love elegy, pursued by poets over harsh terrain at the mercy of their frenzied *amor*.[55]

As in the finale to book 2, therefore, Virgil's programmatic opening to book 3 appropriates the two central elements of Lucretius's language of poetic inspiration, *amor* and Dionysiac possession, and emphasizes the latter's destructive potential. Once again the narrator's association with the forces of irrationality can be seen to call into question Lucretius's conception of poetry as an agent of *ratio*, in line with the Athenian Epicurean tradition, which viewed poetry as an inherently irrational medium inimical to *ataraxia*. And here too the narrator's *furor poeticus* suggests a tension between his medium and his own efforts to promote order and control, signalled by the allusions to Orpheus and Lucretius's Epicurus in the same passage.

It is therefore perhaps no accident that the role of civilizing influence and public benefactor is ultimately denied to the figure of Virgil in the *sphragis* to the *Georgics* – where, I have argued, the poet's 'Muse' Parthenope evokes Epicurus's irrational Sirens of poetry – and it is instead Octavian who fulfils the narrator's ambition to supplant (Lucretius's) Epicurus in the proem to book 3.[56] Thus Octavian's triumphant path to Olympus (4.561–2: *uictor . . . uiam . . . adfectat Olympo*) recalls Epicurus's intellectual conquest of the heavens at *DRN* 1.62–79 (the same passage recalled by the narrator at 3.8–12),[57] while Octavian's pacification and ordering of the world (4.562: *uictorque uolentes | per populos dat iura*), which is presented as the basis of his future divinity, echoes Lucretius's panegyric of his philosophical *deus* Epicurus (*DRN* 5.20–1: *quo magis hic merito nobis deus esse uidetur, | ex quo nunc etiam per magnas didita gentis | dulcia permulcent animos solacia uitae*, 'So with more reason he is considered by us to be a god, from whom the sweet consolations of life, distributed throughout great nations, even now are soothing the minds of men').[58] Of course, the implication that Octavian has now assumed the role of Epicurus might be interpreted as a rejection of Lucretius's claim that salvation can only be achieved through Epicurean philosophy, rather than through political endeavour. However, Virgil's failure to earn the same distinction in the *sphragis*, and his reduction to a passive figure of *otium*, may also illustrate the unattainability of the narrator's own ambition to become a new Epicurus and Octavian's equal in the proem to book 3.

Returning to book 3, the connection between poetry, Dionysiac possession and *amor* is developed still further in the narrator's description of his poetic experience at 291–3:

> sed me Parnassi deserta per ardua dulcis
> raptat amor; iuuat ire iugis, qua nulla priorum
> Castaliam molli deuertitur orbita cliuo.

But sweet love drags me over the deserted heights of Parnassus; it is a delight to traverse the ridges, where no earlier path leads down to Castalia over gentle slopes.

Once again Virgil engages with Lucretius's discussion of his poetic inspiration in the apology, the narrator's *dulcis amor* recalling the *suauis amor musarum* that inspired Lucretius's wanderings through the trackless haunts of Mt Pieria (*DRN* 1.925–6: *suauem ... amorem | musarum, quo nunc instinctus mente uigenti | auia Pieridum peragro loca*). However, the *amor* of the Virgilian narrator now has distinctly negative connotations, as this passage immediately follows a discussion of the destructive effects of sexual *amor* (209–83), which climaxed with the story of Glaucus's dismemberment by his own love-maddened horses. Indeed, the narrator's behaviour here resembles the frenzy of the horses driven by *amor* across mountains and ridges in the preceding passage (252–4, 269–70, 276–7).[59] Therefore, just as at the end of book 2 and in the proem to book 3, Virgil emphasized the dangerously irrational qualities of poetry by reworking the conventional Dionysiac imagery applied to poetic inspiration in Lucretius's apology, he now suggests an analogy between poetic *amor* and destructive sexual *amor*, which also was absent from Lucretius. The *dulcis amor* of poetry is thus simultaneously attractive and destructive, like the *dulces Musae* of book 2 (475) and Epicurus's Sirens of poetry, evoked by *dulcis Parthenope* in the *sphragis* to book 4.

However, lines 291–3 also appear to engage with the Dionysiac imagery in Lucretius's apology, for the poet's journey across Parnassus recalls Bacchus's specific association with mountains,[60] as well as the mountain settings of the Bacchanalia adduced at the end of book 2 and in the proem to book 3.[61] The idea of Bacchic possession is perhaps further reinforced by the substitution of Lucretius's Pieria (*DRN* 1.926) for Parnassus (*G.* 3.291) as the site of the poet's frenzy: while Parnassus was sacred to the Muses and Apollo, it was also co-host of the trieteric festival with Cithaeron, itself adduced in the narrator's discussion of his poetic inspiration in the proem to book 3. With this earlier passage in mind, Virgil may have introduced Parnassus to suggest, once again, the potentially destructive aspect of his Dionysiac inspiration.

Conclusions

As I have argued, Virgil emphasizes the alluring but dangerously irrational qualities of poetry in a series of passages in which the narrator offers his reflections on the nature and function of his own poetic activity, and in the process he frames his discussion as a response to Lucretius's justification for writing Epicurean didactic poetry in the *De Rerum Natura*. Virgil highlights the dangers of Lucretius's approach by problematizing his language of poetic inspiration: whilst Lucretius portrayed himself at the mercy of *amor* and Dionysiac ecstasy to illustrate the powerful allure of poetry, the Virgilian narrator now accentuates his poetry's association with the potentially destructive *furor* generated by *amor* and Bacchus, potentially undermining the authority of his didactic *persona* even as he seeks to cast himself in the role of civilizing influence and public benefactor.

That Virgil should take such a position within a poem that itself purports to teach may seem paradoxical, to say the least, and deserves consideration. On one level, Virgil's engagement with Epicurean poetics can be seen in the context of his broader interrogation of philosophical traditions and systems of thought in the *Georgics*, of which Epicureanism represents an important strand. In this case, however, Virgil stages a confrontation between two competing positions within the Garden itself: between, on the one hand, Lucretius's assertion that the pleasurable aspects of poetry can be harnessed in the service of Epicurean *ratio*, and, on the other hand, the mainstream Athenian tradition beginning with Epicurus himself, which rejected poetry as a mode of *didaxis* precisely because of its dangerously irrational allure. As I have suggested, in drawing out the tension between his message and his medium, Virgil tips his hand in favour of the Athenian Epicurean position.

At first glance this would appear to support Seneca's view that the *Georgics* was not intended to instruct at all, and that Virgil merely aimed to 'delight' (*delectare*) his readers (*Ep.* 86.15). However, Virgil arguably still clings to the hope that Epicurus may be proved wrong, despite persistent doubts about the efficacy of his poetry – one senses this most urgently in the proem to book 3, which expresses in the boldest and loftiest terms the poet's potential to make a difference to his society. But in the end this tension – this Epicurean ambivalence – is never fully resolved, and Virgil is unable to forget the lessons he learned as a young man in the embrace of *dulcis Parthenope*.

PART III
POLITICS AND SOCIETY

CHAPTER 6
DIVINIZATION AND DIDACTIC EFFICACY IN VIRGIL'S *GEORGICS**

Bobby Xinyue

Virgil's *Georgics* offers near-contemporary responses to and repeated meditations on the subject of the divinization of Octavian, the soon-to-be Augustus, who in the wake of his victory at Actium in 31 BCE stood poised to usher in a new political era for Rome.[1] Right from the outset of the poem, Octavian is said to be on his way to becoming a god; yet subsequent explorations of this idea make that prospect seem uncertain or even problematic. The multiple and often contrasting images of Octavian held up by the poet manifestly constitute a challenge for readers who are intent on finding within the *Georgics* some determinate or unified view on Octavian's divinization.

The poem's ambivalence about the proleptic apotheosis of Octavian has been understood by many scholars as a reflection of Virgil's attempt to come to terms with Octavian's supremacy while confessing Roman anxieties about ruler cult and its potential effect on the Roman constitution.[2] Others have taken the poet's recurrent deliberations on Octavian's divinity as a series of political lessons on how to exercise power, aimed directly at the new Caesar, who now possesses the authority 'to initiate, maintain, and bring an end to all manners of phenomena, especially agriculture, poetry, and war'.[3] Different approaches place different degrees of emphasis on the didactic force of Virgil's poem; but they nevertheless share an understanding that the *Georgics* is constitutive of a wider debate in the post-Actian transitional period about Octavian's power, and that, as such, the poem is acutely aware of its own mediating role both within Virgil's poetic corpus and in the transformation of Rome from republic to principate.[4] The present chapter pursues this line of inquiry further by suggesting that discussions of Octavian's divinization in the *Georgics* function as a means by which Virgil considers the effectiveness and relevance of not just didactic poetry, but poetic mediation more generally, in the face of an emergent Augustan regime. It will be argued that Virgil initially seeks to direct Octavian on how to achieve divinity and presents him with a model of divinization based on *cura terrarum*, which encapsulates an idealized relationship between poet, farmer and ruler. As the poem proceeds, however, it becomes clear that the poet's proposal diverges significantly from what is being pursued by Octavian, and this leads eventually to a reflection on the efficacy and nature of poetry in the forthcoming Augustan age. By presenting the divinization of Octavian as a topic unable to be affected by Virgilian didactic, the *Georgics* couches in disarming terms both the inevitability of Octavian's drive towards singular power and the diminishing effect of poetry's mediating role in Rome's shift towards autocracy.

Divinization and *cura terrarum*

The *Georgics* opens with a summary of its four books (1.1–5) followed by a two-part prayer, which is addressed first to a catalogue of agricultural deities (1.5–23), then to Octavian (1.24–42), who, as the poet immediately points out, is not even a god yet (1.24–5): *tuque adeo, quem mox quae sint habitura deorum | concilia incertum est* ('And you above all, it is unclear what company of the gods shall soon claim you'). The word *mox* delays his moment of formal divinization; and the type of divinity Octavian will eventually become is also left unclear.[5] The next section of the prologue suggests that, depending on what responsibility Octavian chooses to exercise (cf. *uelis*, 1.26), he might become the god of land and weather (1.26–8), or the god of the sea (1.29–31), or a new constellation (1.32–5). A fourth possibility – becoming the *rex* of Tartarus (1.36–9) – is firmly rejected. The uncertainty surrounding Octavian's future here lies in what *kind* of divinity he will become and how. The fact that he *will* be divinized is never in doubt.

In the final three lines of the prologue, the poet directly appeals to Octavian and chooses a divine role for him (1.40–2):

da facilem cursum atque audacibus adnue coeptis,
ignarosque uiae mecum miseratus agrestis
ingredere et uotis iam nunc adsuesce uocari.

Grant me an effortless journey and give assent to my bold undertaking, and along with me pity the farmers who do not know the way, come, and even now become accustomed to be called upon by prayers.

The auspicious nod (*adnue*, 1.40) asked of Octavian invests him with a power that traditionally belongs to Jupiter (cf. Hom. *Il.* 1.514, 524, 527). This suggests, in view of Jupiter's conspicuous absence in this prayer, that Octavian has taken the place usually reserved to the supreme god.[6] Equally strikingly, Octavian seems to have replaced the Muses as well. Both Hesiod and Aratus appeal to the Muses for the success of their didactic works (cf. Hes. *Op.* 1; Arat. *Phaen.* 16–18), but Virgil asks only for the blessing of Caesar for his new poetic project. Positioned as such a major determinant of both human existence and poetry, the poet's request for Octavian to show sympathy towards uninformed farmers (1.41) becomes significant, as it focuses in on the kind of influence Virgil would like Octavian to exert. The display of sympathy is a major theme in the *Georgics*, connecting poet, farmer and ruler;[7] here especially Virgil seems to suggest that through shared compassion he and Octavian might provide enlightenment, and the latter is placed in the role of an agricultural protector. The semantically homogenous sequence of *cursum* (1.40), *uiae* (1.41) and *ingredere* (1.42) further intertwines the progress of poet, farmer and ruler, giving the impression that by allowing the *Georgics* to advance, Octavian can enact poetic enlightenment for farmers as well as his own course to divinity.[8] The new Caesar may not be divinized yet (*mox*, 1.24), but in this formulation Virgil already (*iam nunc*, 1.42) makes him a god in his poetry.[9]

Importantly, the request for showing compassion towards the farming community looks directly back to the first of three divine roles proposed to Octavian by the poet earlier in the prologue, when Virgil pictures him as the god of land and weather (1.25–8). Readers do not learn how Octavian will become the god of the sea – he simply 'comes' as one (cf. *an deus immensi uenias maris*, 1.29);[10] while the idea that Octavian 'might add himself as a new star' (*nouum ... sidus te ... addas*, 1.32) appears too politically awkward to contemplate, since this image alludes to not only the divinization of Hellenistic monarchs (with *nouum sidus* evoking the ἄστρον νέον of Callimachus's *Coma Berenices*, cf. *Aet.* fr.110.64 Pf.),[11] but also the apotheosis of the dictator Julius Caesar.[12] By contrast, only the first divine role as the god of land and weather is presented as wholly desirable (1.25–8):

> urbisne inuisere, Caesar,
> terrarumque uelis curam, et te maximus orbis
> auctorem frugum tempestatumque potentem
> accipiat cingens materna tempora myrto

Whether you might choose to watch over cities, Caesar, or the protection of the lands, and the greatest earth would accept you as the guardian of crops and the lord of seasons, with your temples wreathed with your mother's myrtle.

Octavian's choice of watching over cities and terrains, and the world's acceptance of him as an authority, are paratactically set side by side as corresponding events. His welcomed dual-role as *auctor frugum*[13] and *tempestatum potens* (1.27) is imbued with connotations of deification: as the one who causes crops to grow, Octavian would take over the function of Ceres just as Epicurus's benefaction transcends those of Ceres and Liber (Lucr. *DRN.* 5.7–21);[14] and as the lord of the seasons, he would assume the role of Jupiter similar to the weather-controlling Zeus in the prologue to Aratus's *Phaenomena* (10–13).[15] Both the idea of divinization and of Octavian usurping Jupiter's role are present in the final prayers of the prologue as I have shown above. Moreover, given that *cura terrarum* (1.26) is a central topic for the *Georgics* (cf. *cura boum*, 1.3) and *cura* is frequently used to mean the 'cultivation' or 'care' of animals throughout the poem (e.g. 1.216, 1.228, 2.405, 2.415, 3.138, 3.157, 3.404, 4.118),[16] Virgil's request for Octavian to take pity on the farmers lies precisely in his power to protect the land and influence their lives and daily tasks. The correspondence between this divine role proposed by Virgil and the poet's final request for Octavian to sympathize with the rustics who depend on him points to a model of divinization favoured by the poet, namely by means of *cura terrarum*. The attainability of this form of divinization is further highlighted by the temporal relationship between the opening and closing of Virgil's address to Octavian. As *mox* (1.24) becomes *iam nunc* (1.42), it underlines that Octavian – if he should choose to act as the benefactor of farmers, which he is capable of being – can already consider himself divine (*uotis ... adsuesce uocari*, 1.42). The final line of the opening prologue thus emphatically communicates to Octavian that divine status and godlike power for him need not be uncertain or delayed: the future can be now.[17]

My contention in the remainder of this chapter is that this provisional model of deification is subsequently challenged or overlooked at several crucial junctures in the poem.[18] Scenes of Octavian's divinization in the finale of book 1, the opening of book 3 and the poem's *sphragis* ('seal' or 'signature') progressively suggest that Octavian would not subscribe to *cura terrarum* as a means of achieving divinization, and that the Virgilian *didaxis* is not only ignored by Octavian, but also fast becoming irrelevant and therefore unable to effect any change as Rome enters a new political climate. As Gale points out, this strategy of destabilizing or rendering ambiguous what at first appears to be an encouraging and unproblematic notion is typical of Virgil's mode of writing in the *Georgics*, and even the meaning of *cura* becomes complicated as the poem proceeds.[19] Like Horace's *Satires* 2.1, which insinuates that the forthcoming age of Augustus will have a profound impact on the nature of poetic composition, especially on *what* can be said about the new Caesar and *how* it should be said (cf. Hor. *Serm.* 2.1.10–20),[20] Virgil too in the *Georgics* shines a spotlight on these issues by leaving readers in the *sphragis* of his poem with an equivocal image of Octavian soaring unstoppably towards Olympus.

Divinization and *cura triumphorum*

The invocation of the gods in the *Georgics'* prologue is structurally mirrored at the end of book 1, where Virgil appeals to a number of deities to allow a certain *iuuenis* – later revealed as 'Caesar' and addressed directly – to rescue the Roman world from destruction. Prior to this prayer, Virgil firstly recalls the portents that accompanied the death of Julius Caesar and the civil wars (1.466–92),[21] and then looks ahead to a time when a farmer, tilling the fields which once hosted the Battle of Philippi, will one day unearth rusty javelins, empty helmets and the bones of fallen warriors (1.493–7). Between visions of the past and the future, a suggestive gap is left open for the prayer to focus on the present; even though its dramatic setting recalls the turbulent triumviral period, the urgency conveyed by the prayer locates it in the 'now' (1.498–514):

> di patrii Indigetes et Romule Vestaque mater,
> quae Tuscum Tiberim et Romana Palatia seruas,
> hunc saltem euerso iuuenem succurrere saeclo   500
> ne prohibete. satis iam pridem sanguine nostro
> Laomedonteae luimus periuria Troiae;
> iam pridem nobis caeli te regia, Caesar,
> inuidet atque hominum queritur curare triumphos,
> quippe ubi fas uersum atque nefas: tot bella per orbem,   505
> tam multae scelerum facies, non ullus aratro
> dignus honos, squalent abductis arua colonis,
> et curuae rigidum falces conflantur in ensem.
> hinc mouet Euphrates, illinc Germania bellum;

uicinae ruptis inter se legibus urbes   510
arma ferunt; saeuit toto Mars impius orbe,
ut cum carceribus sese effudere quadrigae,
addunt in spatia, et frustra retinacula tendens
fertur equis auriga neque audit currus habenas.

Gods and heroes of my country, Romulus, and Mother Vesta, who guard the Tuscan Tiber and Roman Palatine, do not prevent this young man at least from rescuing a world turned upside down! Long enough already we have atoned for Laomedon's perjuries at Troy with our blood; long enough heaven's realms have envied your presence amongst us, Caesar, and they complain of your care for earthly triumphs, where indeed right and wrong are reversed: so many wars in this world, so many shapes of evil; no worthy honour for the plough: neglected fields robbed of farmers and curved sickles fused into solid blades. Here the Euphrates agitates; there Germany threatens war; neighbouring cities breaking laws to take up arms amongst themselves, as impious Mars rages across the entire world: just like when the chariots stream from the starting gates, add to their speed each lap, and the charioteer, tugging vainly at the bridles, is dragged on by the horses, and the chariot is not responding to the reins.

The manner in which the poet invokes *Caesar* following an appeal to the gods invites comparison with the book's opening prayer to Octavian.[22] In the prologue, Virgil suggests that agricultural salvation, poetic composition and the trajectory of the world at large (cf. *da facilem cursum*, 1.40)[23] depend as much – if not more – on the not-yet-divine Octavian as any god. Here in the final scene one can detect a similar level of dependence: in her struggle to overcome civil strife, Rome places all hope of salvation not in well-established divinities, but in Caesar, a *iuuenis* (1.500–1), whose deification is being delayed (1.503–4).[24]

Virgil's claim that heaven wants Octavian for itself (1.503–4) reinforces another prominent idea of the poem's prologue – that his divinization is inevitable;[25] however, on this occasion the image of Octavian being occupied on earth by his 'care for earthly triumphs' (*hominum queritur curare triumphos*, 1.504) diverges from what is being asked of him by the poet in the book's opening prayer: this *cura* for military distinction contrasts sharply with the *cura terrarum* for which Virgil expresses a preference in the prologue.[26] The undesirability of *cura triumphorum* is not only spelled out immediately in the next line of the prayer, where the poet implies that triumphs obtained in a tumultuous world might be morally ambiguous anyway (cf. *fas uersum atque nefas*, 1.505),[27] but also in the images of disused or misused farming tools and fields deprived of farmers (1.506–8), which virtually call out for the kind of *cura terrarum* envisaged by Virgil for Octavian in the book's opening prayer. The final simile (1.509–14), which strikingly compares a helter-skelter world descending into chaotic violence to a charioteer losing control of his runaway vehicle, not only emphasizes the perils facing Octavian as he attempts to impose order,[28] but also undermines the poet's request in the prologue for an 'effortless journey' (cf. *facilem cursum*, 1.40), since one of the meanings of *cursus* is a chariot ride.[29] As the salvific Caesar morphs into a figure who is fixated on subjugating the world and tries to take control of his own fate by pursuing a *cursus* that is entirely different from what Virgil had in mind, the final scene of *Georgics* 1 figuratively highlights that the poet's attempt to mediate a symbiotic relationship between Octavian and those who rely on his *cura terrarum* is already faltering, and that there appears to be an irreconcilable divergence between Virgil's *didaxis* and Caesar's own trajectory. Admittedly, as I mentioned above, the reader gets a glimpse of a future when agriculture will triumph over war (cf. 1.493–7); but the image of a lone farmer unearthing remnants of the civil wars (1.495–6) and memorabilia of death (cf. *grandiaque effossis mirabitur ossa sepulcris*, 1.497) only seems to adumbrate the futility of 'caring for earthly triumphs'.[30] The farmer who turns the earth and works the land lives on, but men who take part in wars perish.[31] Here at the end of *Georgics* 1 Virgil ostensibly sets *cura terrarum* and *cura triumphorum* as opposite and mutually exclusive choices for the new Caesar.

The triumph of Caesar

The so-called 'proem in the middle'[32] at the beginning of book 3 highlights again that military achievement is being pursued by Octavian, though the poet no longer imagines fatal destruction as a potential outcome. Virgil now looks ahead to enshrining Octavian in a temple and even fantasizes about a triumph of poetry that rivals the politician's literal triumph.[33] The interconnectedness of the poet's literary future and Octavian's divinity is further dramatized in an ekphrasis of the engraved doors and sculptural decorations of the temple (3.26–36). Virgil claims that he will adorn the temple's doors with battle scenes from the Ganges, the Nile, Asia, the Niphates and Parthia (3.26–31) – locations which not only recall Octavian's recent victories but also anticipate further Roman campaigns in its wake.[34] No lessons are to be taught in this vision of the future; beyond the scope of the present poem Virgil can only envisage himself taking on the role of the imperial artist and a celebrant of Caesar's triumph (3.10–18):

> primus ego in patriam mecum, modo uita supersit,   10
> Aonio rediens deducam uertice Musas;
> primus Idumaeas referam tibi, Mantua, palmas,
> et uiridi in campo templum de marmore ponam
> propter aquam, tardis ingens ubi flexibus errat
> Mincius et tenera praetexit harundine ripas.   15
> in medio mihi Caesar erit templumque tenebit:
> illi uictor ego et Tyrio conspectus in ostro
> centum quadriiugos agitabo ad flumina currus.

I'll be the first to return to my country, if life lasts, bringing the Muses with me from the Aonian peak; I'll be the first, Mantua, to bring you Idumaean palms, and I'll set up a temple of marble by the water, on that green plain, where great Mincius wanders in slow curves and clothes his banks with tender reeds. For me, Caesar will be in the middle and own the temple. In his honour, I, the victor, conspicuous in Tyrian purple, will drive a hundred four-horse chariots by the river.

The centre of the Virgilian poem-temple will be occupied by Octavian (3.16), and this will be realized in book 8 of the *Aeneid*. There Octavian stands *in medio* (*Aen.* 8.675; cf. *Geo.* 3.16) on the shield of Aeneas which has the Actian victory as its focal point;[35] and after the battle, the victor surveys a procession of conquered nations (reminiscent of those mentioned here at 3.26–31)[36] from yet another temple – the Palatine Temple of Apollo (*Aen.* 8.720).[37] Indeed, later in this passage of the *Georgics*, Virgil envisages an image of Apollo as part of the decorative programme of his poem-temple (*stabunt et Parii lapides . . . Troiae Cynthius auctor*, 3.34–6).[38] Various commentators have suggested that the reader is here encouraged to connect Virgil's proposed artistic monument with the construction of contemporary architectural projects, perhaps especially the Palatine temple.[39] If so, by drawing this parallel Virgil already gestures towards the moment when state art and poetic art will become two sides of the same coin: the god who occupies the middle of Virgil's epic-in-the-making is also the man who will soon stand at the centre of the religious framework and political discourse of Rome. Seen in this light, the poet's depiction of Caesar as a divinity housed in a metaphorical temple is itself a metaphor for the evolving relationship between Octavian and those who will soon become his subjects, delicately portraying Rome's cultural revolution towards one-man rule as a jubilant scene of thankful worshippers paying tribute to their victory-god.[40] Leading the celebration of Caesar is Virgil himself, a self-styled *uictor* (3.17), gladly driving chariots (3.18) and parading the rewards of *cura triumphorum* in a manner that looks directly back to the failing *auriga* at the end of book 1.[41] The transfiguration of the image of the poet – from that of a power-broker between Octavian and those who depend on him, to a chief-celebrant of the cult of Caesar – not only embellishes in poetic terms the shift of power away from the poet into the hands of Octavian,[42] but also rehabilitates the concept of ruler cult, making the language of divinization and the idea of willing subordination concurrent with the burgeoning of the new regime. By thus aestheticizing Rome's transition from republic to autocracy, Virgil makes himself complicit in it. For the poet for whom 'right now it is a delight to lead the solemn procession to the sanctuary [of Caesar]' (*iam nunc sollemnis ducere pompas | ad delubra iuuat*, 3.22–3;[43] cf. *uotis iam nunc adsuesce uocari*, 1.42), his postponement of the proposed epic – *mox tamen ardentis accingar dicere pugnas | Caesaris* ('Soon I will prepare myself to speak of Caesar's fierce battles', 3.46–7) – is merely symbolic. The use of *mox* here recalls the postponement of Octavian's deification in the *Georgics*' opening prayer (cf. *tuque adeo, quem mox quae sint habitura deorum | concilia incertum est*, 1.24–5); but much like in that prayer, the line between the present and the future is becoming increasingly blurred: *iam nunc* Rome is moving into a new political era centred on the *primus inter pares*, a 'god' amongst men.

Divinization and didactic efficacy

The relationship between the divinization of Octavian and the poetic career of Virgil comes into direct focus again for the final time in the *sphragis* to the *Georgics*.[44] This passage offers a kind of 'parallel chronology' of the lives of *Caesar* and *Vergilius* while reflecting on the contrasting activities each character is preoccupied with. Here the portrait of Octavian clearly and deliberately looks back on his previous appearances in the poem's prologue and the finale of book 1 (4.559–62):

> Haec super aruorum cultu pecorumque canebam
> et super arboribus, Caesar dum magnus ad altum
> fulminat Euphraten bello uictorque uolentis
> per populos dat iura uiamque adfectat Olympo.

> These things I sang about the care of fields, herds, and trees, while mighty Caesar thundered in battle by the deep Euphrates, implemented a victor's laws on willing nations, and took the path towards the heavens.

The juxtaposition of the thematic enumeration of the *Georgics* (4.559–60) and Caesar's thundering (*Caesar . . . magnus . . . | fulminat*, 4.560–1) brings the poem to a full circle. In the prologue, Virgil imagines Octavian as *tempestatum potens* (1.27) and asks him to give a Jupiter-like approval to his new undertaking (*audacibus adnue coeptis*, 1.40). Now as the poem approaches its conclusion, Octavian appears in the guise of the supreme god again: the word *fulminat* invests in him the traditional power of Jupiter (cf. βροντᾶν οὐκ ἐμόν, ἀλλὰ Διός, Callim. *Aet.* fr. 1.20 Pf.), while at the same time hinting at his control over the physical processes of the weather and so picking up *tempestatum* in the prologue. Moreover, having been asked to 'embark' (*ingredere*, 1.42) on a course to divinity, Octavian now 'attempts a journey to Olympus' (*uiamque adfectat Olympo*, 4.562). As this image of Octavian making his way to the sky coincides with the presentation of the unfolding structure of the *Georgics* (4.559–60), the *sphragis* suggests that 'while' (*dum*, 4.560) the poem is being written, Octavian is gradually fulfilling the role of Jupiter assigned to him in the poem's prologue.[45]

Yet the depiction of Octavian's activities here also underlines a process of deification that is manifestly different from the one suggested by the poet in the prologue. Octavian is seen firstly conquering the East (*Euphraten, uictor*, 4.561), then imposing civic order (*uolentis | per populos dat iura*, 4.561–2) and finally heading towards Olympus (4.562).[46] His campaign on the Euphrates and the implementation of legal authority provide a direct response to the finale of book 1, where imminent dangers along the Euphrates (*hinc mouet Euphrates*, 1.509) and the infringement of law (*ruptis . . . legibus*, 1.510) threaten to bring down the Roman world. The correspondence between these two passages adds more force to the description of Octavian here as a *uictor* (4.561), characterizing his journey to Olympus as the divinization of a conqueror through his military and civic virtues.[47] As the *sphragis* portrays Octavian taking the matter of his deification into his own hands and finding success with it, the poem's final image of *Caesar* leaves readers with the impression that Virgil's teaching on divinization has not had its desired effect on its principal addressee. Rather than assuming the role of a compassionate protector and becoming divine by taking part in Virgil's poetic consolation of unenlightened farmers who cannot find their way (*uia*, 1.41), it would seem that the thundering *Caesar* has found his own path (*uia*, 4.562) to immortality.

The idea that Octavian is diverging from the course set by Virgil is highlighted further through the demarcated lives of *Vergilius* and *Caesar*, as the poet's portrait of his own career contrasts sharply with that of Octavian (4.563–6):

> illo Vergilium me tempore dulcis alebat
> Parthenope studiis florentem ignobilis oti,
> carmina qui lusi pastorum audaxque iuuenta,
> Tityre, te patulae cecini sub tegmine fagi.

> At that time sweet Parthenope was nourishing me, Virgil, joyous in the pursuits of lowly leisure, I who toyed with shepherds' songs, and, in youth's boldness, sang of you, Tityrus, in the spreading beech-tree's shade.

Juxtaposed against the heaven-reaching dynamism of Octavian, Virgil's apparent fondness for *otium* (4.564),[48] in conjunction with the nostalgic mention of his youth (*iuuenta*, 4.565) and the citation of *Eclogue* 1.1 (4.566), pointedly emphasizes that the poet has been left behind to languish in an idealized past, and that the *Eclogues* and the *Georgics*, now retrospectively fashioned into a single oeuvre,[49] appear insignificant and even incompatible with the concerns of the new *kosmokrator*. That the poet is fully aware of the limitation of his poetry is also embedded in the way Virgil describes his past poetic activity as *ludere* (4.565). This verb evokes the Callimachean tradition of light verse,[50] and Virgil alludes to this idea in the prologue to *Eclogue* 6, where Tityrus's choice 'to play' (*ludere*, *Ecl.* 6.1) with the 'rustic Muse' (*agrestis Musa*, *Ecl.* 6.8) is contrasted with the gravity of the themes of epic poetry (*reges et proelia*, *Ecl.* 6.3). In fact, the same verb is used in *Eclogue* 1 when Tityrus reveals that the *otium* restored to him by his saviour (cf. *deus nobis haec otia fecit*, 'a god has created this leisure for us', *Ecl.* 1.6) enables him 'to play' with bucolic songs (*ipsum | ludere quae uellem calamo permisit agresti*, 'he allowed me to play what I wished on the rustic reed', *Ecl.* 1.9–10). The use of *lusi* in the *sphragis* of the *Georgics*, therefore, not only draws a parallel between Virgil and Tityrus – the significance of which will be discussed shortly – but also characterizes the poet's art as trivial in a world where *Caesar* dominates. Set against the memorable image of Octavian in the first half of the *sphragis*, Virgil's dismissal of his poetic endeavours as mere 'play' ostensibly conveys his reservation about his poetry's capacity to address the most powerful man of the post-Actian world.[51]

The parallel between Virgil and Tityrus established by the *sphragis* of the *Georgics* has a further implication on how the divinization of Octavian might be interpreted. In *Eclogue* 1, Tityrus promises to deify his saviour – an anonymous *iuuenis* frequently identified by scholars as Octavian[52] – since he had restored *otium* and poetic vocation to members of the bucolic community (*Ecl.* 1.4–6, 42–5). Here in the *Georgics*, Virgil's *otium* clearly evokes that of Tityrus, as the poet recalls his composition of 'songs of shepherds' (*carmina . . . pastorum*, 4.565); indeed, the syntactical ambiguity of the final line of the poem (*Geo.* 4.566) even allows readers to see Tityrus as a Virgilian persona.[53] If the image of Octavian in the *sphragis* is meant to be understood in relation to the *iuuenis* of *Eclogue* 1, then this portrait of Caesar finding a path towards Olympus could be seen as Virgil fulfilling the promise of Tityrus to deify his saviour, and in doing so the poet synchronizes the restoration of *otium* with the transformation of Octavian from obscurity to all-conquering prominence. The conflation of two seemingly incompatible ideological constructs – restoration and transformation, peace and war – will soon find expression in the political discourse of the Augustan regime, a discourse underpinned by the contradictory coexistence of opposites and seeking to maintain the illusion that Rome has been transformed and restored simultaneously by its newly emerged master.[54] In the meantime, however, the poet appears content with his own triviality, readily surrendering his poetic power as if he were one of the 'willing peoples' (*uolentis . . . populos*, 4.561–2) on whom Octavian imposes his rule.[55]

Conclusions

Around the time when the *Georgics* was published, official celebrations and representational media had been put in place to adulate Octavian, who upon his return to Rome in 29 BCE held a three-day triumphal procession commemorating his victories in Illyricum, Actium and Egypt. The archaeological evidence from Nicopolis near the site of Actium shows that Octavian attributed his victory to Mars and Neptune, as well as of course to Apollo;[56] and Octavianic coinage minted between 31 and early 27 BCE fostered his link to the divine even further, with the iconography of one issue of *denarii* casting him in the role of a victorious god of war.[57] In the period between the news of the victory at Actium reaching Rome and the eventual triumphant return of Octavian from the East almost two years later, the Senate also lavished Octavian with numerous honours: some of these, such as the senatorial decree that priests and priestesses were to pray for Octavian (as well as the Senate and people) and that a libation was to be poured to him at all public and private banquets, placed him on a par with Olympian deities.[58] These 'god-equalling honours' (ἰσόθεοι τιμαί)[59] gave the impression that Octavian was not just any homecoming Roman general: he was to be seen as the saviour of Rome, a godlike provider of stability and peace after more than two decades of war. In light of this set of evidence, which points to a systematic effort to highlight the connection between triumphal and divine glory on the one hand, and a centralized attempt to instil within Roman society a perception of total dependence on Octavian on the other, Virgil's discussion of Octavian's divinization in the *Georgics* must constitute a response to this top-down operation of accumulating power in and around the new Caesar.

From the outset of the *Georgics* Virgil captures the idea that the Roman world is reliant on Octavian by attaching the fate of farmers, cities and communities, and even the progress of the present poem, all to the apotheosis of Octavian. As the poet requests that Octavian join him on a journey of agricultural enlightenment while embarking on a path to divinity, Virgil fashions his didactic poem as an act of political mediation. Yet subsequent reflections on his divinization in the *Georgics* challenge the impression that Octavian's route to unrivalled status is subject to contestation or persuasion. The poem's opening hymnic appeal to the quasi-divine Octavian, which implies the possibility of establishing an efficacious relationship with the addressed god who is (or at least might be) listening, is displaced in the *sphragis* by a far more descriptive account of the all-conquering authority of Caesar; and this change in the *mode* of interaction underlines that Virgil appears to abandon hope in the poem's capacity to effect a change in trajectory of Octavian's career. Indeed, as the poet depicts himself undergoing a dramatic transformation from questioning to endorsing the notion of 'divinization through conquest', it renders the poem's discourse on the divine status of Octavian closer to that of the emergent regime, signalling that poetry too must play a part in the accumulation of Augustan power. By finally characterizing his poetry as songs of leisure, soon to be surpassed by a proposed Augustan epic, Virgil's disarming articulation of the insignificance and inefficacy of his poetry encapsulates in palatable terms that Octavian is on an unstoppable course to obtaining ultimate power; that the new Caesar and those who will soon become his subjects already occupy two different ends of the power scale (and can only drift further apart from each other); and above all, that persuasion and mediation have ceased to have an effect on the godlike man who is intent on taking Rome, as well as the poet, into uncharted territory.

CHAPTER 7
BUNTE BARBAREN SETTING UP THE STAGE: RE-INVENTING THE BARBARIAN ON THE *GEORGICS*' THEATRE-TEMPLE (*G.* 3.1–48)
Elena Giusti

As with every middle, the so called 'proem in the middle'[1] of Virgil's 'poem in the middle' is the pulsating and ever-shifting pivot of a much bigger structure, a *mise en abyme* that allows us to 'plunge into the abyss . . . from which there can be no escape to a place from which we can view the totality of a structure having a clearly delimited beginning and an ending'.[2] The passage lies not only at the core of the *Georgics*, and of Virgil's entire poetic career, but it can also be recast as a momentous transitional piece on the crucial edge between the not yet bygone times of the Republic and the upcoming rise of the empire. It is, as it were, in a watershed between two eras, locating the continuously shifting 'here and now' of the *Georgics* at some kind of fluctuating threshold between the age of republican triumph, envisaged in the procession to the theatre-temple, and the future triumphal expansionism of Augustus's empire, unravelled in its monumental ekphrasis. This temporal liminality posits both proem and poem in the middle of a poetic continuum between the epics of Naevius and Ennius and the future Virgilian 'monument' that will be destined to replace them. Following the tenets of the Augustan revolution, this is an attempt to emphasize continuity with (as much as 'restitution' of) the *Res Publica* while downplaying the extent of Augustan innovation: the two eras converge in foreign politics, just as they agree on the poetic means of staging the past and future conquests of Rome's paradoxically imperial republic. And in the middle's middle's middle, as has often been recognized,[3] is no less than Caesar (3.16: <u>*in medio*</u> *mihi Caesar erit templumque tenebit*, 'I will put Caesar <u>in the middle</u> and he will occupy the temple'), the same name that also frames the two concluding lines of the proem (3.46–8: *Caesaris et nomen . . . ab origine Caesar*). He is both the centre of Virgil's *opus*, and the 'alpha and omega' of the future epic.[4] But what 'Caesar' spelled in the impermanent present of this proem has been open since its very inception to redefinition and renegotiation.

Within this larger twofold directionality, the proem also offers a striking, paradoxical image. Barbarians – Britons – raise the crimson curtain of this poetic and political stage, a curtain in which they are themselves inwoven (3.25: *purpurea intexti tollant aulaea Britanni*). In this chapter, I focus on this image as representative of the language of foreign policy in the Augustan age, and notice how it recurs both in the figurative language of the time and in Virgil's simultaneous treatment of Carthaginians in the *Aeneid*. At the same time, I shall argue that the connection between barbarians, triumph and theatre is also inherently imbedded in mid-republican culture, so that the *intexti*

Britanni are in turn at the crossroads between the mid-republican theatrical productions and the epic poem that Virgil will compose, and interweave with drama, in order to exalt the new imperial era.

Staging the barbarian[5]

Both Greece and Rome have a long history of dragging barbarians on stage. As Edith Hall has shown in her ground-breaking monograph, drama can be recognized as the privileged locus for the so-called 'invention of the barbarian'.[6] In the Roman context, it is interesting to notice that those Greek plays that dealt with barbarian themes (especially versions of *Medea* and *Bacchae*) appear to have been popular among the early Latin tragedians during years of foreign conflicts such as those against Hannibal, Philip V or King Antiochus.[7] This may indicate that, just as previously at Athens, at Rome too these plays would hold the community tight around a sense of collective cohesion through the development of an anti-barbarian ideology, borrowed from fifth-century Athens, that may have already existed in the Middle Republic and that was certainly operative in the Augustan era. Indeed, the Augustan discourse on foreign policy clearly exhibited, in both its artistic and literary production, direct emulation of fifth-century Athenian discourse on the Persian barbarians, with the obvious mediation of the Hellenistic kingdoms.[8] It suffices to think about the recurrent imagery of Amazonomachies, Gigantomachies, Titanomachies or Centauromachies in the iconographic and poetic works produced under Augustus,[9] or the entertaining restaging, in 2 BCE, of the Battle of Salamis in a specially excavated arena by the Tiber.[10] We can confidently link what Spawforth has recognized as 'a persistent theme in the Roman representation of eastern policy under the empire'[11] not only with the well-established equation between Persians and Parthians[12] but also, and most pressingly, with the shaping of the Battle of Actium as a success of the Roman West over the barbarian East.[13] This trend of establishing a continuum between classical Athens and Augustan Rome in terms of Eastern policy also ends up encompassing the enemies of the republican past, such as the Carthaginians, who, as latter-day Phoenicians, become implicated into such a process of othering to the point that the Punic Wars turn into a symbolic example of the foreign wars that Augustus himself will wage in the foreseeable future in order to avoid further shedding of brotherly blood.[14] Among these contemporary and future wars, Augustus's conflict with Parthia receives a privileged place in the ideological language of future conquest, as the Roman counterpart of Greece's conflict with Persia.[15]

It is possible to imagine that the connection between Carthaginians and Persians was established at the same time as this renewed enthusiasm for fifth-century Athenian ideology in the Augustan age, but it is more plausible to believe that the link was already operative, with all due contextual differences, at the time of the Punic Wars, and perhaps present, explicitly or implicitly, in the now fragmentary epics of Naevius and Ennius, and possibly also in the mysterious Roman historical dramas, the *fabulae praetextae*, and in those *cothurnatae* that adapted Greek tragedies dealing with the theme of barbarism and otherness. After all, the connection between Persians and Carthaginians was clearly operative in the fifth-century Greek world, both in mainland Greece and in its Western department: it is witnessed both by the artificial synchronization, on the very same day in 480 BCE, of the battles of Himera and Salamis, or Himera and Thermopylae,[16] and by the evidence from fifth-century Sicily, where the assimilation served the primary purpose of legitimating the Sicilian tyrants as defenders of the Hellenes, as in Pindar's first Pythian Ode[17] and in the post-Himera iconography. This is the case of the massive temple of Olympian Zeus at Agrigentum, which has long been connected to a fragment of Naevius's *Bellum Punicum* (fr. 8 Blänsdorf) that many have interpreted as evidence for a representation of Carthaginians as Giants in early Latin literature.[18]

If it appears reasonable to suppose that Naevius and Ennius represented the fight against Eastern enemies and Carthaginians in their epic poems in cultural continuity with fifth-century Athenian anti-barbarian ideology, and in a recognizably Hellenistic fashion, one is left to wonder whether similar interests in themes of alterity and otherness would have been conveyed in their tragedies, which were staged for the community precisely while Rome was in the grip of the conflict against Carthage. Indeed, early Roman theatre may have functioned as a powerful tool for passing on collective messages and gathering the community while Rome was under threat of foreign invasion: it is telling that the first Latin *fabula* was produced for the *ludi Romani* in the year after the end of the First Punic War (240 BCE) by Livius Andronicus,[19] the same poet who would later be chosen to compose the propitiatory hymn to Juno Regina in the year of the Battle of the Metaurus (207 BCE).[20] Nor can it possibly be a coincidence that the Hannibalic war and its successful conclusion saw a striking multiplication and increase in length of public festivals and their attendant *ludi scaenici*, occasions to confirm, in Gesine Manuwald's phrasing, 'Rome's national identity as well as its cultural competence and political unity'.[21] It would be reasonable to assume that the *praetextae*, the Roman historical dramas, would have looked like the most suitable genre to host themes related to the Punic Wars, but while there is almost no evidence for themes related to the Carthaginians in the *praetextae*,[22] we witness a striking interest in topics related to barbarism and otherness in the tragedies based on Greek models, the Roman *cothurnatae*.[23]

But while the mid-republican period provides no more than scanty evidence for the connection between theatre, triumph and staged representations of barbarians, Virgil's poetry shows since the *Georgics* that there is a palpably clear connection between theatrical representations and foreign politics, a nexus that might be inherited from those epic and tragic predecessors that his work aimed at surpassing and replacing, but that is also, and more certainly, a product of the cultural propagandistic issues of his time. The proem to the third *Georgic*, a text that Alessandro Barchiesi has defined as crucial for the understanding of how Virgil's poetic programme works hand in hand with the Augustan *Macht der Bilder* in 'an age of intervisual appropriation',[24] plays a key role in this debate: it joins explicit references to mid-republican culture and literature with a possible evocation of the temple of Palatine Apollo in the ekphrasis of its theatre-temple monument, the so-called 'Caesareum in Mantua'.[25]

The passage has received a great deal of critical attention,[26] and its status as an anticipatory text of both the *Aeneid*[27] and the forthcoming figurative programmes of Augustan art has already been emphasized. In what follows, while I recapitulate some of the arguments already proposed, I focus on its treatment of foreign conquest under three specific but interconnected aspects, all contributing to show the intrinsically liminal nature of this text: the theatricality of triumph, the use of conquered barbarians as willing contributors to their own conquest, and the dissolution of differences between these conquered Easterners and the ancestors of the Romans.

Bunte Barbaren setting up the stage

The proem to the third Georgic marks a strong caesura between the age of republican triumph, envisaged in the procession to the theatre-temple, and the future triumphal expansionism of Augustus's empire, explicated in the ekphrasis. In poetic terms, this caesura is rendered by means of allusions to both *fabulae praetextae* and epic, positioning the text between Ennius's double epic *and* theatrical production and Virgil's own *Aeneid*, which will incorporate theatre *within* the epic. Both in historical and in poetic terms, the passage looks simultaneously backwards and forwards in time.

Since the beginning of the parade, Virgil presents himself as a second and better Ennius, not only *uiuus*, but *uictor* (see 3.9: *uictorque uirum uolitare per ora*, '[I may ...] fly victorious on the lips of men', an echo of the epitaph that Ennius was thought to have written for himself, *Epigr.* 18 V.: *uolito uiuus per ora uirum*, 'I fly, alive, on the lips of men')[28] and envisages the completion of his poem in terms of a triumphant return from a military campaign, with the Hesiodic Muses as foreign captives led in train (3.11: *Aonio rediens deducam uertice Musas*, 'I shall lead the Muses back with me from the Aonian peak', where both *rediens* and *deducam*, together with the repetition of *uictor* at lines 9 and 17, clearly point to the *pompa triumphalis*).[29] Virgil's poetic success will be immortalized in strongly Pindaric terms[30] with the erection of a marble temple (3.13: *uiridi in campo templum de marmore ponam*, 'on the green plain I shall set up a marble temple') and the institution of *ludi* in honour of Octavian (3.19–20: *cuncta mihi Alpheum linquens lucosque Molorchi* | *cursibus et crudo decernet Graecia caestu*, 'for me, all of Greece, leaving Alpheus and the groves of Molorchus, shall compete in races, and with the raw-hide boxing gloves').

Connections between triumphal processions, epinician poetry accompanying the games, propitiatory rituals at the founding of a temple, theatrical performances and visual representations of the subjugated enemy are established after the instauration of the games (3.21–33):

ipse caput tonsae foliis ornatus oliuae
dona feram. iam nunc sollemnis ducere pompas
ad delubra iuuat caesosque uidere iuuencos,
uel scaena ut uersis discedat frontibus utque

purpurea intexti tollant aulaea Britanni.   25
in foribus pugnam ex auro solidoque elephanto
Gangaridum faciam uictorisque arma Quirini,
atque hic undantem bello magnumque fluentem
Nilum ac nauali surgentis aere columnas.
addam urbes Asiae domitas pulsumque Niphaten   30
fidentemque fuga Parthum uersisque sagittis;
et duo rapta manu diuerso ex hoste tropaea
bisque triumphatas utroque ab litore gentis.

I myself, my forehead adorned with shorn olive-leaves, shall bring the gifts. Now comes the joy to lead the solemn procession to the shrine, and to see the slaughter of the oxen, or to watch how the stage retreats when the fronts have rotated, and the interwoven Britons raise the purple curtain. On the doors I shall make, in gold and solid ivory, the battle of the Gangarides[31] and the arms of victorious Quirinus, and here the Nile, swelling with war and flowing in its greatness, and columns towering with bronze prows. I shall add the cities of Asia, all conquered, and the subdued Niphates, and the Parthian, trusting in his flight and with his arrows shot backwards, and two trophies snatched perforce from widely distant foes, and nations twice triumphed over, on either shore.

Virgil's victory over Greek poetry[32] is matched with the victories of Octavian over the peoples of the East[33] in a text that exploits allusions to Ennius and specific characteristics of the Roman triumph mingled with Pindaric echoes and allusions to Greek games in order to display a type of festival that is ultimately Roman.[34] The mention of a *scaena* (24) after the ritual sacrifices (22–3) evokes the republican inclusion of *ludi scaenici* within *ludi triumphales*, echoing the occasions for specific Roman plays such as the *praetextae*.[35] A very likely allusion to the triumphal return of M. Fulvius Nobilior from Ambracia in 187 BCE,[36] which involved his relocation of the Muses to Rome (Plin. *Nat. Hist.* 35.66 *inde Musas Fuluius Nobilior Romam transferret*, 'from there Fulvius Nobilior transferred the Muses to Rome') and the foundation of the *aedes Herculis Musarum*[37] strengthens the links between Virgil and Ennius, who celebrated his patron not only in the *Ambracia* (a *praetexta* probably performed for the occasion) but also, it has been suggested, in the close of his *Annales*.[38] Greek poetry and art, symbolized by the subjugated Muses, have been transplanted to Rome in order to extol the military achievements of Quirinus together with the properly Roman *columnae rostratae* (29) such as that (or those) of Duilius.[39] Artistic motifs stolen from fifth-century Athens will serve the purpose of celebrating not only success over the Parthians, the Roman equivalent of the Persians (31), but victories over enemies located at the opposite ends of the world (32–3).

Barbarians play a key role in this old/new *praetexta*. After the *scaena* is rotated to let the play(s) begin (24: *uel scaena ut uersis discedat frontibus*, 'or how the stage retreats when the fronts have rotated'), it will be eventually, once the show is over,[40] the duty of enslaved barbarians to introduce the audience to the visual staging of their own defeat. Ironically, and in a deeply humiliating way, they are woven into the same curtain that they are forced to raise in glorification of Rome's success (25: *purpurea intexti tollant aulaea Britanni*, 'the interwoven Britons raise the purple curtain'),[41] thus acting like captives in a triumphal procession, as 'both the humiliated and defeated enemies of Rome and at the same time new participants, in whatever role, in the Roman imperial order'.[42] To the humiliation Virgil adds the scorn of casting no less than the Britons in the role of the 'painted' barbarians: those people whose very name (Greek *Prettani* or *Pritani*) is thought to be Celtic for 'painted' or 'tattooed'[43] are now themselves interwoven (so in some way painted *and* tattooed) in the purple curtain which is being raised in order to signal the closure of the celebration of their own defeat.

If we are to imagine inwoven figurines of the blue-painted Britons on the theatre-temple's purple curtain, the blue-purple technicolor also highlights the fictionality of Caesar's allegedly objective narrative, where the self-painting Britons had already been depicted by their conqueror (Caes. *Gal.* 5.14: *omnes uero se Britanni uitro inficiunt, quod caeruleum efficit colorem, atque hoc horridiores sunt in pugna aspectu*, 'all the Britons, indeed, dye themselves with woad, which produces a blue colour, and makes their appearance in battle more terrible').[44] The mockery was also not spared by Cicero, when begging his brother Quintus to describe Caesar's invasion of Britain so that he might turn it into a poetic subject: 'just give me Britain, so that I may paint it in your colours, but with my own brush' (Cic. *Q. fr.* 2.15a.2: *modo mihi date Britanniam, quam pingam coloribus tuis, penicillo meo*). Interestingly, the poetic work on Caesar's expedition that Quintus then seemed to have been expecting to co-write with Cicero (Cic. *Q. fr.* 2.16.4, 3.6.4) has recently been argued by Peter Kruschwitz to be not an epic poem but rather a *praetexta*,[45] perhaps the historical and Western counterpart to the mythological tragedies that he was simultaneously composing on the Trojan theme.[46] The façade of both Quintus's and Virgil's spectacle may still be Republican, but its contents, as Kruschwitz suggests, elicit the conquests of Alexander,[47] while also anticipating themes that will reappear in the presentation of both Augustus's 'victory' over the Parthians after the recovery of Crassus's standards in 20 BCE, and in the picture of the Carthaginians at the beginning of the *Aeneid*. On the one hand, the mention of a link between barbarians and theatrical performances and the representation of the fleeing Parthians on the temple frieze strongly testifies to their Greek influence, from both classical Athens and Alexander's conquest, but on the other hand the representation of these apparently willing *Britanni* is entirely new and looks forward to the future: both to those three kneeling pavonazzetto Parthians (the 'Bunte Barbaren') that Rolf Schneider has interpreted as supports for a monumental bronze tripod in honour of Augustus's Parthian 'victory',[48] and to the Parthians of Augustus's triumphal arch, which will be represented in a 'radical new construction of Rome's enemies … like contributors to peace rather than its opponents'.[49]

Connections can also be established between the overall structure of the proem and the *Aeneid*: the beginning of the *Aeneid* will 'rotate the stage' to Libya and set its actors on a *scaena* whose curtain is made of glittering frondage (*Aen.* 1.164: *siluis scaena coruscis*, 'a stage of glittering woods');[50] Venus will enter shod with the traditional *cothurnus* (*Aen.* 1.337),[51] as a θεὸς προλογίζων come to deliver the prologue to a tragedy (*Aen.* 1.338–68).[52] Carthaginians, rather than Britons and Parthians, will ironically lay the foundations of one or more theatres that are metaphorically destined to stage the death of their queen (*Aen.* 1.427–9: *hic alta theatri*[53] | *fundamenta locant alii, immanisque columnas* | *rupibus excidunt, scaenis decora alta futuris*, 'here others lay the deep foundations of a theatre, and hew out of the cliffs enormous columns, high adornments for future stages'). Like the Britons, these unwitting barbarians will also 'raise' a temple whose engravings display in Pheidias's style their own subjugation to the Romans: namely, an Amazonomachy (*Aen.* 1.490–3). This is inserted within the pictures of a capture of Troy that may well be reminiscent of the Olympieion in Agrigentum, the temple on which the Carthaginians themselves may have figured as painted giants, if Dufallo is right that we may hear an echo of the Phoenician purple dye in Naevius's giant *Purpureus* (fr. 8 Blänsdorf).[54] Moreover, after Dido's death and the symbolic fall of Carthage at the end of book 4, properly Roman *ludi* accompanied by rituals will be performed – namely in honour of Anchises, but with historical hindsight in honour of this military success, and a temple will be founded: that of Venus Erycina (*Aen.* 5.759–60), ancestor of the one vowed by Quintus Fabius Maximus on the Capitol in 215 BCE, symbolic of Rome's 'national heritage' and propitiatory of military victory over the Carthaginians.[55] This time, Aeneas-as-Augustus-as-Virgil[56] will take care to carry out the rites:

ipse caput tonsae foliis ornatus
oliuae dona feram.

(*G.* 3.21–2)

ipse caput tonsae foliis euinctus oliuae
stans procul in prora pateram tenet . . .

(*Aen.* 5.774–5)

I myself, my forehead adorned
with shorn olive-leaves, shall
bring the gifts.

He himself, his forehead bound
with shorn olive-leaves, standing
apart on the prow, holds the cup . . .

Yet there is one last aspect in which the theatre-temple anticipates themes that will become of primary importance in both the *Aeneid* and in Augustus's *Macht der Bilder*, and which complicates the straightforward polarity between Romans and barbarians: namely, the similarity between the Parthians and Rome's Trojan ancestors, attested both by the interaction between Trojan and Parthian iconography[57] and by the use of orientalistic stereotypes to describe not only Parthians or Carthaginians, but the very ancestors of the Romans. The ekphrasis on the *Georgics'* theatre-temple also shows the Trojan ancestors following directly after the representation of the conquered Easterners (*G.* 3.34–6):

stabunt et Parii lapides, spirantia signa,
Assaraci proles demissaeque ab Ioue gentis
nomina, Trosque parens et Troiae Cynthius auctor.

Here there shall also stand, in Parian marble, statues breathing life, the offspring of Assaracus and the glorious names of Jupiter's race, our father Tros and Apollo Cynthius, maker of Troy.

Virgil initially seems to act, according to this new cultural agenda, as if he was unaware of how problematic the theme of Eastern conquest had always been in the Roman Republic for the definition of what was to be considered purely Roman. And yet some intra- and intertextual echoes seem to point instead towards a problematization of the topic.

When establishing the Greek games, 'resplendent in Tyrian purple' (3.17: *Tyrio conspectus in ostro*), Virgil acts not only as a Roman magistrate[58] but also as a hero on stage (cf. Hor. *AP* 227–8: *heros | regali conspectus in auro nuper et ostro*, 'a hero [brought upon the stage], whom we have just beheld in royal gold and purple') and an actual *triumphator*,[59] whose conquest over the East might be underlined by the indication of the Tyrian/Carthaginian provenance of the scarlet dye.[60] This use of the adjective *Tyrius* (commonly used metonymically for 'purple')[61] is traditional, but it acquires added resonance once connected to the much more refined synonym *Sarranus*,[62] which had been applied to *ostrum* towards the close of *Georgics* 2.[63] Here Virgil, in what has been recognized as a kind of paradoxical reversal of the triumphalism displayed in the subsequent proem,[64] shows the benefits of rustic life by way of a sharp contrast with the anxieties that beset those who are involved in the politics of cities. The purple is used first to indicate royal status (2.495: *purpura regum*, 'purple worn by despots') that should not affect the *fortunatus* countryman, then as the actual symbol of decadence, greed and ambitious imperialism in terms that recall those of the Elder Cato in his rejection of the display of Eastern artefacts (*G.* 2.503–6):[65]

sollicitant alii remis freta caeca, ruuntque
in ferrum, penetrant aulas et limina regum;
hic petit excidiis urbem miserosque penatis,
ut gemma bibat et Sarrano dormiat ostro;

Others urge with the oars unknown seas, and dash upon the sword, or they sneak into the courts and chambers of kings; one wreaks ruin on a city and its wretched homes, in order to drink from a jewelled cup and sleep on Tyrian purple.

Furthermore, if taken together with the metonymic use of *elephantus* for the (Indian)[66] ivory of the temple doors (3.26: *ex auro solidoque elephanto*, 'in gold and solid ivory'), *Tyrius* might reflect the Roman tendency to boast of their access to foreign resources. This is matched in Propertius's description of the temple of Palatine Apollo, where the materials themselves are exploited in order to evoke Eastern conquest,[67] from its 'Punic columns' (Prop. 2.31.3: *Poenis ... columnis*, made of Numidian marble, known as 'giallo antico') to its double-folding doors, whose ivory is periphrastically indicated as 'noble work of Libyan tusk', *Libyci nobile dentis opus* (Prop. 2.31.12). In Propertius, the elegiac poem itself makes author and reader collude in what Alison Keith calls an 'aesthetic "mystification" of Roman militarism' that both 'commemorates and produces' the imperialism on which the poem's very leisure depends.[68] In Virgil, the aesthetic and monumental exploitation of Eastern resources – therefore the merit of foreign conquest itself – must change connotation depending on whether it is inserted within the poetry of *Cosmos* or in that of *Imperium*:[69] rejected in the first case, it is extolled and boasted of in the latter. It is noteworthy that Virgil's pride in wearing the *toga picta* and the subsequent praise of Octavian's achievements in the East will be subject to further problematization in his future epic, where the negative evaluations of *Georgics* 2 will haunt the picture of a proto-Roman hero who 'sneaks into' royal chambers, drinks from Eastern jewelled cups (*Aen.* 1.728–9: *hic regina grauem gemmis auroque poposcit | impleuitque mero pateram,* 'then the queen called for a cup, heavy with jewels and gold, and filled it with wine') and dresses and sleeps in purple from Tyre (*Aen.* 4.262–3: *Tyrioque ardebat murice laena | demissa ex umeris,* 'a cloak hung from his shoulders ablaze with Tyrian purple').

Conclusion

I hope I have shown that this poem is in the middle of middles, lying as it does at the edge between republic and empire. It is a precious document for our understanding of features of both early Roman theatre and Virgil's *Aeneid*: it points to the triumphal contexts of the early theatrical productions and, if taken as a metapoetic description of the *Aeneid* rather than the *Georgics*, it also signals the recognition of the poem's involvement with theatre as a programmatic characteristic of Virgil's new epic. Furthermore, it invites readers to imagine that Augustus's recent and future military achievements over foreign enemies will be one of the key themes of Virgil's expected epic. What is envisaged here is the *Augusteid* that the poet will never compose, but only dis-compose, in the sidestep of the *Aeneid*: the substitution of Britons, Egyptians and Parthians by Carthaginians is a consequence of the more compelling need to replace Augustus by Aeneas, a choice that constitutes, in Philip Hardie's words, 'the crucial point of liberation from the panegyrical straitjacket of historical epic into the freedom to problematise the issues of Roman history and of the principate'.[70]

The proem's image of barbarians raising the crimson curtain that they are woven into in glorification of Rome's success may be interpreted as the missing central link in the shift from republic to empire: these *intexti* barbarians are reminiscent of the old *praetextae* which accompanied triumphal processions, but at the same time they also anticipate the later Augustan imagery of barbarians as unwitting and willing contributors to their own conquest. Moreover, just like the painted Britons depicted by the brushes of Caesar and the Ciceros, *intexti* signposts the theatricality and fictionality of these subaltern barbarians. It is not a coincidence that these lines will be remembered by Ovid in *Metamorphoses* 3, when introducing his readers to the theatricality of his 'barbarian' Theban book by comparing the Sown-Men rising from the ground to figures woven into the curtain rising on the stage (*Met.* 3.111–2: *sic, ubi tolluntur festis aulaea theatris,* | *surgere signa solent*, 'so when on festal days the curtain in the theatre is raised, figures of men rise up').[71] In a post-civil wars era, the artificiality of any representation of foreign enemies deserves particular attention: the fictional nature of these barbarians, their transformation into painted puppets, may indicate their complete subjugation at Rome's hands, but it also highlights, de facto, their non-existence.[72] Cadmus and his readers need not worry if in this strange land that he has landed in there are barbarians springing from the ground and waging war on one another. They may even find it entertaining. Only, this is a journey from East to West, and this land will be called Europe.

CHAPTER 8
FROM *MUNERA UESTRA CANO* TO *IPSE DONA FERAM*: LANGUAGE OF SOCIAL RECIPROCITY IN THE *GEORGICS*
Martin Stöckinger

Absences: the *Georgics* and explicit (socio-)economics

The *Georgics* is and, at the same time, is not a work about agriculture. When looking over the recent bibliography of secondary literature on this poem, one might gain the impression that the *Georgics* is a text essentially about poetry, other Hellenistic and Latin texts, ideology or politics, to name but a few prominent foci of interest. While it is certainly true that these issues are at stake in the text, one cannot deny that its central subject matter are the activities of the farmer. This paradox has long been pointed out. For example, Bernd Effe, in his typology of ancient didactic poems, lists the *Georgics* under the category of 'transparent' poems.[1] In didactic poems of the 'transparent type', the ostensible subject matter is not to be regarded as a single end in itself, but its representation is geared towards additional goals, which are considered more important than the subject matter; for the *Georgics* he assumes political and ideological goals.[2] While Effe's approach can be – and indeed has been – criticized,[3] his general idea that a poem's subject matter (in the case of the *Georgics*: agriculture) and its literary representation are deliberately made transparent so that other themes and purposes can 'shine through' is particularly fitting to describe the complexity inherent to the *Georgics*.

My own contribution sets out to take the *Georgics*' ostensible subject matter of agriculture seriously and to re-examine its role in the text in a particular sense. Though the equivalent German word for agriculture, 'Landwirtschaft', contains stronger economic implications than the English word and its Latin parent (*agricultura*) and Romance siblings,[4] economics – it has long been seen – is nevertheless present in the conception of agriculture in Virgil's times.[5] What is the status of these economic implications in Virgil's poem of land cultivation? In my attempt to answer this question, I will start from the position of Karl Polanyi (famously applied by Moses Finley), who has argued that, in antiquity, the economic sphere should not be seen as isolated from other areas of life, such as religion and society, but rather embedded in these areas.[6] Consequently, in its ancient, and in particular Roman, context the word 'economics' is to be defined broadly and encompasses ideas of monetary exchange and trade as well as gift-giving and other forms of social reciprocity, for instance the patron–client system.

At a first glance at the *Georgics*, it is surprising to see no in-depth depiction of material items being given, traded or exchanged. It is also surprising that Virgil does not include trade and the exchange of gifts among the activities of the farmer. Contrary to Hesiod's *Works and Days*, in which the figure of the neighbour plays a central role, the farmer in Virgil scarcely engages in any social relationships. And although in Hesiod, an ethic of fair-trading is developed, which culminates in a passage about the desired social relationships (*Op.* 341–65), this topic seems entirely absent from Virgil, especially when money is involved. These absences are all the more striking because only a decade or so before the composition of the *Georgics*, another Roman reader, Cicero in *Brutus* 15, had mentioned Hesiod in this very sense as a source for the ethics of reciprocity: *illud Hesiodium laudatur a doctis, quod eadem mensura reddere iubet qua acceperis aut etiam cumulatiore, si possis* ('Scholars cite the admonition of Hesiod to repay with what measure you have received, or if possible with larger'). And Hesiod is not the only major influence on Virgil, where an ethic of wealth and economic exchange features so prominently that Virgil's relative silence on this issue comes as a surprise: in his treatise *On Property Management*, Virgil's teacher Philodemus contrasts an expert manager of a villa estate with an Epicurean manager. While the former exclusively concentrates on gaining profit and avoiding loss, the latter considers wealth as a precondition for, but not as an equivalent of, a good life.[7]

As Philip Thibodeau and Stephen Spurr have shown, these absences of reciprocity and trade from the world of the *Georgics* do not arise from the topos of the self-sufficient farmer, but rather the farmer (regardless of whether he runs a villa estate or a farm) is at times depicted as the head of a large *familia* who gives instructions to the servants.[8] Yet such a depiction of the farmer would only be logical if he maintained relationships with business partners and carried out trade: while even the shepherds Tityrus and Meliboeus in the first *Eclogue* offer their products in the city on the market (*Ecl.* 1.34–5),[9] the farmer of the *Georgics* exchanges his products only occasionally for other goods but not for money (*G.* 1.273–5),[10] and he would rather keep his goats for further nourishment than slaughter them and sell their fur (3.305–7).[11]

The depiction of the gardener in book 4 (116–48) is yet another passage where one could expect trade or some other form of exchange, but where such elements are remarkably absent: scholars have wondered if the phrase *seraque reuertens | nocte* ('when he [i.e. the gardener] returns home late at night', 132–3) means that Virgil's gardener has a day job, such as selling honey and flowers in the city at the market.[12] A particularly pragmatic interpreter of these lines has even suggested that the *inemptae dapes* ('unbought banquet', 133) consumed by the gardener only cover his needs partially, since he only produces honey, flowers, fruits and some vegetables; according to this interpretation, the passage implies that the gardener 'must have purchased grain and wine'[13] for his other meals in addition. These conjectures about the gardener's diet go perhaps a little too far, but it is interesting to observe that already the poet of the pseudo-Virgilian *Moretum* must have felt the silence about the gardener's economic relations and, in a technique typical for *Pseudepigrapha*,[14] filled this *blanc* by making his gardener conduct trade, however modest it may be (cf. *Moretum* 78–81).[15]

These observations about explicit (socio-)economics do not necessarily mean that gifts, trade and other forms of reciprocity are not of importance in Virgil's *Georgics*. Neil Coffee's monograph on Roman epic and Phebe Bowditch's on Horace[16] have demonstrated that economics and reciprocity, even if not depicted directly, are present at a deeper level as discourses in Roman literature, and in this way shape the texts of the Augustan and early imperial period. It can be argued that the *Georgics* is also a poem decidedly about gift-giving and exchange. In the following sections, I will selectively examine a few passages of the *Georgics* in which Virgil writes about social reciprocity metaphorically, and try to establish the purpose of these exchanges. In particular, I will argue that gift-giving and social reciprocity function in the *Georgics* at a poetic level and at a social level in more or less the same way: they bring about relationships. They always involve, however (and this is an important distinction), relationships between unequal elements that would otherwise remain apart.

Metaphors: man and nature

Numerous metaphors from the field of social and economic reciprocity can be found which describe man's relationship to nature and the gods of cultivation. Already in the proem of the work, the deities of the first two books (Ceres and Bacchus) are praised for their 'service' (*uestro munere*, 1.7) in the development of farming, and after the invocation to the Fauni and the Dryads (who seem to represent the third book), we find the sentence *munera uestra cano* ('your gifts I sing', 1.12). Similar wordings can be found in the proems to the second and fourth books, but this time it is the products of nature – in this case wine and honey – that are referred to as 'gifts' (*munera*, 2.5, and *dona*, 4.1). The golden age, however, when the land brought forth its gifts spontaneously, or, as Ovid fittingly puts it, *immunis* (cf. *Met.* 1.101: 'exempt'),[17] seems in Virgil to have passed. In the first book and after the proems of the second and fourth, it quickly becomes clear that these gifts require the *labor* of the farmer.

Perhaps the clearest example of this reciprocal relationship between man and nature can be seen in lines 1.219–24:

at si triticeam in messem robustaque farra
exercebis humum solisque instabis aristis,   220
ante tibi Eoae Atlantides abscondantur
Cnosiaque ardentis decedat stella Coronae,
debita quam sulcis committas semina quamque
inuitae properes anni spem credere terrae.

But if for harvest of wheat and for hardy spelt you ply the ground, and if grain alone is your aim, first let the daughters of Atlas pass from your sight in the morn, and let the Cretan star of the blazing Crown withdraw before you commit to the furrows the seeds due, or hasten to trust the year's hope to the reluctant soil.

The participle *debita*, which has a strong socio-economic colouring, describes the two-way relationship between the earth, which yields its harvest to the farmer, and the farmer, who gives seeds to the earth.[18] The time before the sowing is therefore the time when the farmer 'owes' seeds to the earth. If this meaning of the word *debita* can be accepted, one can assume that *credere* in the next line continues this theme.[19]

In addition to the metaphorical references to gifts and debts, booty is also used as a metaphor (2.60: *et turpis auibus praedam fert uua racemos*, 'the grapes bear foul berries as booty for the birds'). It suggests that birds and plants were at war with each other and had to fight for their supply. The absence of social reciprocity between men and the parallel metaphoric use of socio-economic vocabulary to describe the relations between man and nature and between animals and plants suggest that, through the exchange of gifts, unequals can be brought into a relationship.

Poisoned gifts: man and Jupiter

This supposition is confirmed, when one observes how the relationship between man and god, or indeed between animal and god, is represented (4.149–52):

> Nunc age, naturas apibus quas Iuppiter ipse
> addidit expediam, pro qua mercede canoros   150
> Curetum sonitus crepitantiaque aera secutae
> Dictaeo caeli regem pauere sub antro.

> Come now, the qualities which Jove himself has given bees, I will unfold – even the reward for which they followed the tuneful sounds and clashing bronzes of the Curetes, and fed the king of Heaven within the cave of Dicte.

Before the description of the bee kingdom, in which the division of labour and the sociality of the bees is described in anthropomorphic terms (4.153–205), the relationship of Jupiter to the bees is presented as reciprocal: because they have nourished him with honey, he gives them their social character 'as a reward' (*pro . . . mercede*, 4.150). It has been noted that the choice of words in these lines, which lead up to the description of the bee kingdom, strongly recalls a passage in the first book, where the transition from the golden age to the later ages is narrated (1.118–46).[20] Amongst the bees, this development proceeds in reverse: whereas humans initially worked for the community (1.127: *in medium quaerebant*, 'they made gain for the common good'), with this changing only after Jupiter's intervention, it is through Jupiter that the bees are capacitated towards collective action (4.157: *in medium quaesita reponunt*, 'they garner their gains into a common store'). The key sentence *Iuppiter ipse addidit* (4.149–50) inverts the train of thought from book 1. There, it is first expressed with similar wording that 'the father himself willed it, that the way of the farmer should not be easy' (*pater ipse colendi | haud facile esse uiam uoluit*, 1.121–2). A little later, the father of gods makes another appearance with the same verb as in book 4: *ille malum uirus serpentibus addidit atris* ('he it was who put the noxious venom into deadly snakes', 1.129), which is then linked to the keyword of this aetiology (and perhaps of the entire *Georgics*): *mox et frumentis* <u>*labor additus*</u> ('soon, the corn, too, was given *labor*', 1.150). Whereas the verb *addere* in the passage from book 4 expresses a benefaction from Jupiter, the same verb is used in book 1 to depict a tainted gift from Jupiter for man and nature.[21]

These observations possibly support the view that the *Georgics*' aetiology of *labor* (1.118–46) depends also upon Hesiod's Pandora myth (*Op.* 47ff.)[22] and not just upon the alternative explanation of the world's ages (*Op.* 106: ἕτερον λόγον), which is usually considered the dominant pretext for Virgil's passage in book 1.[23] In the myth of the ages, Zeus himself is subject to the historical development and makes his first appearance in the already-deteriorated silver age, whilst nothing is revealed as to why he made the third, fourth and fifth races of man in the manner that he did. In contrast, in both the Pandora myth and the Virgil passage, the creation of evil is depicted as a voluntary intervention from the father of the gods in the intact state of nature. In both cases, however, evil is described as something given by the father of the gods. Leaving that aside, the main point of the above discussion was to demonstrate that, in the *Georgics*, through the giving of gifts, unequals, whether man and nature, animals and plants, man and gods, or nature and gods, are brought into relationships with each other. The sacrifices which man offers up to the gods throughout the *Georgics* lend further support to the hypothesis that there are strong inequalities between the exchange partners, from the humble to the high.[24]

Approaching the future: the narrator and his patrons

Along this vertical axis of giving, one can also imagine the relationship of the narrator[25] with Maecenas, who functions as one of the poem's addressees, and with the political ruler Octavian (referred to as *Caesar*). This relationship in the *Georgics* is far more complex than in Hesiod, where Perses, the addressee of the didactic poem, is encouraged to establish relationships on a horizontal axis with those of equal rank, whilst kings and unjust men are vilified as 'devourers of gifts' (cf. *Op.* 39, 220 and 263: δωροφάγοι).[26] In Virgil, a more unconditional, but less straightforward relationship to the ruler Octavian is established.

In the proem, Virgil calls Caesar 'benefactor' or, to be etymologically exact, 'increaser of fruits' (*auctor frugum*, 1.27). This address, which may anticipate the honorary title 'Augustus',[27] places the ruler in a hierarchical yet direct relationship both to the farmer and to Virgil, who bestows honour upon him with the introductory hymn.[28] In the *sphragis* at the end of the poem (4.559–66), Octavian is referred to as the law-giver over other peoples. Just as the sole ruler Dido in book 1 of the *Aeneid* organizes the society of Carthage through her legislation and judicature, so too does the equivalent power of Octavian, albeit over a larger area, announce itself in these lines (cf. 562: *uolentis | per populos* <u>*dat iura*</u>, 'he bestows laws over willing people' with *Aen.* 1.507: <u>*iura dabat legesque*</u> *uiris*, 'laws and ordinances she gave to her people').

The most complex of all the references to Octavian, however, is the one from the proem to the third book. The narrator aspires to construct a temple and consecrate it with games (3.12–25):

primus Idumaeas referam tibi, Mantua, palmas,
et uiridi in campo templum de marmore ponam
propter aquam, tardis ingens ubi flexibus errat
Mincius et tenera praetexit harundine ripas.   15
in medio mihi Caesar erit templumque tenebit:
illi uictor ego et Tyrio conspectus in ostro
centum quadriiugos agitabo ad flumina currus.
cuncta mihi Alpheum linquens lucosque Molorchi
cursibus et crudo decernet Graecia caestu.   20
ipse caput tonsae foliis ornatus oliuae
dona feram. iam nunc sollemnis ducere pompas
ad delubra iuuat caesosque uidere iuuencos,
uel scaena ut uersis discedat frontibus utque
purpurea intexti tollant aulaea Britanni.   25

First I will bring back to you, Mantua, the palms of Idumaea, and on the green plain will set up a temple in marble beside the water, where great Mincius wanders in lazy windings and fringes his banks with slender reeds. In the midst I will have Caesar, and he shall possess the shrine. In his honour I, a victor resplendent in Tyrian purple, will drive a hundred four-horse chariots beside the stream. For me all Greece will leave Alpheus and the groves of Molorcus, to compete in the foot race and with the brutal boxing glove. My brows graced with leaves of cut olives, I myself will bring offerings. Even now I long to escort the stately procession to the shrine and witness the slaughter of the steers; and see how the scene on the stage changes as the sets revolve and how Britons raise the crimson curtain they are woven into.

The building of the temple is usually interpreted as a symbol for a major literary project.[29] It is particularly noteworthy that the narrator appears in several roles: first as victorious poet (cf. *referam ... palmas* and *ego uictor*), then as builder (*templum ponam*), later as master of ceremonies at the consecration festival (*agitabo ... currus* and *cuncta mihi ... linquens ... Graecia*) and as prominent participant in the procession (*ipse ... dona feram* and *sollemnis ducere pompas*) and finally as a spectator at the festival (*iuuat ... uidere*).[30] All of these activities are ultimately directed towards the honour of Caesar, the deity of the temple. This relationship to Caesar is expressed programmatically in the pronouns in the dative of verses 16–17: *mihi Caesar* is followed by *illi ego uictor*.[31] Just as it is in Virgil's interest for Caesar to be the guardian deity of the temple, so too it is in Caesar's interest to be honoured by Virgil.[32]

It is interesting to observe that the beginning of this relationship with Caesar is presented as an event in the future. In lines 12–22, verbs appear in the future tense, and since Pindar features prominently in this passage,[33] one might construe them as 'Pindaric futures'.[34] Only when the narrator envisages himself in attendance at the festival in Caesar's honour does he revert back to the present (*iam nunc ... iuuat*). The prophecy is in this way performative; the narrator's vision of a future, in which he will be brought closer to Caesar, is self-fulfilling, starting at the very moment of the utterance. The sentence preceding the switch into the present sparks this performative aspect. The phrase *ipse . . . dona feram* is of particular importance here. Given its difficulty, I would like to discuss it in some detail.

Most translators, commentators and critics tend to understand the phrase *ipse . . . dona feram* (21–2) as the narrator awarding prizes after the games (cf., e.g., Rushton Fairclough's translation 'I myself will award the prizes'). Damien Nelis and Jocelyne Nelis-Clément have argued that in the proems to books 1 and 3 the historical context of a *pompa circensis* is evoked, and that in the proem to book 3 there is a transgression in line 22 to a sacrificial *pompa*, which makes it possible to read the word *pompa* at line 22 still as part of the allusions to a *pompa circensis*, although it syntactically already belongs to the sacrificial context of the next lines.[35] Yet, for a variety of reasons, it is possible and, I would argue, more attractive, to put this argument the other way around and to regard the preceding sentence, and especially the phrase *ipse . . . dona feram*, as part of the sacrificial passage. I find four arguments for this reading.

(i) While it is true that *Aen.* 5.774, which famously picks up line 21 (*ipse caput tonsae foliis ornatus oliuae*), is part of the book of games, it does *not* refer to Aeneas awarding prizes to athletes, but occurs where he presides over a sacrifice *after* the games.

(ii) As has been shown, the phrase *dona feram* can productively be read in tandem with 2.476 *quarum* [sc. *Musarum*] *sacra fero*; Philip Hardie, who proposed this reading,[36] interprets these phrases as part of an initiatory context, which unfolds both on a religious and poetical level and which is later found in Ov. *Pont.* 1.1, especially lines 45–8 (47: *locum date sacra ferenti,* 'make way for the bearer of the sacred objects'). Whereas in book 2 we read of a reciprocal relationship between the poet and the Muses, in the proem to book 3 the narrator is seeking access to the temple of his (deified) super-patron Caesar.

(iii) Yet another parallel, which supports a sacrificial meaning of *ipse . . . dona feram*, is identified by John Miller.[37] He demonstrates that Ascanius's prayer to Jupiter in *Aen.* 9.625–9 shows significant parallels to both *G.* 1.40 (*audacibus adnue coeptis*) and 3.21–3, when the boy promises Jupiter gifts and sacrifices (cf. 626–7: *ipse . . . feram sollemnia dona | et statuam ante aras . . . iuuencum,* 'I myself shall bring you solemn gifts and set before your altar a steer').

(iv) Finally, there are intertextual links to the depiction of the triple triumph on the shield of Aeneas in *Aen.* 8, where Octavian in the guise of a quasi-deity sits in front of the temple of Apollo reviewing the gifts the conquered people present to him (720–21: *ipse sedens niueo candentis limine Phoebi | dona recognoscit populorum*): the clearest parallel is the animal sacrifice in the direct context of the gifts (cf. *G.* 3.23: *ad delubra iuuat caesosque uidere iuuencos,* with *Aen.* 8.719: *ante aras terram caesi strauere iuuenci,* 'before the altars slain steers covered the ground'), but there are further similarities, most notably the fact that the narrator of *G.* 3 plans to depict scenes of Roman victories similar to the victory celebrated at the triple triumph (see, e.g., the importance of rivers in *G.* 3.27–9 and *Aen.* 8.726–8).

To sum up my points so far: even if we are to assume that when read as a sentence in its own right the exact meaning of *ipse . . . dona feram* at 3.21–2 is obscure, we have to concede that Virgil, by recycling elements of these lines in *Aeneid* 5, 9 and 8, at least retrospectively wanted to implement a sacrificial meaning; he thus retrojects a relationship of exchange between the poet and Octavian back into the *Georgics*.[38] Read in this way, the text presents the narrator stepping out of the crowd of those honouring Caesar in order to bestow him with gifts. The future is made present through the presentation of gifts.[39] Perhaps we can imagine the presentation of gifts taking place directly at or even in the temple, where (the statue of) Caesar is located. Although the other actions explicitly take place in the vicinity of the temple, a physical nearness to the deity seems in this case most likely.

It has become a commonplace that Virgil adopts for himself a middle position in the *Georgics*. Socially he seeks to draw close to the still largely unknown new ruler but is reluctant to position himself too close. Poetically he soars into the territory of epic panegyric at the start of the third book (3.8–9), only to revert back to the actual subject of the *Georgics* towards the end of the proem (40–8). The *interea* (40) is therefore a key word. Maecenas functions in both areas as a central figure, socially as an influential connoisseur of political relations, and poetically, far from being of little importance, as the one who keeps Virgil on a central course by bringing the literary topic back down to earth when it becomes too lofty, as we see at the start of book 3,[40] or by elevating its importance when it seems too small, as in the proem to book 4.

Acquiring symbolic capital: Virgil and his audience

So far, this chapter has examined relationships inside the poem. The prominence of Octavian and Maecenas inevitably broadens the perspective of this enquiry, since, as historical figures, they also exist outside the poem. In this section I would therefore like to ask whether and how the relationship between Virgil and his explicit and implicit addressees chimes in with the reciprocal yet asymmetrical paradigms we observed in the previous three sections of my discussion. When raising such an issue one is immediately confronted by the vexed question of who is to be regarded as the poem's addressee and, related to that, the actual audience. It is clear that not many of the actual instructions uttered in the second person are directed to Octavian and Maecenas, who are the only addressees mentioned by name. Unlike its predecessors in the didactic tradition, the *Georgics* lacks an explicit addressee who can act as a pupil.[41]

Many attempts have been made to solve this problem. Recently, Peter Wiseman has suggested first performances of the *Georgics* at games run by Agrippa in 33 BCE and reconstructs an audience[42] that actually consists of farmers: 'Traditionally, the games were the time when country people might come in to their city; and the games were about education as well as entertainment.'[43] This idea, however enchanting it may be, can hardly be proved right or wrong, since there is no evidence for these performances of the *Georgics*. Other interpreters have therefore undertaken more literary approaches, such as William Batstone, who explains the various implicit and explicit addressees by assuming a 'multiplicity of Virgil's subject' and 'the many voices and perspectives of Virgil's praeceptor.'[44] According to Batstone, this tendency is rooted in Varro's *De Re Rustica*, where the reader is also confronted with a great variety of conversants and their different educational backgrounds, interests in and perspectives on agriculture.[45] While this model seems to describe the complexity inherent in the *Georgics* better, it has the disadvantage that it overemphasizes the disintegrating tendencies of the poem and consequently cannot explain its unifying forces. Therefore, it is undoubtedly the case that there are strong tensions within the poem, but it is difficult to imagine that a text could have been so attractive for different audiences within Roman society if it fell apart into different elements that could not form, or contribute to, a larger whole. I would therefore like to opt for a more integrative model, one that acknowledges the text's different perspectives, but one that, at the same time, does not dismiss ideas of coherence per se.

The *Georgics'* subject – agriculture – and its depiction via ideologically laden metaphors serve as such a means of integration for the Roman audience: Octavian might have been attracted by the religious aspects of it;[46] for a cultural politician such as Maecenas, who famously sponsored poets with property in the countryside, the poem's frequent references to villa estates must have been very appealing; Virgil himself is traditionally said to have chosen the subject for his career development from pastoral poverty to the heights of narrative epic; his fellow poets and other literati may have been most interested in the text's learned allusiveness; the military elite and the veterans may have been flattered by the military metaphors that illustrate the farmer's activities throughout the four books;[47] people from the upper and middle class, such as landowners (*domini*) and estate managers (*uilici*), can act as implicit addressees of the instructions at various points; and, finally, smallholders or dependent farmers can identify with the *agricolae* as they are depicted in the poem. All these views are not particularly new, but they illustrate that agriculture, whether understood in one of its 'realistic' components or in a literary or even metaphorical way, is a large foil onto which Romans can project their own experiences, hopes and interests.

Lucretius, in the proem to the *De Rerum Natura*, calls his work and its Epicurean doctrine 'gifts' to Memmius and hopes they will not be rejected by the pupil (*DRN* 1.50–3):

Quod super est, uacuas auris animumque sagacem
semotum a curis adhibe ueram ad rationem,
ne mea <u>dona</u> tibi studio disposta fideli,
intellecta prius quam sint, contempta relinquas.

. . . for the rest, do thou [Memmius], lend empty ears and a keen mind, severed from cares, to true philosophy, lest, before they are understood, you should leave aside in disdain my gifts set forth for you with unflagging zeal . . .

Text and trans. by Bailey

In another famous programmatic passage, Lucretius uses the simile of a cup which is filled with bitter medicine but sweetened by a honey-coated rim to describe his didactic poetry (1.936–50 = 4.11–25); as a medic presents this cup to children, so does the didactic poet present his text to the audience.[48] In the *Georgics*, no such gift imagery can be found when Virgil talks about his didactic undertaking. The obscure expression *ipse ... dona feram* (3.21–2), as discussed above, is the closest one gets to it; for such a reading, however, one would have to understand the phrase allegorically as a literary offering by the poet to *Caesar*, who, as we have seen, is not the only addressee. Lucretius's poem, by contrast, features an individual pupil addressee, namely Memmius. And although in the cup simile a collective audience lurks in the background of Lucretius's address to his pupil,[49] this would be a homogeneous group, since its members are all equally to be enlightened and guided towards the Epicurean doctrine.[50] As opposed to this, Virgil addresses a heterogeneous audience and therefore has to offer various modes of reading. That the didactic goal of the *Georgics* is not as clear as Lucretius's is an advantage rather than a weakness for this kind of project. It renders the *Georgics* a poem that is attractive to many readers, and it also renders Virgil a poet who – just like the *princeps* – tries to unify the various groups of Roman society, not by politics but by means of literature. It is this way of inclusive writing – which goes beyond blunt classifications as 'optimistic' or 'pessimistic' – that secures Virgil symbolic capital in return for his poem as a gift.

Conclusion: reciprocity at the time of Actium

The manner in which gifts and social reciprocity occur in the *Georgics* reflects the complexity of social relationships at the time of Actium, and the complexity of Virgil's poetic project. Concerning the social complexity, Miriam Griffin has shown in her studies on Seneca's *De beneficiis* that the rise of the principate fundamentally complicated social reciprocity, and that a pervasive sense of uncertainty, particularly among the elites, held sway over the norms of giving and receiving.[51] In traditional philosophical discourse, giving and receiving is a practice among equals,[52] but now of course, even before Actium, Roman society had become highly stratified. The rise of Octavian at Actium intensified this stratification, and we learn from Tacitus (*Ann.* 1.2.1) and other historical sources that Octavian made use of generous gifts to consolidate his power.[53] Notionally he maintains the political system of the republican era with an influential class of senators, but among the senators he paradoxically acts as the *primus inter pares*, slowly implementing a quasi-monarchical system. For the social and political actors within this process, the old republican 'currencies' such as ancestry or political merit become less important; what counts now is their personal reciprocal, yet asymmetrical, relationship with the *princeps*.

One result of these changes is an increasing feeling of uncertainty towards social and economic dealings, which one can already sense in the *Georgics*. The fact that gift-giving and social reciprocity are themes evoked metaphorically throughout the poem can be ascribed to the complex poetic objectives. The *Georgics* are simultaneously didactic and epic; they are Hesiodic and Roman; they deal with the farmer and his difficult relationship with nature and the gods; they deal also with the history of culture and of human *labor*;

and above all else they deal with the poet and his relationship with his patron and Caesar, the latter superior to both. The reciprocal processes in the *Georgics* are carried out in a vertical rather than a horizontal line: between the farmer and the earth, birds and plants, Jupiter and the bees, and between Virgil and Octavian. Gifts and social reciprocity, whether concrete or metaphorical, cannot remove these tensions in the poem, but they act as the glue that holds the conflicting elements together.[54]

PART IV
ROMAN RESPONSES

CHAPTER 9

'PULPY FICTION': VIRGILIAN RECEPTION AND GENRE IN COLUMELLA *DE RE RUSTICA* 10

Sara Myers

Interpretations of Virgil's garden in *Georgics* 4.116–48 have flourished as vigorously as the plants in the old man of Tarentum's fertile plot. The small scale of the passage has proved to be no hindrance to the garden's production of meaning. The 'absent presence' of this garden, described in a *praeteritio*, exerted a surprisingly widespread influence on the Latin literary imagination of later authors, and perhaps on none more so than Columella, who took it upon himself to supply the missing garden in the tenth book of his *De Re Rustica*, a hexameter book of horticulture hedged about by the other eleven prose books. This chapter looks at the ways in which Columella may be seen as an interpreter, as well as an imitator, of Virgil and considers why it was specifically his gardening book he chose to versify. I shall argue that to understand Columella's poetic book we need to consider it within his whole project of the *De Re Rustica*, especially his second treatment of horticulture in prose in book 11.[1] It is precisely this generic contrast which allows Columella to explore poetic modes of representation in book 10. Columella's two treatments of gardens, poetry and prose allow him to explore in an innovative manner two different modes of horticultural teaching, as well as the traditions of garden literature. By taking up the work of the garden again in prose, Columella allows his garden poem to eschew pragmatism and to embrace the realm of poetic fictionality elsewhere rejected in the *De Re Rustica*.

After nine books of practical agricultural precepts on soils and planting, arboriculture and viticulture, the care of farm animals, grafting and pruning, and beekeeping, Columella surprisingly announces at the end of book 9 a poetical treatment of horticulture to follow in book 10. Columella's choice of verse for horticulture, he tells us, is due to pressure from his primary addressee Publius Silvinus and a certain Gallio (*RR* 9.16.2).[2] In his prose preface to book 10, Columella reveals that Silvinus's request specifically entails supplementing Virgil's omission of a full treatment of gardening in his *Georgics* (*RR* 10 Praef. 3):[3]

Quare cultus hortorum, quoniam eorum fructus magis in usu est, diligentius nobis quam tradidere maiores praecipiendus est; isque, sicut instotueram, prorsa oratione prioribus subnecteretur exordiis, nisi propositum meum expugnasset frequens postulatio tua, quae peruicit ut poeticis numeris explerem georgici carminis omissas partis, quas tamen et ipse Vergilius significauerat posteris se memorandas relinquere. Neque enim aliter istud nobis fuerat audendum quam ex uoluntate uatis maxime uenerandi

Wherefore the cultivation of gardens, since their produce is now in greater demand, must be taught by us with more care than our forefathers have handed down; and I should be adding it in prose to my earlier books, as I had intended, had not your repeated requests overcome my resolve and charged me to complete in poetic numbers those parts of the *Georgics* which were omitted by Virgil, which, nevertheless, as he himself had intimated, he left to be dealt with by later writers. For indeed I ought not to have dared the task were it not in compliance with the wish of that greatly revered poet.

The use of verse in this book would seem to serve as a signal of the end of Columella's work (10 *Praef.* 1: *faenoris tui . . . reliquam pensiunculam,* 'the small remaining payment of your interest'), as the topic of the garden similarly acknowledges Virgil's closural gestures in the garden *praeteritio* of *Georgics* 4 (116–17: *extremo sub fine laborum,* 'at the end of my labors'; cf. 147).[4]

Despite the strong closural signals of book 10, however, just as surprisingly in the following book Columella announces that yet another treatment of horticulture has been extorted from him by yet another addressee, a certain Claudius Augustalis, this time a prose version (11.1.1: *extudit mihi cultus hortorum prosa ut oratione componerem,* 'he extorted from me a promise to write a treatment in prose on the cultivation of gardens').[5] Columella says that he had been intending all along to do this (11.1.2), before Silvinus's request for poetry. The difference in addressee may be significant, if, as has been suggested, Silvinus is often depicted as a 'text-book farmer', whereas Claudius is an appropriately teachable *adulescens.*[6] Columella 11 contains a list of the monthly chores for the *uilicus,* among which is gardening (11.1.2: *ut holitoris curam subtexerem uilici officiis,* 'to append horticulture to the duties of the bailiff'), which takes up the final section of the book (11.3.1–65). Book 11 provides seasonal instructions for the *uilicus*-gardener for sowing and tending edible plants; gone are the flowers of book 10. While book 10 contains mention of only four months and eight dates, usually expressed in epicizing mythological or astrological periphrases,[7] book 11 abounds in very precise information about dates and planting (11.3.14: *quid quoque tempore uel colendum uel serendum sit,* 'what must be cultivated and sown and at what time'). The supplement of book 11 essentially highlights the ornamental character of book 10; as a didactic poem it does not serve as practical instruction; it can be skipped, as indeed it is in the list of contents provided at the end of book 11.[8]

Aside from his two treatments of gardens, the only other place Columella speaks of external pressure on his choice of content is in book 5. There he responds to Silvinus's complaint that he has omitted instructions on measuring land (5.1.4). Like the geometry of land measurement, gardening evidently does not always find a place in agronomy. In both cases Columella announces and rises to the challenge of comprehensiveness and demonstrates his wide-ranging expertise.[9] At the opening of book 12 Columella similarly justifies his inclusion of a chapter on the chores of the *uilica* by citing Xenophon's

Oeconomicus (and Cicero as translator) as his model (12. *Praef.* 1–7).[10] Such footnoting lends authority to Columella's technical treatise on a subject no longer considered 'gentlemanly' (*RR* 1 *Praef.* 13: *turpi consensu deserta exoleuerit disciplina ruris*, 'the shameful consensus with which rural training has been abandoned'),[11] in the same way his inclusion of verse demonstrates his sophistication and literary ambitions, which are made clear at the beginning of the *De Re Rustica* (*RR* 1 *Praef.* 29–31).[12] As for the choice of genre, Columella understands poetry as stylistically powerful (*RR* 1.1.12): *Virgilium, qui carminum quoque potentem fecit* ('Virgil, who gave agriculture the power of song').

By juxtaposing the two genres of poetry and prose, Columella implies that verse veers towards the fictional, not functional. Though there is much overlap between books 10 and 11, in instructions and in plants (out of the forty-three or so plants in book 11, all but five appear also in book 10, which has a far larger list of plants); in book 11 the garden contains only herbs and vegetables, no flowers. The flowers belong in the verse garden, where they allow Columella his ornamental interlude (cf. *RR*. 9.2.1: *Vergilius poeticis floribus inluminauit*, 'Virgil brightened the subject [apiculture] with the flowers of poetry'). Despite his widespread use of Virgilian quotation throughout the whole of the *De Re Rustica*, Columella clearly understands Virgil's poetical work to be primarily literary, not practical, in much the same way that Pliny and Seneca judge Virgil's aims as those of pleasure (Sen. *Epist.* 86.15): *nec agricolas docere uoluit sed legentes delectare* ('who wanted to not to teach farmers but please his readers').[13] The Virgilian model gives Columella license to diverge from practicality and to demonstrate his literary versatility in encompassing the whole of the agricultural literary tradition, yet the addition of book 11 shows up the salutary difference between poetic and prosaic discourses. I would suggest that the contrast between Columella's two treatments of gardens is meant to demonstrate the superiority of prose for agricultural teaching. Although the book is introduced as fulfilling a practical aim, *RR* 10 seems rather to indulge in the pleasure associated with both poetry and the garden.

De Re Rustica 10 is a didactic poem, responding not so much to Virgil's garden in *Georgics* 4 as to the whole project of the *Georgics*, agronomy in verse form. Columella takes his cue from Virgil's statements in book 4 of the *Georgics* that he is unable to treat the subject of gardening because of the constraints of space imposed by his being about to finish his work (*G.* 4.116–17, 147). Virgil goes on to recall briefly having seen near the southern Italian town of Tarentum the humble, but productive, garden of an unnamed old Corycian (125–46). The Corycian's horticultural activities seem to offer an alternative to the conventional agricultural pursuits that form the subjects of the first three books of the poem, since his land is specifically qualified as not suitable for crops, livestock or vineyards (127–9). The image of the garden seems a positive one of frugal contentment, self-sufficiency and a harmonious relationship with nature; absent from this vision is the *labor . . . improbus* ('insatiable labour', *G.* 1.145–6) and failures of the earlier part of the poem.[14] For some critics Virgil's garden is realistic, for others almost wholly ideal; its function in and implications for the *Georgics* as a whole have long been debated.[15] Proposed identifications of Virgil's *senex Corycius* draw upon many of the different associations of gardens, including an Epicurean or Pythagorean philosopher,[16] an embodiment of Utopian leisure.[17] Many have seen this garden as representing Virgil's intensely personal aesthetic ideals of privacy, imagination and self-sufficiency.[18] A number of scholars have suggested plausibly that a complex literary tradition lies behind many of the elements in Virgil's description.[19]

We should in fact distinguish between Virgil's initial description of horticulture (*G.* 4.116–24, cf. *cura colendi*, 118) and the garden belonging to the *senex* (125–46). Already at the opening Virgil mentions two types of gardens: the utilitarian *pingues hortos* ('fertile gardens', 118) and the decorative *rosaria Paesti* ('rose beds of Paestum', 119). The following ecphrasis notably also combines the edible with the ornamental. In lines 120–4, Virgil mentions typical garden produce such as *intiba* (curly endive), *apium* (probably wild celery) and *cucumis* (cucumber), all of which appear in Columella 10 and 11. Roses, narcissus, acanthus, ivy and myrtle (119–24), however, sound distinctly more ornamental.[20] The Corycian's garden begins with an oddly brief mention of *rarum . . . olus* (130), which is presumably meant to cover all vegetables, usually the most important produce of a productive garden.[21] Virgil does not enumerate the garlic, onions, beets or cabbages of Columella books 10 and 11. And then there are all the flowers: white lilies, verbena, poppies, roses and hyacinths (130–1, 137). Doubtless many of these flowers are for the old man's bees (cf. *G.* 4.183, *hyacinthus* for beekeeping). It is, of course, notoriously difficult to categorize flowers as either decorative, edible or medicinal.[22] Flowers were a cash crop, used also for garlands, and Columella at 10.303–10 tells of the *rustici* who fill baskets with flowers to sell in town and return drunk and cash-laden.[23] In Virgil, however, the commercial realities of horticulture are passed over;[24] his flowers instead evoke the pleasure garden and the poetic tradition, wherein flowers and flower garlands frequently serve as aesthetic and metapoetic symbols.[25] As many have argued, Virgil's garden, with its trees planted *in uersum* (4.144), serves as a fertile metaphor for the artistry of the poet wherein the gardener's activities 'mimic and materialize the process of writing itself'.[26]

Garden descriptions invite this self-reflexivity, with their artificial and artistic arrangement of the raw material of nature. As Nicholas Horsfall has observed, 'the description of the market garden has deep poetic, and indeed metapoetic, roots'.[27] Pliny the Elder reflects the persistent literary associations of gardens in Roman thought by recalling the Homeric garden of Alcinous at the beginning of his discussion of gardens (*Nat. Hist.* 19.49). Virgil's *praeteritio* may acknowledge that horticulture does not in fact have a prominent place in earlier agricultural treatises, such as those of Cato or Varro, although Varro's garden aviary in the shape of a writing tablet in *De Re Rustica* 3.5.9–17 seems to serve as another example of how literary gardens have a tendency to become self-reflexive and closural. Garden descriptions and catalogues belong mainly to verse from Homer onwards, although they also figured in the rhetorical and philosophical traditions.[28] If there were precedents for horticultural teaching in verse, Virgil has displaced them all for Columella.[29]

As in Virgil's *Georgics*, in Columella bees lead to gardens,[30] and, as in Virgil, bees invite mythology and fiction. At *RR* 9.2.2, Columella disavows any interest in questions of the mythical (*fabulose*) origins of bees, which, he says, belong to the realm of poetic license (*poeticae magis licentiae*).[31] In book 10, however, he fully mobilizes the poetic techniques of didactic epic; included are mythological and astrological temporal periphrases, etymological wordplay, chariot metaphors for poetry, catalogues, divine invocations, and storms.[32] Structurally, Columella's admission of myth and poetry into one of the final books of the work reflects Virgil's similar turn to mythological narrative in book 4 of the *Georgics*. The 436 hexameters of Columella's book 10 mark out the garden as a separate world and highlight its special role in his farming and literary enterprise. At the opening of his poem Columella again justifies his choice of topic and genre by citing Virgil's refusal and bequest of the topic of gardens (*RR* 10.1–6), and at its close he recalls Virgil's poetic genealogy from Hesiod (10.435–6), thus placing himself within the agricultural and didactic poetic tradition.[33] Book 10 is closely indebted to Virgilian language, although Boldrer points out Columella's many innovations in vocabulary and syntax, especially the introduction of a multitude of new botanical terms (also in 11), many Greek.[34]

Virgilian influence is evident throughout the *De Re Rustica*. Columella lists Virgil as a source along with some fifty other Greek and Roman agricultural writers in book 1 and cites or quotes him (mostly from the *Georgics*, but also *Eclogues* and *Aeneid*) more than anyone else (some fifty times, up to seven consecutive lines).[35] Virgil is *celeberrimus uates* ('the most renowned poet', 1.1.7), *uir eruditissimus* ('most learned man', 1.3.9), the *Georgics* a *diuinum carmen* ('divine poem', 7.3.9). Although Virgil is on a number of occasions cited for his agricultural authority,[36] most of Columella's citations of Virgil function ornamentally (cf. *RR* 9.2.1: *ornatius*).[37] In book 7, for example, Columella embellishes a discussion of the swelling of pigs' spleens (7.10.8) with the quotation of *Ecl.* 7.54 (on falling fruit in the summer). Columella's verse is both earthier and more erotic than Virgil's. There is a heady linguistic mix of the high and low (often technical), exploiting the contrast between his material and his new genre. Richard Thomas suggests that Virgil's strategy in converting agricultural prose into poetry involved refinement and suppression.[38] A telling contrast between Virgil and Columella can be seen in a comparison between their treatments of composting. At *RR* 10.84–5 (*pabula nec pudeat fesso praebere nouali | immundis quaecumque uomit latrina cloacis*, 'let him not be ashamed to offer to the exhausted fallow-ground whatever the latrine vomits from its filthy sewers') Columella recalls with *pudeat*[39] Virgil's delicate treatment of this topic at *G.* 1.79–81 (*arida tantum | ne saturare fimo pingui pudeat sola neue | effetos cinerem immundum iactare per agros*, 'do not be embarrassed to drench the dry soil with rich manure or to throw filthy ashes over the exhausted fields'), but includes the starkly technical (and non-Virgilian) *latrina* and *cloaca*.

Columella is also keen to display his learning by reproducing rare forms first appearing in Virgil. In a periphrasis for the coming of winter at *RR* 10.52–4, Columella picks up an elegant astrological reference from *G.* 1.221–2 (*ante tibi Eoae Atlantides abscondantur | Cnosiaque ardentis decedat stella Coronae*, 'first let the morning daughters of Atlas be hidden and the Cretan star of the burning crown set'), borrowing the learned *Atlantides* from Virgil,[40] but reversing the setting of the two constellations, Pleiades and Corona Borealis (*RR* 10.52–4):[41]

expectetur hiemps, dum Bacchi <u>Cnosius ardor</u>
aequore caeruleo celetur uertice mundi,
solis et aduersos metuant <u>Atlantides</u> ortus

. . . let winter be awaited, when Bacchus' Cretan 'flame'
in the summit of the sky is hidden in the blue sea
and the daughters of Atlas fear the rising sun's opposing rays.

Columella picks up the latent passion of Virgil's *ardentis* with his *ardor*, underscoring the eroticism of his garden poem.[42] Aside from recalling the opening and closing frame of Virgil's horticultural *praeteritio*, Columella does not engage closely with the garden of *Georgics* 4: there is no Corycian, no Tarentum.[43] Direct quotation of one of the most famous tags in Virgil's passage comes in book 11, where Columella quotes Virgil's 'unpurchased feasts' (11.3.1: *quod ait poeta, inemptas rure dapes*, G. 4.133), now food provided by the overseer from the garden to the master.

Columella's tenth book might profitably be viewed in the context of some of the early imperial poems in the *Virgilian Appendix*, which share bucolic and horticultural themes.[44] Like Columella, these poems represent a 'creative supplementation aimed at expanding canonical texts and filling in their gaps'.[45] Close in theme and time to the Neronian Columella are the pseudo-Virgilian *Culex* and the two anonymous poems *Copa*[46] and *Moretum* (the latter a poem with which Columella seems to be familiar),[47] all of which feature garden descriptions and plant catalogues (*Moretum* 60–84 (garden), *Culex* 123–45 (catalogue of trees), 398–411 (catalogue of flowers), *Copa* 7–22 (garden)) and a similar tendency to make neoteric programmatic statements.[48] The *Moretum* has been understood as exposing the grim reality of Simulus's existence of rural poverty and thereby challenging Virgil's idyllic and idealizing vision of the Corycian's life on a small plot of marginal land in *Georgics* 4.[49] In the moralizing description of the hardworking Simulus's garden in the *Moretum*, no flowers are allowed to grow and the rustic himself eats only very few of his vegetables, while the remaining are sold in town. The *Copa* and *Culex* also offer debased versions of the *locus amoenus*, if not specifically of the garden of *Georgics* 4. Although these texts, and earlier also Horace,[50] seem to represent critical responses to Virgil's idealization of horticulture, Columella's garden does not offer a parody of Virgil, but rather picks up the notes of pleasure in *Georgics* 4. His reading is primarily positive, reinforcing his view of a benevolent and providing earth, a 'love affair between farmer and earth'[51] that borrows Virgilian language of personification. Columella's exuberant interpretation can highlight for us the latent passions within Virgil's brief garden passage, where endive (*intiba*) rejoices (*gauderent*, G. 4.120), myrtles love (*amantis*, 124), flowers have soft hair (*comam*, 137), trees are dressed with fruit (*induerat*, 143) and the fertility threatens to spill over the ecphrasis (*onerabat*, 133, *abundare et spumantia*, 140, *uberrima*, 141).

Columella's garden does not represent a Virgilian ideal of solitude, but of fecundity, sexual reproduction and financial profit. It contains over fifty varieties of plants, ranging from roses to onions. The abundance of flowers does not necessarily define it as solely a pleasure garden; as Katherine von Stackelberg observes, it 'meets Cato's criterion of a garden as a space planted with diverse products'.[52] Columella never loses sight of the economic goals of his work set out in the proem (1 *Praef. 7*).[53] At *RR* 1 *Praef.* 27 Columella suggests that fruits, vegetables and even roses have become an important part of the farmer's revenue (*uectigalia*). This is not a 'dilettante's garden',[54] but rather an encyclopedic and imperializing one, embracing as many varieties of plants as possible, including the very latest type of cabbage (*RR* 10.138; *Turni lacus*; cf. Plin. *Nat. Hist.* 19.141: *nuper subiere Lacuturnenses*).[55] Columella, like Pliny the Elder after him, exhibits all the nationalistic enthusiasm of new horticultural discoveries, with long lists of recently imported plants that demonstrate and display Italy's fertility and horticultural imperialism (*RR* 3.8.5): *Italiam, quae paene totius orbis fruges adhibito studio colonorum ferre didicerit* ('Italy has learned to bear the fruits of almost the whole world when our cultivators have applied themselves to the task').[56] He and Pliny also both tap into the traditional moralizing associations of the humble kitchen-garden (*hortus*)[57] while simultaneously celebrating it as 'a microcosm of the fertility of nature'.[58] Pliny adopts a moral tone in his introduction to gardens at *Nat. Hist.* 19.52: *Romae quidem per se hortus ager pauperis erat* ('At Rome in fact a garden was in itself the estate of the poor man'), but includes in his encyclopedic work all the newest and most exotic imported plant specimens, including Persian, Gallic and Asian peaches (*RR* 10.410–12, *Nat. Hist.* 15.39–40). In his prose preface to book 10 Columella strikes a similar moralizing note, suggesting that garden fare is in greater demand for the poor because they cannot afford dairy and meat (10 *Praef.* 2–3: *plebeia paupertas ... ad uulgares compellitur*, 'plebeian poverty ... is reduced to common food'), but his garden poem often takes him far from basic alimentary concerns.[59]

The dual nature of the garden (sustenance and pleasure) always opens up the possibility of luxury and excess.[60] Moralizing discourse reflects this cultural ambivalence about the garden; often gardener and virtuous farmer differ significantly. Columella in his opening preface extols the virtues of the traditional Roman farmer (1 *Praef.* 14–18, 15: *pristinum morem uirilemque uitam*, 'ancient custom and a virile way of life'),[61] while Manilius, for example, disparages horticultural enthusiasts in his discussion of those born under the sign of Virgo, who, he says, cultivate flowers and effeminate leisure in gardens (*Astr.* 5.254–68). Although absent from *RR* 10 (and 11) are the purely ornamental acanthus, myrtle and plane tree (with its tempting shade) of Virgil's garden in *Georgics* 4, along with the sculpted boxwood of Pliny the Younger's luxuriously curated villa estates (*Epp.* 2.17, 5.6), Columella's invocations of nymphs and naiads (10.263–77), Venus (286–7) and satyrs (428) evoke the typical statuary of the Roman pleasure garden.[62] In a sense, this is what poetry does to Columella's garden: the pleasure principle transforms the garden and makes it into a metapoetic image of its own decorative function within the *De Re Rustica*.

Columella most notably borrows from Virgil's technique in the *Georgics* of animating the natural world, and underlining its subjection to human violence and ministration. Columella, however, eschews the Virgilian military metaphors and instead replaces them with primarily sexual language.[63] The eroticism of Columella's poetic garden has been long recognized. He frequently describes the act of gardening in terms of human sexuality (e.g. 10.68–73, 194–212, 204–8),[64] sometimes verging on the disturbingly violent (*lacerate comas*, 70; *scindite amictus*, 70; *perfode terga*, 71; *eradere uiscera*, 72),[65] which reflects both the traditional use of sexual metaphors in agricultural writing,[66] as well as the erotic associations of the garden in Greek and Roman literature.[67]

Columella's praises of the fecundity of spring at *RR* 10.194–212 exemplify his energetic adaptation of Virgilian language and imagery and also display his combinatory poetics. The passage blends myth with hints of Stoic philosophy (197: *spiritus orbis*, 'spirit of the world').[68] It is stylistically elevated, with epic epithets and periphrases (200: *pater aequoreus, regnator aquarum*), and learned Greek names (201: *Tethyn, Amphitriten*; 205: *Acrisioneos ... amores*).[69] Columella's most important sources are Virgil's so-called 'praises of spring' at *Georgics* 2.315–45 and his passage on the power of *amor* at 3.242–83, along with the Lucretian passages upon which Virgil drew (*DRN* 1.1–20, 248–64).[70] At the same time, numerous verbal allusions to Catullus 64 advertise Columella's neoteric poetic allegiance. *Amphitriten* at the end of *RR* 10.201 is an elegant footnoting of Catullus 64.11 (*illa rudem cursu prima imbuit Amphitriten*) in the only spondeiazon in book 10, and *suam Tethyn* at the beginning of the same line recalls 64.29.[71] Columella borrows from Virgil and Lucretius his language describing the process of spring fertilization as an act of intercourse, as exemplified in the allegorical mythic union of sky (rain) and earth (the motif of the sacred marriage, *hieros gamos, RR* 10.202–8 ~ *G*. 2.324–7 ~ Lucr. 1.250–3, 2.991–8). While in both Lucretius and Virgil this erotic passion proves ultimately dangerous in the natural and human worlds, Columella's sensual garden remains safe (10.278): *hic nullae insidiae nymphis, non ulla rapina* ('here there are no traps for nymphs, no rape').[72] Columella's gesture towards the destructive potential of passion at 211 (*atque Amor ignescit menti saeuitque medullis*, 'and love enflames the mind, and rages in the marrows') leads to fecundity, in contrast to the possibility of infertility (214).

At 10.215–29, in a strategy typical of didactic literature,[73] Columella interrupts and reins in this celebration of the fertility of spring, here with a 'proemio al mezzo' in the form of a *recusatio*, making use of the chariot imagery frequent in didactic (10.215–16):[74] *sed quid ego infreno uolitare per aethera cursu | passus equos audax sublimi tramite raptor?* ('but why have I boldly allowed my horses to fly in an unchecked course through the air carried away on a sublime path?'). The passage is a veritable pastiche of programmatic language, outlining a stylistic antithesis between more elevated epic poetry (216: *audax sublimi tramite*, 217: *maiore deo*, 220: *uatem*) and Columella's humble horticultural project (225: *cura leuiore*, 226: *paruo ... gyro*, 227: *gracili ... filo*, 228: *putator*, 229: *olitor*). Columella aligns his poem with epic verse (225: *mea Calliope*), but also advertises his adherence to Alexandrian aesthetics, by now de rigueur (cf. 10.40: *Pierides tenui deducite carmine Musae*).[75] The elevated, Ennian language (*Epigr*. 18 V) of the opening lines recalls Virgil's statement of his poetic ambitions at the beginning of *G*. 3 (8–9: *temptanda uia est, qua me quoque possim | tollere humo uictorque uirum uolitare per ora*, 'a path must be attempted by which I may raise myself from the earth and fly as victor on the lips of men'), which are checked at 3.40 (*interea*).[76] Columella's *reuocatio* is also similar to Virgil's transitional and proemic manoeuvre at *Georgics* 3.284–94 (286: *hoc satis armentis*, 'this is enough for herds'; 291–2: *sed me Parnasi deserta per ardua dulcis | raptat amor*, 'but a sweet love carries me over the deserted heights of Parnassus'), which follows his section on sexual passion in the animal world (209–83), an important source, as we have seen, for Columella's preceding passage.

Columella recalls himself from pursuing the lofty epic themes of natural philosophy (218–19: *rerum causas, sacra* ... *orgia naturae*, 'the causes of things, the sacred rites of nature') and astronomy (219: *secretaque foedera caeli*, 'the secret laws of the sky'),[77] which he associates with Apolline (217: *Delphica laurus*; 224: *Delie te*) and Bacchic (221–3) inspiration.[78] This *recusatio* also recalls Virgil's own staging of poetic alternatives at the end of *Georgics* 2.475–7, where natural philosophy (*rerum ... causas*, 490; *caelique uias et sidera*, 'the paths of the sky and the stars', 475) and rural themes are juxtaposed.[79] At lines 225–7, Calliope, Muse of epic poetry, plays the somewhat incongruous role of the Callimachean 'warning Apollo',[80] recalling Columella to his humbler themes of horticulture, expressed in typical Callimachean terms (225–9):[81]

me mea Calliope cura <u>leuiore</u> uagantem
iam reuocat <u>paruo</u>que iubet decurrere gyro 🦗
et secum <u>gracili</u> conectere carmina <u>filo</u>
quae canat inter opus Musa modulante putator
pendulus arbustis, holitor uiridantibus hortis

Me my Calliope with a lighter task now recalls
from my wandering and orders me to race a narrow course,
and with her to weave poetry of a slender thread,
which the pruner hanging from a tree and the
gardener in his verdant gardens may sing to the muse's measure
amidst their labour.

Such antithesis between high stylistic level and humble subject matter is characteristic of the poetics of the *Georgics*, as well as the *Moretum* and *Culex*.[82] Columella's conventional vocabulary is also clearly indebted to important programmatic passages in Horace and Propertius.[83] The final two lines associate the poem with the rustic singers of the *Eclogues* (specifically *Ecl.* 1.56: *alta sub rupe canet frondator ad auras*, 'under the lofty rock the pruner shall sing to heaven').[84]

I would suggest that this passage illustrates how much of Columella's allusive programme in *De Re Rustica* 10 springs from his drive for accumulation, collecting and cataloguing; exhibiting in spades the 'compilatory aesthetic' typical of his age.[85] Columella's poetic garden is crammed to satiety with produce and poetry, demonstrating both nature's and Columella's potency. Emily Gowers in her ground-breaking paper on Columella 10 quoted Dallinges's use of the term 'pulpy' to characterize Columella's style in book 10.[86] Richard Martin more recently has called the similarly epigonal *Hesiodic Shield* a 'rather pulpy poem'. As he explains, 'pulp poetics depends on a simple overriding rule: more is more'.[87] This seems to me to fit Columella's competitive engagement with Virgil's poetry and the literary tradition of agricultural teaching.

CHAPTER 10
SERVIAN READINGS OF RELIGION IN THE *GEORGICS*
Ailsa Hunt

Why should classicists read Servius? Cameron's recent judgement on the experience of doing so hardly encourages the Servian-novice to dive in.

> When we read Servius, we are reading the very words a well-known *grammaticus* wrote for his students in an early fifth-century Roman schoolroom. On the whole it is a dispiriting read.[1]

Nor is it hard to see how Servius earned his 'dispiriting' from Cameron. For Servius's commentaries on the *Eclogues*, *Georgics* and *Aeneid* are replete with tedious grammatical explanations, far-fetched etymologies and nit-picking observations which leave many a reader cold, and add little to nothing to their reading of Virgil. Yet these texts have had plenty of readers – within the academy at least – long after they ceased to have a role within the late antique schoolroom. It is an irony of Servian reception that he now rarely attracts readers with a primary interest in Virgil's texts; rather he attracts them because he is *useful*. For in and among the dispiriting mass of observations there will be a detail which, for a particular scholar's purposes, is just what is needed. Thus Servius gets framed as a kind of a treasure store from which we can help ourselves to nuggets of information, whether on an unusual linguistic form, an obscure variant of a myth, or a matter of sacrificial practice.

> For the classicist their sole value is for the jewels of ancient knowledge that lie imbedded in them.[2]

> Servius' commentary on Virgil is widely used by classical scholarship as a source book for antiquarian information of all sorts – mythology, religion, law, social and political history, geography, philosophy, and so on; and it is invaluable for its citations of ancient authors and authorities which we would not otherwise have.[3]

Scholars who dip in and out of Servius for its 'jewels of ancient knowledge' do not, as you would expect, stop to ask questions about the kind of text they are dealing with: information is simply extracted as though Servius offered some kind of neutral encyclopedia of facts. Indeed, questions about the nature of Servius's texts have been taken up and explored by only a handful of scholars, notably Kaster and Cameron, who put pressure on the nature of the text for what it tells us about intellectual culture at the turn of the fifth century CE.[4]

In this chapter I aim to bring these two distinct approaches into dialogue: it is only by asking what *kind* of text Servius's commentaries are, I argue, that we can confidently and meaningfully *use* them. Kaster and Cameron approach Servius with the intellectual priority of obtaining a richer understanding of the culture of late antiquity, but my own concern is to better understand the nature of Servius's text – within the context of the late fourth and early fifth century CE – in order that we as classicists might make better use of it. My focus, naturally for this book, is on Servius's response to the *Georgics*; in particular, I home in on what Servius has to say about religion as he works through Virgil's text.

I begin by painting a picture of Virgil's *Georgics* as an insistently religious text, before turning attention to Servius's response to this text. Broad reflection on the way Servius 'reads' the *Georgics* then leads into a focused exploration of what Roman religion looks like in Servius's eyes, within the pages of the *Georgics* commentary. In particular, I emphasize how his construction of religion within the commentary maps onto the thinking about religion which is present in Virgil's text: a close look at Servius's note on *Georgics* 1.21 will allow us to get our teeth into this rarely discussed material. My first major aim, then, is to better understand the nature of Servius's response to the *Georgics* vis-à-vis his interest in religion. From here, I turn to face the fact that Servius's intense interest in religion has made him temptingly *useful* to scholars of Roman religion, who love to pick out nuggets of religious information from his encyclopedic treasure chest. Expanding the case study of *G.* 1.21 to examine how recent classicists have made use of this one Servian note, I reveal ways in which scholars of Roman religion have unwittingly become Servian readers of Roman religion. Overlooking Servius's idiosyncrasies in his approach to Roman religion, and often his date as well, these scholars have allowed Servius to mould their own portraits of 'classical' Roman religion, presumably thanks to a comforting (but flawed) assumption that in Servius we have a neutral commentary on an Augustan author who is as 'centrally Roman' as they come.

As such, this chapter tells a story about the *seeming* influence of one line of the *Georgics*, via Servius, on a particular branch of classical scholarship, namely the study of Roman religion. For, I argue, the influence that *G.* 1.21 has had on the scholarship of Roman religion owes far more to Servius than it does to Virgil, and a history of failure to realize this has done much intellectual damage.[5] We need, my argument continues, to take a step back from Servius before we can meaningfully use him. For by separating out Servius's thinking about Roman religion from Virgil's, we can hold it up to the light and see it in its own terms; and only then will we start to see how Servian our own readings of Roman religion have become. An immediate aim of this chapter, in short, is to become wary and self-aware readers of Servius, as he reads religion in the *Georgics*: but it also stands as a cautionary tale for all academic use of Servius.[6]

Before we begin in earnest, however, I must deal with a question of terminology, clarifying what I mean when I talk about Servius, and his commentary on the *Georgics*. For the textual transmission of these commentaries is notoriously complex, and they are not straightforwardly the work of a single author. What we do know can be summarized as follows.[7] Some time around the turn of the fifth century, Servius wrote commentaries on the *Aeneid*, *Eclogues* and *Georgics*, in which he drew on a variety of sources, including an earlier fourth-century commentary by Aelius Donatus, now lost. We also possess an expanded version of Servius's commentary, believed to be the work of a seventh-century scholar, possibly from Ireland. This text is known either as Servius Danielis, because it was first brought to light by Pierre Danielis in 1600, or alternatively as Servius Auctus.[8] The nature of the additional material in Servius Auctus has been a matter of debate, but it is now commonly accepted that Donatus's commentary provided most of it. This has been the dominant opinion since an influential article by Rand, published in 1916. Of the scholars who have tackled the question in the last fifty years, Goold, Kaster, Cameron and Stok all essentially agree with the Donatan hypothesis, with only Daintree going out on a limb in objecting to it. For the purposes of this chapter I do not take a strong stance on the origin of the additional material in Servius Auctus, but will refer loosely to the composite text as Servius, remembering that even the 'purer' non-expanded version of Servius is itself a conglomeration of source material; Servius will stand as shorthand for the various commentary traditions which have been synthesized into the text we now have.

Of course, using 'Servius' in this way is not without conceptual difficulties. For one aim of this chapter is to explore a 'Servian approach' to Roman religion, and this is complicated by our positing many different authorial strands to the Servian text, as well as periods of composition. The individual notes which make up the Servian text may have been produced within a grammatical tradition, but in different cultural contexts, and nowhere is this more obvious than in the notes on religious matters. Scholars have observed that Servius's notes on cult practice from the turn-of-the-fifth-century text tend to be in the imperfect tense, whilst those preserved only in Servius Auctus are in the present, reflecting – it is argued – unaltered extracts from Donatus's fourth-century commentary, written at a time when it seems it would have been natural to refer to these cult practices in the present tense.[9] By the time of Servius, it seems, it was not, and this has given scholars a hook on which to hang arguments about the huge changes in religious culture taking place at this time in the Roman Empire.[10] In this chapter the text I engage with is that of Servius Auctus, the expanded version, and in so doing I stay alert to potential differences in the characterization of Roman religion in those notes attributed by Servius to different commentators, or believed – on arguments based on tense – to belong to separate commentary strands. Yet whilst the work and observations of many different commentators have been pooled, and presumably modified and adapted, to form the text known as Servius Auctus, there is also considerable consistency in the thinking about Roman religion which emerges from it, enabling us to engage with this as an 'approach' to Roman religion. This may not be the religious worldview of one man alone, but it is the worldview of a particular academic tradition, which has happened to have its impact under the name of one man, Servius.

It is commonplace to say of Virgil that he was treated like a 'pagan bible' in late antiquity, but this reflects more on his cultural authority than the content matter of his poems.[11]

Certainly the *Georgics* is not the most obvious port of call for those interested in Roman religion, but this idiosyncratic work does offer some rich reflections on human relationships with the divine, especially as mediated through the natural environment. Gods in the *Georgics* tend to make brief appearances: an oak may be called an oak of Jupiter (3.333); literary favour is succinctly requested from the Muses (4.315, 2.475). Individual deities also represent particular georgic topics, and thus enjoy topic-appropriate appearances: book 2 begins, with an exuberant shout, that now it is time to sing of Bacchus, signalling that this is the book on the cultivation of vines; a shift of topic to sheep and goats halfway through book 3 likewise prompts Virgil to state that now he must sing of Pales (3.294).[12] These topic-appropriate invocations also shade into treatments of the divine which are more overtly allegorical: thus savage Mars is let loose to rage throughout the world at the end of book 1 (1.511), whilst later we learn that close-packed soil is better for Ceres, and the lightest type of soil for Lyaeus (2.229). The brevity of references may also leave open whether a deity is present in an allegorical, or more personified, way: thus the phrase *Cereale papauer* ('poppy of Ceres') may be meant to conjure up a cornfield poppy, or remind us of the myth that Ceres took comfort in the poppy when grieving for Proserpina; or, of course, both (1.212). In a similar way, Jupiter takes on 'weather roles' which we might describe as, to varying degrees, 'more personal' or 'more allegorical'; he ranges from being responsible for the weather, to being the weather. Thus we watch Jupiter as impressive father figure hurl thunderbolts from the clouds (1.328–9), but not many lines later he is described as 'wet with south winds' (*uuidus Austris*, 1.418), taking on himself some qualities of the weather. And on another occasion Jupiter is strikingly described as *metuendus* ('to be feared') by mature grapes, in a move which has him fully stand in for the rain (2.419).

Such allegorical colouring of deities in the *Georgics* is one way in which the poem dwells on a potential overlap between the divine and the natural worlds, but only one. For the *Georgics* display a varied and deep-seated interest in how the natural world might communicate the divine to a human audience, and itself be influenced and shaped by the divine. A whole host of portents on the death of Julius Caesar provide one extreme example of divine powers expressing themselves through the natural world: Etna kept erupting, there were earthquakes in the Alps, flocks started talking and rivers stopped flowing (1.469–88). Virgil's interest in the predictive power of the natural world can also be felt when he takes pains to explain that rooks, whilst appearing to be able to predict forthcoming sunny periods with joyous cries, do not have knowledge of fate, nor do they have *diuinitus . . . ingenium* ('wisdom from above'); rather it is the change in atmosphere which rouses different movements in their chests (1.410–23). Other reflections on relationships of causation and influence between the divine and natural worlds are much less dramatic than these, and occur frequently enough that they become part of the texture and tone of the poem. Thus, whilst listing the oak as an example of a tree which springs up naturally from fallen seed, Virgil alludes to the well-known relationship between Jupiter and oaks by briefly, and imaginatively, painting this oak as going to extra special efforts with its foliage for Jupiter (2.15–16). His famous section on the nature of bees, and the functioning of their miniature society, is also prefaced by a brief mythological digression which presents Jupiter almost as author of this particular form of insect life: now it is time to explain the 'qualities' (*naturae*) which Jupiter has given to bees, in thanks for their feeding him whilst an infant hidden in a cave on Mount Dicte (4.149–52). The incredible behaviour of these bees also prompts further reflection from Virgil on their relationship with the divine as he notes – without himself committing on the matter – that some people believe bees to have a share of 'divine intelligence' (*diuina mens*) and enjoy 'drinks of aether' (*haustus aetherios*, 4.219–21).[13] In addition, Virgil's penchant for depicting 'Golden-Age-style' environments – the gulf between contemporary agriculture and Golden-Age spontaneous abundance is an ever-present undercurrent in the poem – extends this interest in ways in which the divine influences the natural environment and the place of humans within it (1.121–4, 2.490–4). Finally, on a rather different note, the *Georgics* is also interested in forging a path towards ruler cult. Here we see attempts to establish ways of talking about Augustus's divine status, just as Augustus himself 'attempts' (*adfectat*) a 'way' (*uia*) to Olympus (4.562); a sycophantic agnosticism colours the most intense and extended of these attempts, as Virgil wonders whether Augustus will choose to be a god of the sea or take on life as a new star (1.24–35).[14] By necessity brief, this discussion of the religious thinking of the *Georgics* has nevertheless established a major interest in the ways in which the divine and natural worlds intersect, and an additional interest in the divine status of Augustus.

And if ever you need a reminder that the *Georgics* is a religious poem, Servius is a good place to start, as he persistently brings its religious aspects to the fore. Indeed, Servius's intense interest in religious matters has prompted Horsfall to observe that he was 'more interested than the poet himself in religious detail': the *Georgics* become more religious in Servius's hands.[15] But before exploring how Servius reads religion in the *Georgics*, I pose a broader question. How does Servius read the *Georgics*? Or, what kind of a text is this in his eyes? Servius gives us no easy answers here, because his commentary does not put forward a 'take' on Virgil's *Georgics*: he reads the poem, but does not offer a reading of it.[16] For Servius is far more engaged with Virgil as an *author* (with all the resonances of the Latin word intended) than he is with the *Georgics* as a text. As many have pointed out before, Servius is driven by an intense concern (shared with other grammarians) to defend Virgil's authority and preserve him from error: 'Servius presupposes . . . Virgil's infallibility'.[17] Consequently, he focuses to such a degree on author over text that he can come across as insensitive even to the simple fact that the *Georgics* is a *poem*. We find him complaining, to give but one example, that the phrase *sidera caeli* ('stars of the sky', *G.* 2.1) is pleonasm, adding with didactic condescension that 'stars can be nowhere other than in the sky'; such a pedantic approach, to borrow Thomas's eloquent phrase, 'flattens out the poem'.[18]

That this is a *georgic* poem also feels largely irrelevant to Servius. Occasionally Servius comments approvingly on, or comes to the defence of, Virgil's agricultural know-how, but no more often than he does to defend him on other matters (with approving comments on his religious expertise outweighing those on agricultural matters).[19] Virgil has *not* made a mistake in referring to the fibres of the endive, and in fact shows himself to be *au fait* with the terms used by genuine country bumpkins (*G.* 1.120); Virgil steers a sensible middle ground between the opinions of Cato and Catullus on the Raetican grape (*G.* 2.95); Virgil has *not* made a mistake in claiming that only India produces black ebony (*G.* 2.116). References to Pliny the Elder may be intended to reinforce an image of Virgil's knowledge and competence, if oddly executed: Virgil's seemingly innocuous reference to the savage offspring of lions is, for example, expanded by turning to Pliny's discussion of lions who are unable to give birth, due to internal trauma caused by their offspring's claws (*G.* 2.151).[20] Yet, as Hackemann argues, Servius has missed many other opportunities to paint Virgil as an agriculturalist par excellence by means of cross references to other authorities, such as Aristotle, Theophrastus or Columella. The reason for which, Hackemann argues, is simple: Servius 'exhibits little or no interest' in such technical writing and 'shunned the specialist writers whom Vergil himself had read and imitated'.[21] And *occasional* attempts by Servius to amplify Virgil with his own specialist-sounding observations are not enough to counter the impression of a reader of the *Georgics* who is largely disengaged with its georgic content matter.[22] Nor does he expect his audience to be otherwise. That Servius is writing for school students, and not for an audience drawn to the *Georgics* out of interest in its subject matter, is nicely illustrated by his clarification that *alnos* (alder) is a 'type of tree' (*G.* 1.136).

In fact, the closest Servius gets to a reading of the *Georgics* as a whole is in his comment on the first line of the poem. Here he emphasizes that, of Virgil's three works, the *Georgics* most breaks away from its literary model, namely Hesiod's *Works and Days*. For Servius, Virgil's innovation lies in his rewriting of Hesiod as a four-book work, which gives him the opportunity to show off his skills 'in expanding narrower themes' (*angustiora dilatando*), as opposed to the contraction job which he did on Homer and Theocritus in the *Aeneid* and the *Eclogues* respectively (*G.* 1.1).[23] The bees are later set up as a prominent example of how Virgil makes 'much' (*magna*) out of 'minor topics' (*minoribus rebus*, *G.* 4.1). If Servius offers us a 'reading' of the *Georgics*, then, it is that the poem is an excellent example of literary amplification. As such, Servius's response to the *Georgics* is not dissimilar to Columella's, as painted by Myers in this volume – namely that Columella is drawn to a 'more is more' quality to Virgil's poem (pp. 134–5, 137). This appreciation of Virgil's poem rather ironically sets the tone for a commentary in which – as I will further argue – Servius often uses the text as a springboard for showcasing his own learning by means of expansive comments, whilst revealing himself to be rather distant from the priorities of the text itself.

This I now aim to prove by exploring how Servius reads religion in the *Georgics*, beginning by asking: how much do Virgil and Servius's religious thinking overlap? Servius's notes do show interest in an imperial cult, roughly reflecting the amount of space Virgil devotes to the debated issue of Augustus's divine status (see, for example, *G.* 1.24–34 and 3.16–27). By contrast, interest in the relationship between the divine and natural worlds is minimal. Outside of allegorical explanations of Virgil's use of some divine names – of Neptune, for example, Servius explains 'he used "the god" for "water"' (*deum pro aquis posuit*, *G.* 4.29) – at best we can point to a note which sets out two different reasons for the myrtle being consecrated to Venus (*G.* 2.64): either because this tree rejoices in shores, and Venus is said to have been born from the sea; or because, as medical authors tell us, this tree is useful for many female 'ailments' (*necessitates*). It is interesting, however, that Servius's excursus is in no way prompted by Virgil's text: Virgil mentions the 'myrtle of Venus' (*Paphiae . . . myrtus*) in the context of a recommendation to graft myrtle onto oak; the question of its relationship with Venus is not his priority here.

Given this disjunct between Virgil's religious interests and Servius's comments, a second question naturally follows (especially when we remember Horsfall's observation about Servius's fixation with religion in his *Georgics* commentary). What *does* loom large in religious terms for Servius, when he reads the *Georgics*? Unsurprisingly, a number one priority is to defend Virgil against any suggestion of error in religious matters. In the note on 1.344, for example, he brands those who say that Virgil spoke 'against religion' (*contra religionem*) in having Ceres sacrificed to with wine as 'unnecessarily picky' (*superfluum*), for in fact the pontifical books do not forbid this. Again, there is precious little in Virgil's text which could be seen to prompt this note, but Servius's response is rooted not in the original Virgilian line, but in a particular aspect of the afterlife of the text, namely a lively tradition of critics and defenders of Virgil's religious expertise. (Servius places himself firmly in the camp which made Virgil such a consummate expert in pontifical law that he is labelled a quasi *pontifex maximus* in Macrobius's *Saturnalia* 1.24.16.)[24] It is ironic, then, that whilst presenting himself as a champion of Virgil's religious thinking, Servius ends up straying far from Virgil's own religious priorities in the *Georgics*.

Another favoured kind of note for Servius is the detailed recounting of myths in response to Virgilian lines, which can at best be said to have alluded to those myths. Here I give but one example. In the grand invocation which opens book 1, we find Virgil invoking Silvanus (1.20), alongside several others whom he is calling to the aid of his poetic task: Silvanus is said to be carrying an uprooted cypress, an act of seeming arboreal violence we might find surprising for this god called Woody. But those who expect Servius to make sense of this for his audience of schoolboys will find his note *ad loc.* a disappointment.[25] Silvanus, he tells us, used to love a boy called Cyparissus, but the affair ended in tragedy: for one day Silvanus killed Cyparissus's pet stag by mistake and the boy died from grief. Also grief stricken, Silvanus had him turned into a cypress, which he now carries around with him. Servius's explanation arguably only enhances the oddity of Virgil's image of Silvanus and his portable cypress, taking this into the realm of the disturbingly surreal. Indeed, Servius's amplificatory tendency when it comes to myth rarely seems to be sensitive to the content and context of Virgil's original line; rather the simple mention of Silvanus prompts in him a kind of reflex instinct to advertise his mythological expertise.

Besides this mythologizing reflex, throughout the Servian commentary there also runs a persistent interest in the nature of the gods. The banality of some of these comments is a salutary reminder that this was a text designed to help children get through their Virgil: of Silvanus, for example, Servius helpfully observes, 'he is a god of woods' (*deus est silvarum*, *G.* 1.20). On other occasions, explanations of the nature of various deities is less run-of-the-mill. At *G.* 1.315 a simple reference to milky grain reminds Servius that Varro mentions a god called Lactans ('Milky') who pours himself into crops. A dating reference to the cold star of Saturn also leads to the striking observation that Saturn is the god of rain, for which reason he is imagined as an old man, because we know that old men are always icy cold (*G*. 1.336). A particularly strong vein within Servius's wide interest in the nature of the gods is a concern with the meaning of divine names. Etymologizing notes are common here – Faunus is so called from *fando* ('speaking', *G*. 1.10) – but he is also interested in alternative divine names: thus an invocation to Pales at the beginning of the third book leads Servius, without prompt from the Virgilian text, to observe that some want her to be known as Vesta, some Mater Deum (*G*. 3.1). On another occasion when Virgil actually does invoke Vesta, Servius observes that Virgil is here speaking 'poetically' (*poetice*), because it is prohibited by sacred law to know the true name of the *numen* who protects Rome (*G*. 1.498). It is hard to see why Virgil's depiction of Vesta having oversight of Rome really needed explaining away in this fashion; once again it seems that Servius's own interests, here in divine names, override the content and purposes of the Virgilian text. Moreover, Servius's instinct to call Vesta a *numen* introduces another Servian obsession: whilst *numen* occurs in the *Georgics* a mere five times, it is omnipresent in Servius's commentary. *Numen* is a slippery word – and one whose multivalency gets overlooked by a current scholarly tendency to translate it as 'spirit' or 'power' – but for Servius this favoured word takes on a handful of meanings.[26] It can be used as an apparent synonym for *deus* ('god'; e.g. *G*. 1.344, where *numina* is used of Liber and Ceres), and of other 'divine figures' whom we might be tempted to put somewhere on a spectrum between god and mortal, such as Glaucus; Servius calls him a 'marine *numen*' (*numen marinum*, 1.437). It is also used to capture the qualities of particular deities: the *numen* of Neptune, for example, is 'swift' (*uelox*) and 'on the move' (*mobile*).

Servius's penchant for *numina* also comes to the fore in his note at *G*. 1.21, on which I now focus attention. Virgil, drawing to a close a grand invocation of deities whom he wants to favour his poem, calls upon 'all gods and goddesses whose interest is the protection of fields' (*dique deaeque omnes studium quibus arua tueri*, 1.21). Predictably enough, given his predilection for amplifying Virgil's text, Servius cannot resist providing the names of these gods (or in his terms, *numina*); these, he claims, are to be found in the pontifical books. I print the text below, with my own translation (*G*. 1.21):

DIQUE DEAEQUE OMNES post specialem inuocationem transit ad generalitatem, ne quod numen praetereat, *more pontificum, (per) quos ritu ueteri in omnibus sacris post speciales deos, quos ad ipsum sacrum, quod fiebat, necesse erat inuocari, generaliter omnia numina inuocabantur.* quod autem dicit 'studium quibus arua tueri', nomina haec numinum in indigitamentis inueniuntur, id est in libris pontificalibus, qui et nomina deorum et rationes ipsorum nominum continent, quae etiam Varro dicit. nam, ut supra diximus, nomina numinibus ex officiis constat inposita, uerbi causa ut ab occatione deus Occator dicatur, a sarritione Sarritor, a stercoratione Sterculinius, a satione Sator. *Fabius Pictor hos deos enumerat, quos inuocat flamen sacrum Cereale faciens Telluri et Cereri: Veruactorem, Reparatorem, Inporcitorem, Insitorem, Obaratorem, Occatorem, Sarritorem, Subruncinatorem, Messorem, Conuectorem, Conditorem, Promitorem.*

ALL GODS AND GODDESSES. He moves from a specific invocation to a general one, so that he doesn't miss out any *numen*, in the manner of the *pontifices*, who, in the old-fashioned manner, in all sacrifices made a general invocation of all *numina*, after the specific gods, whom it was necessary to call to the sacrifice which was taking place. As to him saying 'those whose interest is the care of fields', the names of these *numina* are found in the *indigitamenta*, that is in the pontifical books, which contain both the names of the gods and the reasons for those names, as Varro also tells us. For, as I explained above, it is well known that names are imposed on *numina* from their functions, with the result that the god Occator is so-called because of the word, from *occatio*, Sarritor from *sarritio*, Sterculinius from *stercoratio*, Sator from *satio*. Fabius Pictor lists these gods, whom the *flamen Cerealis* invokes when sacrificing to Tellus and Ceres: Vervactor, Reparator, Inporcitor, Insitor, Obarator, Occator, Sarritor, Subruncinator, Messor, Convector, Conditor, Promitor.

With a reminder that *nomina* ('names') are given to *numina* 'from their functions' (*ex officiis*), Servius mentions four deities who exemplify this statement: Occator, so called from *occatio* ('harrowing'); Sarritor from *sarritio* ('hoeing'); Sterculinius from *stercoratio* ('manuring'); and Sator from *satio* ('planting'). By juxtaposing *numina* and *nomina*, Servius visually reinforces his point that the names and characters of these deities are intimately connected, indeed interdependent. An additional line from Servius Auctus then provides a more comprehensive list of twelve similar-sounding deities, including Vervactor ('First Plougher'), Subruncinator ('Weeder') and Messor ('Harvester'), with the third-century BCE scholar Fabius Pictor cited as the source of this information.[27]

What does Servius – and here I use 'Servius' as the shorthand I outlined earlier – gain from this note? Servius begins his note by explaining that Virgil uses a general, all-encompassing invocation ('*all* gods and goddesses who care for fields') in order not to ignore any *numen* by mistake. In this context, it is hard not to suspect that Servius's note has a tone of academic one-upmanship to it, showing that he knows in intimate detail who these *numina* are, and going beyond Virgil in diligence by listing them. Nor is it only Virgil whom it seems Servius is angling to upstage here. Varro is a very strong presence at this early point in Virgil's text: famously beginning his *De Re Rustica* with an invocation of twelve agriculturally minded deities, Varro provides a model for Virgil's own opening invocation of twelve gods, with Caesar making his impact as the 'surprise' thirteenth. In adding his own twelve-god list of agricultural deities into the mix, Servius invites us to put him, and his antiquarian expertise, on a par with that of Varro.[28] Little in Virgil's line *dique deaeque omnes studium quibus arua tueri* would prompt the reader to start thinking about specific agricultural tasks such as weeding and harvesting, but Servius's note manages to make this line a launch pad for a display of his expertise in divine names and antiquarian knowledge of little-known gods.

Indeed, throughout this sketch of the religious interests which loom large in Servius's commentary on the *Georgics* we have seen how Servius's observations can feel extremely distant from the content and priorities of Virgil's text. Servius imposes on the text very much his own interests and agenda. Nor am I the only one to feel the idiosyncrasies of Servius: for Kaster we see in Servius 'an individual and often decidedly quirky turn of mind' at work, whilst Cameron insists that Servian mythological notes are 'peculiar'.[29] This kind of vocabulary, as well as the glaring gap I have identified between Virgil's text and the comments it prompts from Servius, should make us deeply wary of using Servius as some kind of 'sourcebook' which can illuminate our understanding of Roman religion in Virgil's day, or indeed other periods of Roman history. Yet no such wariness has made itself felt in modern scholarship on Roman religion. Rather, to the contrary, we have developed a tendency not only to pillage Servius's commentaries for nuggets of religious information, but also to frame Roman religion through Servian-centric eyes.[30] This I will now illustrate by examining the use five scholars have made of the note on *G.* 1.21.

Gods were presumed as and when the need for them arose, but the multiplication of functional deities could be carried to ridiculous and quite unreal lengths, especially by professional priests with an urge for systematisation and a liking for lists. Fabius Pictor, historian of the late third century B.C., recorded a list of the gods that the *flamen* of Ceres invoked when he performed a sacrifice to Earth and Ceres: 'First Plougher, Second Plougher, Harrower, Sower, Top-dressor, Hoer, Raker, Harvester, Gatherer, Storer, Distributor (Vervactor, Reparator, Imporcitor, Insitor, Obarator, Occator, Sarritor, Subruncinator, Messor, Convector, Conditor, Promitor: Servius, *On the Georgics of Virgil* I, 21).

Ogilvie 1969:12

Roman religion had a rare proliferation of spirits or *numina*. German scholars called them Sondergötter, or, more picturesquely, Augenblickgötter, gods of the twinkling of an eye. They are powers, involved in or presiding over a limited but necessary operation, and having no existence apart from that operation ... For the agricultural *numina*, Fabius Pictor tells us that the *flamen*, in sacrificing to Tellus and Ceres, invoked the following powers: Vervactor for the first ploughing, Redarator for the second, Imporcitor for the harrowing, Insitor for the sowing, Obarator for the top-dressing, Occator, Sarritor, Subrincator, Messor, Convector, Conditor, Promitor for the later operations. We can add to the list Spiniensis for uprooting thorn-bushes, Sterculius for manuring, Puta for pruning, Nodutus for grain-stalks, Mellonia for bees.

Ferguson 1970: 68–9

Roman religion was especially rich in agrarian spirits ... The fourth-century AD grammarian Servius, in his commentary on Virgil's Georgics, preserves (on 1.21) a plausibly authentic list of a dozen such spirits from the early third-century BC annalist Fabius Pictor; it includes Vervactor (first ploughing), and Promitor (corn distribution).

Phillips 1997: 132

The Roman sense of operational realism made use of the *indigitamenta*; one therefore had to pray to Sterculinius for animal manure, Vervactor for turning over fallow land, Redarator for the second ploughing, Imporcitor for the third, Obarator for a new turning of the soil, Occator for harrowing, Sarritor for weeding, Seia for the germination of seed, Segetia for the corn to grow, Nodutus for the stem to have nodes, Volutina for the sheath of the corn-ear, Patellana for it to open, Hostilina for the corn to be of the same height (to make harvesting easier), Lacturnus for the ears to be milky, Runcina for killing the weeds, Matuta for the ripening, Messia for the harvesting, Convector for the loading, Noduterensis for threshing, Condito for garnering, even Promitor for taking the grain from the granary, but chiefly Tutilina for preserving it (Aug., CG., 4.8; Serv., G 1.21). Even this list is by no means exhaustive.

Turcan 2000: 38

Prayers containing unusually detailed lists of gods survive for some rituals. The best example is provided by the Fabius Pictor whom I mentioned earlier, the writer on pontifical law; the passage happens to be quoted by Servius, the late-antique commentator on Vergil. During the *sacrum cereale*, a ritual held on December 13th each year for the goddesses Tellus (Earth) and Ceres, who was especially concerned with grain-farming (her gifts are *cerealia*, cereals, as in corn-flakes), the priest who conducted the ritual (the *flamen Cerealis*) invoked the following twelve divinities: Vervactor, Redarator, Inporcitor, Insitor, Obarator, Occator, Sarritor, Subruncinator, Messor, Convector, Conditor, Promitor. In translation the names mean: First Spring-Plougher, Second-Plougher, Ridge-Maker, Broadcaster, Seed-Coverer (or Clod-Smasher), Harrower, Manual Hoer, Manual Weed-Root-Remover, Reaper, Grain-Transporter, Granary Protector, Bringer-Forth for Use. This sounds like a pretty thorough list of grain-farming procedures but it could have been much longer . . .

Rüpke 2007: 78–9

Servius's penchant for lists and amplificatory detail has definitely rubbed off on these scholars, who seem to find the most effective way to engage with his note is to repeat, and amplify, his list of gods. Just as Servius's list works, on one level, to upstage Virgil's list, so these scholars try to better Servius's. Not content with citing the whole list given in Servius Auctus, Turcan interpolates other deities mentioned by Augustine (as though introducing details from a polemical mockery of such gods were unproblematic!), before concluding that even this list is not exhaustive. Ferguson too wants to add to Servius Auctus's list, with Spiniensis, Sterculius, Puta, Nodutus and Mellonia; unlike Turcan, he does not even acknowledge that we only know of the existence of these deities, bar Sterculius, thanks to Augustine and Arnobius.[31] For Rüpke too, this list, whilst 'pretty thorough', could have been longer. A strong impression emerges that being able to list as many obscure divine names as possible is how we are fully to understand Roman religion, a way of thinking immediately recognizable from Servius. Indeed, aping Servius in this particular context prompts scholars to slip into a Servian mindset when it comes to characterizing Roman religion more generally: thus Ogilvie imposes on Roman priests 'an urge for systematisation and a liking for lists', which does indeed come across strongly in Servius's commentary; Rüpke's Roman priests also share an unusually strong liking for lists.

I have referred above to Servius Auctus's list, but in fact several of these scholars treat the list not as Servian, but as unproblematically that of Fabius Pictor. Servius's role in preserving the list goes largely unnoticed and it is treated independently of its textual context; Ferguson, for example, adds Sterculius to (what he calls) Pictor's list, apparently oblivious to the fact that Servius had already mentioned his close counterpart Sterculinius earlier in the note. Rüpke, by contrast, does note that Pictor's list 'happens to be' preserved in Servius, but does not stop to question *why* this list might end up in Servius. Yet from our brief look at Servius's obsession with divine names we might think the inclusion is hardly surprising. Rüpke, who is hardly alone in this, does not think about the note on 1.21 in the wider context of the Servian commentary; rather the assumption at work seems to be that it is simply good fortune that our disinterested commentator picked out this factual jewel from Pictor to preserve for posterity. And it is surely the allure of a passage from the early Pictor which has helped to make this passage so irresistible to scholars of Roman religion, the unacknowledged implication being that a source as early as Pictor must give us an insight into 'bona fide' Roman religion.[32] Pictor may be early, but nobody chooses to acknowledge that this list attributed to him is only present in Servius Auctus, namely a text dated to the seventh century CE; and so nobody worries – or at least not openly – that the quotation from the third-century BCE Pictor does not turn up in our surviving sources for approximately a thousand years. Nor is anyone openly worried that Pictor, who wrote in Greek, is here quoted in Latin, suggesting at least one basic level of interference with any 'original' text we might want to attribute to Pictor.

Servius's presentation of these gods as *numina* also strongly influences scholarly enthusiasm for this passage, as well as colouring the way these scholars approach them: that is, they are treated not so much as gods, but as spirits or powers. This way of thinking is overt in Ferguson's introduction to this Servian passage – 'Roman religion had a rare proliferation of spirits or *numina*' – and also in Phillips's idea of 'agrarian spirits'. In so doing, they are not in fact taking their cue from Servius, who gives no indication in this passage that he views *numina* and *dei* as substantially different phenomena: indeed, Servius uses *deus* ('god') of Occator, whilst Pictor is also made to call Vervactor and friends *dei* ('gods'). Rather they are responding to an engrained scholarly tendency to understand *numina* as spirits or powers, thanks to a long history of thinking about this particular term which stretches back to the nineteenth century. Nor is this passage of Servius likely to prompt scholars to reassess this way of thinking: in fact, as I will now argue, it had a great deal of influence in creating this particular pattern of thought.

Roman religion emerged as a discipline in its own right towards the end of the nineteenth century, and grew out of scholarship on comparative religion, for which a major aim was the discovering of the earliest strata of religious experience. These early religious experiences, the orthodox position insisted, were made up of animistic responses to the natural world, or in other words the perception of spirits in your natural surroundings. This was an orthodoxy taken to heart by the first scholars of Roman religion, who held up the word *numen* as quintessential proof that early Roman religion was also primitive and deeply animistic.[33] In addition, gods like Occator and Vervactor – made famous in Usener's *Götternamen* of 1896, and known as Sondergötter (specialist deities) or Augenblicksgötter (blink of the eye deities) – were valued as evidence of a crucial first stage of development by which Roman thinkers managed to emerge from an animistic stage of thought towards an anthropomorphic and polytheistic system; and Servius's list provided the classic examples.[34] As I have argued elsewhere, this early animistic scholarship still has an influence on the way we think about Roman religion, especially religious responses to the natural world.[35] And Servius's note on G. 1.21 has been so attractive, I argue here, because of the way it seems to confirm long cherished narratives about the nature and development of early Roman religion: the combined emphasis on *numina*, specialist gods named after nature-focused 'functions' (*officia*) and the testimony of the early Pictor makes this passage too good to ignore. Yet the thinking here is disturbingly circular, for Servius is being used to give a stamp of approval to scholarly narratives about early Roman religion, without anyone questioning how reliant the scholars who first crafted those narratives were on Servius. Certainly we would not know about Subruncinator and co. if it were not for this Servian passage! Or to put it another way, nobody stops to question whether the focus of G. 1.21 – with its emphasis on *numina* and lists of obscure divine names – tells us more about Servius and his intellectual interests and priorities than it does about anything else. In taking this passage so much to heart, scholars of Roman religion have unwittingly become Servian-minded readers of Roman religion.

This chapter has focused attention on one purple passage from Servius's commentary on the *Georgics*, but there are many more beloved of scholars of Roman religion, be it his note on the consecration of oaks to Jupiter (G. 3.332) or the secret name of Rome (G. 1.498): and this is to pick passages from the *Georgics* commentary alone. The moral of our focused engagement with G. 1.21 is that, if we want to use Servius to inform our thinking about Roman religion, we cannot assume either that he gives us a fleshed-out version of Virgil's religious thinking, or that he offers a useful sourcebook of information with which to supplement our understanding of Roman religion in the centuries prior to Servius. Instead, we need to explore the priorities and intellectual obsessions which Servius brings to his reading of Virgil's text, to be aware of the pet topics and approaches we can expect from this idiosyncratic scholar. In addition, we need to be alert to ways in which our own constructions of Roman religion may already have been shaped by Servian thinking. And crucially, if we want to use Servius's commentaries in a sensitive and productive way, we need – dispiriting as it may be – to read them cover to cover.

PART V
MODERN RESPONSES

CHAPTER 11
THE *GEORGICS* OFF THE CANADIAN COAST: MARC LESCARBOT'S *A-DIEU À LA NOUVELLE-FRANCE* (1609) AND THE VIRGILIAN TRADITION

William M. Barton

Introduction

Among the myriad responses to Virgil's *Georgics* in the early modern period, the name of French lawyer and humanist Marc Lescarbot (*c.* 1570–1641) is seldom, if ever, mentioned. Lescarbot is perhaps best known for his *Histoire de la Nouvelle-France*, first published in 1609. The work offers a history of early French exploration of the Americas alongside an account of Lescarbot's experiences of colonial life at the French settlement of Port-Royal (present-day Annapolis Royal, Nova Scotia, Canada). But the volume also contains a collection of Lescarbot's poetry under the title *Les Muses de la Nouvelle-France*. By the time of the work's final edition in 1617, *Les Muses* contained nearly 2,000 verses and included North America's first theatrical production, the *Théâtre de Neptune*, as well as an *A-dieu à la Nouvelle-France*, a poem of 428 verses which provides a unique perspective on the reception of the georgic tradition in early modern literature.[1]

Despite the apparent popularity of *Les Muses* among its seventeenth-century readership – on top of its three editions, the collection saw two further reprints together with *L'Histoire* and one individual reprint in 1618 – scholarship on Lescarbot's poetry has not been as receptive: René Baudry, biographer and early editor of Lescarbot's work, labelled the poems 'maladroits et forgés à la hâte, [les poèmes] obéissent au mauvais goût de l'époque et n'ajoutent rien à sa gloire' ('clumsy and composed in haste, [the poems] follow the bad taste of the period and contribute nothing to its reputation').[2] With a new critical edition of Lescarbot's poetry on New France in 2014, however, appreciation of *Les Muses* both as literature and as an important record for the early history of Canada has been steadily growing.[3]

This intensification of interest in Lescarbot's verse has led to an increasing number of questions over the character of his poetry and its models. Philip Usher indicated the complexity of this issue in his summary of *Les Muses* as 'un métissage de la culture antique (y compris ses grands genres, l'épopée mais aussi la tragédie) et de la réalité historique du Nouveau Monde' ('a crossbreed of ancient culture (including its important genres, epic but also tragedy) and the historical reality of the New World').[4] The two most detailed overviews of the poetic forms and traditions at work in Lescarbot's oeuvre echo these views, to the effect that *Les Muses* draws heavily on the classical tradition while blending in contemporary history and features from vernacular (French) literature.[5] One group of Lescarbot's poems has, however, thus far eluded a satisfactory analysis of its influences and inspiration: as Pioffet and Lachance put it in the introduction to their edition, 'le ton des "A-dieux" de Marc Lescarbot est quelque peu différent' ('the tone of Lescarbot's *A-dieux* is somewhat different').[6]

The three *A-dieu* poems are the *A-dieu à la France*, penned on departing from the port of La Rochelle in 1606, the *A-dieu aux François retournans de la Nouvelle-France en la France Gaulloise*, written at Port-Royal on the departure of a group of colonists, and – the poem under particular study in this chapter – the *A-dieu à la Nouvelle-France*, written at sea during Lescarbot's return to France.[7] The superficial relationship of these poems to the vernacular tradition of 'Farewell' poems (related, but not identical to classical literature's *propemptika*) has been highlighted in recent studies,[8] but Westra's summary of the aims and influences of the *A-dieu à la Nouvelle-France* in the introduction to his translation underlines the poem's bewildering polyvalence:

> The poem represents a final, almost desperate attempt to 'sell' Port-Royal to his fellow Frenchmen by appealing at one and the same time to their financial, patriotic, imperial, as well as esthetic, moral and religious instincts enhanced by the affective quality of his poetry and carried by the poetic licence of hyperbole in a variety of voices: from lament to praise and from prayer to adhortation … In terms of genre we can add polemic, commercial prospectus, natural history and ethnography to the epic and idyllic elements already mentioned.[9]

In response to this debate, this study of Lescarbot's *A-dieu à la Nouvelle-France* will gather the evidence to show that the poem also constitutes a powerful and innovative instance of the early modern reception of Virgil's *Georgics* and its later tradition. This re-evaluation of the literary background of the *A-dieu* allows us to better understand the poem as a whole and to better appreciate passages unfairly judged by current criticism as 'longues et fréquentes digressions descriptives'.[10] After an overview of the reception of the *Georgics* in early modern France intended to place the *A-dieu* within contemporary understandings of Virgil's agricultural didactic, this chapter will offer a closer look at Lescarbot's engagement with the *Georgics* to negotiate the socio-political challenges presented by European colonization attempts in the New World. In amending our perspective on the passages in the *A-dieu* that modern critics have considered less successful, we thus uncover the appeal of Lescarbot's verses to a contemporary, early modern readership, whilst gaining a fresh perspective on the reception of the *Georgics* and its poetic landscape in the early modern period.

Renaissance and early modern reading and reception of the *Georgics*

In comparison to the popularity of the *Eclogues* and the *Aeneid*, the *Georgics* was the least often studied and imitated of Virgil's three main works in the Renaissance and early modern period.[11] In France the first translation of the *Georgics* (1519) lagged behind the first printed *Eclogues* by three years and the first French translation of the *Aeneid* by a decade.[12] Even at a time when the *Georgics*' stocks were low against those of the *Aeneid*, however, numerous influential figures, including Pierre de Ronsard, Michel de Montaigne and Joachim Du Bellay, read, cited and imitated the poem frequently and at length.[13] In this brief and necessarily superficial overview of early modern responses to the *Georgics* in France, questions of theory will first be approached, followed by the prominent Neo-Latin tradition and finally by examples of vernacular georgic writing.

Broadly considered, the *Georgics* were understood according to two models in early modern literary discussion: on the one hand the *Georgics* were Virgil's 'middle' poem, corresponding to a moderate style of poetry between the *Eclogues*' lowly playfulness and the high, powerful style of the *Aeneid*. The ordering of Virgil's poetry in this way along with the tradition of the *rota Virgilii* goes back to Donatus's *Vita* (58–60) and Virgil's epitaph, which it recorded (36).[14] On the other hand, the *Georgics* were placed alongside the works of Hesiod, Aratus and Lucretius *inter alia*, in the tradition of didactic poetry, a hotly debated issue after the 'rediscovery' of Aristotle's *Poetics* at the beginning of the sixteenth century.[15] The fact that neither of these classifications, however, nor the interplay between them, was by any means straightforward perhaps contributed to the slower uptake of the *Georgics* in France during the period: Ronsard, for example, could appear to leave out the *Georgics* from the poetic curriculum in mentioning only bucolic and epic poetry when he recounted Virgil's career by way of praise for his colleague Jean de Boyssières.[16] And Denys Lambin could write in the dedicatory letter to his edition of Lucretius that didactic poetry belonged to the genre of epic poetry on account of the two forms' shared metre, formal characteristics and their treatment of 'the hidden causes of things and those enveloped by nature',[17] thus complicating the classic tripartite system of styles. As for the debate sparked by Aristotle's exclusion of didactic from classification as poetry in his *Poetics* (1447b), France entered the conversation – begun in Italy after the text's *editio princeps* in 1508 – largely by way of Julius Caesar Scaliger's *Poetices libri VII*.[18] The 'limited Aristotelianism' proposed by Scaliger permitted the sort of artful didactic in early Neo-Latin imitations of the *Georgics*, such as Pontano's *De hortis Hesperidum*, but excluded dry didactic expositions of theory.[19] For the diverse positions of France's contemporary theorists we can look to the *Deffence et Illustration de la langue francoyse* (1549), in which Joachim Du Bellay had seemed not to mention didactic or georgic poetry in his list of favoured forms he proposed for the 'futur poëte'.[20] While in Vauquelin's *Art Poëtique* (1605), a number of France's sixteenth-century poets (explicitly Jan de Baïf and Scévole de Saintemarthe) are celebrated as part of the georgic tradition after Hesiod and Virgil.[21] Despite the vexed questions over the status of the *Georgics*, Virgil's status as the 'prince of poets' – or simply the typical discrepancy between literary theory and practice! – did, nonetheless, lead to a rich tradition of engagement with his didactic work.

While Italy emerged as a hotspot for didactic poetry at the beginning of the sixteenth century with the sort of playful 'recreational georgic' typified in Pontano's *De hortis Hesperidum*, France began to dominate the scene from seventeenth century onwards.[22] At the same time, Jesuits began to engage intensively with didactic poetry and eventually came to dominate the genre. The 'father of Jesuit georgic poetry', René Rapin (1621–87) published his *Hortorum libri IV* in 1665.[23] Rapin's prominence in the early Jesuit reception of the *Georgics*, as well as his work's wide and lasting influence,[24] make his *Hortorum libri IV* a convenient guide for this brief glance at Neo-Latin georgic production: like Pontano before him, Rapin takes his departure from Virgil's garden *praeteritio* in his *Georgics*. Rapin's ideal nature is also a cultivated one, and his poem depicts numerous Ovidian metamorphoses typical of his Renaissance predecessors.[25] Also similar to the earlier Italian reception of the *Georgics* is Rapin's 'modular' or 'episodic' engagement with Virgil's text, apparently separating out the *Georgics'* set pieces for individual imitation or emulation.[26] Thus, for example, the *laudes Italiae* (Verg. G. 2.136–76) become in the *Hortorum libri IV* the *laudes telluris Franciae* (1.474–506);[27] there is a *laus ruris* (Verg. G. 2.245–540; Rapin, *Hortorum libri IV*, 2.676–702) and the weather symbols scene (Verg. G. 1.351–92) is similarly imitated (Rapin, *Hortorum libri IV*, 1.156–90). But Rapin's georgic poetry also innovates in several important ways. First, in contrast to the private and 'miniaturized' version of nature offered to readers in Italian 'recreational' georgic, Rapin brings back the national and public scope of georgic poetry. France vies for supremacy with Virgil's Italy (*Hortorum libri IV*, 1.474–506) and her leaders play a prominent role in securing the prosperity of the nation in the wider context of Europe (*Hortorum libri IV*, 4.793–825). Moreover, in a second, related development, Rapin's poem intensifies the focus on the theme of the Virgilian tag *labor omnia uincit* – already part of humanistic tradition – which now becomes closely associated with France's leaders through mobilization of the *topos* of the labouring ruler (e.g. *Hortorum libri IV*, 1.14–28, 4.793–825) and emphasized, as Haskell has argued, by its connection to the Jesuit ideal of work-in-the-world.[28]

In contrast to the position of Seneca, Rapin believed that didactic poetry should aim to teach in a real sense.[29] Indeed, the Jesuit order produced didactic poetry on an incredibly wide variety of topics from fishing and the science of rainbows through to painting and the New World.[30] In this way, then, the Jesuit didactic, and particularly georgic poetry, captures the spirit in which Virgil's *Georgics* were read and received in the early modern period: Virgil's text was read for the variety of images and information that it offered.[31] In turn, Jesuit didactic expanded exhaustively the topics and individual phenomena sung. Virgil's poem was seen as a storehouse of valuable knowledge.[32] Similarly, early modern didactic celebrated and recorded both knowledge handed down by tradition and the new discoveries of its age. Moreover, in spite of the slow uptake of the *Georgics* among Virgil's oeuvre, the descriptive virtuosity of the work[33] made it increasingly popular, first among Renaissance scholars and connoisseurs, then later more generally.[34] Montaigne, to take a prominent French example, labelled the poem 'le plus accomply ouvrage de la poesie' ('the most accomplished work of poetry'),[35] while early imitator Poliziano (1454–94) praised the poet's resourcefulness in his treatment of the agricultural theme with such style in his *Rusticus* (1483).[36]

Back in France, the years around the establishment of the first Canadian trading companies (1580s) saw an increase in interest in literary engagement with Virgil's didactic, producing poetry with georgic themes, poems inspired directly by the *Georgics* and what might be considered more strictly georgic poetry, as well.[37] *Les Météores* of Jan de Baïf, Du Bellay's *Moretum* and Pybrac's *Les plaisirs de la vie rustique* serve as representative examples of each. To take another particularly well-known example – and an instance of the type of 'episodic' treatment of the *Georgics* highlighted above – Ronsard echoes Virgil's *laudes Italiae* over twenty times in his *Hymne de France*.[38] As Brazeau has shown, the French saw the colonization of New France as a chance to effect a renewal of 'Frenchness' in a 'twin' country, free of the corruption that had taken over in Europe.[39] Lescarbot himself decried 'la lacheté de nôtre siècle' ('the cowardice of our age') at home in France in the opening volume of the *Histoire*, and compared his countrymen unfavourably to other European nations abroad.[40] For many contemporaries like Lescarbot, then, this 'new' France was to be founded on the values of hard, virtuous (agricultural) labour in a land where benevolent nature could be harnessed to the benefit of mankind. Mixed with the colonial and political agenda of this colonization, poets would often find much inspiration for their treatments of these themes in the *Georgics* – just as did Marc Lescarbot.

Lescarbot's *A-dieu à la Nouvelle-France* and the *Georgics*

The text of both *L'Histoire* and *A-dieu* is accompanied, as often in early modern publications, by short notes in the margins. The large number of these notes which refer the reader to Classical literature throughout the volume – together with biblical verses and occasionally also contemporary works – attests to Lescarbot's wide reading, as well as his humanist education.[41] In *L'Histoire*, unsurprisingly, we find from Classical literature a preponderance of references to Pliny the Elder, alongside stories from Livy and allusions to Valerius Maximus, for example. But even in his prose work there are several references to poetry, including Virgil's *Georgics*. The notes alongside the poems in *Les Muses* by Lescarbot were reserved almost exclusively for directing the reader back to his treatments of various subjects in *L'Histoire*, apparently in order to clarify the novel subject matter for the audience. Even if Lescarbot did not mark out the moments in the poem where he was referring to the georgic tradition, a careful reading of the *A-dieu à la Nouvelle-France* does indeed reveal the profound influence of Virgil's didactic poem. For the sake of clarity, a brief overview of the poem is first provided below, before Lescarbot's engagements with the georgic tradition in the *A-dieu à la Nouvelle-France* are addressed in more detail.

The opening verses of the *A-dieu* (1–12) include four rhetorical questions that express Lescarbot's frustration at having to leave the colony. He accuses his compatriots of wasting the time and money invested in the settlement at Port-Royal. After a prayer for safe passage back to France (19–24), Lescarbot next moves into the descriptive and eulogistic mode that dominates the rest of the piece. He opens with an overview of Port-Royal and its surroundings (25–72). Next follows the first in a series of detailed passages dealing with the natural resources available in New France: there are the numerous types of fish and sea creatures (77–128), as well as land animals (141–57) and birds (158–228). The bird catalogue is introduced by an excursus on the duty of the French king to propagate the faith in the New World. Here Lescarbot again regrets the colonists' departure (159–80).

Next comes the praise of the fields, gardens and agricultural potential of *la Nouvelle-France* (239–92), which leads Lescarbot into his treatment of the native populations (293–346). After an interlude, where he paints a memorable image of the harbour at Port-Royal (347–57), Lescarbot moves into a short 'historical' section (358–84) in which the location of the earlier French colony on the Île-Saint-Croix is described, together with its losses. The final part of the poem sees Lescarbot praise Canada's further natural resources in shorter sections: her mineral wealth (385–94), her natural fertility again (395–411) and the hemp plant (412–22). The next six verses include Lescarbot's hope that the French return to New France (423–6), and his sign-off on the waves (427–8).

Four of these final six verses summarize one of the key Virgilian themes upon which Lescarbot draws frequently throughout the *A-dieu*. Lines 425–8 read in Lescarbot's Alexandrines:[42]

> Puisse-je voir bien-tot cette chose arriver,
> Et le François soigneux à tes champs cultiver,
> Arriere des soucis d'une peineuse vie,
> Loin des bruits commun, & de la piperie.[43]

> May I see that thing arrive soon,
> And careful Frenchmen cultivate your fields,
> Away from the cares of a life of hardship
> Far from the noise of the common crowd and from deceit.[44]

Besides a hint of Lescarbot's own personal history – he had decided to join the expedition to Port-Royal after an 'injustice' done to him at court in Paris[45] – the lines also contain a sentiment familiar from Virgil's so-called 'praise of the country life' (*G.* 2.458–540). Lescarbot's lines may even echo some of the images in this set piece, in which the earth, *procul discordibus armis, | fundit humo facilem uictum* ('far from the clash of arms, pours from her soil an easy living', 459–60) and offers *nescia fallere uita* ('a life innocent of deceit', 467). The passage finishes with a similar image (*G.* 2.538–40) of the Golden-Age life that Saturnus led on earth, *necdum etiam audierant inflari classica* ('while no-one had yet heard the war trumpets blown').

Thus in the *laus ruris*, Virgil paints a picture of a 'golden', rustic world uncorrupted by riches and greed, luxuries and ambition. He describes the hectic city life, the ruin that chasing after wealth can bring, and the deceit that comes with it. These images are set in contrast to the husbandman whose simpler existence and dedication to the land protect his happiness (*G.* 2.524: *casta pudicitiam seruat domus*, 'his unstained home preserves its purity'). For Lescarbot, too, no enthusiast of life in his contemporary France, the agricultural opportunities in *la Nouvelle-France* offered the prospect of new Golden Age, or at least the chance to lead a quiet life 'loin des bruits commun' (181–5):

> Ayant à noz labeurs fait selon noz desirs,
> Et iceux terminé de dix-mille plaisirs

Car la terre ici n'est telle qu'un fol l'estime,
Elle y est plantuereuse à cil qui sçait l'escrime
Du plaisant jardinage et du labeur des champs.

Having made our labours commensurate with our desires
And having completed them with ten thousand pleasures
For the earth here is not as a fool would guess
[As] she produces copiously for him who has experience
Of the pleasures of gardening and the labour of the fields.

Part of this 'golden' version of nature in the *Georgics* is the image of the *saturnia tellus* ('Saturnian land', 2.173), praised for its fertility and rich production of cereal crops, wine, olive oil and apples, for example (2.143–4, 2.149–50), in another of Virgil's set pieces, the *laudes Italiae* (2.136–76). In turn, Lescarbot in his poem also idealizes the fecundity of the Canadian landscape and its spontaneous fertility. In doing so, the French author picks up on the *Georgics'* images, such as the passage on abundance of vines in Italy (2.143–4), perhaps even aiming to outdo his Virgilian model (Lescarbot, *A-dieu*, 400–3):

Car en elle [la terre] desja la provide Nature
A le raisin semé si plantureusement,
Et en elle telle beauté, que Bacchus mémement,
Ne sçauroit invoqué lui faire davantage.

For in her [the land] provident Nature has already
Implanted the vine so copiously
And with such beauty, that Bacchus himself,
If invoked, would not know how to improve on it.[46]

Moreover, in praising New France and its natural landscape in this 'golden' mode, Lescarbot also takes inspiration from a technique of argumentation in Virgil's *laudes Italiae*: in the section leading up to the start of the *laudes* – beginning with the famous line *nec uero terrae ferre omnes omnia possunt* ('nor yet can all soils bear all fruits', *G.* 2.109) – Virgil praises the products of numerous other regions' varying soils and climates (2.109–35). For all of their commodities, however, none of these lands can rival the glories of Italy (2.136–9). Moreover, he argues, the exotic products of these foreign lands also bring with them innumerable drawbacks and dangers, which Italy does not (2.151–4). Lescarbot also takes advantage of this comparative technique to throw into greater relief his praise of New France. In particular, Lescarbot adds to his straightforwardly positive comparison of New France with other similar countries by admitting that while other regions may offer benefits, these advantages bring disadvantages with them as well (269–76):

Peuples de toutes parts qui estes loin d'ici
Ne vous emerveillez de cette chose ci,

Et ne vous tenez point comme en region froide,
Ce n'est point ici Flandre, Ecosse, ni Suede,
La mer ici ne gele, et les froides saisons
Ne m'ont oncques forcé d'y garder les tisons.
Et si chez vous l'eté plustot qu'ici commence,
Plustot vous ressentez de l'hiver l'inclemence.

Nations of all parts far away from here
Do not marvel at this
And do not at all consider us as being in a cold region,
[As] this is not at all [like] Flanders, Scotland or Sweden,
The sea here does not freeze over, and the cold seasons
Have never forced me to save the half-burnt firewood.
And if in your country summer arrives earlier than here
You experience winter's inclemency earlier.

It is easy to understand why Lescarbot was keen to downplay the cold of the Canadian winter in the passages of his poem that eulogize New France. The unexpectedly warm climate is also treated in the *Histoire*, and Lescarbot included a note on his verses referencing the chapter that deals with this issue in the prose work.[47] Indeed, the very winter that Lescarbot spent at Port-Royal with De Monts's colony was historically a mild one.[48] But just as the *Georgics* mixes idealization of the Italian land with detailed descriptions of the real difficulties and hard work that face the farmer, so too the *A-dieu*, whose author knew first-hand the challenges of agriculture in a newly-established settlement, represents nature and its cultivation in a more realistic manner.

In these moments Lescarbot reveals himself as sharing another fundamental aspect of his outlook on man's relationship to the natural environment with that presented in the *Georgics*. While Virgil often praised the powers of nature – especially those at work in Italy – they were always better, more effective and more beautiful if helped along by a human hand (*G.* 2.35–7). Cultivation, after all, is what agriculture is all about. Indeed, in the first book of the *Georgics* Virgil sums up his pessimistic view of nature left to her own devices (however fertile she may be (!), 1.147–57) with the image of even the best seeds tending to ruin if not maintained by human intervention, and the memorable simile of a rower struggling against the current (1.193–204).

We have already seen that nature was considered best when cultivated in the poetry of Pontano and Rapin, but even in the wild and spontaneously fertile environment of New France, Lescarbot still stressed that an agricultural landscape was preferable to raw nature. At one of the high points of his praise of New France's fertility, Lescarbot turns his attention to the hemp plant, which grew plentifully in early modern Canada. Despite his praise for the plant (417) and the fibre ('soye', 'silk') which it produces, the passage finishes with an emphasis firmly on a still brighter, cultivated future (419–26).[49] And in another passage, Lescarbot makes his case for the necessity of agriculture even more strongly (247–50):

Hé que sera-ce donc s'il arrive jamais
(Ce qu'il est de besoin qu'on face desormais)
Que la terre ici soit un petit mignardée
Et par humain travail quelquefois amendée?

So what does it matter if it ever happens
(And which it necessarily will do in the future)
That the soil here needs to be made more appealing
And improved sometimes by human labour?

In both Virgil and Lescarbot, this preference for cultivated land over wild nature also expresses itself in the praise of the country life. Indeed, the Virgilian *laus ruris* (alongside the passages from Horace, Ovid and Claudian on similar themes) served as the inspiration in France for a boom of both Neo-Latin and French literature on the rustic life, which eulogized agriculture and the lifestyle of farmers.[50] We have already seen how the theme was taken up in Rapin's *Hortorum libri IV* and mobilized to support his call to France's rulers for action (see n. 27 above). But in Lescarbot's *A-dieu*, the praise of rustic life gains an important new perspective: in addition to the idealization of the beauty and fertility of nature in New France, and the civilizing force of the colonizing 'François soigneux' (426), now the people of the First Nations come to represent, for Lescarbot, an ideal agricultural society. As earlier scholarship has shown, Lescarbot's descriptions of North America's native populations in *L'Histoire* were considerably more optimistic in this than his contemporary Samuel de Champlain.[51] And so it is in the *A-dieu* that the idea of a happy and honest rustic life is employed to depict the First Nations people (287–92):

Ces peuples vagabons qu'on appelle Sauvages
Hôtes de ces foréts et des marins rivages,
Et cent peuples encor qui sont de tous côtez
Au Sud, à l'Oest, au Nort de pié-ferme arretez,
Qui aiment le travail, qui la terre cultivent,
Et, libres, de ses fruits plus contens que nous vivent

These vagabond peoples one calls *Sauvages*[52]
Dwellers of these forests and marine shores,
And a hundred peoples more who are located on all sides
To the south, west and north settled in one place
Who love to work and who cultivate the soils
And who, in freedom, live more contentedly from their produce than we.

Lescarbot detailed his conception of the Amerindian populations as long-lost, uncorrupted brothers of the modern-day French in his *Histoire*,[53] but key for our theme here is the relevance of these lines to the political agenda at work in Lescarbot's georgic project and their parallels in Virgil's *Georgics*: Lescarbot had left France less than a decade after the end of the French Wars of Religion (1562–98), which had devastated the land and country. He went to New France in search of a new start based on what he saw as the pure and honest values of an agricultural existence in a fertile land. Virgil's *Georgics* were also written against a background of civil war. Within that political context, both the opening and the final passages of book 1 describe on the one hand the hoped-for *terrarum ... curam* ('care for the land', 1.25–6) and on the other, the contemporary *euerso ... saeclo* ('generation in ruins', 1.500), in explicitly agricultural terms.[54]

If Caesar Augustus is the hope of the agricultural world imagined in the *Georgics* (1.25–8 and 1.500–1), it is Henry IV of France (reigned 1589–1610) who assumes the role of a singular saviour in Lescarbot's *A-dieu* (5–12, 377–84). Following the pioneering but unsteady support of France's colonial efforts by Francis I (reigned 1515–47), Henry was the next French monarch to encourage exploration of *la Nouvelle-France*. He did so by financing a number of expeditions to America and by offering trade monopolies to merchant-colonizers like Pierre Dugua De Monts (*c.* 1558–1628), the explorer on whose expedition Lescarbot made his way to Port-Royal. As Lescarbot's benefactor, it is to De Monts that he addresses the opening verses of the *A-dieu*. In another instance of the episodic reception of Virgil common at the time, the list of questions to De Monts with which the frustrated Lescarbot begins his poem (1–12) echo the *Georgics*' often imitated and widely-recognized opening sequence.[55] They also serve a similar programmatic and didactic function to Virgil's parallel address to Maecenas (1.1–5). But a number of later passages in the piece also reveal interesting engagements with early modern ideas about didactic, and especially georgic-didactic tradition as a poetic mode.

The theme of *didaxis* moves in two main directions in the *A-dieu*: on a first, explicit level, Lescarbot treats the theme of what he saw as France's duty to instruct the native populations in the Christian faith in a number of passages (293–4, 315–16, 331–4). Here again, it is the simplicity and innocence of the First Nations peoples that Lescarbot emphasizes (331). Closely connected to this need for religious instruction is Lescarbot's call for the civilizing influence of French culture in New France. In the *A-dieu*, as we have already seen, this means explicitly agriculture (327–8):

Seulement il demande un pere qui l'enseigne
A cultiver la terre, à façonner la vigne

Only they need a father to teach them
To cultivate the earth, to cultivate the vine.

The second level of *didaxis* in the *A-dieu* is directed implicitly towards Lescarbot's readers back in France. The expansive *Histoire* must remain Lescarbot's primary work for describing his experiences in New France to interested readers back at home, but in the poetic collection appended to it, Lescarbot was able to live up to the Horatian tag referenced frequently in early modern discussions of didactic literature (Horace, *Ars poetica*, 343–4):[56] *omne tulit punctum, qui miscuit utile dulci | lectorem delectando pariterque monendo* ('He who mixes the useful with the sweet, both delighting and instructing the reader equally, carries off all the points'). Thus he provided a detailed and instructive description of the landscape around Port-Royal in his opening sketch of the region, emphasizing at once the beauty of the region and its unique points of interest, 'singularités' (38), for the European audience.

These 'singularités' were dealt with at length throughout the *A-dieu*, often in the form of lists or catalogues including types of fish and other sea creatures (77–128), the animals which live on land (141–57) and birds (158–228), to mention but the first three. These catalogues echo the lists of trees, vines and wines (*G.* 2.83–109) and list of mythical horses (3.90–4), for example, in Virgil's *Georgics*. Lescarbot even repeats Virgil's affirmations of personal observation – the '*uidi ego*' passages (1.193, 197, 316–18, 4.125–7) – which already reflected the poetic performance of didactic in Lucretius.[57] In addition to emphasizing the didactic mode of the poem, these moments of explicit autopsy perform an extra function in *A-dieu*, assuring the reader of Lescarbot's truthfulness in recounting his tales from the still very exotic and unexplored North American colony. In advertising New France's fertility, Lescarbot writes (63–4):

Nous en pouvons parler, qui de mainte semence
Y jettée, en avons certaine experience.

We [ourselves] are in a position to talk of it, who of many seeds
Sown there have had first-hand experience.

And later, when he describes the enormous schools of Atlantic herring around the Gulf of St Lawrence, he adds 'mes yeux en sont témoins' ('I saw them with my own eyes') (81) to achieve the same effect.

Moreover, Lescarbot adopts a more obviously didactic tone when he comes to describing parts of nature and wildlife which neither he, nor his readers, would have recognized. In these passages, Lescarbot again echoes Virgil's techniques in presenting his information. In his description of the lynx (146–7), for example, Lescarbot uses a parenthetic comparison to something apparently more familiar (the leopard) to bring an accurate image to the reader's mind. This is the same technique that Virgil used in his description of the citrus tree (*G.* 2.130–2), which he described for the benefit of the Italian reader as similar to the bay tree. Lescarbot's didactic tone is perhaps at its clearest when he introduces the names of animals in the native (Mi'kmaq) language. Lescarbot instructs us on the habits and appearance of the '*nibachés*', racoon, at 151–7, and at verses 207–30 he sings the praises of an 'admirable oiselet', 'amazing little bird', which he calls the '*niridau*' (225–30):

Niridau c'est ton nom que je ne veux changer
Pour t'en imposer un qui seroit étranger.
Niridau oiselet delicat de nature,
Qui de l'abeille prens ta tendre nourriture

Pillant de noz jardins les odorantes fleurs
Et de ces rives des bois les plus rares douceurs.

Niridau is your name which I do not wish to change
In order to impose one that would be foreign:
Niridau, delicate little bird by nature,
That takes the sweet nourishment of bees
Syphoning the fragrant flower of our gardens,
And the rarest sweets from the forest edge.

The humming bird (*niridau*) takes on a fascinating, almost mystical, character in Lescarbot's description, to which the unfamiliar Mi'kmaq name lends both an exotic charm and a didactic emphasis. This detailed poetic description of New France with its catalogues of trees, fish, birds, animals and insects, together with the wide-ranging assortment of outstanding features, singled out for more careful explanation to the reader with techniques familiar from didactic literature, gives the *A-dieu* characteristics which correspond to the early modern idea of the georgic tradition. The piece is a veritable storehouse of knowledge, which can offer to teach the reader in a very real way about a startling variety of new and unknown features of the land around Port-Royal while at the same time pleasing his poetic sensibilities.

Conclusions

Marc Lescarbot's *A-dieu à la Nouvelle-France* is obviously not an example of georgic poetry *tout court*. A close reading of the poem in the context of early modern interpretations and reception of the *Georgics* does reveal, however, considerable correspondence between the *A-dieu* and contemporary ideas about the georgic tradition. These moments of overlap can perhaps most helpfully be organized into three groups: first, a number of common techniques and elements of composition, including sections based on the episodic analysis of Virgil's *Georgics* common to early modern literature, and the use of didactic methods of presentation; second, a view of the role of didactic poetry – in Lescarbot's piece corresponding to early modern opinions about the georgic tradition – which puts into practice the idea that poetry should aim to teach in a real sense, and offer an entertaining variety of subject matter to the reader as a kind of storehouse of valuable information; third, a common literary-political perspective on nature, which at once idealizes the land and the life of the farmer, while recognizing the hard labour involved and painting a generally pessimistic image of untamed nature. These ambiguous perspectives are in turn mapped onto an ambiguous view of the author's own historical context, where a single saviour offers a prosperous future with agriculture at its core.

Thus situating the *A-dieu* within the georgic tradition allows us to further our understanding of both the poem itself and the ways in which Virgil's *Georgics* were read and received in early modern literature. As for the poem itself, the passages which earlier scholarship had seen as 'plats, ennuyeux, presentant peu d'intérêt' ('flat, boring and offering little of interest')[58] can now be read as central parts of the text, offering a wealth of knowledge in a pleasant poetic form, which was designed to satisfy a taste for variety and new information. Moreover, previous readers of Lescarbot's *Muses* have identified the influence of epic poetry, for example, as well as the Pindaric ode and elegy in his collected pieces, not to mention the more obviously recognizable dramatic forms.[59] By now adding the georgic tradition, the *A-dieu à la Nouvelle-France* no longer appears to be such an outlier. True, the blend of a framework familiar from 'Farewell' poems with the georgic tradition in the *A-dieu* is evidently novel, but Lescarbot also had the techniques, themes and outlook of the Virgilian georgic tradition at his disposal, too, when he came to write the poem.

The identification of this substantial influence from the georgic tradition in Lescarbot's *A-dieu* also has implications for our understanding of the reception of the *Georgics* in early modern literature. In Neo-Latin literature, didactic poetry and its georgic subset are relatively easy to identify and are frequently discussed. In studies of contemporary vernacular literature, however, georgic poetry frequently disappears from sight, apparently having fallen into the gap between Latin literary tradition and that of the national language. Summing up the accepted view, Kallendorf writes that 'The most curious thing about the Renaissance reception of the *Georgics* ... is that the poem recedes upon closer inspection – i.e. there are fewer signs of influence than one might have expected, and they often prove to have only limited importance once they are investigated.'[60] It is often noted, to take an example we met above, that in his *Deffence* Du Bellay did not mention didactic or georgic poetry among the types that he proposed for future French literature.[61] But modern critics have perhaps made more of these omissions than was done in early modern France:[62] in a representative case for my arguments here, Du Bellay himself finished the *Deffence* with a chapter explaining France's superiority over Italy, which relied on a prose imitation of Virgil's *laus Italiae*. He thus allowed Virgil's middle poem into his manifesto, albeit in a less explicit way than the *Aeneid* or the *Eclogues*.[63] Recognition of the reception of the *Georgics* in vernacular literature, in contrast to the analogous Neo-Latin case, is often compressed in modern literary criticism between acknowledgement of the widespread taste for pastoral literature in Europe during the sixteenth and seventeenth centuries, and the vogue for self-proclaimed georgic literature (especially in England) in the eighteenth century. Thus, to take just one example, *La Savoye* (1572) by Jacques Peletier du Mans, early translator of the *Georgics* and literary theorist who treated the *Georgics* at length in his *Art poëtique*, is rarely discussed in terms of its relationship to the georgic tradition, despite its discernible overlaps in didactic tone, natural and agricultural themes and poetic technique.[64] This position perhaps sounds familiar from that of Anthony Low over thirty years ago: 'If one were to believe historians of the georgic, Virgil's middle poem interested scarcely anyone between the Augustan age of Rome and that of England.'[65] Low's work and that of numerous scholars after him has shown just how mistaken these earlier 'historians of the georgic' were. But in finding the georgic tradition in the work of an underappreciated author writing off the Canadian coast in 1606, the suspicion arises that the influence of the *Georgics* may have travelled still further than currently acknowledged.

Appendix: primary texts from the early modern period cited in this chapter

Amaral, Prudêncio do (1781), *De sacchari opificio carmen*, Rome.

Baïf, Jean de (1567), *Le Premier des Météores*, Paris.

Du Bellay, Joachim (1549), *Deffence et illustration de la langue francoyse*, Paris.

Du Bellay, Joachim (1558), *Divers jeux rustiques et autres oeuvres poetiques*, Paris.

Lambin, Denys (1563), *Titi Lucretii Cari De rerum natura libri VI*, Paris and Lyon.

Landívar, Rafael (1781), *Rusticatio Mexicana libri XV*, Modena.

Lescarbot, Marc (1598), *Actio gratiarum pro pace*, Paris.

Lescarbot, Marc (1617), *Histoire de la nouvelle-France contenant les navigations, découvertes, & habitations faites parles françois és Indes Occidentales & Nouvelle-France*, 3rd edn, Paris.

Melo, José Rodrigues de (1781), *De rusticis Brasiliae rebus*, Rome.

Michel de Tours, Guillaume (1516), *Les bucoliques de Virgille Maron*, Paris.

Michel de Tours, Guillaume (1519), *Les georgiques de Virgille Maron*, Paris.

Montaigne, Michel de (1580), *Essais de Messire Michel seigneur de Montaigne. Livre premier & second*, Bordeaux.

Peletier du Mans, Jacques (1555), *L'Art poëtique*, Lyon.

Peletier du Mans, Jacques (1572), *La Savoye*, Anecy.

Pontano, Giovanni Gioviano (1505), *De hortis Hesperidum sive de cultu citriorum libri II*, Venice.

Pybrac, Guy Du Four de (1574), *Les plaisirs de la vie rustique*, Paris.

Rapin, René (1665), *Hortorum libri VI cum disputatione de cultura hortensi*, Paris.

Ronsard, Pierre de (1549), *L'Hymne de France*, Paris.

Ronsard, Pierre de (1578), *Sur les secondes œuvres de J. de Boyssieres*, Paris.

Saint-Gelais, Octovian de (1509), *Les Eneydes de Virgille*, Paris.

Scaliger, Julius Caesar (1561), *Poetices libri VII*, Lyon.

Strozzi, Tommaso (1689), *De mentis potu, sive de cocolatis opificio libri III*, Naples.

Vauquelin de la Fresnaye, Jean (1605), *Art Poëtique*, Caen.

CHAPTER 12
SHELLEY'S GEORGIC LANDSCAPE
Katharine M. Earnshaw

Percy Bysshe Shelley's translation of a fragment from Virgil's fourth *Georgic* provides a case study in how his ideas on poetry, language, thought, mind and metre in the *Defence of Poetry* are enacted in a densely allusive space. It is a dynamic passage, in which Shelley acknowledges the innovative and experimental poetry-making of Virgil, whilst testing how he himself might 'innovate upon the examples of his predecessors' (*Defence* 1840: 31). It is also overlooked.[1] I offer here some contextual discussion of Shelley's writing on the philosophy of poetry and language before providing a close reading of the fragment against the original. In so doing, I suggest that the poem is viewed not just as one of the few translations out of Latin by Shelley,[2] but as a creative commentary on the reception of Virgil's *Georgics*, in which fundamental questions about the nature of poetry are posed – and answered.

On 17 December 1812, Shelley began a letter to the publisher and bookseller Thomas Hookham with a criticism: 'The Translation of the Georgics you sent is not precisely *in my way*, but I shall keep it.'[3] A few weeks later, on 2 January 1813, the opening line to a subsequent letter to Hookham amends this opinion:

> On reflection I feel rather chagrined that I excepted against the Georgics. I fear it may with[h]old your hand when you would otherwise send me some really valuable work. I assure you that I am quite reconciled to Professor Martyn; Harriet will probably derive some assistance from his translation when she has mastered Horace.[4]

The phrase '*in my way*' does a lot of work in the first letter. Shelley had not yet written his 1821 essay *A Defence of Poetry*, in which he conceptualizes his thoughts on language, poetry and poets, but a concern with 'the idea and fact of language'[5] was happening at the very time these two letters were written.[6] The translation to which he is responding is revealed in the second letter to be that by John Martyn, who first published *The Georgicks of Virgil, with an English Translation and Notes* in 1741, ahead of a similar edition of the *Bucolicks* in 1749. Martyn's version is in prose, and he himself foresees criticism over this choice to avoid a poetic translation. 'I am no Poet myself, and therefore cannot by moved by any envy to their superior abilities' says the Cambridge Professor of Botany; 'The prose translation will, I know, be thought to debase Virgil. But it was never intended to give any idea of the Poet's style; the whole design of it being to help the less learned reader to understand the subject.'[7] Indeed, the fulfilment of this didactic ambition is what

Shelley claims as its usefulness in the January letter (though his revelation that the real concern lies in being cut off by Hookham from other books rather damns the claim with faint praise).

It need not be the case, of course, that '*in my way*' is a criticism of Martyn's work only on the basis of it being prose, given Shelley's later suggestion in the *Defence* that 'the popular division into prose and verse is inadmissible' (*Defence*: 31),[8] but it is perhaps an early articulation of where the real 'division' lies: between texts where 'sounds as well as thoughts have relation both between each other and towards that which they represent', giving it a 'uniform and harmonious recurrence of sound' (*Defence*: 31), and those that do not. Texts that achieve this need not only be those written in poetic form, and he includes Plato and Bacon as examples of those writing in prose who are 'poets'. But one can begin to see the broader metaphysical backdrop creeping in behind these statements, for the notion of 'sound' is part of a longer section in which Shelley is engaging with linguistic and philosophical concerns about 'the nature itself of language':

> Poetry ... expresses those arrangements of language, and especially metrical language, which are created by that imperial faculty ... And this springs from the nature itself of language, which is a more direct representation of the actions and passions of our internal being ... For language is arbitrarily produced by the imagination, and has relation to thoughts alone.

Keach has discussed in detail the slipperiness of 'Shelley's basing his celebration of the verbal medium of poetry partly upon the arbitrariness of linguistic signs',[9] and places it within a wider discussion about the metaphysical relationship between words and thoughts.[10] Shelley's ongoing concern with this can be seen elsewhere in his *Speculations on Metaphysics*: 'Words are the instruments of mind whose capacities it becomes the Metaphysician accurately to know, but they are not mind, nor are they portions of mind.'[11] In his discussion of the importance of 'sound', then, we might understand it to be an aspect of the creative process that combines with 'words' to map out thought in a way that gets closer to an 'eternal truth' (*Defence*: 33).

'Sound' also speaks to the formal and the metrical, of course. Shelley's argument seems to be that poetry manages to capture in the arbitrariness of words, in the sound of language in the broadest sense (utterance and rhythm), a 'truth' about 'the very image of life'. Refashioning that combination through the act of translation is tricky, and it is in this context that he makes his famous declaration on the 'the vanity of translation'. Shelley's suggestion that 'it were as wise to cast a violet into a crucible that you might discover the formal principle of its color and odor, as seek to transfuse from one language into another the creations of a poet'[12] seems often to be taken as a statement about the loss that occurs when the words of one language become the words of another. As we can see, it is more than this. The act of translation itself is framed within a broader contextual questioning of what language is, and how that might be something in flux with itself, so that the identity of thought with the language that it signifies is non-trivial. The higher questions about whether one can ever translate 'thought' as it is reified in poetry becomes wrapped up with the question as to whether the combination of word and metre in one language can ever really be rendered in another. However, Shelley gives us hope: if the task is to be attempted, 'every great poet must inevitably innovate upon the example of his predecessors in the exact structure of his peculiar versification' in order to achieve success. His later 'criticism' of Virgil in the *Defence* (50) should be seen in this context:

Virgil, with a modesty that ill became his genius, had affected the fame of an imitator, even whilst he created anew all that he copied.

It is not that Virgil *was* an imitator, but that the adoption of the guise of imitator distracts from the brilliance of Virgil's achievements. He manages to achieve this difficult aim, to 'copy' (or perhaps 'translate') earlier poetry and makes something new – and therefore 'true' – in the process. This makes his work part of the procession of the 'infinite' line of poetry, for poetry is not singular, but 'as the first acorn, which contained all oaks potentially':

A great poem is a fountain forever overflowing with the waters of wisdom and delight; and after one person and one age has exhausted all its divine effluence which their peculiar relations enable them to share, another and yet another succeeds, and new relations are ever developed, the source of an unforeseen and an unconceived delight.[13]

Poetry and thought are aligned within the symbol of water. Elsewhere in his poetry and prose Shelley makes clear the metaphorical connection between water imagery and the mind, such as in his *Mont Blanc*: 'The everlasting universe of things | flows through the mind, and rolls its rapid waves ...' (1–2).[14] Here in the *Defence* we see 'poetry' elide with the concepts of 'idea', 'thought', 'the mind'. Poetry is simply 'the expression of the imagination' (*Defence*: 26). It is reified thought. For Shelley, the language of poets is 'vitally metaphorical', allowing for the 'unapprehended relations of things' to be marked (*Defence*: 28), and it is but a metaphysical step further on from this depiction of poetry as a body of water to symbolize the mind as a cave in which the course runs, as he does in the *Speculations*:[15]

Thought can with difficulty visit the intricate and winding chambers which it inhabits. It is like a river whose rapid and perpetual stream flows outwards ... The caverns of the mind are obscure, and shadowy; or pervaded with a lustre, beautifully bright indeed, but shining not beyond their portals.

Of course, the symbol of the cave also marks one of the clearest indications of Shelley's Platonic engagement. It is with this acknowledgement of the potential symbolism contained within the image of the river and the cave, together with the philosophical underpinnings to the act of translation, that we now turn to the passage from the *Georgics*.

Some time between late 1818 and August 1819,[16] Shelley translated his fragment from book 4 of Virgil's *Georgics*. The excerpt, published only posthumously, describes the moment when Aristaeus visits his mother, Cyrene, under the waters (*Georgics* 4.360–73):[17]

At illum	360

curuata in montis faciem circumstetit unda,
accepitque sinu uasto, misitque sub amnem.
iamque domum mirans genetricis, et umida regna,
speluncisque lacus clausos, lucosque sonantes,
ibat, et ingenti motu stupefactus aquarum,   365
omnia sub magna labentia flumina terra
spectabat diuersa locis, Phasimque, Lycumque,
et caput, unde altus primum se erumpit Enipeus,
unde pater Tiberinus, et unde Aniena fluenta
saxosumque sonans Hypanis, Mysusque Caïcus   370
et gemina auratus taurino cornua uultu
Eridanus; quo non alius per pinguia culta
in mare purpureum uiolentior effluit amnis.

FROM VERGIL'S FOURTH GEORGIC[18]

And the cloven waters like a chasm of mountains   1
Stood, and received him in its mighty portal
And led him through the deep's untrampled fountains

He went in wonder through the halls immortal
Of his great Mother and her humid reign,   5
And groves profaned not by the step of mortal

Which sounded as he passed, and lakes which rain
Replenished not, girt round by marble[19] caves;
By the soft watery motion of the main

Half wildered, he beheld the bursting waves   10
Of every stream, beneath the mighty earth:
Phasis and Lycus which the starred sand paves,

The chasm where old Enipeus had its birth,
And father Tiber, and Aniena's flow,[20]
And whence Caicus', Mysian stream, comes forth   15

And rock-resounding Hypanis, and thou,
Eridanus, who bearest like empire's sign
Two golden horns upon thy taurine brow,

Thou than whom none of the streams divine
Through garden-fields and meads with fiercer power   20
Burst in their tumult to the purple brine.

A possible first section, taken from *Georgics* 4.317–18, is often excluded from those edited volumes that contain the translation, partly due to the editor Locock having dismissed it when he first published the poem in 1903; this was due to its cancellation in the original notebook and the different verse rhyming scheme.[21] Given the significance of the *terza rima* form (discussed below), I would suggest that this omission is correct. The reader embarks upon the fragment *in medias res*, uncertain of whose journey is being described, or in which landscape they are located.

Translations of the *Georgics* had a particular vogue in the long eighteenth century, beyond the edition published by Martyn. De Bruyn outlines the many that appeared during this period, naming '1808 as a kind of *annus mirabilis*, when three new versions appeared', a 'fascination … [that] continued into the middle of the nineteenth century'.[22] It is perhaps surprising in this context that so little discussion has been generated on Shelley's translation, nor has it been considered in connection to the popularity of the 'georgic' mode at this time, including for the Romantic poets.[23] Yet, despite being fragmentary, the translation speaks to many of the complexities outlined above. The words and the sound are innovative and experimental, and when seen alongside the symbolic potential of the landscape, the imagery of water as poetic inspiration, and the construction of the cave as mind, the fragment becomes a place where we witness a key performance of Shelley's philosophy of poetry. Shelley renews the *Georgics* through careful meditation on the poetic sensitivity of the Virgilian original, and creates a space in which the conceptual crossover of thought, poetry and language are explored.

From the outset, the spatiotemporal framework of Shelley's translation nudges away from the Virgilian original. The connective opening – 'And' – immediately posits a looking backwards; by beginning *in medias res*, Shelley demands that his version is considered both against and within the original. Temporal markers throughout are absent,[24] and the corresponding timelessness becomes amplified through the lack of context. The reader is set wandering at an unspecified time, through an unknown landscape, companion to an unidentified figure. The first stanza reveals that the landscape too is subtly different to that found in the *Georgics*. At *G.* 4.360–3, Virgil describes the parting of the water, which is the means of allowing Aristaeus to enter his mother's underwater domain. The description of the water's mountainous shape[25] captures the size and the interaction from a ground-level perspective: the *curved* waves stand *around* Aristaeus (*circumstetit*, 361), and receive him, host-like, before despatching him to his mother beneath (362).[26] In Shelley's translation, there is an elemental crossover, a disconnect of sorts, from the beginning: the water is 'cloven' (1), as if it were solid, earth-like.[27] Rather than the curve of the water marking the point of comparison to a mountain, the body of water is itself made mountain, and the fissure between is likened to a 'chasm'. This minor alteration ensures that the emphasis is not as much on what *is* there (a wave as big as a mountain: *curuata in montis faciem*, *G.* 4.361), but on what is *not* (the absence of water in the cleft: 'like a chasm of mountains', line 1), whilst (almost conversely) rendering the content of the line simultaneously more substantial and material.[28] Indeed, the overall size has been scaled up to stress the enormity of the breach, with the Virgilian singular *in montis faciem* ('into the form of a mountain') becoming the plural 'mountains'. Shelley thus opens his translation with an emphasis on the divide; in a poem dense with intertextual allusion it seems to be the divergence from the Virgilian original, the gap between, that is given emphasis.[29] It is not that the translation departs substantially in content from the original, but that the conceptual changes invite a perceptual adjustment. The Shelleyan waters are still sentient; he maintains the sense of *accepit*[30] ('received') and *misit* ('led'), yet reduces the softness of *sinus*[31] (present even when coupled with *uastus*, a word which captures both 'empty of human presence' and 'awe-inspiringly vast'), and replaces it instead with something more constructed, majestic and potentially less organic in his 'mighty portal'.[32] The certainty that *sinus uastus* (362) refers to the hollow of the wave is gone, but something of the meaning and the affective force of Virgil's original remains. We are left with the impression of having arrived at a gateway between two worlds; which, of course, we have. In recognizing this, one cannot help but recall Shelley's other use of 'portal' in the *Speculations* passage above, where the word seems to denote the entry points to the mind.

It is also here that I believe we can see the influence of Martyn on Shelley. Whatever the aesthetic or philosophical qualms about Martyn's translation, by 1817 there seems to have been some improvement in Shelley's assessment of the work; or at least a willingness to spend money on it. On 3 August of that year[33] he wrote to his publisher Charles Ollier to send him a manuscript – Mary Shelley's *Frankenstein* – and in the postscript requests that he 'Be so kind as to tell me also, is Martyn's Georgics of Virgil printed in a very large Octavo Edition to match with the Eclogues.' It is unclear if this request converted into a purchase, but I would like here to suggest that Martyn's edition is understood to be a contributing factor in Shelley's translation of this section of the *Georgics*. Whilst it is uncertain if Martyn's translation improved on Shelley, his edition also contained accompanying notes on the text, and it is there a connection can be discerned. Indeed, Martyn's note may even have been the catalyst for Shelley's interest in choosing this particular passage. On line 4.363 Martyn includes a long note, which in part recounts Servius's comments on the line about Egyptian rites related to groves under the earth and the 'immense water ... from which everything is procreated'. Martyn goes on to note that,

Homer makes the ocean to be the source of all rivers ... But Plato, whom Virgil seems to follow here ... supposes all the rivers to rise from a great cavern, which passes through the whole earth, and is called by the poets *Barathrum* and Tartarus.

He then proceeds to quote Plato's *Phaedo* (111e6–12a5), in which Socrates describes the geography of the underworld. The quote includes Socrates' claim that one of the χασμάτα ('chasms') under the earth is larger than the rest, and it is into and out of here that all rivers flow. It is thus the beginning and the end of everything. This inclusion of the reference to 'chasm' (and again at line 13) seems to me to explain its seemingly odd inclusion in Shelley's translation, and, in so doing, prompts a reading of the Virgilian passage through Plato's dialogue. Martyn's paratext helps us to recognize the philosophical framework in which this space is situated, the 'metaphysical liminality' of the riverscape, 'be it in geographical space or historical time'.[34] It also helps to introduce the notion that this landscape might be eschatological.

Shelley's translation augments the sense of admittance to an otherworld, and potentially an underworld, over the subsequent lines. The coupling of 'the deep's untrampled fountains' (3; an expansion of *amnem*, 'river', 362) and 'halls immortal' (4) with the figure's sense of 'wonder' (4) seems to whisper that this is the first admittance of a mortal (or perhaps anyone) to these realms; Aristaeus's 'semidivine'[35] status is mitigated by the anonymous opening. Virgil's text also focalizes through Aristaeus, but the emphasis falls on the oddity of the situation: that of a son who has seemingly never entered his mother's home. The line *iamque domum mirans genetricis et umida regna* ('And now, awe-struck at the home of his mother, and the humid kingdom', 363) slows down metrically at *mirans* to stress the marvelling moment, with the encircling *domum ... genetricis* indicating where the focus of the awe should rest: the first sight of this divine realm by a (not-quite) mortal. Shelley retains this awe, but establishes a secondary point of wonder: that of the unfrequented landscape. His Aristaeus goes 'in wonder through the halls[36] immortal | of his great Mother ... | *And* groves profaned not by the step of mortal' (4–6), projecting the astonishment forward in space. In fact, the very notion that the groves are unvisited by mortals is a significant addition by Shelley to the original; the idea does not appear here in Virgil's text.[37] Shelley's tactile 'untrampled' of line 3 sets up his expansion in lines 6–7 of the compressed Virgilian *lucos ... sonantes* (364), where it is explained that the cause of these 'echoing groves' are the footsteps of Aristaeus as he passes. The kinetic is made aural, and the echo sounds throughout the text with the rhyming pattern of the *terza rima* form, given extra emphasis at this moment with the homonyms 'reign / rain' (5, 7). This elaboration of the Virgilian text is stressed, coming, as it does, at the centre of a series of negatives ('untrampled', 3; 'groves profaned not by the step of mortal', 6; 'lakes which rain replenished not', 7–8), a familiar Shelleyan technique.[38] The translation thus lends particular focus to the untrodden landscape and the gap between mortality and immortality: two tropes associated with the very act of poetry writing.

This particular passage is already a creatively and intertextually significant space within the Virgilian corpus. Morgan extends the notion of the underground origins of life, discussed above, and proposes that 'Aristaeus' descent to Cyrene's cave and subsequent capture of Proteus ... dramatizes Virgil's mastery of Homeric poetry, the highest possible form of literary inspiration, the source of all other poetic inspiration ... a return to the *beginnings* of poetry'.[39] Shelley maps a realm that holds the potential for both origin and renewal, proceeding from Virgil, and his utilization of the 'untrodden path' offers an extension to this poetic dissonance: the poet creates 'anew', but within a landscape crafted in part by his literary ancestors. That the most famous examples of the (Hesiodic) untouched path come from Lucretius, the *translator* of Epicurean material into Latin, adds weight to the idea that the act of translation provides an opportunity for innovation and creation.[40] At *De Rerum Natura* 1.925–8, Lucretius describes his pathless landscape, and its watery topography: 'I feel, I rising feel, Poetick Heats, | And now, inspir'd trace o'er the Muses Seats, | Untrodden yet: 'tis sweet to visit first | Untouch'd and virgin Streams, and quench my Thirst.'[41] Virgil has alluded to this passage earlier in the *Georgics*;[42] Shelley's translation prompts us to read Virgil's Aristaeus passage as another moment in this mould, where space becomes self-definition, where untouched landscape is equivalent to new poetic ambition.

The person who walks these untrodden ways is almost always the poet-narrator. In resituating his translation as a fragment Shelley un-names Aristaeus, rendering him anonymous. In so doing, the figure begins to look both like Aristaeus and a surrogate poet, one who repeats the walk through an allusive, untouched landscape. Such a combination has neat implications for Shelley's position in the hierarchy of poet-narrators, and plays on the surrounding concern with mortality and immortality. The figure of Aristaeus holds a peculiar position within the *Georgics*: his status is uncertain, his divinity insecure.[43] Cyrene claims *fas illi limina diuum | tangere* ('it is permissible for him to ['touch', or perhaps just 'reach'] the threshold', 4.358–9), a statement which clarifies almost nothing beyond elevating him somewhat above standard mortality. He is frequently called a 'semidivine hero',[44] one who succeeds where Orpheus fails precisely because of some intangible godliness, though the point at which he transitions from man to god is unclear: 'Aristaeus was a deity; in this story he is a shepherd and still mortal (though with expectations)' claims Mynors.[45] Such an indeterminate identity may suit the Romantic writer: he figures himself as demi-god and poet, immortal visitor and mortal interloper, not yet, perhaps, equal to *diuinus poeta noster Virgilius* ('our divine poet Virgil'),[46] but fostering a potential for emulation beyond imitation.

Shelley's Aristaeus perhaps seems closer to mortality, in part, through being alone. Separated from his mother (their reunion is not translated, and thus denied), and deprived of the catalogue of nymphs that precedes the passage in the Virgilian text, he becomes emblematic of the archetypal Romantic hero: isolated, a wanderer, connected to nature (though somehow alienated from it), potentially rebellious,[47] and having 'a tendency to respond to the world through feeling rather than rational cogitation',[48] an observation substantiated by the Aristaeus-figure's only given reactions being his 'wonder' (4) and 'half wildered' gaze (10). The shift from a divinely populated landscape in the *Georgics* to a differently divine yet unpopulated landscape (the space is not for gods now, but poets) is perhaps a subtle change, but a striking one. Such a progression may mark the transition from the implicit engagement with the sublime that we find in Virgil,[49] to it being foregrounded in the eighteenth-century version. In this context the earlier emphasis on mountains can be seen anew: through the mountainous imagery,[50] the water, and the overwhelming sense of awe, Shelley's fragmentary translation becomes a sublime tableau. He uncovers the aesthetic in Virgil's work, and amplifies as he translates. In so doing, he makes the fragment into a contemporary piece, which is aligned to the concerns of (for example) Wordsworth's *Prelude*, and similarly shaped by the potential of the imagination.[51]

The anonymization of person in Shelley's translation extends also to place. Whereas Virgil signposts the geographic location of Aristaeus for us (*G*. 4.317–19), there is no map at the beginning of Shelley's fragment to locate ourselves within the text; no title, beyond the utilitarian and non-specific one attached later. Tally Jr describes the 'sense of disorientation, [the] sort of cartographic anxiety or spatial perplexity' that supervenes when a work of literature begins in the middle, as here.[52] The topography is also ambiguous, drawing our attention to the complexity already intrinsic to the *Georgics*: the setting is either under a river, in a palace of sorts or walking through groves – or all three. The elongation of 'And groves profaned not by the step of mortal | Which sounded as he passed' (6–7) over not just a line, but the break between stanzas, allows for the maximum amount of surprise, whilst seeming almost to freeze Aristaeus's foot in mid-air just as it seeks placement. It lends a pause just long enough for us to wonder why this waterscape seems to be populated with trees.[53] In English, 'groves' certainly does denote a wooded area,[54] and *lucus* too would seem to indicate a wood (*G*. 4.364).[55] Mynors suggests that 'caves … make it easier for the reader's imagination to accept the "groves loud with waters", which are at home really in the upper air'.[56] Yet it is also the case that a landscape placed under the earth, in which one encounters 'groves' and a river, may immediately recall underworld topography.[57] The anonymity of Shelley's Aristaeus exaggerates this confusion, allowing other possible scenarios to suggest themselves: without the title we could briefly imagine ourselves to be reading about Moses and the Red Sea, for example; with it, we might expect to encounter Orpheus. The shadowy characterization amplifies the surrounding spatial uncertainty and reflects a textual ambiguity in the *Georgics*, for Shelley is here accessing and augmenting the infernal hints in Virgil's text, and, in so doing, evokes in his translation two underworld episodes: that of the descent to Hades by Orpheus, and the descent to Hell by Dante.[58]

First, Orpheus. The Aristaeus episode in the *Georgics* encircles a longer narrative, the climax of which is a description of Orpheus's descent to the underworld in an attempt to rescue Eurydice (*G*. 453–527). The Orpheus section has always been celebrated: Low claims that in the seventeenth century the episode was one way 'the *Georgics* survived', due in part to the significance of Orpheus as poet-figure.[59] By the Romantic period, Wordsworth had produced his own translation of this 'most imitated and translated part of the *Georgics*', which 'offered the young poet an attractive opportunity to measure himself against the English poetic tradition'.[60] Like Shelley, Wordsworth's translations remained unpublished; indeed, Wu describes their unfinished state as 'the great lost project of Wordsworth's Cambridge years'.[61] Importantly, Graver suggests that Wordsworth's translation of the Orpheus passage offers a space in which to think about poetry itself, and, whilst it is uncertain how widely known Wordsworth's project was, it is tempting to see here a conversation between the older Romantic poet and the younger about poetry via the passages they have chosen.[62] Shelley does not translate the Orpheus scene directly, but situates himself referentially 'before' Wordsworth by translating the precursory Aristaeus episode. The section does not figure as a highlight of the *Georgics* by contemporary literary standards (the Proteus episode and the Ages of Man seem to be the next most popular passages), and yet it is one which is fundamental to our understanding of the wider Orphic narrative, for the Aristaeus scene in the *Georgics* contextualizes why Orpheus must undertake his short epic adventure, and reflects the second descent within the *Georgics* both structurally and thematically. Both missions require that they 'seek' something lost; each offers a contrasting outcome related to their success or failure in following instructions; both heroes must approach 'subterranean deities'.[63] By responding to the intratextual connections in the *Georgics*, as well as to contemporary receptions, Shelley's translation intensifies the readers' awareness that Aristaeus's trip is also an underworld journey of sorts, though crucially for a renowned atheist, an underworld which hints at, but largely avoids, religious counsel.

Shelley's reading of the Orpheus scene through the Aristaeus episode is especially clear through his depiction of the landscape. On his way to Hades, Orpheus *Taenarias etiam fauces, alta ostia Ditis, | et caligantem nigra formidine lucum | ingressus* ('He even entered the mouth of Taenarum, the lofty [or 'deep'] entrances of Dis, and the grove glooming with black dread', *G.* 4.467–70). The details recall Virgil's Aristaeus scene, and are augmented through Shelley's fragment. Orpheus must pass through the *alta ostia*, reminiscent perhaps of the 'mighty portal' of the translation; one might even remember that *ostium* can be applied to the mouth of a river.[64] He must then pass through a grove, before arriving in the vicinity of the king and queen. Cyrene, a relatively middling goddess, has both her power and surroundings expanded in Shelley's version. Her domain is elevated to a palatial grandeur akin to Persephone's in the first three stanzas: 'mighty portal' (2), 'halls immortal' (4), 'Great Mother'[65] (5), 'humid reign' (5), 'marble caves' (8), this latter an upgrade from Virgil's more modest *pumex* ('pumice', 4.374). The episode is made grander, more significant in the retelling, a reading that deftly and subtly maintains the Orphic scene within the translation, reminding the reader that the Aristaeus episode is the *first* descent in *Georgics* 4. By eliding the Aristaeus and Orpheus episodes just enough, Shelley manages to triangulate the three textual moments, to set the echoes sounding. The Romantic poet becomes the vatic narrator, inheritor of the classical role: a mortal showing us the immortal realms.[66]

The construction of space connects the two passages, even when the motivation for the excursion is lost. Whilst in the *Georgics* Aristaeus and Orpheus both descend because 'they both lose what is most precious to them',[67] such provocation is absent from Shelley's translation. There is no bee mystery, and no Eurydice here. As it stands, the culmination of the journey is the discovery of the waters and the source of the rivers. The translation is balanced and falls into two exact halves: the first ten lines are concerned with Aristaeus's journey through the underwater landscape; a middle line transitions from sight to description (11); the final ten lines comprise the catalogue of rivers. It is in this latter section especially clear how the fragment not only speaks to Shelley's ongoing concern with water, but offers a way of reading this engagement against a longer reception of classical material. His catalogue again enhances as it translates; for example, the sibilant sounds of Virgil's text are maintained, but there is greater variation given to the auditory than is heard in the *Georgics*. The addition at line 9 of 'the soft watery motion of the main' allows one better to appreciate the crescendo of sound in lines 16 ('rock-resounding Hypanis') and 20–1 ('with fiercer power | Burst in their tumult to the purple brine').

At line 12 *Phasimque Lycumque* (*G.* 4.367) is extended to 'Phasis and Lycus which the starred[68] sand paves'. It is slightly ambiguous as to whether 'starred' is written in the notebook here, and a lacuna between 'the' and 'sand' is sometimes suggested. Whilst 'starred' is often used to mean 'decorated' (as at *The Revolt of Islam* XX.9), there is a spatial distancing, a dislocation that is invited through the astral connection which disorients the reader.[69] In line 13, Shelley translates *caput* as 'chasm', thereby repeating the 'chasm' of line 1 and denying the reader the satisfaction of visualizing the very place from whence Enipeus springs.[70] There is then an alteration in order: *saxosumque sonans Hypanis Mysusque Caicus* (*G.* 4.370) becomes 'And whence Caicus', Mysian stream, comes forth | And rock-resounding Hypanis' (15–16). In itself, this might be attributed to a readjustment for the rhyming scheme; as it falls within such a metapoetical setting, one might wonder whether the delay of Hypanis is to bring it closer to the Eridanus, now in the same stanza and separated by only two words. The intertextual background to these rivers is carefully articulated by Heyworth, who explains their coupling in Propertius 1.12 through their connection to Catullus, and especially to Gallus,[71] arguing that we should see the Hypanis as ultimately representative of elegiac poetry, and the Eridanus of epic. That Shelley recognizes the epic embodiment of Eridanus is made clear in his expansion of Virgil's *Georgics* 4.371–2, which at lines 16–18 becomes 'and thou, | Eridanus, who bearest like empire's sign | two golden horns upon thy taurine brow'.[72] The river bears 'empire's sign', due to its being both the largest and most forceful river here, and the Italian Po; it is thus representative of epic, and particularly Virgilian epic. The sudden interpolation of 'garden-fields and meads' at line 20 is a deliberate move away from the Latin (*per pinguia culta*, 'through fertile lands', 4.372), and the shift towards a particularly English phraseology[73] unsettles our prospect. Rather than the Po forming the climax to the catalogue, the land intrudes in the final stanza, landscape that has suddenly altered from Italianate to English. The change is temptingly suggestive: in poetic terms, the enduring influence of Classical texts can be discerned in the English literary landscape. At the same time, the well-watered earth now generates not georgic *culta*, but smaller, fragmentary, gardens.

Virgil's watery underworld already brings the symbol of the river into symbiosis with the act of writing poetry. Homer was long associated with large bodies of water,[74] and the image was perpetuated in the Hellenistic period, most memorably by Callimachus in the opening to his *Hymn to Apollo* (105–13).[75] Morgan argues that the riverscape of Virgil's Aristaeus scene is a locus of complex intertextuality, a space that features significant interplay between the Homeric and the Callimachean.[76] At *Georgics* 4.285–6, Virgil makes clear the aetiological connection between watery and poetic sources, and the catalogue of rivers extends this idea, becoming 'at once an epic device and a reference to Hellenistic scholarly traditions'.[77] In other words, the Aristaeus scene is already a space in which poetic time converges, where poetic sources are rendered in topographical terms, and where Virgil demonstrates his ability to create an original landscape within a complex tradition.

Just as the concepts of *imitatio* ('imitation') and *aemulatio* ('emulation') are core to the Virgilian passage, so Shelley makes them central to his translation. In so doing, Virgil's text becomes a source in itself, the fount to which Shelley returns. The renewed motivation for the descent of Shelley's Aristaeus is to gaze on this confluence of poetic rivers. No wonder that he finds himself 'half wildered' at the overwhelming poetic landscape.

That Shelley's fragment is a creative renewal is made clearer when we consider the other text that he imitates and emulates through the translation: Dante's *Inferno*. The fragment follows the unusual *terza rima* structure – a form devised by Dante – and the 'continuous flow'[78] of its rhyming structure (aba, bcb, cdc), 'technically, [with] ... no beginning or end',[79] suits exactly the narrative description of the rivers. The importance of Shelley's instruction, discussed above, that 'every great poet must inevitably innovate upon the example of his predecessors in the exact structure of his peculiar versification' is here demonstrated, as form becomes a way of referencing as much as recreating. And Shelley's choice of form is particularly innovative; though there are a handful of earlier examples, *terza rima* was still experimental in the eighteenth century.[80] Whilst in Italy in late 1818, Shelley began re-reading Dante intensely; then, and in the period following, he tested the *terza rima* scheme in several poems.[81] At the same time that Percy was reading Dante, Mary Shelley was reading the *Georgics*, and the two of them spent time in Naples visiting the surrounding countryside and relating aspects of the scenery to Virgil's descriptions.[82] Webb suggests that 'For Shelley, of course, Virgil was not so much a classical as an Italian poet',[83] and it may be this which inspires the elision between translation and rhyme scheme. Yet it must also be true that the very act of rendering Virgil's words within a Dantean scheme forces the Roman poet into this Italian role, one that is politically subversive[84] as much as it is poetically ambitious. The alteration in the metrical medium points to the gap of time between Virgil's *Georgics* and Shelley's version of the *Georgics*, and to the other receptions that have occurred in between. Shelley's mastery of a difficult rhyme scheme aims to surpass the Virgilian original, creating it 'anew', whilst consciously introducing Dante's *Inferno* thematically, as well as structurally, into his *Georgics* landscape.

Shelley's synchronization of the *Inferno* with the *Georgics* helps to illuminate in the earlier texts the repeated theme of descent, the significance of water, the poet as both innovator and imitator, and the density of poetic allusion, as much as in his own. The very opening of Dante's *Inferno* features the famous depiction of dislocation that the narrator feels upon finding himself in an unknown wood, *una selva oscura*:

Nel mezzo del cammin di nostra vita
mi ritrovai per una selva oscura,
ché la diritta via era smarrita.

Ahi quanto a dir qual era è cosa dura
esta selva selvaggia e aspra e forte
che nel pensier rinova la paura!

Dante, Commedia: Inferno, *Canto I.1–6*

At one point midway on our path in life,
I came around and found myself now searching
through a dark wood, the right way blurred and lost.

How hard it is to say what that wood was,
a wilderness, savage, brute, harsh and wild.
Only to think of it renews my fear!

Translation by Robin Kirkpatrick

Dante articulates the emotional turbulence of finding oneself in the middle of a bewildering landscape, a disorienting effect conveyed to the reader by the structural choice to begin *in medias res*. Shelley reprises this confusing opening, but transmutes the affective charge from fear to wonder. Dante's text, as in Shelley's fragment, is devoid of geographical markers, yet potent in its use of topography: the significance of waking in a wood may play on the metapoetical connotations of trees in Latin poetry (where *silua* can refer to the composition of poetry, alongside 'trees'),[85] especially given that certain of the ancient poets are later discovered in this very grove (*Inf.* IV.64ff.). At *Inf.* I.13, Dante describes reaching the foot of a hill, which will mark the entrance to the underworld; Shelley's mountainous opening thus stands within Dante's landscape as well as Virgil's. Dante is of course reworking the various Virgilian descents to the underworld, though one might more immediately recall Aeneas's katabasis in book 6 of the *Aeneid*. In drawing the Dantean and the Virgilian texts together in his translation, Shelley reminds the reader that Virgil wrote other descents to other underworlds, and displaces the *Aeneid* with the 'original' descent: the first Virgilian underworld, that of Aristaeus in the *Georgics*. As a consequence, the Aristaeus episode becomes the source for those that follow. Shelley's engagement with Dante in his translation supports the idea of the underworld as a geocritical space in which different texts are brought into dialogue with each other, and, more immediately, compounds the misdirection (in part through the rhyming scheme) that his descent will reveal an eschatological underworld. In fact, Shelley's underworld will contain a revelation: that the texts themselves provide a metaphorical space in which poets possess an afterlife.

Dante famously animates his poetic predecessor within his *Divina Commedia*. Virgil is his guide throughout the landscape of the *Inferno* and *Purgatorio*,[86] and upon meeting and recognizing the Latin poet in the *Inferno*, Dante employs a (now familiar) watery image of Virgilian authority:

'Or se' tu quel Virgilio e quella fonte
che spandi di parlar sì largo fiume?',
rispuos'io lui con vergognosa fronte.

Dante, Commedia: Inferno, *Canto I.79–81*

'So, could it be,' I answered him (my brow,
in shy respect, bent low), 'you are that Virgil,

whose words (a river running full) flow wide?'

Translation by Robin Kirkpatrick

His admiration for Virgil, and the inspiration he has provided for his work, is articulated through the image of a river. Dante recognizes here the shift that has occurred since the *Georgics* was written: Virgil has equalled Homer in renown, such that a large body of water now represents the Latin as much as the Greek poet. The metaphor employed by Virgil to express his own debt and competition with his predecessors is used to render the poetry and the poet synonymous with each other. In the *Georgics*, the passage is already a poetic space where the authority of previous poets (Homer, Callimachus) converges; in Dante, we see that Virgil's ability to weave together texts, creating a new poetic unity in the process, makes his very person symbolic of that densely allusive approach. Shelley's translation of the river passage thus becomes a way of placing the figure of Virgil within his own text. Whilst Dante's poetry can also be seen as part of that 'infinite' fountain of poetry, it is perhaps worth recalling the related metaphor Shelley employs later in the *Defence* to describe it, as 'the bridge thrown over the stream of time, which unites the modern and the ancient world' (*Defence*: 48). In the translation, this is rendered quite literally: the structure of the poem becomes a metrical 'bridge' that unites the ancient material with modern English via the *terza rima* form. Shelley's translation becomes part of a successive reworking through the act of reading and re-reading poetry, such that 'new relations are ever developed', and the waters within the poetic landscape flow fuller and faster.

To exemplify Shelley's mastery in not allowing this river trope to become turgid, let us reverse course briefly to the earlier stanzas. 'Groves profaned not by the step of mortal' (6) sustains the pathless motif already discussed, and coupled with the 'untrampled fountains' (3) seems to alienate the figure in the landscape from the landscape itself. The word 'untrampled', as well as the concept, are unusual; it appears in Shelley's poetry only here and in his *Stanzas written in Dejection, near Naples* (also written in this period). Given the philosophical, and especially Platonic, engagement in this fragment and throughout Shelley's work, it is tempting to think through the image in relation to Heraclitus's claim, as recorded by Plato, that one cannot step into the same river twice.[87] The analogy is, of course, meant to convey something of the metaphysical nature of the universe, and its state of flux; it also comprises a literary response in itself.[88] The Heraclitean image of the river has its own long reception, and one is worth noting here. Hume, an important influence on Shelley,[89] repeats the idea in his *Treatise of Human Nature* (1.4.6):

> Thus as the nature of a river consists in the motion and change of parts; tho' in less than four and twenty hours these be totally alter'd; this hinders not the river from continuing the same during several ages.

Hume's point, as Heraclitus's (made clear by fragment B12), is that the river is subject to continual change, yet remains in essence what it was. There is stability alongside flux. Hume's claim forms part of a wider discussion on personal identity 'as it regards our thought or imagination', and, in particular, on the stability of identity over time. Though concerned with the notion of the self, the question of 'sameness' ('uninterrupted or invariable' through time) or 'diversity' ('several different objects existing in succession, and connected together by a close relation') maps well onto the related question of the origin(s) of thoughts and imagination; in this case, that a literary landscape is continually evolving, and yet retains elements that are recognizable and stable. Shelley's translation probes at these deeper questions regarding the nature of allusion and textual reworking. Virgil's poem is both a transformation and a continuation of Homeric and Hellenistic poetry; Dante's poem incorporates these[90] and more, and situates the figure of the poet (Virgil) within a version of his own landscape. Shelley's translation offers a clear identification of his source, but, like the proverbial river, it is both the same and different over time. The very form and structure of a translation allows for these broader philosophical questions, as well as the related metaphysical points discussed earlier on the nature of language, to be posed in a way that would be different had Shelley written an 'original' piece. As poet, he walks through landscapes that remain pristine, untrodden, despite multiple visitations; by the time his figure reaches the catalogue of rivers, we might understand that one reading is to see these as new waters running the same courses; another is to see the river as the same. This, then, perhaps indicates some of what Shelley means by a translation 'in my way'.

Shelley's choice of episode reflects his close scholarship on the material, and his recognition of the Aristaeus scene as central to the *Georgics*. Yet the passage also afforded him the opportunity to approach differently the symbol of the river, employed elsewhere in his poems as a means of representing life, death and the mind. The unnamed figure in Shelley's translation becomes poet-by-proxy, frozen in a perpetual present within which he is surrounded by the metaphorical poetry of the past and of the future. In choosing the Aristaeus passage over the similar Orpheus episode,[91] there is perhaps another self-reflexive move to consider with regard to Shelley's own pretensions: one might remember that Aristaeus is ultimately successful, whereas Orpheus is not. The choice of passage, and the manner in which he enacts that choice, helps us to reimagine Virgil's poetic landscape within Shelley's own. Yet Shelley also positions himself as the successful inheritor and interpreter of the Virgilian 'divine effluence', one who is 'delighted' to gaze, 'half wildered', at the sublimity of the new vista he has created.

CHAPTER 13
WOMEN AND EARTH: FEMALE RESPONSES TO THE *GEORGICS* IN THE TWENTIETH AND TWENTY-FIRST CENTURIES

Susanna Braund

One of the most striking phenomena of the translation history of Virgil is how very few women have translated his poems. The publication in 2008 of Sarah Ruden's translation of the *Aeneid* was, astonishingly, the first complete version in English by a woman. Preceding centuries can only offer the French prose version of Books 1–4 by Hélisenne de Crenne (1541), selections in French verse by Marie de Gournay (1620), and Irishwoman Mary Leadbetter's 1808 translation of book 13, the Renaissance supplement to the *Aeneid*.[1] Against that backdrop, it is remarkable, given that the *Georgics* is much less often translated, that there are more published translations of the *Georgics* by women than there are of the *Aeneid*. Besides the 1949 translation by the Dutch poet Ida Gerhardt,[2] there are three twenty-first-century translations by American women: Kristina Chew (2002), Janet Lembke (2005) and Kimberley Johnson (2010). Prior to these is Vita Sackville-West's 1926 phenomenal epic poem *The Land*, which is not a translation but is deeply interwoven with the *Georgics* and is central to any discussion of the reception of the *Georgics*.

In this chapter, I consider Lembke's translation and Sackville-West's original poem, paying particular attention to their use of language and their representation of nature and landscape. On the question of language, the central issues are register (is it elevated or colloquial?) and degree of modernization (is it archaizing or contemporary?). On the question of nature and landscape, the central issue is authenticity. These focal points of my discussion lead me to propose that these two writers achieve similar effects and have a shared sensibility with Virgil which makes them excellent receivers of the *Georgics*. As a coda, I ask whether it is possible that female responses to the *Georgics* offer something unavailable in versions by male translators. Finally, I propose that Sackville-West and Lembke be viewed as precursors of ecofeminist theory. I am not claiming that this approach could not be applied to other responses to the *Georgics*, but that the congruence between the works of Sackville-West and Lembke shines a valuable light on issues of gender and the land in modern responses to Virgil's poem.

Janet Lembke: 'a classical naturalist'

Janet Lembke's 2005 translation of the *Georgics* matches the Latin line for line thanks to a long line without metrical tics but with fine assonance and alliteration. It is these *sounding* qualities of her language that impress; they are palpable in the following examples, where we see her particular strength in evoking the senses to which Virgil appeals. For example, she summons the sound of a sick hive (4.260–3):

> Then, a heavier sound is heard, a slow susurration,
> as sometimes the chilly South Wind whispers in the woods,
> as the restless sea hisses when the waves recede,
> as consuming fire sizzles in closed-up furnaces.

She evokes sight and texture (3.280–2):

> the viscous 'mare-madness,' as herdsmen rightly name it,
> oozes slowly from the vulva – mare-madness, the creamy
> mucus ...

The senses of taste and touch are manifest in Virgil's digest of soils in book 2. Salty soil can be detected by a test (2.246–7):

> But taste will present undeniable evidence,
> its sour nature puckering the testers' hapless mouths,

while this is the test for 'rich, friable soil' (2.249–50):

> it hardly crumbles under kneading hands
> but rather, like pitch, sticks to the fingers when it's held.

Thus Lembke crafts a fitting match for Virgil's mid-range register which is unpretentious and controlled yet capacious enough to discuss beetles and dung along with woodland nymphs and rural deities. Unlike Cecil Day-Lewis in his 1940 *Georgics*, Lembke never makes the mistake of delving into colloquialisms.[3]

The poet and wordsmith in Lembke finds the right register to render Virgil's didactic epic of the land, but it is the naturalist in her that ensures she truly *sees* the land. Janet Lembke (1933–2013) was known as much as a naturalist as a classical translator; indeed, this is how she presents herself in the title of one of her earliest books on the natural world, *Looking for Eagles: Reflections of a Classical Naturalist* (1990). She begins this book by explaining the significance of the phrase, claiming that her mentors are not so much Thoreau, Muir and Aldo as Aristotle, Pliny and 'a few ancient poets' and by explaining, in characteristically vivid and forceful prose:

> I live at the confluence of two broad streams. One is wet, salty, and huge: the lower
> Neuse, more southerly of the two muscular rivers that pour into North Carolina's
> Pamlico Sound. The second runs invisible but hardly silent, though ears cease
> to hear it as they cease to hear traffic or the ticking of a clock. It's the Greco-Roman

tributary that flows with steady, unobtrusive force through Western languages and culture.

Lembke 1990: 1

Lembke wrote a dozen books on nature alongside her classical projects – a study of early Latin poetry and translations of the *Georgics* and three Greek tragedies. She mischievously depicts her work with classical literature as 'pok[ing] into and under old poems and plays' in a woodswoman's terms, as 'an exercise something like turning over old logs to see what wiggles beneath the decaying wood'.[4]

Lembke's books on nature range through water and birds and gardening and pests (she was a Master Gardener), and human relations with other species. In *Looking for Eagles*, she demonstrates her close powers of observation focused upon her North Carolina home along with a profound sense of continuity, qualities which equip her well to translate the *Georgics*:

> A thousand years ago, Indians saw much the same maritime forest that meets our eyes – sweet gums, pines decked in untidy swags of greenbriar and trumpet vine, live oaks and baldy cypress bearded with grey Spanish moss, stands of yaupon holly, wax myrtles, and palmettoes ... Brown pelicans perched on pilings and towhees calling from hedgerows find equal welcome ... Migrating monarch butterflies mingle in season with the ubiquitous swallowtails. Black-and-yellow argiope spiders weave blatant webs while black widows lurk in cinderblocks ...

Lembke 1990: 2–3

And Virgil is a palpable presence in her 2006 book *From Grass to Gardens: How to Reap Bounty from a Small Yard*. This is not surprising, as she was writing this while finishing her translation. Here she writes:

> In the last few years, I've divided my time between two worlds: the world that daily greets my senses – the one that rains or snows, the one that blooms and produces fruit, the one that daily purrs ... [her two cats] – and another world that's located on the farthest edge of the Christian millennia, the world of Italians working family farms in the first century B.C.

Lembke 2006: 32

She then introduces Virgil's poem to her readers and expresses her deep connection with him for his love of gardens. She quotes her own translation of 4.118–24:

> perhaps I should also sing what careful cultivation
> adorns rich gardens and the rose beds of twice-bearing Paestum,
> and how endives rejoice in the streams that they drink

and the green banks, in celery, and how the cucumber
sprawling through the grass swells into a paunch. Nor should I be
silent about late-blooming narcissus or the flexible
twigs of acanthus, pale ivy, and shore-loving myrtle,

Lembke 2006: 32–9

then comments:

As I read, imagination sees my own climbing red 'Blaze' roses, watches the
cucumbers in the front yard produce their fine, fat, pickling-sized paunches, and
picks the fragrant 'King Alfred' daffodils on the backyard terrace.

Lembke 2006: 35

She goes on to report with 'delight' that Virgil 'gives perfectly valid instructions for
tests to see what kind of soil you're working with'.[5] For example, after digging a sizeable
hole, you replace the soil in the hole; if the soil no longer fills the hole, it is loamy soil,
but if it is impossible to get all the soil back in the hole, it is compact and clayey. Another
of Virgil's examples corresponds exactly to that 'prescribed by the Rodale Press's *Garden
Answers* book';[6] this is the squeeze test mentioned above. In other words, for Lembke
the *Georgics* is a poem delivering *practical* instructions along with the higher message
that 'only at our gravest peril do we fail to husband the resources on which our lives
depend'.[7]

Time and again in *From Grass to Gardens* Lembke finds continuity with the past. She
offers a valuable discussion of companion planting (protective pairings of flowers and
vegetables to keep weeds, fungi and pests in check) in which she reproduces the table
devised by the US Department of Agriculture;[8] but she prefaces that by praising Virgil's
knowledge of companion planting, evinced in his description of the garden of the old
man of Tarentum (4.130–3):

Nonetheless, here amid brambles, planting vegetables in rows,
white lilies, curative vervain, and slender-stemmed poppies,
he equaled the wealth of kings in spirit and, coming home
late at night, loaded his tables with an unbought feast.

And she shares Virgil's view of tools as 'militant farmers' weapons' in a battle that must be
waged:

And weapons they are, fighting weeds, keeping entropy at bay. Our battles are just,
for they support the causes of sprouting, bloom, and fruition, of human need and
human delight. Gardens past, gardens present, and gardens to come – the tools we
use connect each one to every other.

Lembke 2006: 53

While her profound sympathy with Virgil's views grounds her translation as authentic and reliable, Lembke's views tend to be more optimistic than those expressed in the *Georgics*, especially in the darker books 1 and 3. Consider her note on 1.199–203, the passage where Virgil deploys the image of someone rowing against the stream and getting carried downstream if he relaxes his efforts: 'These lines comment on entropy. Even the hardest work is not always enough to keep nature at bay. Yet the human obligation under the Jovian regime is to keep on doing our best.'[9] This is a little too upbeat and determinedly cheerful. But, while I agree with reviewer Benjamin Stevens that Lembke under-translates the crucial lines *labor omnia uicit | improbus* (1.145–6) as 'Relentless work conquered | all difficulties', I think it is unfair to say that she 'drain[s] the poem of its venom'.[10] She acknowledges the necessity of toil and failure alongside joy.

Lembke starts her brief 'Translator's Note' by attributing her groundedness to her father: 'I have made this translation in homage to my father, himself a farmer, who taught me to love cows and vegetable gardening.'[11] She acknowledges the need 'to bridge the gap between then and now, to make the poem more accessible and less remote' and explains her strategies with place names (calling Virgil's lakes Larus and Benacus by their modern names, Como and Garda respectively) and nymph names, where she creates 'rough English equivalents' to the Greek names, generating 'Woods Girl and Golden and Clear Voice and Fancy Leaf' to translate 4.336, *Drymoque Xanthoque Ligeaque Phyllodoceque*, one of the poem's most challenging lines for a modern translator.[12] She implicitly contrasts her deeply informed translation with the versions 'rendered in British English by men who know much about poetry but little about farming'.[13] She asserts, with obvious sincerity, 'My pleasure has been to use American English. In with grain, out with corn! Out with truncheons and buskins, in with sturdy twigs and boots!'[14] The 'truncheons' and 'buskins' she rejects I located in the unimaginative prose translation of 1934 by J. W. Mackail, an amateur Virgil scholar who was Oxford Professor of Poetry; these archaic words are barely understood in British English. Lembke translates with joy and with an eye on her particular, contemporary American, audience. To this degree her translation is certainly modernizing, but it refrains from descending into the ephemeral slang which characterizes Day-Lewis's version. It is possible to imagine Lembke's *Georgics* being read with pleasure for decades to come.

I close this discussion by presenting two passages where Lembke's sympathies align extremely closely with Virgil's. The first urges quick preventative action by the farmer upon observing the signs of sickness in an individual sheep. The Latin reads (*G.* 3.464–9):

quam procul aut molli succedere saepius umbrae
uideris aut summas carpentem ignauius herbas
extremamque sequi, aut medio procumbere campo
pascentem et serae solam decedere nocti—
continuo culpam ferro compesce, priusquam
dira per incautum serpant contagia uulgus.

Lembke's translation captures every word of the Latin with accuracy (for example, 'nibble listlessly' for *carpentem ignauius*) and with the unshowy elegance we have seen above in her prose and poetry alike:

> If you should see a sheep often head far away
> into soft shade, or nibble listlessly at the tops of grass
> while lagging behind, or fall in the middle of the field
> as it grazes and go off alone late at night, check
> the problem immediately with the knife before the dire
> infection spreads contagion through the whole heedless flock.

The second passage concerns the bees (*G.* 4.25–9):

> in medium, seu stabit iners seu profluet umor,
> transuersas salices et grandia conice saxa,
> pontibus ut crebris possint consistere et alas
> pandere ad aestiuum solem, si forte morantes
> sparserit aut praeceps Neptuno immerserit Eurus.

Here Lembke enhances Virgil's Latin to ensure that his sympathetic focalization from the bee-perspective is not lost:

> In the midst of the water, be it still or free-flowing,
> place willows across it or stones that look huge to the bees,
> so that they can alight on bridges placed close together
> and spread their wings to the summer sun if a sudden East Wind
> has sprinkled those that dally or plunged them into Neptune's realm.

Virgil is here reworking a passage from the agricultural treatise by his contemporary Varro in which he describes placing pebbles (*lapilli*) or shards of pottery (*testae*) in a shallow pool to allow bees to alight and drink. Virgil sees the world from the bees' perspective: Varro's 'shards' and 'pebbles' become *grandia . . . saxa* and the tiny pool takes on the dimensions of the Ocean thanks to the epic-style metonymy *Neptunus*.[15] Lembke sees all this and accordingly retains the exaggeration of 'Neptune's realm' and elaborates Virgil's *grandia* into 'that look huge to the bees'.

Lembke's translation comes from a place of deep sympathy with the natural world, a sympathy that she shares with Virgil and that is grounded in her authentic connections with the landscapes and soils where she has lived. By the time she undertook the translation, she had more than a decade of nature writing under her belt. The love of the land, the close observations of nature and the evocative descriptive powers of her dozen books on the natural world are manifest in the translation too. She has managed to craft a vivid, unpretentious, elegant style that fits precisely Virgil's mid-level linguistic register, wisely eschewing pompous archaic terminology and modern slang.

Her middle way enables her to fulfil her aspiration 'to bridge the gap between then and now'.[16]

Vita Sackville-West: a gardener poet

I now move backwards in time to Vita Sackville-West's epic poem *The Land* which celebrates its relationship with the *Georgics* through its four-book structure, through Virgilian echoes in its opening and closing lines, and through its explicit invocation of Virgil in the closing panegyric, 'O Mantuan! that sang the bees and vines, | The tillage and the flocks . . .'.[17] Published in 1926 and immediately acclaimed, *The Land* was Sackville-West's most successful work: it was reprinted twenty-two times, won the Hawthornden Prize in 1927 and led to her name being mentioned as possible successor to Poet Laureate Robert Bridges in 1929.[18] The complicated and exotic life and loves of the aristocrat Victoria (Vita) Sackville-West (1892–1962) have been well documented in biographies and in studies of her relationship with Virginia Woolf.[19] Sara Watson gives an overview of Sackville-West as a writer of poetry, travel books, columns and essays on gardening, biographies (including Joan of Arc and her grandmother Pepita, a Spanish dancer), essays on literary history, a history of Knole, the Sackville family home, and especially her many novels; the list of her publications fills three pages.[20] Her relationship with gardens, including those at Knole in Kent, where she was born and raised but which English law, devastatingly for her, did not permit her to inherit, and her passion for the gardens that she and her husband Harold Nicolson created at Sissinghurst Castle, also in Kent, are explored by Jane Brown in *Vita's Other World*.[21] We must not underestimate her passion for gardens and for her corner of England, the county of Kent and specifically the Weald, when we consider *The Land* and its relationship with Virgil's *Georgics*. As Rebecca Nagel says in her fundamental article on *The Land* and *The Garden* and Virgil's *Georgics*, Sackville-West was 'primarily a gardener'.[22] Indeed, her expertise later won her the Veitch Gold Medal of the Royal Horticultural Society.[23]

That there is a relationship with Virgil's poem we cannot doubt. On opening *The Land*, we find a Latin epigraph from *Georgics* 3.[24] Her poem itself starts:

> I sing the cycle of my country's year,
> I sing the tillage, and the reaping sing,
> Classic monotony . . .
>
> *Sackville-West 1926: 3*

which reworks the crops (*segetes*), the turning of the soil (*terram uertere*) and the singing (*canere*) of the opening of the *Georgics* (1.1–5).[25] A few lines below, she resumes:

> I sing once more
> The mild continuous epic of the soil,
> Haysel and harvest, tilth and husbandry;

I tell of marl and dung, and of the means
That break the unkindly spirit of the clay;
I tell the things I know, the things I knew
Before I knew them, immemorially;
And as the fieldsman of unhurrying tread
Trudges with steady and unchanging gait,
Being born to clays that in the winter hold,
So my pedestrian measure gravely plods,
Telling a loutish life.

Sackville-West 1926: 3–4

These passages convey that Sackville-West's poem is certainly a *reception* of Virgil, as the epigraph announces and as her description 'mild continuous epic of the soil' implies.[26]

The four books of *The Land* are named for the seasons, starting with 'Winter'. In length it is similar to the *Georgics*, being about 2,500 lines long, but its structure is looser: within Sackville-West's chosen framework of the year, from December (8) to 'autumn like the Janus of the year' (88), she incorporates lyric poems, some of which were published earlier elsewhere,[27] interspersed with her iambic measures.[28] To demarcate these poems and to offer variety she often uses devices such as italic type, rhyme and shorter lines.[29] 'Summer', for example, includes five five-line stanzas on August, the 'Weod-monath',[30] starting:

This is the month of weeds.
Kex, charlock, thistle,
Among the shorn bristle
Of stubble-drop seeds.
This is the month of weeds,

Sackville-West 1926: 75–6

while 'Spring' includes her reworking of Virgil's *laudes Italiae* in her poem 'The Island', a celebration of England, which starts with the well-known line, '*She walks among the loveliness she made . . .*'.[31]

By writing 'I sing once more' at the start of her poem she deliberately sets herself in the long literary line that leads back to Virgil and, before him, Hesiod, and that glances at all the 'georgic literature' inspired by Virgil, especially in eighteenth-century England.[32] She explicitly celebrates the knowledge of the ancients in 'Autumn':

Homer and Hesiod and Virgil knew
The ploughshare in its reasonable shape,
Classical from the moment it was new,
Sprung ready-armed, ordained without escape,
And never bettered though man's cunning grew . . .

Sackville-West 1926: 89

And she concludes the entire poem by celebrating the continuities with 'Homeric waggons' and 'Virgilian litanies'.[33] On the last page, when a powerful mind's-eye image of 'my English weald' in the moonlight strikes her with pangs of absence as she completes her poem far away in Iran, she addresses Virgil directly:[34]

> O Mantuan! that sang the bees and vines,
> The tillage and the flocks . . .

Sackville-West 1926: 107

– words which echo Virgil's own summary of the topics of his poem in the *sphragis* (*G*. 4.559–60). Even more telling are her four final lines:[35]

> Then thought I, Virgil! how from Mantua reft,
> Shy as a peasant in the courts of Rome,
> Thou took'st the waxen tablets in thy hand,
> And out of anger cut calm tales of home.

Sackville-West 1926: 107

Here she identifies with the country-lover's imagined resentment at being taken away to court from his rural roots, as we can see, for example, from a diary entry which conveys her love of the solitude at Long Barn which allowed her to work on her poem.[36]

Virgil thus frames her project but he is also implicitly present, as 'the Roman' who understands, for example, the importance of the rotation of crops.[37] It is tempting to suggest that when Sackville-West describes the 'humming hive' and the 'swarm' of workers busy with threshing grain in her fourth book, she is inspired by Virgil's focus on bees in his fourth book.[38] Near the end of 'Autumn' she evokes the Roman vintage, which she introduces as 'Another harvest, not beneath this sky | So Saxon-fair':

> Down from the hill the slow white oxen crawl,
> Dragging the purple waggon heaped with must,
> Raising on sundered hoofs small puffs of dust,
> With scarlet tassels on their milky brows . . .
> The wooden shovels take the purple stain,
> The dusk is heavy with the wine's arm load;
> Here the long sense of classic measure cures
> The spirit weary of its difficult pain;
> Here the old Bacchic piety endures,
> Here the sweet legends of the world remain.

Sackville-West 1926: 105–6

With this picture, redolent of the celebration of Bacchus in *Georgics* 2, Sackville-West invites the observer to:

roll the centuries back
And feel the sinews of his soul grow hale,
And know himself for Rome's inheritor.

Sackville-West 1926: 106

She clearly sees herself as 'Rome's inheritor', as well as following in the footsteps of Hesiod and Homer.

Sackville-West's husband Harold Nicolson had seen the parallel with the *Georgics* from the start,[39] but apparently she later said:

> I had never read one line of the *Georgics*, either in Latin which I was never taught or in any translation, until I had got halfway through *The Land* and showed a bit of it to a friend of mine who then said 'But you are copying the *Georgics*.' I denied indignantly and truthfully that I was copying anything . . . He then gave me Lord Burghclere's translation and also the Loeb edition of the *Georgics*, and I was appalled to see that my poem must appear to be a fake or an imitation. It wasn't fake. Neither was it an imitation.[40]

This looks like error, or revisionism, on her part, because in her very first novel, *Heritage*, published in 1919, Sackville-West uses a Latin quotation from the *sphragis* to the *Georgics* as her epigraph.[41] It is possible that her publisher inserted the epigraph without her knowledge, but the choice of a *Latin* epigraph, from the *Georgics*, seems to contradict her later protests of ignorance. Whatever the case, she embraced the like-mindedness as an opportunity: *The Land* is continually in dialogue with the *Georgics* and it continually renews it thanks to her groundedness in the soil of Kent.

Many of the topics addressed by Sackville-West recall passages in the *Georgics*; for example, her sections (mostly advertised by marginal headings but here I indicate the pages in parentheses) on sowing crops (31), pests, orchards (35, 98), the care of livestock (37, 63, 64, 66), the bee-master (39), the gardener (44, 92), stars and constellations (50–1, 52, 56–7, 102), the harvest (67), ploughing (89) and the vintage (105).[42] Some of the topics peculiar to Sackville-West are attributable to the differences between Italy and England: different craftsmen, including the thatcher, and different crops, especially cider and hops. Themes that recall the *Georgics* include the inevitability of toil and imagery of combat with nature. These are both introduced early in 'Winter', the opening book: 'to live men labour';[43] 'I see | Only the battle between man and earth, | The sweat, the weariness, the care, the balk';[44] 'I then, who as a wrestler wrought with earth, | Bending some stubborn acres to my will . . . Nothing but toil';[45] in 'Winter Song', a nine-stanza poem,[46] the farmer who 'plots | To get the better of his lands again; | Compels, coerces, sets in trim, allots, | Renews the old campaign'.[47] Sackville-West maintains these themes throughout the poem, for example, in 'Spring' with the 'constant war' against the pests in the orchard,[48] and in 'Autumn':

Nature's an enemy who calls no armistice.
Mistrust the seeming truce, that in the pyre

Of distant woods, and in the gardens' fire,
In pheasants running bronze on furrowed mould,
Burnishes autumn with a coat of gold.
Therefore towards the stubble turn your plough;
Cut gashes new across the healing earth;
Spare not your servant, since to man austere
No respite comes, but bend beneath your vow
Reluctant fields, and bring new life to birth.

Sackville-West 1926: 35

This language of violence, struggle and toil vividly recalls that in *Georgics* 1, especially the crucial lines (1.145–6): *labor omnia uicit | improbus et duris urgens in rebus egestas.*[49]

While Sackville-West is as realistic as Virgil about adversity and violence, she appears less sentimental. Virgil tends to anthropomorphize animals – obvious cases are the collapsed ox in book 3 and the bees in book 4 – whereas Sackville-West sees a levelling commonality between humans and animals.[50] Her worldview produces the 'brusque and practical heartlessness in the rabbit scene'[51] and delivers this memorable long line to conclude a section that starts 'Man's not the only harvester': 'To hedge-hogs, squirrels, badgers, men, mice, moles'.[52] Sackville-West brilliantly refuses to privilege humans, as the more obvious ending 'mice and men' would have done.[53] This less sentimental perception of the natural world fits with her celebration of cycles and universality which knits the poem together into this 'mild continuous epic of the soil': the work is the same 'whether oats in Greece | Or oats in Kent', whether the shepherd and his flocks are 'As once at Thebes, as once at Lombardy'.[54] A favourite word is 'immemorial', introduced at the start.[55] Accordingly, she draws towards a close by saying:

Now I have told the year from dawn to dusk,
Its morning and its evening and its noon,

Sackville-West 1926: 97

and she evokes again all the work undertaken through the year by shepherd, tiller, sower, reaper.

One of the most striking features of *The Land* is the very 'particularity' of the landscape in her poem, an element that is in tension with the universality I just mentioned and which outweighs those claims.[56] From early in the poem she leaves us in no doubt that she is grounded in her part of Kent:

Hear first of the country that shall claim my theme,
The Weald of Kent, once forest, and to-day
Meadow and orchard, garden of fruit and hops,
A green, wet country on a bed of clay ...

Sackville-West 1926: 11

She calls this by its ancient name, 'Andredsweald', and she devotes the next pages to imagining its primitive inhabitants and its gradual transformation into 'The Weald of Kent'.[57] With fine ring-composition, she returns to celebrate Kent's specific crops at the end of the poem: 'Apples and hops made Kent's clean autumn wine'.[58] *The Land* is undoubtedly a celebration of the land that Sackville-West worked and loved. Where Virgil places his celebration of 'his' (idealized) particular place – the river Mincius flowing through his home town of Mantua – right at the centre of his poem (at the start of book 3), Sackville-West uses her (idealized) part of Kent to frame her poem. But both move between the particular and the universal in a productive tension.

Sackville-West and Lembke: a common worldview and a common style

Lembke does not mention Sackville-West in her *Georgics*, but she seems to share her worldview. Sackville-West, like Lembke, knows her soil and how to work it: this is clay, 'catchy clay', 'that yellow enemy', a 'wet and weeping soil' that 'rots', 'sucks' and 'spoils' 'with yeavy spite'.[59] Sackville-West, like Lembke, values knowledge: she repeats the word 'know' from the very beginning (quoted above) where she says: 'I tell the things I know, the things I knew | Before I knew them, immemorially'. Sackville-West, like Lembke, understands the difference between superficiality and profound understanding (my emphasis):

> The country habit has me by the heart,
> For he's bewitched forever who *has seen,*
> *Not with his eyes but with his vision,* Spring
> Flow down the woods and stipple leaves with sun . . .
>
> *Sackville-West 1926: 5*[60]

And Sackville-West, like Lembke, is gifted with powers of observation which appeal to all the senses: 'The shifting, munching cattle in the dark | And aromatic stalls';[61] or the early bee, venturing out on a clear day in February:

> Crashing through winter sunlight's pallid gold,
> His clumsiness sets catkins on the willow
> Ashake like lambs' tails in the early fold.
>
> *Sackville-West 1926: 41*

Then there is the matter of chosen style. At the opening of *The Land*, Sackville-West introduces her poem as 'The mild continuous epic of the soil'. The word 'mild' denotes aptly the middle style that Sackville-West achieves in her poem and Lembke in her translation; this middle style is characteristic of Virgil's *Georgics* too, as famously noted by Joseph Addison in the opening paragraph of his 1693 essay which appears in Dryden's 1697 translation of the works of Virgil. By using vocabulary in this opening passage such as 'trudges', 'pedestrian', 'plods' and 'loutish', she presents the work as unglamorous.[62] That said, Sackville-West's 'mild' epic is more capacious than Lembke's line, since it can accommodate an elaborate poem such as 'Nocturne' with which she closes 'Spring',[63] a poem which celebrates the nightingale's song and the music of the spheres, alongside her efforts 'to document the age-old Kentish skills and processes and the Kentish landscape', such as castrating the male lambs ('He shall turn little rams to little tegs') and carting manure ('the dung-cart with its reasty load').[64] Crucial to Sackville-West's style is her incorporation of country words still in use, such as East Anglian 'haysel' to mean the hay harvest,[65] along with old place-names and field-names of the Weald, and words falling into disuse, such as 'droil', 'yeavy' and 'reasty'.[66] For example, January is 'the wolf-month, shrammed and gaunt'.[67] This 'lexical parochialism', as Ian Blyth calls it,[68] has the effect of authenticating Sackville-West's language in lived experience and challenging the non-expert reader with unfamiliar, but usually guessable, terminology.[69] This amounts to an extreme form of domestication which is at the same time foreignizing for the non-local reader.

The resourcefulness of her language signifies Sackville-West's self-confidence as poet and as fieldsman. In *The Land* she stands shoulder to shoulder with 'the fieldsman of unhurrying tread' whose steady trudge matches her 'pedestrian measure'.[70] And she identifies with the many craftsmen whose knowledge and skill she celebrates at the close of 'Summer' when she says:

> All things designed to play a faithful part
> Build up their plain particular poetry.

Sackville-West 1926: 81

She speaks of 'language, smithied at the common fire' and aligns the poet's work with that of the artisan wielding his tools.[71] And so, for her and the other craftsmen alike:

> Much goes to little making – law and skill,
> Tradition's usage, each man's separate gift;
> Till the slow worker sees that he has wrought
> More than he knew of builded truth.

Sackville-West 1926: 83

Furthermore, I suggest that Sackville-West's identification of the work of craftsman and of poet – slow work that is grounded in knowledge and skill – applies equally to Lembke's translation of the *Georgics*, although she does not have the chance to articulate this idea as Sackville-West can in an original poem. Their commonalities are grounded in language and landscape. In terms of *language*, both Sackville-West and Lembke have successfully created a middle voice that accommodates the varied matter of farming along with passages of praise, celebration and complaint. This middle register avoids the potential perils of pomposity and colloquialism. Both have a profound knowledge of working the land and a profound devotion to the natural world. This means that both respond to

Virgil's evocation of Italy by articulating their devotion towards their own beloved landscapes: the county of Kent for Sackville-West, and North Carolina for Lembke. This knowledge and devotion is the source of the palpable authenticity of both poems and of their successful modernization of Virgil's world.

To close – a provocation. Are these features peculiar to Sackville-West and Lembke as *women* writers? Is it possible that *female* responses to the *Georgics* offer something unavailable in versions by male translators? First, I should say that I am confident that no sweeping claims can be made that the female reception of the *Georgics* is feminist. I know from personal acquaintanceship that Janet Lembke would have rejected this idea. Sackville-West is more complicated. The masculinist perspective of *The Land* is obvious: she prefers the masculine pronoun, she appears to identify with the masculine position and she virtually excludes women from the poem.[72] In a letter to her husband she reports that Robert Bridges, the Poet Laureate, congratulated her for having her 'feet on the ground – nothing woolly there – not a woman's writing at all – damn good'.[73] And, as Nagel nicely puts it, 'Vita both in real life and in her writing . . . sometimes cross-dresses', a fact reflected in Woolf's bisexual portrayal of her in *Orlando*.[74] But none of this makes her response a feminist response.

But is it possible that a female modesty, whether intrinsic or culturally determined, might make the middle register of Virgil's *Georgics* more attractive to female translators than the preciosity of the *Eclogues* and the elevated register of the *Aeneid*? I realize that I am walking into the marsh of essentialism by raising this question.[75] So I here appeal to Sarah Ruden, the first woman to translate the entire *Aeneid* into English. Ruden dismisses any feminist agenda in her translation work. She does, however, think that female translators have 'an edge over their male counterparts' because they develop 'a sense of personal connection': 'Women get more involved. The authors are more real to us. We develop relationships with them'.[76] I suggest that both Sackville-West and Lembke show this connection.[77]

Do I then deny that a man could match the modesty of the middle register or the love of the land that I find in Sackville-West and Lembke? Not necessarily. One candidate is Robert Wells, whose translation was published in 1982. Wells sets out to 'rescue' Virgil's poem from the eighteenth-century English georgic[78] and plumbs his own experience for inspiration, saying, 'I have worked on a farm, in England and in Italy. The sick sheep that lingers apart from the others and is slow to follow is standing in a high-hedged field on the Exmoor coast'.[79] But for the most part, Lembke was right when she rejected the versions 'rendered in British English by men who know much about poetry but little about farming'.[80] Day-Lewis, for example, wrote his translation when he retreated from London to the Devon countryside precisely in order to *find* some roots, not to articulate them.[81] But if we look further west, we find a phenomenon different from the Englishmen ignorant of the land in the Irish responses to Virgil's *Georgics* by Patrick Kavanagh (1904–67) and Peter Fallon (1951–), as manifested in Kavanagh's long poem 'The Great Hunger' (1942) and Fallon's 2004 translation.[82] Cillian O'Hogan in his excellent study of 'Irish Versions of Virgil's *Eclogues* and *Georgics*' shows how these poets, along with Seamus Heaney, use the resources of Hiberno-English (dialect forms, local idiom, slang) 'to relocate the Virgilian poems in a recognizably Irish landscape'.[83] O'Hogan demonstrates the peculiar tension in this linguistic strategy: choices that localize and domesticate for an Irish audience at the same time make the text *less* comfortable and familiar for an English audience.[84] Fallon, in his 'Afterwords' to his translation, demonstrates a groundedness in the realities of rural life in County Meath that aligns him closely with both Sackville-West and Lembke: this affinity merits future study. For now, at a moment when Western culture is reminding us to check our privilege,[85] it is somehow satisfying to see that it is *outsiders* to the white male British hegemony – Sackville-West, Lembke and Fallon – who form the strongest connection with Virgil's *Georgics* through their knowledge and their groundedness in their local language and landscape.[86]

Ways ahead: how ecofeminism could illuminate *The Land*[87]

My discussion is at this point complete, but because I have raised the question of feminism in these closing pages, I wish to suggest a potential line of future study of the *Georgics*, namely ecofeminist readings of the poem.[88] My proposal can be read alongside Tom Geue's brand new 'Marxish' reading of the *Georgics*, hot off the presses as we go to print, in which he explores the 'blindspots and absences' in the text by exposing its fantasies which see everyone but the pampered elite addressee doing the actual hard work, while leaving the toiling labourers more or less invisible or, where they are acknowledged, happily and voluntarily submitting to their tasks.[89] Geue's reading is compelling, although it is more or less relentlessly masculine; of the invisible female labourers in the *Georgics*, the only one he credits is Cyrene, who 'spoon-feed[s] the hero [her son, Aristaeus] silly'.[90] His 'Marxish' reading leaves plenty of room for the insights of feminist theory to be applied to the *Georgics*. I shall here indicate what I see as a fruitful prospectus for future work, although I declare myself unqualified to undertake it and do not even attempt it here.

There is of course a sizeable literature on the different phases and strands of feminism, how they deal with the risk of essentialism and how they risk reinforcing the binaries that they contest.[91] Of greatest relevance to my essay is the ground (pun intended) where feminism meets environmentalism. Further study of *The Land* might profitably be framed through the lens of ecofeminism, along the lines of the study of 'Renaissance Soil Science' (treatments of earth/soil/ground/land/mud/muck in early modern English literature) in the collection of essays called *Ground-Work*.[92] According to Val Plumwood in *Feminism and the Mastery of Nature*, one of the central problems of the dualistic view of the world is 'the western construction of human identity as "outside" nature'.[93] I suggest that both Sackville-West and Lembke offer a different view. Plumwood proposes that ecofeminism can help us perceive the assimilation of the oppression of women with the domination of nature, challenge the 'negative cultural value' placed by Western thought on the connection between women and nature, and replace it with reframed concepts of continuity and difference; her 'Introduction' could valuably be applied to Sackville-West's project.[94] Susan Griffin's *Woman and Nature: The Roaring Inside*

Her (1978), written associatively in what she describes as poetic prose[95] and which proposes a reconceptualization of the relationship between woman, nature and language with a movement from silence to speech, could also offer fruitful intersections with Sackville-West's interest in silence; the book calls for 'interdependence and renewal' in place of 'hierarchy and division'.[96] Finally, Linda Holler proposes breaking the habit of looking *at* the world and explores different models of *knowing*; she closes:[97] 'One general principle, the unity and affirmation of life, marks the beginning of concrete knowledge and grounds the promise of every particular disclosure.' It strikes me that Vita Sackville's epic poem puts into practice *avant la lettre* these important elements of ecofeminist theory.[98]

NOTES

INTRODUCTION

1. Seneca, *Ep.* 86.15: *Vergilius noster, qui non quid uerissime sed quid decentissime diceretur aspexit, nec agricolas docere uoluit sed legentes delectare* ('our Virgil, who considered not what to say most truthfully but most elegantly, did not wish to instruct farmers but to delight his readers').

2. For an analysis of scholarly approaches to the *Georgics* from 1970s to 2000, see esp. Gale (2000: 1–6) and Volk (2008: 1–13).

3. On the 'Harvard School' approach to the *Aeneid*, see Harrison (1990: 5–6); and to the *Georgics*, see Volk (2008: 3–4, 7).

4. In addition to the studies of Klingner and Buchheit, the work of Otis, *Virgil: A Study in Civilized Poetry* (1964), which considers the *Georgics* as a preliminary to the narrative patterns and explorations of human values in the *Aeneid*, also expresses a broadly optimistic view of the poem, arguing that the Aristaeus story in particular underlines the importance Virgil attaches to moral strength; see Otis (1964: 144–214) and also, much later, the study of Kramer, *Vergils Weltsicht: Optimismus und Pessimismus in Vergils Georgica* (1998).

5. In addition to Putnam (1979), see also Boyle (1986: 36–84), Ross (1987) and Thomas (1988).

6. The editors hasten to add that while Thomas's affiliation with both the 'Harvard School' and its namesake university is demonstrable, his commentary generally spares itself from using the term 'pessimism/pessimistic'.

7. See also Miles (1980).

8. Another example of revisionist optimistic reading is offered by Powell (2008: 239–44, 254–71), who suggests that the subject matter of the *Georgics* is aimed at generating retrospective support for Octavian's policy of land settlements for veterans by showing what they could achieve now that they have become farmers. Similarly, Erren (2005) treats the *Georgics* as a commissioned poem written with the aim of restoring the morale of veterans.

9. The works of Farrell (1991: esp. 3–25) and Hinds (1998) come immediately to mind as the most powerful examples of the extent to which intertextual reading has changed the complexion of Latin literary scholarship, especially of Virgil and Ovid.

10. Volk (2008: 6).

11. Volk (2002: 34–40).

12. Volk (2002: 2). Original emphasis.

13. Volk (2002: 136–8).

14. Volk's reading of the *Georgics* – that it is ostensibly about farming, but really about something else – is an extension of Effe's categorization of the *Georgics* as an example of the 'transparenter Typus' of didactic poetry; see Effe (1977: 80–97).

15. Henkel (2014).

16. For similar readings of the poem's agricultural instructions, see also Pucci (1998: 99–108) and Clément-Tarantino (2006). Henkel's work is also indebted to an essay by Gowers (2011) on the language and imagery of trees in the *Aeneid*.

17. Nappa (2005: 2).

18. See esp. Nappa (2005: 3–8).

19. Nappa engages with Gale (2000) throughout his book.

20. Nappa (2005: 2–3).

21. Batstone (1997), esp. 125 and 139–141 (on the 'failure of allegory'); compare with Schiesaro (1997: 63–89).

22. Nappa's starting point is an episode recorded in Donatus's *Vita Vergili* 27, that Virgil read the *Georgics* to Octavian over four days at Atella when the latter was on his way back to Rome after his victory at Actium. Donatus's account may be factually true, of course, but many critics prefer to take the more cautious view that such biographical details may simply be derived from retrospective readings of Virgil's text; see Nelis (2013: 248) and Horsfall (2001a: Ch.1).

23. Kronenberg (2009: 3).

24. Kronenberg (2009: 23). Original emphasis.

25. Kronenberg (2009: 22).

26. See esp. Kronenberg (2009: 137–8).

27. On Hesiod and Aratus, see Farrell (1991); on Lucretius, see Gale (2000).

28. Thibodeau (2011: 4).

29. Quotations are from p. 39 and p. 5 of Thibodeau (2011), respectively.

30. Thibodeau (2011: 38).

31. Sen. *Ep.* 86.15: *Vergilius noster, qui . . . quid* decentissime *diceretur aspexit*.

32. Thibodeau (2011: 40).

33. Thibodeau (2011: 74–115).

34. Thibodeau (2011: 115). For a similar interpretation of the *Georgics*, see Morgan (1999).

35. The transitional nature of the *Georgics* has been interpreted variously. For example, Otis (1963: 144–213) argues that the *Georgics* sees Virgil moving from non-narrative (*Eclogues*) to narrative poetry (*Aeneid*). Thomas (1985) sees a transition from pastoral Callimacheanism to national epic in the *Georgics*. Nelis (2004a) reads the end of book 2 and the opening of book 3 together and argues that this two-part midpoint offers readers a highly complex and detailed meditation concerning the position occupied by Virgil's oeuvre within the whole tradition of Greek and Roman epic.

36. Nelis (2013), esp. 249 and 262.

37. Geue (2018). In an earlier essay, Geue (2013) has shown that in the *Georgics* and the *Aeneid* Virgil retrospectively crystallizes ideas and identities that the *Eclogues* leave ambiguous in order to create the impression that Octavian-Augustus was 'always already there' even before his rise to power, thereby normalizing political change. By contrast, Powell (2008) reads the *Georgics* as fully committed to the Caesarian cause and renouncing the doubts raised by the *Eclogues*.

38. The term was coined by Conte (1980: 122–36). For a recent collection of a diverse range of intertextual readings of the 'proem in the middle', see Pieri (2011).

39. Henderson (2004: 133) argues that Seneca's quotation and discussion of the *Georgics* in his epistle tell us more about how Seneca 'would see himself as always putting Truth above Decorum, if obliged to choose' than how readers should regard Virgil and his work.

40. Thibodeau (2011: 152–201).

41. Ancient reception of the *Georgics* (i.e. in the first 150 years after the poem's publication) forms the final chapter of Thibodeau's monograph. See also Christmann (1982) and Horster (2005).

42. Wilkinson (1969: Ch. 10), Jenkyns (1998: Ch. 15), Ziolkowski and Putnam (2008).

43. Wilson-Okamura (2010), Haskell (2003), Ziolkowski (1993). On the anti-aristocratic 'georgic spirit' of sixteenth-century English poetry, see Low (1985), who examines in sequence major poetic works from the second instalment of Spenser's *The Faerie Queene* (1596) to Milton's *Paradise Regained* (1671). There is still scope for the examination of the *Georgics*' reception in the seventeenth century. In England, for example, there was Abraham Cowley's verse translation of Virgil's *O fortunatos* passage (*Geo.* 2.458–540), appended to his essay *Of Agriculture* (1668), as well as his earlier Neo-Latin poem *Plantarum Libri Sex* (1662), which explicitly engages with the *Georgics* throughout; on this poem, see Moul (2012 and 2017). In Europe, Neo-Latin garden-poems formed a subspecies of their own; by far the most important 'georgic' poem of the few produced in the seventeenth century was René Rapin's *Hortorum Libri IV* (1665); on this poem, see Barton (Chapter 11) in this volume.

44. On the reception of the Virgilian Orpheus, see esp. Segal (1989). On the Virgilian *laudes Italiae* in Renaissance Italy and elsewhere, see Houghton (2015).

45. On the English 'georgicists', see Wilkinson (1969: 296–30) and Ziolkowski (1993: 104–20).

46. Ziolkowski (1993: 26).

1 THE STORY OF YOU: SECOND-PERSON NARRATIVE AND THE NARRATOLOGY OF THE *GEORGICS*

1. De Jong (2014) offers a useful introduction and survey including bibliography which space constraints exclude from this chapter. The seminal works on narratology are Genette (1980 (1972)) and Bal (2009 (1977)), the subsequent bibliography immense.

2. De Jong (1987), Winkler (1985).

3. Fowler (2000a: 206), citing Benveniste (1971 (1966)) and Genette (1980 (1972)) for the distinction.

4. Plague: Penwill (1996), P. Fowler (1997); *Aristaeus*: Perutelli (1980), Bartels (2004: 166–90), Baier (2007).

5. Thibodeau (2011: 170–5), though its subsection is entitled 'Narratology', makes no use of narratological theory or terminology.

6. Gale (2004), Fowler (2000a), Trépanier (2007: esp. 254–76).

7. On adventure gamebooks, see now Wake (2016).

8. Richardson (1991), Fludernik (1993), Wiest (1993); *Style*: Fludernik (1994a), including notably Cornis-Pope (1994), Fludernik (1994b), Herman (1994), Kacandes (1994), Nance (1994), Phelan (1994 = 1996: 135–53), Richardson (1994).

9. Conversational: Mildorf (2012); digital, IF and computer games: Montfort (2003), Ryan (2005), Harrigan and Wardrip-Fruin (2007), Bell and Enslin (2011), Enslin and Bell (2012), Punday (2012), Salter (2014).

10. Akujärvi (2012: 354–6), de Jong (2014: 23–5).

11. Richardson (1991: 313).

12. On the authority of the narrator of 'how-to' second-person narratives, see DelConte (2013/14: 59).

13. 'For a text to be considered as a second-person narrative there has to exist a (usually fictional) protagonist who is referred to by an address pronoun.' Fludernik (1994b: 302). It makes sense to substitute second-person verbs for address pronouns in languages, like Latin and Greek, which only sparingly use nominative and vocative pronouns.

14. Trollope (1999 (1864–5): 384).

15. DelConte (2003: 207–8), original italics. Cf. Nance (1994: 367).

16. On the *Georgics*' addressee(s) and/or audience(s), see esp. Effe (1977: 87), Schiesaro (1993), Rutherford (2008 (1995)), Horsfall (2001a: 65–70), Volk (2002: 129–39), Reay (2003), Nappa (2005: 6–9) and Thibodeau (2011: 17–73).

17. Phelan (1996: 137).

18. Horsfall (2001a: 70).

19. On the sort(s) of farmer implied by the tasks assigned, see Horsfall (2001a: 67–9), Reay (2003) and Thibodeau (2011: 17–73).

20. Pucci (1998: 99–108), Clément-Tarantino (2006), Henkel (2014).

21. Volk (2002: 136), original italics.

22. Phelan (1994: 146).

23. Herman (1994), cf. Herman (2002: 331–71). Classics and deixis: e.g. Danielewicz (1990), Felson (2004), Edmunds (2008) and Hutchinson (2010).

24. Herman (1994: 390).

25. Herman (1994: 389, 402).

26. Cf. Effe (1977: 93–4) on the *Georgics* as an example of the 'transparenter Typus'.

27. On *didaxis* as the true object of the *Georgics*' *didaxis*, see Schiesaro (1997) and Hardie (2004c).

28. Richardson (1991: esp. 310; 2006: 17–36, esp. 18). For a useful critique and suggestions for a revised typology, see Reitan (2011: 151–60).

29. For example, Bal (1996: 181–2).

30. Gibson (1997: esp. 70–3).

31. Solomon and Reinheimer (2012: 71)

32. McInerney (1984: 41).

33. Gibson (1997: 90).

34. Richardson (1991: 320–2; 2006: 30–2).

35. Volk (2002: quote from 124, definition at 13–24).

36. Lucr. 1.265–9 (*accipe*), 1.921 (*cognosce*), 2.333–5, 730–1, 4.110–11, 269–70, 722–3, 6.535–6 (all *percipe*).

37. Lucr. 2.62–6, 6.495–7, 738–9 (all *expediam*); 1.953–4 (*euoluamus*), 3.417–20 (*pergam disponere*), 4.176–80 (*edam*). 4.673–4 is particularly bold in combining imperative *age* with future *agam*.

38. Richardson (1991: 319–20; 2006: 28–30).

39. Fludernik (1996: 171).

40. Vogel (2011: 76).

41. Phelan (1994: 359).

42. Schofield (1997: 98).

43. On game books, see Wake (2016).

44. Ryan (2005: 519). See n. 9 for further bibliography.

45. Volk (2002: 13–24).

46. Volk (2002: 124).

47. McInerney (1984: 27).

48. Updike (1979 (1972): 43–4, 45 *bis*).

49. 2.274–7. Putnam (1979: 114) catches the paradox, writing of 'the alternatives necessity forces upon us'.

50. '[the *Georgics*] make their reader participate in an experience of mutability and shifting perspectives', Batstone (1988: 242).

51. Nappa (2003: 54).

52. Cf. 3.525: *quid labor aut benefacta iuuant?*; Thomas (1988: *ad loc.*): 'The words ... imply, as much of the poem has implied, the futility of *labor* when such destruction is visited on its practioners.'

53. Moore (2008 (1985): 577).

54. DelConte (2003: 214), Richardson (1991: 320).

55. 'a caustic parody of the glowing self-help manuals they pretend to imitate', Richardson (1991: 320), Phelan (1994: 359), Vogel (2011).

56. Barthes (1977: 94).

57. Quint (1992: 9).

58. War imagery: Betensky (1979), Gale (2000: 232–69). Epic: Farrell (1991), Grilli (2002), Harrison (2007: 149–67).

59. Sideshadowing: Bernstein (1994), Morson (1994); in Classical epic: Armstrong (2002), Cowan (2010).

60. Richardson (1991: 314 = 2006: 23).

61. Houston (1990: 103).

62. Enn. *Ann.* fr. 20 Sk., Verg. *A.* 1.530, 3.163, 7.563.

63. *Od.* 22.299–300, with Thomas (1988: *ad loc.*).

64. Thomas (1988: 1.145–6, original emphasis): 'in this poem (as in life) toil does *not* overcome all difficulties: the farmer's crops are destroyed by sudden, unseasonable storms ... the oxen succumb to plague *in spite of* their toil'.

65. Love, snakes, plague: Putnam (1979: 184–6), Ross (1987: 157–63), Thomas (1988: 3.150–1, 152–3), Erren (2003: 626–7).

66. Erren (2003: 629).

67. Batstone (1988: 232, n. 13): 'Vergil continually questions the effectiveness and propriety of his own didaxis.' Cf. Putnam (2008 (1975): 141, n. 1) on 2.158: 'the near *praeteritio* ... helps us to see beyond the mere rhetorical question, to entertain firmer doubts about any positive thrust in the poet's continuing list'.

68. Nappa (2003: 51).

69. Thomas (1988: 124, 1.335–50): '[O]bservation of the calendar and the signs is of no avail against storms, and there is no suggestion in the *Georgics* that piety is of any use in the struggle between man and his environment.'

70. Rutherford (2008 (1995): 85).

71. Cf. Lovatt (2013: 263) on Hector's corpse at Hom. *Il.* 22.369–75 and '[t]he strong contrast between active action hero and passive object of the gaze'.

72. See n. 58.

73. On second-person narrative as 'radical narrative apostrophe', see Kacandes (1994).

74. Versions of this chapter were delivered at the UCL conference, the University of Sydney Classics and Ancient History seminar, and Homer Seminar VIII at ANU. I am grateful to all three audiences for their comments and to the volume editors for their support and insight.

2 CLEARING THE GROUND IN *GEORGICS* 1

1. Cf. Nelis (2004a), an essay much concerned with beginnings, as well as middles and ends; see especially pp. 75–80.

2. Nelis (2004a: 86) stresses the run of future verbs in this passage.

3. Cf. Farrell (1991: 104–13).

4. See, e.g., Morgan (1999: 105–8).

5. This is what is transmitted, but *iratus* is a participle that Virgil uses nowhere else, and I suspect it has displaced another epithet, such as *ingratus*: see Heyworth (2015: 230–1).

6. As well as exploring how Virgil transforms the simile, Thomas (1988: *ad loc.*) notes the military language in *comminus . . . insequitur . . . ruit*. Ross (1987: 48), Cramer (1998: 16–18) and Gale (2000: 253) see such diction as starting with *iacto* in 104 (seeds/spears are cast before hand-to-hand combat begins); we might add *sequentis* in 106 (the streams are presented as troops following the commander).

7. The words in bold are the translation of Wilkins.

8. Similarly Papillon: 'from the brow of a sloping ravine'.

9. 'In a sloping area', *Il.* 21.262.

10. Word order, with *ad* separated from the accusative noun and epithet, strongly implies that the ablative *molli tramite* modifies *decliuem*.

11. *OLD moles* 8, but playing on sense 3, 'earthwork'.

12. Similar are the instances where *trames* is used for other channels, e.g. the wind-pipe at Plin. *Nat. Hist.* 11.176.

13. On the other hand the translation, in vol. 1, reads 'sieh da, da entlockt er dem First der Gefällstrecke eine Flutwelle!' ('Look, there he elicits a flood of water from the ridge at the top of the incline').

14. According to Erren *ad loc.*, 'Die "Braue" . . . bezeichnet eigentlich einen Weg am oberen Rand eines steilen Abhangs' ('*Brow* indicates simply a path on the upper edge of a steep slope').

15. Cf. *limine* at Prop. 1.18.12: *limine formosos intulit ulla pedes* ('any woman has brought her beautiful feet in via the doorway'), and Heyworth 2007 *ad loc.*

16. Apuleius perhaps wrote *iuxta supercilio*, 'nearby on the top of the bank'.

17. So de la Cerda, in his *explicatio*, though he has no plausible account of *cliuosi tramitis*: 'agricola elicit undam ex supercilio (cacumine) in quo est trames cliuosus (id est, molliter et leuiter fastigiatus, per quem unda deducatur)'.

18. Cf. the Livy passages already cited: 34.29.11: *supercilio . . . tumuli*; at 27.18.10 the previous sentence contains the word *tumuli*. Prudentius, *Peristephanon* 12.31: *supercilio saxi liquor ortus* ('water rising from the top of a rock') is conceivably indebted to Virgil's phrasing here; but given that Servius is confused, it is hardly surprising that his contemporary was too.

19. 'Hillock' at Hyginus Gromaticus, *De Generibus Controuersiarum*, page 91, line 19; 'ridge' at Frontinus, *Contr.* 5; Siculus Flaccus, *De Condicionibus Agrorum*, page 102, line 17; Siculus Flaccus, *De Condicionibus Agrorum*, page 115, line 23, for example.

20. Thus he glosses *ecce* at *Aen.* 2.203. *ecce* gives lively expression to a sudden action or revelation also at 3.515, *Ecl.* 3.50, *Aen.* 3.687, 6.337, 8.81, 11.448, 12.319. Cowan, as he mentions in the previous chapter, has plans to explore such quasi-apostrophes in the *Georgics*.

21. 'der den entscheidenden Wink gibt . . . das Wasser wie einen Trupp Menschen herbeieilen zu lassen' ('who gives a decisive wink to let the water rush over, as if to a contingent of men').

22. Or perhaps, as Erren implies, like soldiers accepting orders from their general; cf. the military diction earlier in the sentence.

23. Similar is Quintilian, *Inst. Orat.* 11.3.78–9 on the orator's use of the eyebrows.

24. Note the use of the adverbial ablative *superciliis*, like the singular at *Ars* 1.500: *multa supercilio . . . loquare* ('you may say much with an eyebrow'). Cf. also *Am.* 2.5.15, *Her.* 17.82; Prop. 3.8.25; Martial 9.37.5–6.

25. Cf. also Cicero, *Sest.* 19; *Priapea* 1.2 (and Bianchini *ad loc.*); SHA, *Aurel.* 27.5.

26. As Damien Nelis suggested to me at the UCL conference.

27. DServ. on *Aen.* 3.175 says the dragging was done by the *pontifices*.

28. It echoes the use of the phrase at *Ecl.* 10.74 where Virgil is carefully preparing the ground for the *Georgics*. Lucretius' *De Rerum Natura* also begins in spring (explicitly so at 1.10): see Gale (2002: 59); Hesiod's calendar begins in September (*Works and Days* 414).

29. For *seges* in this sense see *OLD* 2, and, as Servius notes, e.g. 4.128–9: *nec fertilis illa iuuencis | nec pecori opportuna seges nec commoda Baccho* ('that ground is not fertile for oxen to plough nor suited to pasture nor fit for Bacchus [i.e. planting with vines]'); likewise Cicero, *Hortensius* frag. 24: *segetes agricolae subigunt aratris multo ante quam serant* ('farmers work fields with ploughs long before they sow'); Tibullus 1.3.61: *fert casiam non culta seges* ('the untilled ground bears cinnamon').

30. Mynors (1990: 10).

31. So the ninth-century MS γ, where the antique MSS have *ac*: in support of *at*. see Cramer (1998: 9, n. 31).

32. Columella has a version of this at 11.3.11: *ut aut hiemis frigoribus aut aestiuis solibus et glaeba soluatur et radices herbarum necentur* ('so that the soil may be broken up either by the cold of winter or the heat of summer and the roots of weeds may be killed off').

33. See ThLL *frigus* 1335.30–47 for further examples, beginning from *Rhet. ad Her.* 4.61: *ita ut hirundines aestiuo tempore praesto sunt, frigore pulsae recedunt* ('just as swallows are present in the summer season, but disappear driven away by the cold'), and including an example of the plural from *Georgics* 1.300.

34. Erren *ad loc.* (2.48): 'Der frühe Termin bedeutet aber nicht, daß im gleichen Frühjahr noch gesät und in Sommer geerntet werden könnte. Vielmehr liegt jedes Feld jedes zweite Jahr brach und wird fleißig immer wieder gepflügt (Cato *agr.* 61.131, . . .). Das Halbjahr, in dem gepflügt wird, sollte für den Acker seit der letzten Ernte das vierte sein. Dann darf man eine reiche Ernte erwarten.' ('The early date does not mean, however, that in the

same spring one can sow and then harvest in the summer. Rather each field lies fallow every other year and is diligently ploughed time after time … The sixth-month period in which it is ploughed will be the fourth for the field since the last harvest. Then one may hope for a generous crop.')

35. Klingner (1967: 194) sees that the text here offers resumption combined with qualification; cf. also Cramer (1998: 14, n. 55).

36. On the organizational complexity of this passage, see Miles (1980: 74–5). However, Kraggerud (2017: 100–9) makes a strong case for taking *inaratae* as 'ploughed in'; this would reprise 79–81, as 82 summarizes 73–9.

37. A didactic parallel for the importance of having started already comes at Vitruvius 2.3.2: *maxime autem utiliores erunt, si ante biennium fuerint ducti* (on bricks; similarly 2.7.5, on stone).

3 AESTHETICS, FORM AND MEANING IN THE *GEORGICS*

1. I would add that the reviewers for the current volume had no such criticism.

2. Lentricchia (1980: xiii), cited by Jancovich (1993).

3. Jancovich (1993: 4).

4. Hickman and McIntyre (2012: 25).

5. Samuels (1996: 2).

6. Things started to change with the appearance of Altevogt (1952), a work which effectively argued that the notion of toil as a consistently positive force in the poem was untenable in the light of details in the poem itself.

7. Wellek (1978), as his title announces, gives the pros and cons on the New Criticism. His conclusion anticipates the sort of return to aesthetics and to the importance of form that is to be found in Martindale (2005), whose argument for the 'aesthetic turn' Wellek desiderates and predicts (1978: 624): 'I will not conceal my own conviction that the New Criticism has stated or reaffirmed many basic truths to which future ages will have to return: the specific nature of the aesthetic transaction, the normative presence of a work of art which forms a structure, a unity, coherence, a whole.' Forty years after these words were written we see what has been lost in Wellek's prophetic final words: 'The humanities would abdicate their function in society if they surrendered to a neutral scientism and indifferent relativism or if they succumbed to the imposition of alien norms required by political indoctrination. Particularly on these two fronts the New Critics have waged a valiant fight which, I am afraid, must be fought over again in the future.'

8. Batstone (1997: 129).

9. Watkins (1995) 199–200.

10. Mynors (1990: 252).

11. By which I mean the tabbing in to indicate degrees of subordination, each clause subordinate to the one immediately to its left, a useful way of depicting complexity of hypotaxis.

12. See Heyworth in the previous chapter.

13. Mittsdörffer (1938).

14. Noticed by Ewald (1990).

15. Among other treatments, see Danielewicz (2013), with further bibliography.

4 *GEORGICA* AND *ORPHICA*: THE *GEORGICS* IN THE CONTEXT OF ORPHIC POETRY AND RELIGION

1. References to Orphic Fragments marked '*OF*' refer to the enumeration in Bernabé (2004–7). References to the fragments of Empedocles refer to their enumeration in Diels and Kranz (1951–2). I am most grateful to Barney Taylor, Fiachra Mac Góráin, Peter Agócs and the editors for their astute comments on this chapter.

2. Most notably, the Derveni papyrus, which was discovered in 1962; An anonymous edition of part of the papyrus appeared on separately numbered pages at the end of *ZPE* 47 (1982) but the full *editio princeps* was only published as Kouremenos et al. (2006). There have also been a number of publications of newly discovered gold tablets, which have made clearer their association with Bacchus. Note especially the Hipponion tablet (*OF* 474, first published in 1974), which mentions the 'sacred road which initiates and famous *Bacchoi* follow' (lines 15–6); and the two tablets from Pherae (*OF* 485–6, first published in 1987) and the tablet from Amphipolis (*OF* 496n, first published 2001), which mention Bacchus.

3. Bernabé (2004–7).

4. On Bacchus in the *Georgics*, see Freer's contribution to this volume, as well as Gowers (2016) and Mac Góráin (2014).

5. See Bremmer (2014: 55–80), and note Hdt. 2.81.

6. West (1983: 28–9, 37–8) dates the *Hymns* to the second or third century CE, and the *Argonautica* no earlier than the fourth.

7. West (1983: 36–7).

8. Norden (1927: 5, n. 2). Perhaps Norden's strongest evidence for his argument is the similarity between *Aen.* 6.120 and a line from the fifth-century CE Orphic *Argonautica* (42), which occurs in a passage which may refer to an earlier *Katabasis* of Orpheus.

9. Horsfall (2013) *ad Aen.* 6.548–636; Bremmer (2014: 187–93).

10. See Bremmer (2014: 187–93).

11. On the tablets, see Graf and Johnston (2013) and Bernabé and San Cristóbal (2008). The latter present good reasons for accepting the traditional interpretation that Orpheus was believed to be their author (179–89).

12. The most clear and detailed attempt to reconstruct the interrelation of the different Orphic theogonies circulating in antiquity is still West (1983), although he is perhaps overconfident in his reconstructions: see the review by Graf (1985). For a full bibliography on Orphic theogonies, see Bernabé (2004–7), fasc. 1 XXVIII–XLII.

13. The above is a cursory summary of the main findings of West (1983), followed largely by Bernabé (2004–7), although West goes further to suggest two further Orphic theogonies: an original 'Protogonos Theogony', of which the Derveni theogony is supposed to be an abbreviation; and a 'cyclic' theogony which stood at the beginning of the epic cycle and which lay behind the myth at the beginning of Apollodorus's *Bibliotheca*. These views, however, have found less support; see Graf (1985).

14. *In Phd.* 1.3 = *OF* 304 I; 313 II; 318 III; 320 I.

15. *Ap.* Philodemus *On Piety* 192–3 (ll. 4956–69) = *OF* 59. The fragment is printed in Lightfoot (2009: 270–1).

16. See Graf and Johnston (2013: 66–93).

17. Cicero *DND* 1.107 with West (1983: 246–51) (cf. also *DND* 1.40–1) and Nigidius *ap.* Serv. *In Vergilii Bucolicon Librum* 4.10.1.

18. Philodemus mentions 'Orphic hymns' in *On Piety* PHerc. 1428 fr. 3 (for a text of which see Obbink (1994)) and alludes to episodes from Orphic theogony at *On Piety* 192–3 (ll. 4956–69) and, apparently, *On Poems* 181, Janko (on which see the editor's comment).

19. For the surviving fragments of Linus, see Bernabé (2004–7), Fasc. 3 54–104 or, with discussion, West (1983: 56–67).

20. Cf. Hesiod *Op.* 109–26 (the golden race) and 217–24 (Justice personified as the maiden Δίκη). Although these parallels are with the *Works and Days* rather than the *Theogony*, the *Works and Days* is generically similar to theogonical works (such as those attributed to Linus and Orpheus) as it explains the origins of man, recounting two myths on the subject: that of Prometheus and Pandora (42–105) and the myth of the races (106–201).

21. As noted, for instance, by Clausen (1994: 176–7). Orpheus's song in Apollonius's *Argonautica* is based on Empedocles' cosmology – as discussed by P. Hardie (1986: 62), Nelis (1992: 157–60) and Hunter (1993: 162–7, 177) – and has been seen as an indicator (among other evidence) that Empedocles' poem itself can be seen as an Orphic text, on which see Riedweg (1995) and Rodríguez (2005).

22. Morgan (1999) and A. Hardie (2002). See also Johnston (1977, and especially 2009). On Virgil and mystery religion more generally, see Luck (1973). On Dionysiac mysteries, see Burkert (1987: 21–3).

23. For the λικνοφόροι, see Mynors (1990) *ad loc.*, who cites Callim. *Cer.*126. For Iacchus, see Graf (2006).

24. See A. Hardie (2002: 178). On the apotheosis of Octavian in 1.20–42, see also Xinyue in this book.

25. See Morgan (1999: 153–4).

26. For Orpheus and Eleusis, see Graf (1974); for the connections and distinctions between Orphism and Bacchism, see Burkert (1982) and Parker (1995). Cf. Hdt. 2.81 for the early association between Orphism and Bacchism/Dionysism (and Pythagoreanism).

27. See, similarly, Morgan (1999: 195).

28. On the prominence of Orphism in southern Italy, see Parker (1995) and, for the grave at Cumae, Bremmer (2014: 72).

29. West (1983: 127–8). The Orphic theogony he suggests was available to them is the 'Eudemian theogony'.

30. Although, in the Gurôb papyrus, the drums are in imitation of the Coybantes/Couretes guarding the infant Dionysus, a myth that also occurred in the *Rhapsodic Theogony* (*OF* 212–13). See Janko (2000: 401) *ad* fr. 181, and, on the Gurôb papyrus, Hordern (2000).

31. Thomas (1988: *ad loc.*).

32. *de Mund.* 401 a 25 (= *OF* 31B).

33. On the two and the distinctions between them, see Burkert (1982). On the early connections between Orphism and Pythagoreanism, see Riedweg (2005: 51–5), who argues that the early Pythagoreans derived their doctrines from allegorical interpretations of Orphic poems. Note Hdt. 2.81 and Ion of Chios B2 (= D.L. 8.8) and Cicero *DND* 1.107.

34. For example, Cic. *DND* 1.40–1; Plut. *De defectu orac.* 415ff. See further West (1983: 113, 193–6).

35. P. Hardie (1986: 83–4).

36. Hesiod *Op.*109–26; Empedocles B128; *OF* 216B (= Procl. *in Plat. Remp.* II 74, 2).

37. Blessed afterlife: Pindar fr. 137, *OF* 488, 474, 476, 477, 485, 486, 489, 490. Reincarnation: Empedocles B117 and B137; Plato *Resp.* 10.617d ff. and *Phd.* 70c ff. *OF* 488.5, Pindar fr. 133. Divinization: Empedocles B112.4, B146, *OF* 484, 487 and 491.

38. The description of the Golden Race at *Op.* 109–26 is echoed in the language describing the just city at 225–37. See the classic treatment of Vernant (1983 (1965)).

39. On the inconsistencies between the *laudes Italiae* and depiction of Italy in the rest of the poem, see Thomas (1988: 179–80), who writes 'V. presents obvious fictions, demonstrably in conflict with the reality of Italy as it exists in the "technical" sections of the poem' (180). For connections (via Aratus) between the golden age imagery in the *Georgics* and that in Empedocles, see Nelis (2004b).

40. Plato *Resp.* 364b2–365a3. See also Eur. *Hipp.* 952–4. A papyrus decree from one of the Ptolemies (*BGU* 1211), ordering those who perform initiations for Dionysus in Egypt to present their 'sacred accounts' (ἱεροὶ λόγοι), may also refer to this type of text, on which see Parker (2011: 16–7). For the possibility that the Derveni theogony was used as a 'sacred account' in this sense, as part of initiation rituals, see Obbink (1997).

41. See Graf and Johnston (2013: 66–93).

42. A. Hardie (2002: 178) argues that the divinization of Augustus at 1.24–42 evokes the Eleusinian mysteries. Note also the amazing way (* *mirabile dictu*, 2.30) that a living olive root shoots out from the dry (dead?) wood (*truditur e sicco radix oleagina ligno*, 2.31) in the Bacchic book 2.

43. An explanation already suggested by Macrobius *S.Sc.* 1.2.17ff. See further, Burkert (1987: 78–88).

44. On allegory in book 4 of the *Georgics*, see further Morgan (1999).

45. That is, those that purport to be intended to instruct. For the distinction between 'formally' and 'finally' didactic texts, see Heath (1985: 253). Formally didactic texts may not *actually* be intended to instruct, just as most commentators today do not believe that the *Georgics* was intended to be of practical use to farmers.

46. Nelis (2013: 253–4).

47. See, e.g., Thomas (1988: *ad loc.*), and Morgan (1999: 50–101), who suggests that it is the *Georgics* itself. See also Xinyue and Giusti in this volume.

48. Compare with Xinyue's reading in this volume.

49. For further connections between the *bugonia* episode and the end of book 1, see Morgan (1999: 200–2).

50. Cf. also Hor. *Carm.* 1.7, 3.6; *Epod.* 7.

51. Note especially *OF* 488.5 and *OF* 348.

5 VIRGIL'S *GEORGICS* AND THE EPICUREAN SIRENS OF POETRY

1. See, e.g., Gigante (2004: 92–5), La Penna (1977) and Alfonsi (1959).

2. See esp. Gale (2000) and Farrell (1991).

3. Cf. Gale (2000: 185–92).

4. Virgil appears as a dedicatee in several fragments of Philodemus recovered from Herculaneum; see here Gigante (2004, 85–6) and Gigante and Capasso (1989). See Armstrong, Fish, Johnston and Skinner (2004) for a collection of essays exploring Virgil's engagement with the works of Philodemus.

5. The *Georgics*' status as a work of *didaxis* is also addressed by Mackenzie in this section of the book.

6. See Thomas (1988 *ad* 4.559–66).

7. As Fowler (1989: 83) remarks, the *sphragis* 'retrospectively fashions the two works into an oeuvre'.

8. Morgan (1999: 215) notes that *carmina pastorum* may also refer to the *Aristaeus* episode that precedes the *sphragis*, for Aristaeus (317) and Proteus (395) are both strictly *pastores*.

9. Kyriakidis (2002: 284–5).

10. Schmid (1983: 317–8).

11. Gale (2003: 326–7).

12. See Sider (1997: 213) for a bibliography of secondary literature on Parthenope/Naples.

13. Parthenope appears as Virgil's final resting place in the epitaph attributed to the poet by Donatus (*Vit. Verg.* 36: *Mantua me genuit, Calabri rapuere, tenet nunc | Parthenope; cecini pascua rura duces*, 'Mantua bore me, Calabria snatched me away, and now Parthenope holds me; I sang of pastures, the country, and leaders'). Donatus also reports that Virgil was given the nickname 'Parthenias' ('Maiden') in Naples due to his modest character (*Vit. Verg.* 11); see Korenjak (1995).

14. Cf. also Plin. *Nat. Hist.* 3.62.

15. Gale (2003: 327); see also Miles (1980: 293) on Parthenope as the poet's 'Muse' in the *sphragis*.

16. Diog. Laer. 10.6.

17. Epicurus's condemnation of *paideia* is also attested in Plut. *Non posse* 1094d and Ath. *Deip.* 13.588a.

18. The Sirens were associated with poetry throughout antiquity; see Kaiser (1964: 111–36).

19. Cf., e.g., Plut. *Non posse* 1095c.

20. Poetry and myth were widely regarded as inseparable in antiquity; see Gale (1994: 9, 15).

21. *Non posse* 1087a. Heraclitus (*Quaest. Hom.* 79) and Athenaeus (*Deip.* 5.187c) both align Epicurus with Plato as critics of Homer who also emphasized the dangers of poetry and myth. However, it is worth noting that Plato does not invoke the Sirens in connection with the harmful effects of poetry.

22. Cf., e.g., *De mus.* 4. 18.16–19 Delattre. See Obbink (1995) for a collection of essays on Philodemus's views on poetry.

23. Cf. *De poem.* 5. 36.29–32 Mangoni. For discussion of Philodemus's views on the psychagogic power of poetry, see Halliwell (2012: 324), Chandler (2005: 147–67) and Wigodsky (1995: 65–8).

24. Philodemus describes himself as μουσοφιλής (*Ep.* 27.2, 'loved by the Muses'); see Sider (1997 *ad* 27.2).

25. *De mus.* 4.10.13–18 Delattre (dirges), 4.120.5–11 (love songs).

26. *De poem.* 5.4.18–20 Mangoni..

27. See Asmis (1995: 21).

28. This may have been due to the belief that poetry and myth are inseparable (see n. 20), although Epicurus also may have argued that poetic language and diction lack the clarity necessary for effective philosophical instruction (in contrast to plain prose); see here Asmis (1995: 21) and Gale (1994: 14–15). Philodemus likewise questions poetry's power to teach or persuade; see Asmis (1995: 28).

29. According to Diogenes Laertius, Epicurus said that the wise man ποιήματά τε ἐνεργεῖν οὐκ ἂν ποιῆσαι (10.121b). Emending ἐνεργεῖν to ἐνεργείᾳ, Usener (1887: 42) understood Epicurus to

mean that the sage will not make poetry 'in actuality' (i.e. not at all). However, as Asmis (1995: 21) observes, Usener's ἐνεργείᾳ and the transmitted ἐνεργεῖν could also be translated as 'being busy at' or 'practicing energetically' (i.e. the wise man will not devote excessive effort to poetic composition). Whether or not Epicurus endorsed the latter interpretation, his followers may have used this reading to justify their own poetic endeavours as an occasional pastime alongside the serious pursuit of philosophy. This may explain why Philodemus confined his own poetic activity to the genre of light epigram; see Sider (1997: 32).

30. Clay (2004: 26–7).

31. The authenticity of the *Catalepton* remains an object of debate: Peirano (2012: 74–116) and Holzberg (2004), for example, view the entire collection the work of a later imitator, while Clay (2004) and Longo Auricchio (2004) suggest that at least some of the poems are authentic Virgilian compositions.

32. Cicero (*De fin.* 2.119) identifies Siro as one of the leading contemporary Epicureans, along with Philodemus, and a fragment from Herculaneum attests to Siro's presence in Naples (*PHerc.* 312 col. 14). Siro also figures prominently elsewhere in the Virgilian biographical tradition; in line with *Catalepton* 5, Donatus identifies Siro as Virgil's teacher (*Vit. Verg.* 79), while Servius in *Eclogue* 6.13 allegorizes the satyr Silenus as Siro and the boys Chromis and Mnasyllus as his disciples Virgil and Varus. The eighth poem of the *Catalepton* famously portrays Virgil as the heir to Siro's villa.

33. Sider (1997: 19).

34. Clay (2004: 26). Interestingly, the narrator's invitation to the Muses to return *pudenter et raro* ('modestly and rarely', *Cat.* 5.14) is consistent with the approach to poetic composition possibly endorsed by Philodemus; see n. 29. Longo Auricchio (2004: 40–1) has identified a further parallel with *Catalepton* 5 in a passage from Philodemus's *On Rhetoric* (*PHerc.* 463 fr. 13), which contrasts participation in public life through the practice of rhetoric with the εὐδαίμων βίος enjoyed by those who have sailed into the Epicurean harbour of philosophy.

35. Gale (2000: 192).

36. Gale (2000: 185–6). For the allegorical reading of Orpheus's supernatural powers cf. esp. Hor. *Ars* 391–3.

37. Cf., e.g., Diog. Laert. 1 prol. 4; Quint. *Inst.* 1.10.9.

38. See here Gale (2000: 186–7).

39. As Hardie (1986: 40–1) shows, *accipiant* and *monstrent* in G. 2.477 also recall the language of religious initiation and revelation employed by Lucretius in his apology.

40. See Kronenberg (2000: 346–8).

41. For the Bacchic associations of this passage, see Miles (1980: 153–4).

42. The two passages are linked by references to Bacchus's 'gifts' (4–5: *tuis hic omnia plena* | *muneribus*; 454: *Baccheia dona*).

43. Gale (2000: 44). See Mac Góráin (2014) on the ambivalence of Virgil's portrayal of Bacchus in the *Georgics*: 'While Bacchus is mostly a god of fertility and abundance in the *Georgics* ... his dangerous and menacing aspect in the end proves irrepressible' (26).

44. For this point, see Gale (2000: 44–5, 191–2).

45. See Conte (1992) on the 'proem in the middle' as a traditional locus for reflections on poetry in Latin literature. Nelis (2004a) and Hardie (1986: 48–50) examine the connections between the end of book 2 and the proem to book 3.

46. Ennius (*Epigrams* 18 V.): *uolito uiuus per ora uiuum* ('I fly still living on the lips of men'); Lucretius (*DRN* 1.117–9): *Ennius ut noster cecinit, qui primus amoeno* | *detulit ex Helicone*

perenni fronde coronam, | *per gentis Italas hominum quae clara clueret* ('As our own Ennius sang, who first brought down from delightful Helicon a garland of perennial foliage, to win him brilliant fame throughout the peoples of Italy').

47. 1.66–76: *primum Graius homo mortalis* <u>*tollere*</u> *contra* | *est oculos ausus* <u>*primus*</u>*que obsistere contra* ... *ergo uiuida uis animi per*<u>*uicit*</u>*, et extra* | *processit longe flammantia moenia mundi* | *atque omne immensum peragrauit mente animoque,* | *unde* <u>*refert*</u> *nobis* <u>*uictor*</u> *quid possit oriri,* | *quid nequeat* ('It was a Greek man who first dared to raise mortal eyes against it [religion], and who first dared to confront it ... And so the vigour of his mind prevailed, and he sallied far beyond the flaming ramparts of the world, journeying in thought throughout the limitless expanse of the universe; from where he brought back to us, victorious, knowledge of what can arise and what cannot'). See Gale (2000: 13–14) for discussion of Virgil's Lucretian allusions in the proem to *Georgic* 3.

48. Thomas (1988: 3.40–1) notes that Virgil's *intactos* is equivalent to Lucretius's *integros* (*in-* + *tango*). Virgil borrowed language from the same Lucretian line in the discussion of natural-philosophical poetry towards the end of book 2 (*G.* 2.483: *naturae* <u>*accedere*</u> *partis*; *DRN* 1.927: *iuuat integros* <u>*accedere*</u> *fontis*); see Hardie (1986: 38).

49. Scholars have tended to overlook or dismiss the association between these locations and Bacchus; Mynors (1990: 187), for example, asserts that a connection between Cithaeron and Bacchus in this context would be 'entirely out of place'.

50. Cf. Dodds (1960 *ad* 661–2). Note that Bacchus's gift, wine, is explicitly associated with death by dismemberment at *G.* 3.511–4, where it drives diseased horses to tear themselves apart.

51. Segal (1997: 32).

52. See Thumiger (2006) on the language and imagery of hunting in Euripides' *Bacchae*. The mountain hunt for Pentheus and the various hunting metaphors of the *Bacchae* are also important models for the hunt of Dido and Aeneas in *Aeneid* 4; see here Weber (2002: 333–5).

53. Euripides' maenads respond like hunting dogs, standing to attention and looking around at the sound of their master's voice (1086–7).

54. See here Weber (2002: 334–5).

55. Fowler (2002: 156). The idea of hunting as a cure for love – another frequent topos in Latin love elegy – may also be latent in this passage. Virgil himself exploited this motif in *Eclogue* 10, where Gallus dreams of hunting to quell his love for Lycoris (56–7); see Clausen (1994 *ad Ecl.* 10.55).

56. The *sphragis* is the only other passage in the poem, apart from the proem to book 3, where the figures of the poet and Octavian are explicitly juxtaposed.

57. See n. 47.

58. Hardie (1986: 51, n. 42).

59. Cf. Miles (1975: 188) on 3.289–93: '*Amor* has lost the particular meaning which it had in Virgil's discussion of the animals [i.e. sexual *amor*] and has become, rather, a convenient term to designate anything which destroys or replaces self-control.'

60. Phanocles refers to Dionysus as 'mountain-roaming' (ὀρειφοίτης, *Collectanea Alexandrina* fr. 3).

61. Virgil places much greater emphasis on the mountain-climbing aspect of the poet's journey than Lucretius. As Hardie (1986: 166) observes, this reinforces the parallel with the mountain-ranging horses in Virgil's discussion of *amor*, although I would argue that it also calls attention to the Dionysiac element of the poet's inspiration.

6 DIVINIZATION AND DIDACTIC EFFICACY IN VIRGIL'S *GEORGICS*

* This chapter has benefitted from the valuable feedback of the anonymous readers and (far too many) colleagues. Amongst the latter, I thank in particular Nick Freer, Tom Geue, Elena Giusti and Fiachra Mac Góráin.

1. There is widespread agreement that the *Georgics* were published in or around 29 BCE. It has been argued that Virgil originally composed a 'Hesiodic song' consisting of the current books 1 and 2 only, which he read to Octavian in 29 BCE, and subsequently composed books 3 and 4 between 29 and 27 BCE. See Martin in Della Corte (1984–91: 666–8).

2. See especially Perkell (1989: 150–2), Cole (2001: 69–74) and Nelis (2013: 245–6). Gale has consistently argued that Virgil's discussions of deification and political ambition in the *Georgics* evince a Lucretian ambivalence, which hints at an underlying concern about the divine aspirations of Octavian. See Gale (2000: 26–31, 35–6, 194; 2003: 325–32, 348–9; and 2013: 288–90, 296).

3. See especially Nappa (2005: 2–8); quotation comes p. 7.

4. Cole (2001: 68–70) and Nappa (2005: 30–3, 39–43, 65–7, 217–32).

5. White (1993: 174) and Cole (2001: 71) argue that *mox* anticipates posthumous deification, which of course became the standard practice for future emperors. But Virgil's *mox* is unusual in comparison to the more standard formula of delaying deification, which asks for a 'late' apotheosis; cf., e.g., Hor. *Carm.* 1.2.45: *serus in caelum redeas*.

6. See also Thomas (1988: 68), Nelson (1998: 111), Morgan (1999: 93–4) and Cole (2001: 71). Cf. Hor. *Carm.* 1.12.51–2: *tu secundo | Caesare regnes*, where *secundus* is both 'second in command' and 'under the auspices of'. But Nappa (2005: 33) sees Octavian as a parallel to Jupiter rather than supplanting the god's position. It should be noted that when Jupiter appears for the first time in the *Georgics*, the supreme god is far from kind to the rustics: *pater ipse colendi | haud facilem esse uiam uoluit* (1.121–2).

7. See Perkell (1989: 46–50); though she finds this plea for pity 'discordant' with the tone of the rest of the prologue (150).

8. My reading here shares some similarities with the notion of 'poetic simultaneity' discussed by Volk (2002: 13–24). *Cursus* (1.40) can evoke the notion of poetic progress; see *OLD cursus* 9. Erren (2003: 42) reads *da facilem cursum* (1.40) as a 'Fahrtmetapher'. Nelis (2008: 504) points out that *ingredior* is often used with *uia* to mean 'take the first steps on a path or journey'; see *OLD ingredior* 2. Tandy (1985: 54–5) and A. Hardie (2002: 178) argue that *ingredere* is often used of rising stars and so looks ahead to Octavian's catasterism, which has been suggested earlier in line 32, *anne nouum tardis sidus te mensibus addas* ('or whether you add yourself to the slow months as a new star').

9. The idea that Octavian is already the subject of prayers even before his deification evokes the senatorial decree of 30 BCE requiring priests and priestesses to pray for Octavian (Dio 51.19.7).

10. Nappa (2005: 31) also finds the images of Thule's servitude and the 'purchase' of Octavian by Tethys troubling (cf. 1.30–1).

11. Thomas (1986: 177; 1988: 1.32–5). Cf. Catul. 66.63–4: *me | sidus in antiquis diua nouum posuit*.

12. On the so–called *sidus Iulium*, see Plin. *Nat. Hist.* 2.93–4; Suet. *Iul.* 88; Dio 45.7.1; DServ. *ad Ecl.* 9.46. For discussions of Octavian's tendentious interpretation of the comet as Caesar's apotheosis, see Weinstock (1971: 399–401), Osgood (2006: 40–1) and Pandey (2013). The curious celestial location proposed for the new star of Octavian (cf. 1.33–5) receives attention from Whitcomb (2018).

13. *auctor* seems to anticipate the future title 'Augustus'. See Thomas (1988: *ad loc.*) and Nelis (2013: 260–1), and, more generally, Schwindt (2013).

14. Gale (2000: 29). Virgil's request for Octavian to pity farmers who do not yet know the way of life also recalls Epicurus's enlightenment of the mind.

15. Note also that *urbis . . . inuisere* recalls Arat. *Phaen.* 2: μεσταὶ δέ Διὸς πᾶσαι μὲν ἀγυιαί. Divine visitations are often conveyed by the verb *inuisere*, cf. Verg. *Aen.* 4.144: *Delum maternam inuisit Apollo*; Catul. 64. 384–5: *praesentes namque ante domos inuisere castas | heroum et sese mortali ostendere coetu.* Powell (2008: 260) notes that Octavian's double command over *fruges* and *tempestates* precisely reverses his public image before the victory at Naulochus as the bringer of famine and victim of heaven-sent storms.

16. Gale (2000: 160, n. 45).

17. Therefore, as Tom Geue suggested to me, it is not so much 'poetic simultaneity' (cf. Volk 2002: 13–24), but 'poetic instantaneity'. This is of course one of the many possible readings of Virgil's final requests in the prologue. For alternative interpretations, see, e.g., Gale (2000: 26–31), A. Hardie (2002: 182–4) and Nelis (2008: 502–3). The correspondence between the divinization of Octavian in the *Georgics* and that of the *iuuenis* in *Eclogues* 1 will be discussed later.

18. That Virgil discusses Octavian's deification at key turning-points of the poem further underlines the tied-up progress of his poetry and the apotheosis of Caesar.

19. See esp. Gale (2000: 24, 57, 146–7, 159–62, 173–4).

20. Freudenburg (2001: 71–82) calls this a 'totalitarian squeeze' on poetic freedom and finds correspondences between the literary advice given by Trebatius to Horace in *Serm.* 2.1 and Virgil's proposal to compose panegyrical epic in *Geo.* 3.8–39. See also Lowrie (2009: 311–48).

21. On historical flashbacks in the *Georgics*, see Nelis (2013: 255).

22. Other commentators have also noted the echoes between the opening and closure of book 1. See, e.g., Perkell (1989: 150–2), Gale (2000: 32) and Nelis (2008: 505–10).

23. *Cursus* (1.40) evokes a variety of images, including the movement of heavenly bodies, the path of life, a nautical journey and, as mentioned above, poetic progress; see *OLD cursus* 5a, 5b, 6a, 8b and 9.

24. Kronenberg (2009: 138): 'By the end of book 1 . . . the stage has been set for human beings to rely on human powers.'

25. Note the similar phrasing of *caeli . . . regia* in 1.503 and *deorum concilia* in 1.24–5.

26. The claim that 'to care for earthly triumphs' actually delays divinization is contrary to the contemporary Roman perception of a strong link between triumphal and divine glory. On the connotation of divinity in the Roman triumph, see Beard (2007: 237–8).

27. See also Putnam (1979: 75).

28. For example, Gale (2000: 35–6; 2013: 290) argues that the simile alludes to the death of Phaethon. The similarity with Phaethon can also be added to the proem of *Georgics* 1 through Ovid's reading of the Phaethon myth in *Met.* 2, where Phaethon crashes in that space in the zodiac (between Scorpio and Libra, *Met.* 2.195–200) where Virgil had imagined Octavian to ascend to heaven as a star at *Geo.* 1.32–5; see Barchiesi (2009) 166–70.

29. See also Nelis (2008: 508).

30. On the ambivalence of Virgil's picture of the future, see Lyne (1974: 61) and Gale (2000: 34–5). See also Mynors *ad* 1.493–7: 'All human actions, heroic or disastrous, in the end come to dust.'

31. Rimell (2015: 235) notes well that the image of buried *grandia ossa* evokes the underworld-dwelling giants, whose birth from the earth is mentioned at 1.278 and who are the very opposite of the celestial gods.

32. The terminology and concept are originally developed by Conte (1980: 122–36; 1992; 2007: 219–31). See also Freer and Giusti in this volume.

33. See also Giusti in this book (Chapter 7) on the depiction of barbarians and theatre in the triumphal scene at 3.24–5.

34. See Mynors (1990: 26), Erren (2003: 576–7), Miller (2009: 3) and Nelis (2013: 259).

35. Casali (2006: 200) notes that the shield may be read as a surrogate *Aeneid* and Vulcan a surrogate Virgil (*Aen.* 8.439–41): 'tollite cuncta' inquit '*coeptosque auferte labores*, | *Aetnaei Cyclopes, et huc aduertite mentem:* | *arma acri facienda uiro.* Both the shield and the temple are ekphrastic objects.

36. On further points of comparisons between *Geo.* 3.26–31 and *Aen.* 8.714–28, see Mynors (1990: 184).

37. Nappa (2005: 121) focuses on Heracles's role in the Olympian and Nemean games (cf. *Geo.* 3.19–20) and suggests that Virgil casts Octavian in the role of a Herculean civilizer and pacifier of the world. See also Lundström (1976).

38. Gros (1993) argues that the *Parii lapides* (3.34) can be either free-standing statues in the temple or its precinct, or figures on the pediment. See also Erren (2003: 581).

39. See Drew (1924), Kraggerud (1998: 13) and Miller (2009: 3). Alternatively, Koortbojian (2013: 44) suggests that the phrase *in medio . . . Caesar* (3.16) alludes to the prominent position of the cult statue in the Temple of Divus Julius. Harrison (2005: 185) argues that Virgil's description of the temple's location (3.10–18) recalls the Mausoleum of Augustus. Lundström (1976), A. Hardie (2002: 194–8) and Heslin (2015: 257–60) claim that Virgil's temple recalls the *Aedes Herculis Musarum*, established by M. Fulvius Nobilior around 187 BCE.

40. Elena Giusti pointed out to me that at *Aen.* 8.722 *uictae gentes* walk in front of Apollo-Caesar. On the temple and Octavian's status here, see also Mackenzie and Stöckinger in this book.

41. *quadriiugos* and *currus* (3.18) recall *quadrigae* (1.512) and *currus* (1.514) respectively, while *agitabo* (3.18) contrasts with *fertur* (1.514).

42. On the redefinition of the relationship between poet and *Caesar*, see also Lowrie (2009: 150, 155–6), Miller (2009: 3–6, 140, 147–8) and Bergmann et al. (2012: 12–14).

43. See also Stöckinger in this book on *iam nunc*.

44. The *sphragis* is a common vehicle for reflexive discussions of poetry and the poet's literary achievement; see Thomas (1988: 4.559–66). On the depiction of Octavian in the *sphragis*, see also Mackenzie and Freer in this volume, as well as Gale (2003: 348–9) and Nappa (2005: 217).

45. Geue (2018: 137) argues that Virgil's use of *dum* is redolent of political fudging, making a purely temporal relationship out of something far more symbiotic between the poet and Caesar. I read it as implying a separation between spheres of activity, setting the *sphragis* up for the exploration of the divergence between political reality and poetic idealism. For further discussion, see P. Hardie (1986: 50–1) and, again, Volk's idea of 'poetic simultaneity'. Additionally, it may be relevant that a series of post-Actian *denarii* of 29–27 BCE (*BMCRE* I (East), 628–30) depict a laureate bust of Octavian with a thunderbolt behind his head.

46. Mynors (1990) *ad* 4.561–2 suggests that the word *uolens* not only portrays Octavian's *imperium* as agreeable and benign, but also implies the rule of an immortal: cf. Xen. *Oec.* 21.12: οὐ γὰρ πάνυ μοι δοκεῖ ὅλον τουτὶ τὸ ἀγαθὸν ἀνθρώπινον εἶναι ἀλλὰ θεῖον, τὸ ἐθελόντων ἄρχειν ('For I reckon this gift is not altogether human, but divine – this power to win willing obedience').

47. Hollis (1996) and Gale (2003: 327–8) suggest that the expression *uiamque adfectat Olympo*, set against the backdrop of warfare (*bello*, 4.561), aligns Octavian's mission with the Gigantomachy. But the poet dissociates Octavian from any guilt by describing him in the process of establishing order rather than overthrowing it.

48. The mention of *Parthenope*, *studia* and *ignobile otium* in quick succession evokes the Epicurean pursuit of the quietist and contemplative life, λάθε βιώσας; see also Gale (2003: 326–7) and Freer in this volume. On the contrast between the active and the contemplative life throughout the *Georgics*, see esp. Perkell (1989: 25–89) and Gale (2003: 329–32).

49. Fowler (1989: 82) sees the final line of the *Georgics* as an example of a 'supertextual closure', which he defines as the concluding section of a literary work that closes the text in a way that has 'an effect beyond the immediate text'.

50. Clausen (1994) on *Ecl.* 1.10. Wagenvoort (1956: 30–42) offers a useful survey of the topos of *ludus poeticus* in Latin literature.

51. See also Perkell (1989: 58–9).

52. Alternative interpretations of the identity of the *iuuenis/deus* of *Eclogues* 1 are suggested by Liegle (1943: 219–26), Grisart (1966), Berkowitz (1972: 26, n. 26), Wright (1983), Mayer (1983: 20–6) and Cairns (2008: 70–4), amongst others.

53. As Nauta (2006: 308) notes, line 566 could be translated as either 'I sang you, Tityrus, (you who were) in the shade of the spreading beech'; or 'I sang you, Tityrus, (I who was) in the shade of the spreading beech'. The identification of Tityrus with Virgil is also encouraged in *Eclogue* 6 of course.

54. The interactions between dialectical notions (such as tradition and innovation, continuity and novelty) which helped to legitimate and sustain the new regime constitute the subject of a number of scholarly works on the Augustan age; see, e.g., Kennedy (1992).

55. Geue (2018: 125, 137) argues that Virgil's description of peoples as 'willing' subjects of the empire is a sign of the poem's naturalization of the ideology of oppression. See also Giusti in this book on the *intexti Britanni* at *G.* 3.25 willingly staging their own subjection.

56. See Murray and Petsas (1989), Zachos (2003; 2007) and Lange (2009: 95–124).

57. *RIC* 1^2 271. It depicts a statue of Octavian on top of a column, nude except for a billowing cloak, carrying a sword in one hand and a spear in the other – two weapons often identified with Mars. The column could be a close-up of the four-column monument set up by Octavian in the Forum Romanum after his conquest of Egypt (cf. Serv. ad *G.* 3.29); see Lange (2009: 162–3) and Pollini (1990: 348).

58. Cf. Dio 51.19.7; Hor. *Carm.* 4.5.31–6; Ov. *Fast.* 2.635–8; Petron. *Sat.* 60. Dio 51.20.1 (cf. Aug. *R.G.* 10.2) also reports that the Senate arranged for the name of Octavian to be included in public hymns equally with gods. Lange (2009: 125–58, esp. 129) analyzes in detail the honours bestowed upon Octavian between 31 and 29 BCE.

59. Gradel (2002: 25–9).

7 BUNTE BARBAREN SETTING UP THE STAGE: RE-INVENTING THE BARBARIAN ON THE *GEORGICS'* THEATRE-TEMPLE (G. 3.1–48)

1. Gian Biagio Conte's definition: Conte (1980: 122–36; 1992; 2007: 219–31).

2. Hardie (2004a: 26). This is Philip Hardie's interpretation of Fowler (2000b) in the introduction to the collection of essays on middles in Latin poetry dedicated to Don Fowler by

Kyriakidis and De Martino (2004). On Virgilian middles, see also Thomas (1983, 1985 and 2004).

3. See Thomas (2004: 130), Hardie (2004b: 181) and Xinyue in this volume.

4. Hardie (2004b: 181–2). Yet in these lines Caesar also seems to be again 'in the middle', between Tithonus and a distant future; see Nelis (2004a: 88–9).

5. Note that this section provides a very condensed version of a complex and speculative argument, on which see Giusti (2018: 22–75).

6. Hall (1989); cf. also Hall (1993).

7. See Manuwald (2000) and Giusti (2018: 70).

8. Zanker (1988), Spawforth (1994 and 2012) and Hardie (2007a).

9. On the Amazonomachy of the temple of Apollo Sosianus, see La Rocca (1985); for a bibliographical survey on the topic of Giants and Titans in republican and Augustan Rome, see Galasso (1995: 136–7); on Gigantomachy in the *Aeneid*, see Hardie (1986: 85–156).

10. *RG* 23, Dio 55.10.7, Ov. *Ars Am.* 1.171–2 with Spawforth (1994: 238) and Hardie (2007a: 129).

11. Spawforth (1994: 24).

12. At least from 57 BCE (Cicero, *De domo sua* 60 refers to the Parthians as *Persae*); see Spawforth (1994: 237) and Hardie (2007a: 127).

13. Zanker (1988: 84): 'just as in the heroic victories of Athens, Actium was Augustus's triumph over the so-called eastern barbarian'; Hardie (2007a: 130). Actium itself was apparently represented as a Centauromachy; see Prop. 4.6.49 and the Medinaceli reliefs with Schäfer (2013), Hardie (2016: 17).

14. So I have argued in Giusti (2018).

15. See the association between Carthaginians, Britons and Parthians in Horace's *Epode* 7; on Horace's urgent requests to Augustus to undertake foreign war against the Parthians in accordance with Sallust's theory of *metus hostilis*, see especially Seager (1980).

16. Hdt. 7.166; Arist. *Poet.* ch.23.1459a24 (Salamis); Diod. 11.24.1 (Thermopylae).

17. See Giusti (2018: 58) with bibliography.

18. See Giusti (2018: 58–61) with bibliography. On the association, in mid-republican Rome, between Carthaginians and Persians, see Feeney (1991: 117–20; 2007: 56–7; and 2016: 124–5), Dufallo (2013: 16–20) and Biggs (2014: 239–40). Dench (1995: 72–3) also suggests a concurrence of Persian and Carthaginian stereotypes in Plautus's *Poenulus*, but see *contra* Prag (2010: 53).

19. According to Cicero, *Brut.* 72–3 (see also *De Sen.* 50; *Tusc. Disp.* 1.3), who nonetheless also mentions that Accius said that Livius's career as a dramatist began only in 197 BCE, a chronology usually rejected by modern scholarship. See Giusti (2018: 67) with bibliography.

20. Liv. 27.37.

21. Manuwald (2011: 48). Cf. Boyle (2006: 15–6). See Giusti (2018: 68) with bibliography.

22. Even if Ennius's *Scipio* was a *praetexta*, as recently re-proposed by Russo (2007: 199–208), we have no way of tracing the representations of Carthaginians in this work, supposing there were any.

23. On Bacchic themes, see (possibly) Livius Andronicus's *Ino* and *Antiopa*, Naevius's *Lycurgus*, Ennius's *Athamas*, and later Pacuvius's *Pentheus, Antiopa* and *Periboea* and Accius' *Stasiastae/ Tropaeum Liberi, Bacchae* and *Athamas*. Medea was one of the favourite characters of the early Latin stage, both in her Euripidean form (Ennius's *Medea Exul*), in the Apollonian version (Accius's *Medea siue Argonautae*) and in her specific role as ancestor of the Persians (Ennius's

Medea and Pacuvius's *Medus*). Thrace also played a major role, as in Livius Andronicus's, Pacuvius's and Accius's *Tereus*. See Giusti (2018: 70) and especially the collection of essays in Manuwald (2000).

24. Barchiesi (2005: 299).

25. See Drew (1924), and the reception of his suggestion that Virgil had witnessed the dedication of the temple in 28 BCE in Wilkinson (1969: 170), Thomas (1988: 44) and Mynors (1990: 181). The temple is described (and yet not described, as emphasized by Welch (2005: 79–80)) by Propertius in *Elegies* 2.31 and 4.6.

26. See Drew (1924), Wilkinson (1969: 165–72; 1970), Buchheit (1972: 92–159), Lundström (1976), Thomas (1983; 1988: 36–49), Mynors (1990: 178–88), Balot (1998), Kraggerud (1998), Morgan (1999: 50–101), Hinds (1998: 52–63), Gale (2000: 11–14), A. Hardie (2002), Nappa (2005: 115–24), P. Hardie (2007b), Pieri (2011: 31–53), Meban (2008), Lowrie (2009: 150–7), Biggs (2014: 244–61), Heslin (2015: 257–60), Citroni (2015) and Xinyue in this book.

27. Thomas (1988: 36), Hinds (1998: 53), Horsfall (2001a: 96–7), Citroni (2015: 50); but see *contra* Morgan (1999: 50–101), followed by A. Hardie (2002: 195). See Nelis (2004a: 83–4) in favour of a 'deliberate ambiguity'.

28. See Lowrie (2009: 154–5): 'Vergil retains the performative moment . . . unlike Ennius, he is not living despite death: he simply still lives.' Cf. *G.* 3.10–1: *primus ego patriam mecum, modo uita supersit,* | *Aonio rediens deducam uertice Musas*; the same claim had been made by Lucretius of Ennius at *DRN* 1.117–9: *Ennius ut noster cecinit, qui primus amoeno* | *detulit ex Helicone perenni fronde coronam* | *per gentis Italas hominum quae clara clueret*; see Hinds (1998: 53–63). The connections between Virgil and Lucretius's Ennius and Epicurus in terms of '*primus* language' are pushed further, and beyond Lucretius, by Meban (2008: 160–7). For the suggestion that Ennius may have already represented his poetic achievement through the image of the *triumphator*, see Hardie (2007b).

29. See Wilkinson (1969: 168).

30. See *Ol.* 6.1–4 and *Pyth.* 6.7–14 for the comparison of a poetic tribute to a victor and a building, with Wilkinson (1970) and Balot (1998). On the metapoetic interpretation of Callimachus's very lacunose fr. 118 Pf. as describing two temples, one well finished and the other rougher, see Thomas (1983: 97–9).

31. Cf. n. 66.

32. For the rejection of Callimacheanism in Callimachean terms, see Thomas (1983 and 1988: 36–8) and Gale (2000: 14).

33. Balot (1998: 91).

34. Cf. Wilkinson (1969: 168): '*Strangely mingled* with this symbolism of the Greek games is that of the Roman Triumph', my emphasis. On Roman practice in the proem, see Meban (2008: 152–4).

35. Such occasions must have been funerals, triumphs, *ludi magni uotiui* or *ludi* for the dedication of a temple; see Flower (1995).

36. First suggested by Lundström (1976: 176–7) and endorsed by Hinds (1998: 55, 59–63), Morgan (1999: 59–60) and A. Hardie (2002: 195–200).

37. Restored and provided with a columned hall by L. Marcius Philippus the younger (Augustus's step-brother and uncle) around 28 BCE, after his triumphal return from Hispania in 33 BCE; see Lundström (1976: 176–7), Hardie (2007b: 138–9) and especially Heslin (2015: 197–254, 257–60).

38. Skutsch (1968: 18–29; 1985: 144–6, 553, 649–50). On the similarity between Fulvius's *aedes* and Ennius's *Annales* in 'construct[ing] a "unified" vision of Roman history', see Gildenhard (2003: 94–7).

39. Erected on the forum in 260 BCE after Rome's first naval triumph against the Carthaginians at Mylae (Degrassi *Insc. It.* 13.3, n. 69; see Pl. *NH* 34.20, Quint. *Inst.* 1.7.12, Sil. 6.663–6, Serv. *ad G.* 3.29). Augustus's interest in Duilius and in his column is testified by his *elogium Duilii* located in the *Forum Augusti* (Degrassi *Insc. It.* 13.3, n. 13). On the use of the Battle of Mylae in Augustan ideology, see Roller (2013: 120–6) and Biggs (2014: 244–61), the latter arguing for a re-semanticizing of its rostra in a conflation of both Naulochus and Actium.

40. The raising of the curtain signalled the end of the performance: Thomas (1988: 44) and Mynors (1990: 183).

41. This reading would follow Servius's interpretation, who, believing that Augustus had conquered Britain, says he forced many of the captives to work in the theatre, but Wilkinson (1969: 168), Thomas (1988: 44) and Mynors (1990: 183–4) all agree in reading the scene as if the figures of the Britons woven into the curtain, rising, only *seem* to be raising it. Cf. Lowrie (2009: 152) on how the image 'lends animation to the inert'.

42. Beard (2007: 140).

43. See 'Britons' and 'Picts' in Cannon (2002). Note that tattoos are not attested until much later (Herodian, third century CE). On the 'painted' Britons, see Caes. *Gal.* 5.14, Prop. 2.18c.23, Mart. 14.99.

44. The Britons are again *caerulei* in Sil. 17.416, Mart. 11.53.1, but green (*uirides*) in Ov. *Am.* 2.16.39.

45. Kruschwitz (2014: 283–88) *contra* Allen (1955). The argument is intriguing but tenuous: Quintus was writing tragedies at the time, and Cicero's description of Quintus's description of Britain at Cic. *Q. fr.* 2.16.4–5 focuses on emotions (fear and hope) and is called a ὑπόθεσις *scribendi*, which may be a technical term for indicating the plot of a tragedy, but not necessarily.

46. Cic. *Q. fr.* 3.6.7 with Kruschwitz (2014: 287).

47. See Kruschwitz (2014: 287, n. 36) for a speculative but intriguing connection between Quintus's possible *praetexta* for Caesar and Alexander's practice of organizing Dionysia with dramatic performances during his Indian campaigns.

48. Schneider (1986), arguing that the original model had to be recognized in the tripod-column set up at Delphi in celebration of Plataea. See also Spawforth (1994: 238) and Rose (2005: 24, n. 22).

49. Rose (2005: 28).

50. For *scaena* here being a keyword for introducing readers into the 'Carthaginian theatre', together with *fronte* (*Aen.* 1.166) and *sedilia* (1.167), see E. L. Harrison (1972–3; 1989: 4–5) and Pobjoy (1998: 43).

51. See E. L. Harrison (1972–3).

52. See Fernandelli (1996).

53. Mynors (1969) prints *theatris*.

54. Dufallo (2013: 18, n. 13). *Purpureus* is generally identified with Πορφυρίων, king of the Giants; see Pind. *Pyth.* 8.12.

55. See Gruen (1992: 46–7).

56. On the identification/exchange between Virgil and Octavian in the proem to *Georgics* 3, see Nelis (2004a: 88) and Lowrie (2009: 155–6).

57. On which see Rose (2005, especially 33–4). Note that the ancient term for pavonazzetto, after all, is 'Phrygian marble'.

58. The magistrates conducting the games were dressed in scarlet and gold; see Mynors (1990: 182).

59. Cf. the theatrical description of Scipio Africanus in Silius's account of the triumph of 201 BCE (Sil. *Pun.* 17.645–6), with Boyle (2006: 5–7).

60. Cf. Kraggerud (1998: 9): 'the city that had been conquered by Alexander after a long siege contributes with its splendour to the great triumph'. Beard (2004: 124; 2007: 136) makes a similar point on the Sidonian purple which glitters on a captive leader in Ov. *Tr.* 4.2.27 (*hic, qui Sidonio fulget sublimis in ostro*), noticing that it pinpoints interchangeability between barbarian prisoner and Roman *triumphator*.

61. OLD *s.u. Tyrius* 1c.

62. Sarra is an old name for Tyre (possibly from the Hebrew name *Tsor*) used by Ennius (fr. 472 Sk. *Poenos Sarra oriundos*, Probus *ad G.* 2.506); see Skutsch (1985: 631–2).

63. The finale to book 2 and the proem to book 3 forming 'the great central block' of the *Georgics* (Gale (2000: 44)) have been recognized as related to each other by a number of thematic and intertextual correspondences; see Buchheit (1972: 45–148), P. Hardie (1986: 33), Gale (2000: 8–15), A. Hardie (2002: 194) and Nelis (2004a).

64. See A. Hardie (2002: 195).

65. See Cugusi *OR* fr. 139 = *ORF* fr. 185 (Fest. p. 282 Lindsay) for Cato's condemnation of *pauimenti Poenici*; cf. Plut. *Cato* 4.4 for his refusal of an ἐπίβλημα δὲ τῶν ποικίλων βαβυλώνιον, with Gruen (1992: 70–1).

66. For the suggestion that *Gangaridum* (27) must be taken with *elephanto* rather than with *pugnam*, see Pieri (2011: 31–41).

67. See Welch (2005: 85–6).

68. Keith (2008: 149).

69. See Hardie's reading of the twofold 'central block' of the *Georgics* (1986: 49–50). For a similar opposition between the proem and the close of *Georgics* 1, see Xinyue in this book.

70. Hardie (1997: 319).

71. See Hardie (1990: 226, n. 14) and more generally on Ovid's Thebes as an anti-Rome, Barchiesi and Rosati (2007: 142).

72. The emphasised fictionality of these barbarians also turns the spotlight of the fictionality of the ekphrasis, and its temple, as a whole. As an anonymous reader suggests to me, this may also be interpreted as Virgil's hint at his refusal to write the *Augusteid* that the theatre-temple is meant to stand for.

8 FROM *MUNERA UESTRA CANO* TO *IPSE DONA FERAM*: LANGUAGE OF SOCIAL RECIPROCITY IN THE *GEORGICS*

1. Effe (1977: 80–97). 'Transparent' poems are to be distinguished from 'subject-oriented' didactic poems ('sachbezogen' in Effe's words) on the one hand, where the entire text is geared towards an efficient presentation of the subject matter (such as Lucretius's *De Rerum Natura*), and poems of a 'formal type' on the other, where authors have searched for a particularly unpoetic topic, in which they are not interested, but instead are using it to demonstrate their literary

mastery (such as Nicander's poems; cf. Effe 1977: 61). Effe's example for 'transparent' poems is Aratus's *Phaenomena*, which not only teaches about the stars, but also, and more importantly, about man's relation to a divine power (Effe 1977: 40–56, esp. 51).

2. Effe (1977: 86–93). This is in accordance with Hardie's (2004c) interpretation.

3. Sistakou (2014: 118) and Volk (2002: 4).

4. 'Landwirtschaft' is composed of the modifier 'Land' and the noun 'Wirtschaft', which the *Oxford Duden German Dictionary* translates as 'economy' (811), so that the compound means literally 'economy of the land'.

5. Spurr (2008 *passim*).

6. Polanyi (1944/2013: 71–95), applied by Finley (1973). For the ongoing influence of these concepts, cf. Alonso-Núñez (2002: 540) and the introductory remarks in Von Reeden's survey (2009: 211–13), who later on presents other models of how to think about ancient economy.

7. Cf. the account in Tsouna (2007: 163–94), and here esp. sections III and IV (177–87). I owe thanks to Nicholas Freer for pointing me to Philodemus's treatise.

8. Thibodeau (2011: 23–33) and Spurr (2008: 25–32). On this motif, see also Heyworth in this volume.

9. (Sc. *quamuis*) *pinguis et ingratae premeretur caseus urbi,* | *non umquam grauis aere domum mihi dextra redibat* ('though . . . many a rich cheese was pressed for the thankless town, never would my hand come home money-laden').

10. *saepe oleo tardi costas agitator aselli* | *uilibus aut onerat pomis, lapidemque reuertens* | *incusum aut atrae massam picis urbe reportat.* ('Often, too, the driver loads his slow donkey's sides with oil or cheap fruits, and as he comes back from town brings with him an indented millstone or a mass of black pitch').

11. *hae quoque non cura nobis leuiore tuendae,* | *nec minor usus erit, quamuis Milesia magno* | *uellera mutentur Tyrios incocta rubores* ('These goats, too, we must guard with no lighter care, and no less will be the profit, albeit the fleeces of Miletus, steeped in Tyrian purple, are bartered for a high price'). Cf. Thibodeau (2011: 61–5 and 267, n. 61), who makes a distinction between agricultural yield (*fructus*), which in the socio-economic system of the *Georgics* is regarded as a legitimate goal, and economic profit (*pecunia, pretium, lucrum*, etc.), which is banned.

12. Fiachra Mac Góráin brought up this point during a discussion at the UCL conference. See also Spurr (2008: 29).

13. Spurr (2008: 29, n. 41).

14. Cf. the introduction in Peirano (2012: 15–16), who argues that *Pseudepigrapha* are part of a literary culture in which canonical works were treated 'as points of departure, providing clues to be expanded, developed or twisted to create situations that were outside of the realm of the original text'.

15. For the influence of G. 4.116–48 on *Moretum* 60–84, cf. Höschele (2005: 255–9); for the element of trade in the *Moretum*, cf. Höschele (2005: 251–2).

16. Coffee (2009) and Bowditch (2001).

17. *OLD immunis* 2.

18. For the economic colouring of *semina debita*, cf. Erren (2003), Mynors (1990), Thomas (1988: *ad loc.*) (and *OLD debeo* 1–4, *TLL* 5/1,85,77–107,37 *debeo*, esp. 86,16ff. I. *cum obiecto de condicione eius qui pecuniam mutuam accepit*).

19. For an economic notion of *credo*, see *OLD* 2: 'To lend money, to make loans, give credit.'

20. Cf. Thomas (1988: *ad loc.*).

21. On the productive wordplay of German 'Gift' ('poison') and 'Gabe' ('gift'), and its Indo-European equivalents, which bear equally ambivalent meanings (e.g. Gk. δόσις), cf. Benveniste (1969/1993: 55) and Ecker (2008: 12–14).

22. Cf. the Pandora myth in Hesiod, *Op.* 57: τοῖς δ' ἐγὼ ἀντὶ πυρὸς <u>δώσω κακόν</u> ('but I will give men as the price for fire an evil thing'). For further connections to the Pandora account, cf., e.g., Gale (2008: 102), Farrell (1991: 144–7) and Erren (2003) in his introductory remark on 1.118–59.

23. See, e.g., the introductory remark of Thomas (1988) on 1.118–46.

24. On sacrifices at the end of the *Georgics* and during the plague in 3.486–93, cf. Hardie (1998: 52) with further bibliography.

25. I use the term 'narrator' to distinguish between Virgil's persona in the *Georgics* and the historical Virgil, though I am aware that these two are not in every case sharply distinguishable. By this usage I do not necessarily mean to imply that there is a narrative within the *Georgics*; on this issue see Cowan in this book.

26. Cf. West (1978) *ad* Hes. *Op.* 39.

27. G. 1.27: *auctorem frugum tempestatumque potentem* (with Thomas 1988: *ad loc.* and Nelis 2013: 260–1). Schwindt (2013) discusses a range of other literary depictions of Octavian/ Augustus, where the ruler's name is suggestively connected to words with the root *aug-*.

28. For example White (1993: 173–5) reads Octavian's ascension to Olympus as an affirmative gesture by Virgil, but the proem allows other interpretations as well, cf. the curious sequence of indirect questions in G. 1.25–39 or the word *mox* at line 24 (which was found disturbing already by Servius).

29. For a recent metapoetic interpretation, see Harrison (2007: 149–56); further references can be found in Giusti's chapter in this volume.

30. On these and other problems related to the proem to *Georgics* 3, see Mackenzie, Freer, Xinyue and Giusti in this book.

31. Cf. Thomas (1988: *ad loc.*): 'the chiastic syntax underscores the close relationship between poet and ruler'.

32. On the mutual reliance between *Caesar* and Virgil, see also Mackenzie in this volume.

33. Wilkinson (2008).

34. For this concept, see Lowrie (1997: 225): 'The so-called Pindaric future postpones praise even as it enacts it' (with reference to Slater 1969); for discussion of a very prominent case of such a Pindaric future in Horace (*Carm.* 4.5.32), see Lowrie (1997: 349).

35. Nelis and Nelis-Clément (2011: 26).

36. Hardie (2008: 169–71).

37. Miller (2009: 151–2).

38. For this kind of Virgilian self-interpretation with special regard to the *Eclogues*, see Geue (2013) with further bibliography.

39. Derrida (1991) discusses the etymological link between present ('gift') and present (sc. tense), as well as the general connection of gifts and time.

40. For Maecenas as a figure of ethical and literary moderation, see also Propertius 3.9.

41. On the issue of the poem's addressee, see also Cowan in this volume.

42. While I normally use the word 'audience' in a general sense in this chapter, one that also covers readers, it may be understood here in the proper sense of the word as 'listeners'.

43. Wiseman (2015: 122–5), quotation at p. 123. The games celebrated the completion of Agrippa's aqueduct and are attested in Plin. *Nat. Hist.* 36.121.

44. Batstone (1997: 133).

45. Batstone (1997: 133–5).

46. For the importance of *religio* in the *Georgics* and especially in book 1, see Kronenberg (2009: 157–9), though I do not share her argument that Virgil adopts a critical view on *religio* as a means for understanding life. For Augustus's interest in religious matters and the fact that it had started long before he finally became *princeps*, see Scheid (2005). Ailsa Hunt's chapter in this book examines Servian interpretations of Virgilian *religio* in the *Georgics*.

47. Powell (2008: 239–45).

48. On the importance of gifts and reciprocity in Lucretius, see Tutrone (2018). In section III (37–53), he gives a detailed analysis of the cup simile.

49. Memmius is supposed to follow a doctrine which is rejected by the mass, cf. *DRN* 1.945–7 = 4.19–21: (sc. *quoniam*) *retroque* | *uolgus abhorret ab hac, uolui tibi suauiloquenti* | *carmine Pierio rationem exponere nostrum* ('since the multitude shrinks back away from this philosophy, I have desired to set forth to you my reasoning in the sweet-tongued song of the muses').

50. On the complex relationship of Lucretius's internal and external addressees as well as his audience, see Tutrone (2018: 37–9).

51. Cf. Griffin (2003: 106–11; 2013: 46–87) on the uncertainty among Roman elites. Griffin's considerations have recently been complemented by Coffee's (2017) study, which describes the changing attitudes towards reciprocity between the early republic and the principate.

52. Cf. Griffin (2013: 66–7) and, with regard to friendship, Konstan (2005: 345–6).

53. Cf. Goodyear (1972) and Koestermann (1963) *ad* Tac. *Ann.* 1.2.1, who list further sources and who observe that gifts of this kind were a normal and necessary means in the political system.

54. This chapter is a significantly extended and modified English version of chapter 1.3.1 of my German book *Vergils Gaben. Materialität, Reziprozität und Poetik in den* Eklogen *und der* Aeneis (2016). I wish to thank both Winter Verlag and Bloomsbury Publishing for granting permission for the present publication. I am especially grateful to the editors, Nicholas Freer and Bobby Xinyue, for their patience and valuable criticism; to George Spann who translated my initial paper into English; and last but not least to Tom Geue for sharing his thinking and his recent article on the *Georgics* with me prior to its publication.

9 'PULPY FICTION': VIRGILIAN RECEPTION AND GENRE IN COLUMELLA *DE RE RUSTICA* 10

1. Henderson (2002: 114): 'the two gardens gloss each other'.

2. Carroll (1976: 785) argues that the appropriately named Silvinus is fictitious, like Varro's Fundania; cf. Boldrer (1996 on 10.1), Fögen (2009: 157). Gallio, usually identified as Seneca's relative, is not mentioned again.

3. Latin cited from Rodgers (2010). Translations are my own.

4. The late-antique writers Palladius (*De Insitione*) and Marcellus Empiricus (*De med. Praef.* 7) both end their works with verse. See also Thibodeau (2011: 286, n. 42) on gardening in final sections of agronomical treatises, cf. Cato, *Agr.* 156–7, 161; Varro, *RR* 3.5, *Culex* 398–411.

5. *RR* 11.1.2 acknowledges the addition.

6. Carroll (1976: 786), Noè (2002: 47). *Augustalis* identifies Claudius as a member of the collegial association devoted to the imperial cult. Henderson (2002: 114, n. 18) suggests the name may constitute a pun on closure (*claudo*) and supplementation (*augeo*).

7. For example, 10.41–4, 54, 56, 79, 150, 312, 400–1.

8. At the end of book 11 lists of contents are given for books 1–9 (10–11 titles only); see Henderson (2002: 111–13) and Riggsby (2007). At 11.3.65, Columella may suggest that it is specifically the *uilicus* who may need the index; see Christmann (2003: 129). At *RR* 1 *Praef.* 27 gardening topics appear at the end of a list of agricultural topics.

9. Henderson (2002: 119): 'advertising a challenge'. Cf. *RR* 1 *Praef.* 21 on the enormity of agricultural knowledge.

10. See Milnor (2005: 275).

11. Cf. Riggsby (2007: 105–6) on similar strategies in Vitruvius (*De Arch.* 1.1.4–11) and Quintilian (1.10.1); also Milnor (2005: 268) and Fögen (2009: 164). See Mayer (2005: 233) on Columella's desire to create an 'attractive literary style'.

12. Cf. Columella's review of earlier Latin agricultural writing at *RR* 1.1.12.

13. See Doody (2007: 194) on Pliny's objections to Virgil. Cf. Plin. *Nat. Hist.* 14.7, and Cicero on Aratus and Nicander as inexpert didactic poets at *De Orat.* 1.69 and *De Rep.* 1.22.

14. Kenney (1984: lvi); cf. Thomas (1992: 201–2).

15. See Perkell (1981: 172), Grimal (1984: 388–92) and Ross (1987: 200–6) on the garden's unrealistic nature; cf. Thomas (1988: *ad loc.*). Thibodeau (2001: 180–1) argues that the passage of time makes the gardener's feat credible. See Kenney (1984: xxxvii) and Perkell (1981: 171) on the non-commercial nature of the garden.

16. La Penna (1977), Gale (2000: 180–3) and Johnson (2004) – Epicurean; Kronenberg (2009: 169–70) – Pythagorean.

17. For identifications, see Servius on *G.* 4.127 and the recent summary in Kronenberg (2009: 167–76).

18. Clay (1981). Perkell (1981), Ross (1987: 200–6).

19. Thomas (1992): Philetas; Leigh (1994): Parthenius; Harrison (2004): Nicander; Kronenberg (2009): Leonidas of Tarentum.

20. Acanthus, myrtle, verbena (*G.* 4.131) and plane tree (146) are not in *RR* 10 (but see 10.241: *tortos imitatur acanthos* (taken as a Virgilian allusion by Gowers (2000: 146, n. 53)); myrtle is at 11.2.30 and myrtle wine at 12.38.1–8. Cf. Horace's condemnation of an unproductive garden at *Carm.* 2.15.4–6: *platanusque caelebs | ... tum uiolaria et | myrtus*; Mart. 3.58.2–3: *otiosis ... myrtetis | uiduaque platano*; Quintilian (on unnatural ornament), *Inst.* 8.3.8: *lilia et uiolas et anemonas sponte surgentes ... sterilem platanum tonsasque myrtos*; Plin. *Nat. Hist.* 22.76: *acanthi topiariae et urbanae herbae ... duo genera sunt.*

21. Thomas (1988: *ad loc.*) translates as 'spaced-out vegetables', i.e. 'in rows'.

22. See Plin. *Nat. His.* 21.13ff.: flowers, chaplets and medicinal values; 21.70ff.: flowers for bees.

23. Cf. Varro *RR* 1.16.3: *itaque sub urbe colere hortos late expedit, sic uiolaria ac rosaria*, Cat. *Agr.* 8.2; see Jashemski (1979: 411) on commercial flower gardens; Scheidel (1990: 264) on *rusticus* as a neutral term in Columella.

24. Cf. Stöckinger in this book.

25. See Prioux (2013) and Roberts (1989: 47–55) on metapoetic flower imagery; Kronenberg (2009: 172).

26. Fitzgerald (1996: 411); also Clay (1981), Perkell (1981: 177).

27. Horsfall (2001b: 308).

28. See Kenney (1984: xxxiv–xxxvi), Grimal (1984: 64–72, 411–15), Perutelli (1983: 28ff.) and Myers (2018). Earlier Latin treatises on gardens, cited by Varro and Pliny, do not survive (for the Augustan authors M. Valerius Messalla Potitus and Sabinius Tiro, see Keyser and Irby-Massie (2008: s.v.v.)).

29. Nicander is mentioned only at 9.2.4; his *Georgika* fr. 74 Gow and Scholfield consists of a list of flowers.

30. Boldrer (1996: 16).

31. See Henderson (2002: 121).

32. Toohey (1996: 177).

33. Cf. *RR* 1.1.1–14 for a review of agricultural literature (1.1.7 (Hesiod), 1.1.12 (Virgil)).

34. Boldrer (1996: 28–32), also Maggiulli (1980).

35. Weinold (1959), de Saint-Denis (1971: 330–3), Cossarini (1977).

36. For example, *RR* 2.2.4, 3.1.9, 7.3.9, 7.5.10; see de Saint-Denis (1971: 337), Cossarini (1977), Christmann (1982) and Doody (2007: 189).

37. Dumont (2008: 55), Thibodeau (2011: 222).

38. Thomas (1987). See also Thomas's contribution in the present book.

39. Rodgers prints *pigeat*; Boldrer (1996: *ad loc.*) defends *pudeat*.

40. Thomas (1987) on *G.* 1.221 observes that this is the 'first occurrence of the plural form in Greek or Latin'. The two constellations set at different times (early and late November).

41. At *RR* 11, Columella is much more straightforward (11.2.78): *V Kal. Nov. Vergiliae occidunt, hiemat cum frigore et gelicidiis.* Cf. 11.2.77, 2.84.

42. Henderson (2004b: 128).

43. Contrast Horace *Epist.* 1.16.8–11 (*Tarentum*), *Carm.* 2.6.10–11: *Galaesi | flumen*; Propertius 2.34.67: *umbrosi ... Galaesi*; and Petronius (*Anthologia Latina* 469 Shackleton Bailey = Courtney (1991: 54–5)), *Corycium ... olus.*

44. See Peirano (2012: 20). On the *Appendix Vergiliana*, see Holzberg (2005).

45. Peirano (2012: 10).

46. Tarrant (1992) argues for a post-Augustan (possibly Flavian) date for the *Copa*, whereas Goodyear (1977) argues for a date soon after 16 BCE.

47. See Kenney (1984: xxv), who cautiously suggests Columella as the borrower; so also Perutelli (1983: 15) and Boldrer (1996: 25).

48. Ross (1975: 252): 'all the tired clichés of Augustan neotericism are here'.

49. Kenney (1984: lii–lvii), Fitzgerald (1996). Kronenberg (2009: 175–6) suggests that Virgil's garden *praeteritio* itself is 'a parody with a serious purpose'.

50. See Thomas (1982: 13–27) on the 'ideal landscapes' in Hor. *Epist.* 1.16, and Watson (2003) on the 'unrealizable dream of a rustic idyll' in Hor. *Epod.* 2.

51. Spencer (2010: 86).

52. von Stackelberg (2009: 45); cf. La Penna (1977: 57) on the garden's combination of utility and decoration.

53. Cf. 10.142, 308, 310 (~ *Ecl.* 1.35, *Moretum* 78–9), 317, 327.

54. Gowers (2000: 137).

55. On such 'botanical imperialism', see Pollard (2009), von Stackelberg (2009: 138) and Marzano (2014: 221–2). Henderson (2002: 128, n. 46) suggests *Turni lacus* is a Virgilian allusion.

56. For example, *RR* 10.169–75, 410–12. Syrian radishes are praised by both authors (Plin. *Nat. Hist.* 19.81 [*non pridem*], Col. 10.114). See Marzano (2014: 228) on the Augustan professionalization of horticultural expertise. Pliny in *Nat. Hist.* 1 cites Columella and Virgil as sources for book 19 on gardens. Beagon (1992: 89) links Pliny's and Columella's emphasis on nature's variety.

57. See Kenney (1984: xxxv–vi, xxxviii–xl). On the philosophical topos of *uictus tenuis*, see Watson (2003) on Hor. *Epod.* 2.49–60, and Kier (1933: 5–19).

58. Beagon (1992: 89). Cf. *RR* 1 *Praef.* 2 on nature's inexhaustible fertility.

59. See Noè (2002: 44–5) on Columella's ambiguous attitude towards *iucunditas* and *urbanitas* in the *RR*, and Noè (2003) on Pliny and Columella's alimentary moralizing. Varro *RR* 1.4.1 claims that agriculture should aim at both profit and pleasure and lists *pomaria ac floralia* ('orchards and flower gardens') as pleasurable (*fructuosa propter uoluptatem*, 1.23.4). On Columella's moralizing as an 'essential authorizing gesture', see König and Whitmarsh (2007: 24).

60. Beard (1998: 24), also Purcell (1996), Gowers (2000: 135–7), von Stackelberg (2009: 95–100).

61. See Noé (2002: 327–35), Milnor (2005: 264–5).

62. Gowers (2000: 138).

63. On martial imagery in the *Georgics*, see Thomas (1988) on *G.* 1.99; cf. Manilius 2.20: *militiamque soli.*

64. See Gowers (2000: 137–8), Henderson (2002: 128–30; 2004: 13–19) and Milnor (2005: 279–81).

65. Cf. Varro *RR* 1.29.2: *terram cum primum arant, proscindere appellant*; Verg. *G.* 2.399: *solum scidendum*, 408: *fodito*, 236: *terga.*

66. See Thomas (1988) on *G.* 2.325–35, on sexual metaphors as 'part of agricultural tradition'. Cf., e.g., Cic. *Sen.* 51, Plin. *Nat. Hist.* 17.103, 134. Conversely, agriculture is also a standard metaphor for sexual intercourse, e.g. Lucr. 4.1107; see Adams (1982: 24ff., 82–5, 154ff.).

67. von Stackelberg (2009: 97–9), Myers (2018: 264–6).

68. On the Stoic *anima mundi*, see Verg. *Aen.* 6.726, *G.* 4.219–27, Cic. *ND* 2.19, Manil. 2.64: *spiritus unus.*

69. Horsfall (2000) on *Aen.* 7.410, *Acrisioneis ... colonis*, notes Virgil's similar placement of this learned mythological adjective.

70. *RR* 10.196, *nunc sunt genitalia tempora mundi* ~ Lucr. 2.1105, *mundi tempus genitale* ~ *G.* 2.324, *uere tument terrae et genitalia semina poscunt*. *RR* 10.197, *coitus* ~ Lucr. 1.185. *RR* 10.209–10, *hinc maria, hinc montes, hinc totus denique mundus | uer agit: hinc hominum pecudum uolucrumque cupido* ~ Lucr. 1.254–7, *hinc ... hinc ... hinc*, 1.17, *denique per maria ac montis* ~ *G.* 3.242–4. The triple *nunc* at the opening of the passage recalls *Ecl.* 3.56–7, whence also comes the clausula at *RR* 10.413, *parturit arbos* (Boldrer 1996: *ad loc.*), which contains Columella's only use of the poetic *arbos* (vs. *arbor* in prose; at 9.5.4 a quote from *G.* 4.27–9 also has *arbos*). Clausen (1994) on *Ecl.* 3.56 observes that this metaphorical use of *parturio* is found only in these two passages and *G.* 2.330, *parturit almus ager* (~ Lucr. 2.993–4 *mater ... terra ... feta parit*).

71. The poetic adjective *aequoreus* (*RR* 10.200) is also first attested at Cat. 64.15 (Boldrer 1996: *ad loc.*), cf. Verg., *G.* 3.243, *Culex* 357, *TLL* I, 1027.56ff.

72. Coppolino (2003: 69); Toohey (1996: 178) detects a 'notable tension between sensuality and "purity"'. Milnor (2005: 258) suggests that the addition of books 11–12, for *uilicus* and *uilica*, rehabilitates Columella's moral project after the excesses of book 10.

73. See Volk (2002: 141–44); Gibson (2003) on Ovid, *Ars* 3.467–8.

74. Cf., e.g., Lucr. 6.92–4 (a similar invocation to Calliope); Verg. *G.* 1.512–14, 2.541–2; Ov. *Met.* 15.453–4, *Rem.* 397–8, *Ars* 3.467–8; Man. 2.58–9, 138–9, 5.8–11.

75. Gowers (2000: 135).

76. Echoes of Lucretius's lines on Phaethon (*DRN* 5.397–8) also have been detected. *audax* underlines Columella's daring in venturing epic verse, cf. *RR* 1 *Praef.* 3. See Brink (1971) on Hor. *Ars* 9–10 on *audere, audacia*, etc. as a literary topos 'often denoting ventures of style'; cf. Verg. *G.* 2.175, Hor. *Carm.* 1.3.25.

77. Cf. Columella's earlier rejection of such natural-philosophical speculations as unprofitable at *RR* 9.2.5. At *RR* 1 *Praef.* 22 Columella, however, claims that the agricultural expert *sit oportet rerum naturae sagacissimus.*

78. On natural-philosophical themes in the *recusatio*, see Innes (1979) and La Penna (1995). Columella, like Virgil, here clearly associates the topic with Lucretius. Manilius (who associates his poetry with Apollo at *Astr.* 1.19) *Astr.* 5.8–11 contains much of the same imagery and language (e.g. *me properare etiam mundus iubet omnia circum* | *sidera uectatum toto decurrere caelo,* | *cum semel aetherios ausus conscendere currus.* | *summum contigerim . . . culmen*).

79. *G.* 2.476: *sacra fero*; 483: *naturae . . . partis.* The religious-mystical language is a 'traditional metaphor in Stoicism' (Hadot 2006: 170; cf. Seneca *NQ* 7.30.6: *rerum natura sacra*; Plin. *Nat. Hist.* 2.77: *secreta naturae*; Lucan 1.639: *secreta caeli*).

80. Koster (1988: 96); see Call. *Aet.* fr. 1.21–4 Harder.

81. Cf. Verg. *Ecl.* 10.71: *gracili . . . hibisco*; Prop. 2.13.3; *Culex* 1: *gracili modulante Thalia*, 2: *tenuem . . . orsum*, 7: *leuior*; Manil. 1.851: *ardua . . . gracili tenuatur semita filo*.

82. Cf. *RR* 10 pr. 4: *adgressi sumus tenuem admodum et paene uiduatam corpore materiam.* See Thomas (1985 and 1988) on Verg. *G.* 3.290–4 (290: *angustis . . . rebus*; 294: *magno nunc ore sonandum*), cf. *G.* 4.1–6. See Toohey (1996: 5–7); also Horsfall (2001b: 309–10) on the *Moretum.*

83. Cf. Hor. *Carm.* 2.20.1–3: *ferar . . . per liquidum aethera* | *uates*; *Epist.* 2.1.182: *audacem . . . poetam*; 225: *tenui deducta poemata filo*; *Epist.* 2.2.51–2: *paupertas inpulit audax* | *ut uersus facerem*; *Carm.* 1.1.36: *sublimi . . . uertice*; 3.4.2 *Calliope*, 3.25.1: *quo me rapis?*; 3.30.15: *mihi Delphica* | *lauro cinge*; 4.2.31–33: *operosa paruus* | *carmina fingo* | *concines maiore poeta plectro.* Prop. 3.1.1–12 (1: *sacra*; 4: *orgia*; 5: *tenuastis*; 8: *tenui pumice*; 9–10: *me Fama leuat terra sublimis . . . equis*; 11: *in curru*), 3.3.21: *praescriptos . . . gyros.*

84. See also *G.* 1.293–4, 2.417: *iam canit effectos extremus uinitor antes*; *Moretum* 29–30: *modo rustica carmina cantat* | *agrestique suum solatur uoce laborem.* The verb *modulor* frequently denotes pastoral poetry, cf. *Ecl.* 5.14, 10.51; Tib. 2.1.521–4; Ov. *Met.* 11.54, 100; Nemes. *Ecl.* 1.71.

85. König and Whitmarsh (2007: 3). Further on Columella's poetic sources, especially Ovid and Horace, see Kleberg (1932), Weinold (1959) and Boldrer (1996: 22–6).

86. Gowers (2000: 140), Dallinges (1964: 151).

87. Martin (2005: 158–9).

10 SERVIAN READINGS OF RELIGION IN THE *GEORGICS*

1. Cameron (2011: 571).

2. Daintree (1990: 65).

3. Williams (1966–7: 50).

4. Kaster (1980), Cameron (2011).

5. A similar moral can be extracted from Thomas (2009: 93–121), who explores the suppression of anti-Augustan voices in Servius, further illustrating how this has 'succeeded in influencing the lexicographical tradition' (97).

6. Heyworth's discussion in this volume also reveals commentators and textual critics to be guilty of a tendency to *use* Servius by extracting salient observations from his text, rather than *reading* him – a phenomenon which I set out and explore with particular reference to historians of Roman religion.

7. Maltby (2005: 207–10) provides a succinct and useful overview of the text's history.

8. It is now standard editorial practice to print the expanded version of Servius's commentary, with passages found only in Servius Auctus in italics.

9. For example, Stok (2012: 472).

10. For example, Jones (1961: 224) and Fowler (1997: 77–8).

11. Cameron (2011: 567) terms this a 'modern doctrine', albeit one with which he is uneasy.

12. This model is established by the poem's opening roll call of deities and fabled humans who have either invented, or have care for, a particular topic covered in the *Georgics* (1.1–23).

13. See Richter (1957: *ad loc.*), Thomas (1988: 187) and Mynors (1990: 285) on the philosophical background of this theory about bees, with its blending of Stoic and Pythagorean elements.

14. On this, see also Mackenzie and Xinyue in this volume.

15. Horsfall (1991: 242).

16. Ironically, as this chapter argues, this is replicated in the way modern scholars of Roman religion read Servius. Cf. Cameron (2011: 572) who argues that 'his commentary represents less research than a drastic and systematic reduction of the learned material assembled by his predecessors' – in other words this is not a reading of Virgil's text at all!

17. Stok (2012: 477). For discussion, see, e.g., Stok (2012: 477–80), Keeline (2013: *passim*) and Cameron (2011: 590–4).

18. Thomas (2009: 105).

19. An unusual note also paints Virgil as invested in his subject matter, having pondered for a long time the relative merits of a life devoted to philosophy or rural affairs (*G.* 2.475).

20. Pliny is also made to support Virgil's claims about fungi (*G.* 1.392) or the whiteness of animals by the River Clitumnus (*G.* 2.146), although disproves his claims about rooks (*G.* 1.414).

21. Hackemann (1940: 15, 54). Hackemann (1940: 61) admits that Servius has a reasonable knowledge of viticulture, 'but even here his lack of interest made itself felt in his comments'.

22. For example, *G.* 2.23, where he clarifies a distinction between *plantae* (shoots taken from trees) and *plantaria* (shoots grown from seed), or *G.* 3.55, where he provides additional information concerning the horns of cows.

23. An agricultural reason for this structural decision is also added (with venerable backing from Varro), namely that the topic of agriculture falls neatly into four parts. Servius then continues, at various points throughout the commentary, to defend Virgil against criticisms of his structural choices (e.g. *G.* 2.177). For further discussion of which, as well as the focus on structure in *G.* 1.1, see Goodfellow (2015: 56–60). Servius's only other claim about the whole text is that it is in 'the middle style' (e.g. *G.* 1.391), on which see Goodfellow (2015: 57) and Maltby (2011: 65).

24. Cameron (2011: 590–4) discusses Roman academic debates over Virgil's ritual correctness, which start as early as C. Iulius Hyginus, a freedman of Augustus.

25. Dorcey (1992: 15–16), characteristically uncritical of his source material, simply notes of this passage that Servius provides our 'longest mythological account of Silvanus' (15).

26. Indeed, whilst the word *numen* once generated much scholarly controversy – arguments hinged on whether it referred to a primitive impersonal spirit, or a more anthropomorphic deity – today the word commands little notice: my arguments as to why this is a mistake are formulated in part at Hunt (2016: 177–90), and are to be expanded in a future article.

27. Presumably the similarity in agriculturally-specific divine names prompted Servius Auctus to include this additional list which, he claims, draws not on the pontifical books, but the prayers of the *flamen Cerealis*.

28. My thanks go to Stephen Harrison for pointing out this connection with Varro's twelve-god list. Varro's presence is further reinforced by the fact that Servius has already gestured to him in this passage as supporting authority for his claims about the pontifical books.

29. Kaster (1988: 171), Cameron (2011: 571).

30. See also Heyworth in this book for presentation of Servius as a reader of the *Georgics* who is out of touch with Virgil's real intent (producing readings which at their worst can be described as 'nonsense'), but one who strongly influences modern commentators on Virgil's text. As such, both chapters work together to highlight the intellectual dangers of ignoring Servius's eccentricities.

31. Spiniensis (Augustine *CD*. 4.21), Puta (Arnobius *ad Nat*. 4.7), Nodutus (Augustine *CD*. 4.8 and Arnobius *ad Nat*. 4.7), Mellonia (Augustine *CD*. 4.34 and Arnobius *ad Nat*. 4.7). For Sterculius, see Macrobius *Sat*. 1.7.25, Servius *ad Aen*. 9.4 (here called Sterculinius) and Augustine *CD*. 18.15 (here called Stercutus).

32. See Davies (2004: 4) on the instinct among scholars of Roman religion to view early Roman religion as 'genuine' Roman religion.

33. See Hunt (2016: 43–9, 177–90) on the animist orthodoxy in early scholarship on Roman religion and the popularity of the word *numen*.

34. See, for example, Warde-Fowler (1911: 160–4) and Bailey (1932: 52–6), who explains that 'it is one of the marks of the Roman religion as a 'higher animism' that it was able to conceive of spirits not merely attached to a particular object or spot, but in a wider sense as concerned with a definite function' (52).

35. Hunt (2016: 17–19, 62–70).

11 THE *GEORGICS* OFF THE CANADIAN COAST: MARC LESCARBOT'S *A-DIEU À LA NOUVELLE-FRANCE* (1609) AND THE VIRGILIAN TRADITION

1. The poem's title, including its hyphenated forms, follows that given in the modern edition of Lescarbot's poetry on New France: Pioffet and Lachance (2014). See also note 43 below.

2. Baudry (1986). For Baudry's edition of an assortment of Lescarbot's work, see Baudry (1968). Thierry (2001) is not much more sympathetic (101–2).

3. Pioffet and Lachance's new edition of Lescarbot's poetry and smaller works on New France appeared, as we have seen (note 1) in 2014. Representative of the new appreciation of

Lescarbot's poetry is Carile (2000), who made his opposition to traditional criticism of Lescarbot's literary ambitions clear (51). Some of Lescarbot's poetry has also recently been translated into English by Haijo Westra (2015).

4. Usher (2012).

5. Pioffet and Lachance (2014: 27–37), Emont (2004: 20–60).

6. Pioffet and Lachance (2014: 35).

7. For the marine composition, see the final couplet of the *A-dieu à la Nouvelle-France* (429–30).

8. Pioffet and Lachance (2014: 35, nn. 109 and 110).

9. Westra (2015).

10. Carile (2000: 71).

11. Wilson-Okamura (2010: 77). See also Power (2014).

12. The most complete study of Virgil in the period remains Hulubei (1931). The first printed French *Aeneid* was translated by Octovian de Saint-Gelais (1509). The *Eclogues* appeared in 1516, translated by Guillaume Michel de Tours, who also translated the *Georgics* in 1519.

13. Usher and Fernbach (2012: 4–7).

14. For a useful overview of the idea of Virgil's poetic career in the Renaissance and the tradition of the *rota*, see Wilson-Okamura (2010: 87–93).

15. Huss (2000: 90–3).

16. 'Virgile, pour essay chanta sa Bucolique, | Puis le Troyen Aenée: Ainsi premierement, | Boyssieres a chanté son amoureux tourment | et ores son Hercull' d'un long vers Heroique'; 'Virgil, sang his Bucolic as a trial, | And then of the Trojan Aeneas: Thus, | Boyssieres has first sung of his agony in love, and | Now he sings his Hercules in a longer heroic verse'; Ronsard (1578). This passage is cited in Fernbach (2012: 94–5).

17. Lambin (1563), a2: *rerum causas occultas atque a natura involutas*. On Lambin and the inclusion of the *Georgics* along with the *Aeneid* as types of epic, see Cave (2001: 207–9).

18. For an excellent overview of the uptake of the debate over Aristotle from Italy via Scaliger's *Poetices libri VII* (1561), see Chevrolet (2007: 397–417). A Latin translation of the *Poetics* was produced by Lorenzo Valla in 1498 and the first edition of the Greek text by Aldus Manutius in 1508.

19. Chevrolet (2007: 401–3), Scaliger (1561) III.25.115b.

20. The genres and types of poetry proposed by Du Bellay are in the fourth chapter of the *Deffence* (1549): 'Quels genres de poëmes doit elire le poëte françois'; 'What genres of poetry should the French poet choose?' We will return to this example in the conclusion below.

21. Chevrolet (2007: 405). Vauquelin's verses are cited here.

22. For the category of 'recreational georgic' and the well-kempt, cultivated natural environment that it described, see Haskell (1999). On France's prolific production after 1600, see Haskell (2003: 4) and Ludwig (1989: 155).

23. Haskell (2003: 2). She gives Rapin this title at p. 18.

24. See Monreal (2010: 27–34) for an overview of the numerous editions and translations of the work.

25. For the Ovidian character of early Italian didactic, see Ludwig (1982: 160). For the ideal of cultivated nature, see Haskell (2003: 26–8). For the metamorphoses in the *Hortorum libri IV*, see Monreal (2010: 109–14).

26. Wilkinson (1969: 294).

27. For the reception of the *laudes Italiae* in the period in general, see Houghton (2015).

28. Haskell (2003: 32–8).

29. Cf. Seneca, *Ep.* 86.15. Rapin weighed in against Seneca's position in the introduction to the second edition of the *Hortorum libri VI*; Haskell (2003: 31–2).

30. In 2003 Haskell counted around 250 didactic poems by Jesuits. Three georgic poems were composed by Jesuits in South and Central America: José Rodrigues de Melo (1781) published together with Prudêncio do Amaral (1781) in Rome. Again in 1781, but this time in Modena, Rafael Landívar's *Rusticatio Mexicana* (1781) was also published. Tommaso Strozzi published a didactic poem on drinking chocolate: Strozzi (1689), with a georgic book on the cultivation of cacao. On de Melo, Amaral and Landívar, see Haskell (2003: 315–20). Landívar has been studied in Laird (2006), Strozzi in Haskell (2003: 82–101).

31. Wilson-Okamura (2010: 78).

32. Wilson-Okamura (2010: 81–2).

33. Wilkinson (1969: 11).

34. Fernbach (2012: 96).

35. Montaigne (1580: II.10).

36. The *Rusticus* constituted the preface to Poliziano's course on the *Georgics*. The standard edition is Bausi (1996). For contemporary praise of Virgil's poem for its poetic resourcefulness, see Wilson-Okamura (2010: 98).

37. Hulubei (1931: 62–3). For an example of this literary engagement with georgic themes in France, on the basis of Joachim Du Bellay's *Divers jeux rustiques* (1558), see Fernbach (2012: 93–114).

38. Usher (2013: 125), Wilkinson (1969: 301).

39. Brazeau (2009: 4–11). The first Jesuit missionary to Canada, Pierre Biard (1567–1622), arrived at Port-Royal in May 1611, five years after Lescarbot. Biard described the concept of New France's twinhood with France in his *Relation* of 1616; Campeau (1967: 461).

40. Lescarbot (1617) 1.234, 1.218. On Lescarbot's negative assessment of his contemporary France, see Brazeau (2009: 71–4).

41. Lescarbot performed a Latin speech in Vervins in 1598; Lescarbot (1598). He also translated a handful of contemporary Latin works, for which see Thierry (2001: 74–86).

42. The *A-dieu* follows the standard pattern of rhyming Alexandrines in the scheme aaBB (*rime plates* or *suivies*). The Alexandrine took over, to some extent, the duties of the hexameter in Latin.

43. For the text of Lescarbot's *A-dieu à la Nouvelle-France*, I follow the edition of Pioffet and Lachance (2014), who take as their basis the edition of 1609. In using Pioffet and Lachance's text, I also follow their reproduction of early modern French forms and spelling.

44. Westra's 2015 prose translation of the *A-dieu* is accurate and readily available. I use it here for all translations of Lescarbot's text, except where stated otherwise.

45. Lescarbot (1617: 502).

46. Cf. also *A-dieu*, 67–8, for the same idea that nature produces copiously on her own.

47. Lescarbot (1617: 624).

48. On the mild winters of 1605–7, see Brazeau (2009: 25–6).

49. In the same way that Virgil's mention of (what he thought to be) a silk plant at *G.* 2.121 inspired the didactic poems of Vida (1527) and Lazzarelli (*c.* 1505), it is tempting to see in Lescarbot's addition of Canadian 'silk' to his poem another instance of the thematic influence of Virgil's *Georgics* and its later reception.

50. Hulubei (1931: 62).

51. Brazeau (2009: 69–95). On Champlain and Lescarbot's relationship, as well as their approaches to the native populations, see Thierry (2004: 121–34).

52. Later in the poem (323) Lescarbot expands on the distance he puts between himself and the word 'sauvage' in this line. The chapter he dedicates to the native peoples in New France, Lescarbot (1617: book 4), is described by Brazeau (2009: 70) as 'an in-depth and perceptive hymn to the peoples of the new colony'.

53. Pioffet (2007), Gosman (2001), Brazeau (2009: 69–95).

54. See also Xinyue in the present volume.

55. For the imitation of these lines as 'the most frequently employed shorthand for didactic content', see Moul (2017: 183).

56. Moul (2017: 180).

57. For the moments of autopsy in Virgil's *Georgics*, see Spurr (2008: 24).

58. Baudry (1968).

59. Carile (2000: 52).

60. Kallendorf (2014: 1073).

61. Du Bellay (1549: ch. 4).

62. Cf. the summary of the reception of didactic poetry in the *Histoire du vers français*: 'Il est utile de signaler que Du Bellay n'a point parlé de ces poèmes dans sa *Deffence*, qu'ils ne font point partie du programme primitif de la Pléiade'; 'It is worth noting that Du Bellay did not mention these poems in his *Deffence*, as they did not form part of the basic program of the Pléiade'; Lote (1991: 49).

63. On Du Bellay's final chapter, see Mackenzie (2011: 39).

64. Schmidt (1970 (1938)) noted the extensive influence of the *Georgics* in *La Savoye* (81), but in later studies of Peletier's conception of nature, cf. Wilson (1954) and Arnaud (2005), this is all but forgotten. For the *Georgics* in the theoretical works, see Peletier (1555) 1.15–16.

65. Quoted from Low (1983: 231). Low's monograph on the topic attempts to amend this view for English literature; Low (1985).

12 SHELLEY'S GEORGIC LANDSCAPE

1. The brief exception to this is Webb (1976: 329–33), who traces echoes of some of the underwater imagery in sections of Shelley's poetry.

2. Robinson (2006: 115) suggests that 'Latin literature hardly occupies Shelley's translation interests at all', given we have in total only a fragment of Virgil's tenth *Eclogue*, and a fragment from the fourth *Georgic*. I would suggest that the opposition of Latin and Greek is unhelpful here.

3. Jones (1964: 340), original italics.

4. Jones (1964: 347).

5. Keach (1984: 1).

6. On 24 December 1812 (Jones 1964: 343–4) he requested editions from Clio Rickman, bookseller, of three of the 'most important English theorists and philologists of his day', which Keach takes as evidence for his long-standing interest in, and familiarity with, linguistics and the 'study of language' (1984:1). One is Lord Monboddo; see below.

7. Martyn (1746: xv–xvi).

8. Given the evidence that Shelley requested classical texts to be 'original and translation, if possible, united' (Jones 1964: 344), it is unlikely that his criticism is founded upon his not requiring a translation.

9. Keach (1984: 16), though the whole of his discussion in Chapter 1 is of relevance here.

10. For an excellent discussion of 'Shelley's view of language [as] caught between being-for-itself and the representation of being', see Milnes' 2004 article (this quote from p. 18). It is worth noting very briefly one further point here from Keach: he suggests that Shelley is influenced by Monboddo's 'incisive discussion' on the subject, and especially Monboddo's discussion of Plato's *Cratylus* (401e). In the Platonic passage Socrates wonders whether the men who first attached words to things were influenced by Heraclitean theories of flux, and discusses this with particular reference to the names of Ocean and Tethys. Below we shall see how the notion of 'origin' attached to rivers becomes a way of talking about poetic origins, as well as spatial and temporal origins. It is striking that these same passages lie behind the Platonic passage, and are here used to engage in a conversation about etymology, and the nature of words. Compare Morgan (1999: Chapter 2) and Ademollo (2011: 181–256). The connection to Heraclitus is revived below.

11. Ingpen and Peck (1930: 63).

12. Shelley (1840: 10).

13. Shelley (1840: 40). For the purposes of this essay it is perhaps of significance that Shelley is referring here to Dante.

14. On the symbolism of water in his works, see, for example, Farnsworth (2001: esp. 69–116) and Yeats (1961: 80). On the image of the cave as denoting the 'introspective' turn of the mind, see Butter (1954: 47–8).

15. Ingpen and Peck (1930: 64).

16. As estimated by, e.g., Reiman (1986: 152), based on the *terza rima* form and the surrounding context from the notebook; Webb (1976: 330–1).

17. The text is taken from Martyn's edition.

18. This is the title by which it is commonly known, though it was not titled in Shelley's notebook. The text here follows Everest and Matthews (2000), though the line numbering is changed (see note 21).

19. Note that 'girt round by marble' is written in Shelley's notebook alongside 'enclosed in glimmering', with neither cancelled. I include marble here, as I understand it to add to surrounding imagery in creating the impression of a built landscape (see below), but one could just as well include 'glimmering', if one recalls the 'lustre' of the mind's cave in the *Speculations* passage, above, or compares *The Revolt of Islam* I.51.584 and the similarity there in topography and journey.

20. See Webb (1976: 331 n.1).

21. Given as follows:

> [[The shepherd Aristaeus, as fame tells,
> Losing his bees by hunger, fled
> Tempe, and to Peneus
> Mothers Cyrene [
>
>]]]

On a similar combination of geographical locations, see also *Hellas* 1068–70.

22. De Bruyn (2005: 152). De Bruyn's excellent article outlines different purposes behind the translations, with a particular focus on the scientific.

23. On the georgic and Romanticism, see especially Goodman (2004).

24. Virgil identifies the Aristaeus story as an *aetion* (cf. *G.* 4.315–16), thereby setting it within the (albeit flimsy) time frame of the mythological past.

25. *G.* 4.418–20 – the description of Proteus's cave – offers the reverse of this situation: a mountain where waves enter.

26. The sentience of the water may be amplified too by *accipio* and *mitto*; also by the source from which the passage ultimately derives: the description of the rape of Tyro by Poseidon in the *Odyssey* (11.243ff.), where the god disguises himself as the River Enipeus (cf. Mynors 1990: *ad loc.*).

27. The word is particularly appropriate, of course, at the start of a translation from a poem more usually about the earth, harvesting and cutting. In addition, it often has satanic overtones: cf. *OED* s.v. A.c. on the allusive properties of the word 'cloven' as indicating the Devil. Such an infernal aspect is important given the suggestion that this comprises an underworld descent of sorts.

28. It is possible that Shelley was influenced in his emphasis on the 'chasm' by Dryden's famous translation: 'Two rising Heaps of liquid Crystal stand, | And leave a Space betwixt, of empty Sand.'

29. Indeed, it should be noted that 'chasm' can be figurative in its meaning rather than literal, potentially rendering this line even more metatextually loaded than I have suggested; see *OED ad loc.* 5a: 'A break marking a divergence, or a wide and profound difference of character or position, a breach of relations, feelings, interests, etc.'

30. The *TLL* (I.312.19–20) draws a parallel between this use of *accepit* at *G.* 4.362 and that found at Virg. *Aen.* 9.817 (note that the *TLL* contains an error: the line is 817 and not 814 as stated). There, Turnus is welcomed by the Tiber after his rampage and returned to his comrades. The connection may serve to highlight the sentient landscape in both instances; it also aligns Turnus and Aristaeus such that the Homeric aspects of the *Georgics* section are more easily apprehended.

31. On the 'nurturing' aspect of the phrase, see Thomas (1988: *ad loc.*). *Sinus* here refers to the hollow of a wave (*OLD* s.v. 8), and seems to have been used in this sense for the first time in the *Georgics* (at 3.238). More usually, the primary meanings of *sinus* relate, e.g., to the folds of clothing and fabric (s.v. 1), or figuratively to a 'bosom, refuge or shelter' (s.v. 3).

32. Whilst the *OED* does allow for the application of portal to 'a natural entrance, as of a cave, a mountain pass, etc.' (s.v. 1d), the more predominant usage is as 'a door, gate, doorway, or gateway, of stately or elaborate construction; the entrance to a large or magnificent building' (s.v. 1a), and it seems likely that a pluralistic reading is applicable here.

33. The letter is erroneously dated 1818; see Jones (1964: 549) for the full text.

34. Morgan (1999: 39). There is much more that could be said here on the connection between the *Phaedo* passage and Morgan's excellent discussion of Ocean in the *Georgics*.

35. Miles (1980: 257). On the ambiguous divinity of Aristaeus, see below.

36. 'Halls' too seems to capture a grandeur that lacks the homeliness of *domus*.

37. It is perhaps inspired by Cyrene's earlier claim at *G.* 4.358–9.

38. See Webb (2002).

39. Morgan (1999: 48–9).

40. On Shelley's engagement with Lucretius, cf., e.g., Turner (1959) and Roberts (1997).

41. Taken from Thomas Creech's translation of Lucretius, 'the standard full-length English Lucretius throughout the eighteenth century' (Hopkins 2007: 256). Creech helpfully lists the various places where the motif occurs in the note to (his) *DRN* 1.933.

42. *G*. 3.289–93.

43. Importantly, Aristaeus is 'clearly original to V[irgil]'; see Thomas (1988: 4.315–32).

44. Miles (1980: 257).

45. Mynors (1990: *ad* 4.317).

46. Dante, *De Monarchia* 2.3.6. Shelley is responding to Dante's reception of 'Virgil' as well as his poem; see below.

47. Here the transgression occurs within the 'untrampled' setting, as well as the metapoetic transgression resulting from the alteration to Virgil's poetry.

48. Cf. Williams (2004: 8). His entire section on the Romantic Hero is useful here (8–13).

49. On the Virgilian and the Lucretian sublime, see Hardie (2009); on retrospectively considering the ancient sublime in a post-eighteenth-century environment, see Day (2013).

50. On mountains as an especially sublime trope, see, e.g., Day (2013: 4).

51. On sublimity and Wordsworth's *Prelude*, cf., e.g., Shaw (2007: 101), who also discusses the 'Romantic Sublime' more comprehensively.

52. Tally Jr (2013: 1).

53. See p. 181 on the metapoetic significance of trees.

54. *OED* s.v. 1a: 'A small wood; a group of trees affording shade or forming avenues or walks, occurring naturally or planted for a special purpose. Groves were commonly planted by heathen peoples in honour of deities to serve as places of worship.' The final sense of this definition may help to access a 'heathen' and semi-religious undertone to the choice of wording in the translation. It is also of significance to a consideration of Dante (below), given the ancient poets are to be found in a wood (*Inf.* IV.65–6).

55. The *TLL* indicates that its primary meanings are 'wood' (*silua*; VII.2.1751.22), or a sacred wooded grove (*TLL* VII.2.1751.52); the usage here is put in the 'stylistic appendix', where attention is drawn to the fact that the end of the line, *lucosque sonantis*, is repeated at *Eclogues* 10.58 and *Ciris* 196 (*TLL* VII.2.1754.4–5). *Eclogue* 10 is of significance to the study of Shelley, as it represents the *only* other published Virgilian – indeed, Latin – poem that he translates. One might imagine a deliberate connection between the translations, especially given the Servian suggestion that *Eclogues* 10 and *Georgics* 4 are connected through the figure of Gallus. The translated sections are also those which figure (explicitly or implicitly) Arethusa, on whom Shelley composed his poem *Arethusa*.

56. Mynors (1990: *ad loc*.). Virgil may also be responding to Lucretius's depiction of the topography below the earth's surface (*DRN* 6.536–42), which includes lakes and pools.

57. As exemplified in the Sibyl's description of the underworld descent at *Aeneid* 6.131–2.

58. One might as easily suggest 'at least' two underworlds: Socrates' depiction in the *Phaedo*, above, the famous underworld in Virgil's *Aeneid* and Hell in Milton's *Paradise Lost* certainly provide infernal texture.

59. Low (1985: 17). One must also account for the influence of Ovid's versions of the myth, of course, when considering its popularity. In *Metamorphoses* 10, he omits the Aristaeus episode altogether; in the *Fasti* (1.363–80) he omits the descent of Aristaeus. It makes the episode a particularly Virgilian moment, emphasizing the focus of Shelley's piece.

60. Graver (1991:146).

61. Wu (1990).

62. Graver (1991: 146).

63. Hardie (1998: 46); see also, e.g., Thomas (1988: 4.315–558).

64. Cf. *TLL* IX.2.1152.85.

65. Shelley's translation of *genetrix* (*G.* 4.363) as 'great Mother' (5) seems almost to metamorphose Cyrene into Cybele, the Roman *Magna Mater*.

66. A trope seen elsewhere in his work; cf., e.g., *Alastor*.

67. Hardie (1998: 45–6).

68. 'Starred' is a slightly odd choice here. The editors remind me that Virgil's Orpheus is singing *sub astris* ('beneath the stars') at *G.* 4.509 in some manuscript traditions, so could form another connection across the episodes. Another, more tentative, suggestion is that one might recall the constellation of Aries, given these rivers appear in Apollonius's *Argonautica* (4.131–4) at the moment when the Golden Fleece is stolen.

69. It is possible that this speaks again to a symbolic rendering of the mind, as Shelley frequently uses the idea of marks on the sand to represent thought.

70. A sly acknowledgement, perhaps, of what the wanderer might find there were he to look; see n. 26 on Poseidon. See also above on Platonic 'chasms'.

71. 'The Hypanis alludes to Gallus, whose only surviving line until 1979 was a description of the river preserved by Vibius Sequestus' (Heyworth 2007: 59). Heyworth connects Gallus to this passage in the *Georgics*; the association is triangulated by the fact that Shelley's only other translation of Virgil is a passage concerning Gallus, 'From Virgil's Tenth Eclogue'. It is clear the two Virgilian translations should be considered more closely together.

72. Note also that the final stanza dramatically shifts as the narrator swims into focus and apostrophizes the Eridanus, a particularly epic form of address.

73. 'meads' = meadows: *OED* s.v. 'mead', n. 2.

74. In particular, the Ocean; Morgan (1999: 32–3) has a useful summary.

75. Also his treatise on rivers; see Thomas (1988: 4.333–86).

76. Morgan (1999: 37–40); as does Thomas (1988: 4.333–86).

77. Jones (2005: 85).

78. Baer (2006: 130). On Shelley's use of *terza rima* in *Ode to the West Wind*, and especially this quality of 'fluidity', see Mahoney (2011: 54–8).

79. Ravinthiran (2011: 156).

80. See the detailed history of *terzetti* in English poetry up to Shelley in Reiman (1984: 151–60).

81. This fragment represents an early example. By coincidence, Byron is also writing in *terza rima* in the same period; see Bone (1982) and Reiman (1984: 157–9).

82. Webb (1976: 332–3).

83. Webb (1976: 329).

84. For Byron, at least, Dante is 'the poet of liberty' (Medwin 1824: 195). See also his *Prophecy of Dante*, written in *terza rima*. Byron was also engaged with his own reception of the *Georgics*, claiming that 'The Georgics are indisputably – and I believe *undisputedly* even – a finer poem than the Æneid. – Virgil knew this – he did not order *them* to be burnt' (Nicholson 1991: 143).

85. See Henkel (2014: esp. 38–41).

86. It is worth noting that early commentators saw an echo of Orpheus's cry to Eurydice (*G.* 4.525–7) in Dante's cry to Virgil at the moment he realizes his departure in the *Purgatorio* (XXX.49–51); cf. Parker (1997: 247, 252). Shelley's encouragement to read the *Georgics* into the opening of the *Inferno* would mean that Virgil is defined by that text at his entrance and exit.

87. *Cratylus* 402a. The Heraclitean fragments (B12, B49a, B91) underline the point even more neatly. It is uncertain that Shelley could have accessed all those directly, though Hume seems to have had B12 in mind. Shelley certainly owned a copy of Thomas Taylor's translation of the *Cratylus* (cf. Keach 1984: 239, n. 36), and his sustained dialogue with Plato and Hume is well recorded, as is his metaphysical philosophy; cf., e.g., Howe (2012) and Notopoulos (1949). See also note 10.

88. Socrates claims the idea is analogous to a point in Homer (*Cratylus* 402a).

89. See, e.g., Howe (2012).

90. Dante did not have access to Homer's works directly, but read them 'through' quotations and allusions by other authors, hence the appearance of Homer in the grove.

91. See also Keach (1984: xvi) and the discussion of Shelley's 'perpetual Orphic song' (*Prometheus Unbound* 415–17) as being non-indicative of his approach to language, which may be relevant.

13 WOMEN AND EARTH: FEMALE RESPONSES TO THE *GEORGICS* IN THE TWENTIETH AND TWENTY-FIRST CENTURIES

1. Kallendorf (2012) catalogues translations down to 1850. Things are shifting: since the publication of Ruden's *Aeneid*, we have Patricia Johnston's 2012 translation, and there are at least two more translations by American women in progress.

2. For an introduction to Gerhardt, see Verstraete (2014); Gerhardt fairly closely resembles Lembke in that she had received a training in classics but was more renowned for her original writing. I discuss Gerhardt in Braund (forthcoming).

3. On Day-Lewis's descent into a register too low to represent Virgil accurately, see, e.g., Thomas (2001: 121–5).

4. Lembke (1990: 2).

5. Lembke (2006: 38).

6. Lembke (2006: 38). *Rodale's Garden Answers*, by Fern Marshall Bradley and Linda A. Gilkeson, is a title of enduring popularity first published in 1995 by Rodale Press, which was founded in 1930 by J. I. Rodale (1898–1971) with a focus on gardening and sustainable agriculture. My thanks to Emma Hilliard for researching this.

7. Lembke (2005: xiii).

8. Lembke (2006: 116–19).

9. Lembke (2005: 82).

10. Stevens (2005).

11. Lembke (2005: ix–xi), quotation from ix.

12. Quotation is from Lembke (2005: ix); examples from x and xi; Stevens (2005) praises the latter highly.

13. Lembke (2005: x); she names Dryden, Day-Lewis and Wilkinson.

14. Lembke (2005: x). She is right to reject 'corn' which in British English designates grain in general and often wheat in particular, whereas for Americans it denotes 'maize' (what the British call corn-on-the-cob).

15. Varro *RR* 3.16.27; Thomas (1988: *ad loc.*) thinks that the metonymy may have been clichéd, in epic at any rate; Virgil avoids this metonymy in the *Aeneid*.

16. For a stark contrast, see Kristina Chew's 'ultra-modernist' version, published in 2002 (the label is that of Verstraete 2014: 42). For discussion, see Braund (forthcoming).

17. Sackville-West (1926: 107). I discuss below the structure and closing panegyric of her poem.

18. For the immediate acclaim of *The Land*: Blyth (2008: 20, and n. 7 for reviews). On the book's reprintings: Pomeroy (1982: 269). On being awarded the Hawthornden Prize: Glendinning (1983: 172). On Sackville-West being considered a possible successor to the Poet Laureate: Glendinning (1983: 213). Sackville-West's husband Harold Nicolson wrote to her, 'Your fame … is anchored in *The Land*' (Watson 1972: 59). In 1935 Sackville-West made gramophone recordings of *The Land* (Blyth 2008: 20–1), some of which can be accessed on YouTube, e.g. https://www.youtube.com/watch?v=AjXvkRhoXXs (accessed 2 July 2018). That she was in tune with her times is suggested by the fact that the Council for the Preservation of Rural England was founded in the same year, 1926 (see Blyth 2008: 28). For the title as a riposte to T. S. Eliot's *The Waste Land*, published in 1922, see Ames (1978: 16) and Pomeroy (1982: 281).

19. The 1983 biography by Victoria Glendinning is especially useful. On Woolf and Sackville-West, see especially Raitt (1993); Sackville-West was the model for Woolf's Orlando in the novel of that title (1928). Especially famous is her son Nigel Nicolson's *Portrait of a Marriage*, which portrays her affair with Violet Trefusis. The name 'Vita' distinguished her from her mother Victoria.

20. Watson (1972).

21. Brown (1985: 19–39 on Knole; 109–55 on Sissinghurst). They purchased Sissinghurst and its 400 acres in 1930. On her bitterness about her 'exile from Knole', see Ames (1978: 12–13). Sackville-West wrote *The Land* based at Long Barn, a fourteenth-century cottage near Knole, next to which was their farm, Brook Farm (see Brown 1985: 89–97), including a photo of the room where Sackville-West wrote). The manuscript drafts of *The Land* reveal late changes, such as from third to first person and from past to present tense: see Pomeroy (1982), including 274 on these changes. I have been privileged to visit both Knole and the Sissinghurst Castle Gardens while writing this chapter and I cannot recommend them strongly enough; I am grateful to the National Trust curators who met with me for their insights.

22. Nagel (2004: 12). *The Garden* (1946) was a companion poem which also won a major prize.

23. Watson (1972: 12).

24. Sackville-West (1926: 2). *G.* 3.289–90: *nec sum animi dubius uerbis ea uincere magnum | quam sit et angustis hunc addere rebus honorem.* In Lembke's translation, 'Nor does my heart doubt how glorious it is to conquer | these matters with words and give their humbleness grace.'

25. It is possible that her words also echo the opening of the *Aeneid*.

26. I discuss the implications of 'mild continuous epic' and 'pedestrian measure' below.

27. Glendinning (1983: 122), Blyth (2008: 23).

28. See the quotation from Sackville-West pp. 3–4 on pp. 191–2 here.

29. Variety: Pomeroy (1982: 281).

30. On Anglo-Saxon Weod-monaþ, see Blyth (2008: 25).

31. Sackville-West (1926: 45–6).

32. Blyth (2008: 21) has a list. James Thomson's *The Seasons* (1726–30) is especially salient, given its organizational mode; because of its phenomenal popularity, Sackville-West must have known it (thus Blyth 2008: 30, n. 31). For book-length studies of the English tradition of georgic poetry, see Durling (1935), Chalker (1969) and Goodridge (1995). Ziolkowski (1993: 104–19) in his discussion of 'The Modern Georgicists' persuasively proposes that Dryden put the *Georgics* at the centre of English poetic consciousness (109) when he described it as 'the best Poem of the best Poet'.

33. Sackville-West (1926: 106).

34. She signs off with 'Isfahan, April 1926', but we know that she actually completed the poem in Tehran where she was correcting the final proofs; see Glendinning (1983: 157).

35. Although there is no evidence that Sackville-West had read the *Eclogues*, these lines perhaps evoke the displacement and yearning articulated for example by Meliboeus in *Eclogue* 1.

36. Glendinning (1983: 146). The diary entry is for 30 September 1925.

37. Sackville-West (1926: 34).

38. Sackville-West (1926: 90–1).

39. Glendinning (1983: 119): writing in 1921, Harold said 'Vita has an idea of writing sort of English Georgics.'

40. Quoted by Glendinning (1983: 166), and dated 18 June 1940; according to Nagel (2004: 3), this interview took place in 1929.

41. I do not believe this has been noticed previously. The lines quoted start with *Haec super ... bello* (4.559–61) and continue with *Carmina ... fagi* (565–6). Glendinning (1983: 103) notes that this first novel was a great success. Sackville-West was an adept linguist whose mother spoke French, and who corresponded with her husband in Italian, as we see from her letters.

42. Sackville-West 'actually populates her poem with vignettes of people at work: Yeoman, bee-master, shepherd, thatcher, craftsman, and more' (Pomeroy 1982: 280), possibly inspired by a remark that no one now writes poems about occupations (Glendinning 1983: 119).

43. Sackville-West (1926: 7).

44. Sackville-West (1926: 7).

45. Sackville-West (1926: 8).

46. Sackville-West (1926: 9–11).

47. Sackville-West (1926: 22).

48. Sackville-West (1926: 35).

49. I find Sackville-West rather less optimistic than does Nagel (2004: 13), but readers must make up their own minds about the balance between celebratory and gloomy material in the poem.

50. Nagel (2004: 14).

51. Nagel (2004: 17).

52. Sackville-West (1926: 76).

53. She may have been imitating Dryden's occasional use of alexandrines to conclude sections in his heroic couplets.

54. Sackville-West (1926: 3); see Pomeroy (1982: 288). The mention of the shepherd's 'Boeotian forebear' here is a clear reference to Hesiod.

55. Immemorial: 4, 43, 90; cf. 'the centennial concerns' of the fieldsman (7) and the celebration of continuity in 'Spring': 'The law of life and life's continuance' (52) and 'a permanent common

thing' (55). Ames (1978: 15) aligns this concern with continuity with Sackville-West's concept of good stewardship.

56. I borrow 'particularity' from Nagel (2004: 1).

57. Sackville-West (1926: 11–15).

58. Sackville-West (1926: 98): her final headings (98–105) before she widens her scope again with her closing section on 'Vintage' are 'Orchards', 'Making Cider', 'Hop Garden' and 'Oast'.

59. Sackville-West (1926: 13).

60. Cf. the change from winter to spring which is 'Not visible to eye, (not visible | Save in close seeing, . . .)' (Sackville-West 1926: 32). In this insistence on understanding, rather than just observing, Virgil takes over one of the central themes of Lucretius's *De Rerum Natura*; for an in-depth study of the relationship between those two poems, see Gale (2000).

61. Sackville-West (1926: 8).

62. Although 'loutish' seems to have a similar charge to its present-day value, the word 'lout' can denote a servant or worker, thus 'loutish life' (used again at 6, cf. 'loutish hands' at 91) points more to unpretentiousness than to misbehaviour.

63. Sackville-West (1926: 56–7).

64. Sackville-West (1926: 19, 20).

65. Blyth (2008: 24).

66. Glendinning (1983: 166); Pomeroy (1982: 270) asserts that she uses words that are 'obsolete, invented, prickly, tart, a highly personal mixture of archaic and local terms'; Blyth (2008: 24–6) offers detail. She consulted an encyclopedia of agriculture given her by her husband (Pomeroy 1982: 277), farming treatises and the local oral tradition (Blyth 2008: 25). It was reported that a farmer wrote to her that there was nothing wrong with her farming knowledge; see Pomeroy (1982: 281–2).

67. Sackville-West (1926: 20); on Wulf-monaþ as Anglo-Saxon, see Blyth (2008: 23); on 'shrammed' (numbed with cold), a word used by Hardy, see Blyth (2008: 24).

68. Blyth (2008: 24).

69. Lembke obviously had less scope to introduce such language, but one word which was new to me was 'a passel of weeds' (2.252).

70. Sackville-West (1926: 4).

71. Sackville-West (1926: 81–2).

72. Raitt (1993: 98–102).

73. Quotation in Nagel (2004: 8).

74. Nagel (2004: 8–9).

75. See 'Ways Ahead' at the end.

76. These and the following quotations are from Howard (2008).

77. This informs Robert Bridges's question to Sackville-West, 'but how, then, have you got this Virgilian *bite*? eh?', quoted by Nagel (2004: 8).

78. Wells (1982: 15).

79. Wells (1982: 25). The passage is discussed above in Lembke's translation.

80. Lembke (2005: x). Similarly, Michael Cummings, in his review of Kristina Chew's 2002 strikingly modern translation, mentions 'the occasional whiff of formaldehyde' in her predecessors.

81. Day-Lewis, *On Translating Poetry*, 6–7 (my emphasis): 'When I began to translate the *Georgics* of Virgil, in 1939, I had just moved house from an urban to a rural area. As I worked on into the summer of 1940, I felt more and more the kind of patriotism which I imagine was Virgil's – the natural piety, the heightened sense of the genius of place, the passion to praise and protect one's roots, or *to put down roots somewhere while there is still time*, which it takes a seismic event such as war to reveal to most of *us rootless moderns*.' Although Day-Lewis was born in Ireland and described as Anglo-Irish, he was raised in London from the age of two. There is a different story to be told of L. A. S. Jermyn's translation, *The Singing Farmer*, which was written while he was interned by the Japanese in the years 1942–45; for discussion, see Braund (forthcoming).

82. The opening of Kavanagh's poem, 'Clay is the word and clay is the flesh', echoes Sackville-West's obsession with clay, but in the grimmer context of the Irish potato famine. On Virgil, Kavanagh and Heaney, see Thomas (2001: 143–7).

83. O'Hogan (2018: 399).

84. O'Hogan (2018: esp. 399–400 and 411).

85. Insert 'white' / 'male' / 'straight' / 'thin' / 'western' / 'able-bodied' / 'Christian' / 'American' etc., as appropriate.

86. The anonymous reader rightly challenged me on this assertion by observing that all three of these 'outsiders' are white, one is male and one British. But that leaves plenty of outsider-hood for these three poets: Sackville-West was an aristocrat but was excluded from inheriting her beloved Knole by virtue of her sex; the American naturalist Lembke was kept at arms-length by the Classical academy; and Fallon understands as well as the next Irishman the alienation of the Irish from British hegemonic culture. I am confident in my demarcation of these three authors as outsiders, in their different ways.

87. I am grateful to Vin Nardizzi for guidance on feminist and ecofeminist theorization of the land.

88. I welcome this opportunity afforded me by the editors to close this exciting volume by asking such questions.

89. Geue (2018: quotation from 117, n. 19).

90. Geue (2018: 132).

91. Plumwood (1993: 1, 8, 6 respectively).

92. Eklund (2017); see especially Eklund's 'Introduction' (1–19) and Dolan's chapter on treatises on gardening and composting (2017). For a recent overview of ecofeminism, see Laroche and Munroe (2017: 1–15) on 'Introduction: Ecofeminism and the seeds of time'.

93. Plumwood (1993: 2).

94. Plumwood (1993: 1–18).

95. Griffin (1978: xv).

96. Quotations from Cantrell's review essay of Griffin; see Cantrell (1994: 235).

97. Holler (1990: 20).

98. I am deeply grateful to the editors for their receptiveness to my ideas and their suggestions for improving the chapter, and to the anonymous reader for her comments.

BIBLIOGRAPHY

Adams, J. N. (1982), *The Latin Sexual Vocabulary*, London: Duckworth.

Ademollo, F. (2011), *The Cratylus of Plato: A Commentary*, Cambridge: Cambridge University Press.

Akujärvi, J. (2012), 'One and "I" in the Frame Narrative: Authorial Voice, Travelling Persona and Addressee in Pausanias' *Periegesis*', *Classical Quarterly* 62: 327–58.

Alfonsi, L. (1959), 'L'epicureismo nella storia spirituale di Virgilio', in E. Bignone (ed.), *Epicurea in memoriam Hectoris Bignone: miscellanea philologica*, 167–78, Genoa: Università di Genova.

Allen, W. Jr. (1955), 'The British Epics of Quintus and Marcus Cicero', *Transactions of the American Philological Association* 86: 143–59.

Alonso-Núñez, J. M. (2002), 'Wirtschaftsethik', in *Der Neue Pauly* 12, no. 2: 540–3, Stuttgart: Metzler.

Altevogt, H. (1952), *Labor Improbus: Eine Vergilstudie*, Münster: Aschendorff.

Ames, C. (1978), 'Nature and Aristocracy in V. Sackville-West', *Studies in the Literary Imagination* 11, no. 2: 11–25.

Armstrong, D., Fish, J., Johnston, P. A. and Skinner, M. B. (eds) (2004), *Vergil, Philodemus, and the Augustans*, Austin: University of Texas Press.

Armstrong, R. (2002), 'Crete in the *Aeneid*: Recurring Trauma and Alternative Fate', *Classical Quarterly* 52: 321–40.

Arnaud, S. (2005), *La voix de la nature dans l'œuvre de Jacques Peletier du Mans (1517–1582)*, Paris: Classiques Garnier.

Asmis, E. (1995), 'Epicurean Poetics', in D. Obbink (ed.), *Philodemus and Poetry: Poetic Theory and Practice in Lucretius, Philodemus, and Horace*, 15–34, Oxford: Oxford University Press.

Baer, W. (2006), *Writing Metrical Poetry*, Cincinnati: Writer's Digest Books.

Baier, T. (2007), 'Epische Erzählen in Vergils *Georgica*: Struktur und Funktion der Proteus-Geschichte', *Rheinische Museum für Philologie* 150: 314–36.

Bailey, C. (1932), *Phases in the Religion of Ancient Rome*, Oxford: Oxford University Press.

Bal, M. (1996), 'Second-Person Narrative', *Paragraph* 19, no. 3: 179–204.

Bal, M. (2009 (1977)), *Narratology: Introduction to the Theory of Narrative*, trans. C. van Boheemen, Toronto: University of Toronto Press.

Baladié, R. (1974), 'Sur le sens géographique du mot grec ὀφρύς des ses dérivés et son équivalent latin', *Journal des savants* 1974, no. 3: 153–91.

Balot, R. K. (1998), 'Pindar, Virgil, and the Proem to *Georgic* 3', *Phoenix* 52, no. 1: 83–94.

Barchiesi, A. (2005), 'Learned Eyes: Poets, Viewers, Image Makers', in G. K. Galinsky (ed.), *The Cambridge Companion to the Age of Augustus*, 281–305, Cambridge: Cambridge University Press.

Barchiesi, A. (2009), 'Phaethon and the Monsters', in P. Hardie (ed.), *Paradox and the Marvellous in Augustan Literature and Culture*, 163–88, Oxford: Oxford University Press.

Barchiesi, A. and Rosati, G. (2007), *Ovidio Metamorfosi Volume II Libri III–IV*, Milan: Valla.

Bartels, A. (2004), *Vergleichende Studien zur Erzählkunst des römischen Epyllion*, Göttingen: Duehrkohp & Radicke.

Barthes, R. (1977), 'Introduction to Structural Analysis of Narratives', in *Image, Music, Text*, trans. S. Heath, 79–124, London: Fontana Press.

Batstone, W. (1988), 'On the Surface of the *Georgics*', *Arethusa* 21: 227–45.

Batstone, W. (1997), 'Virgilian didaxis: value and meaning in the *Georgics*', in C. Martindale (ed.), *The Cambridge Companion to Virgil*, 125–44, Cambridge: Cambridge University Press.

Baudry, R. (1968), *Marc Lescarbot. Textes choisis*, Montreal: Fides.

Baudry, R. (1986), 'Lescarbot, Marc', *Dictionnaire biographique du Canada / Dictionary of Canadian Biography*, Quebec and Toronto: University of Toronto Press.

Bausi, F. (1996), *Angelo Poliziano. Silvae*, Florence: L. S. Olschki.

Beagon, M. (1992), *Roman Nature: The Thought of Pliny the Elder*, Oxford: Oxford University Press.

Beard, M. (1998), 'Imaginary *horti*: Or Up the Garden Path', in M. Cima and E. La Rocca (eds), *Horti Romani*, 23–32, Rome: L'Erma di Bretscheider.

Beard, M. (2004), 'Writing Ritual: The Triumph of Ovid', in A. Barchiesi, J. Rüpke and S. Stephens (eds), *Rituals in Ink: A Conference on Religion and Literary Production in Ancient Rome Held at Stanford University in February 2002*, 115–26, Stuttgart: F. Steiner.

Beard. M. (2007), *The Roman Triumph*, Cambridge, M A: Harvard University Press.

Bell, A. and Ensslin, A. (2011), '"I know what it was. You know what it was": Second-Person Narration in Hypertext Fiction', *Narrative* 19, no. 3: 311–29.

Benveniste, E. (1971 (1966)), *Problems in General Linguistics*, trans. M. E. Meek, Coral Gables, FL: University of Miami Press.

Benveniste, E. (1993 (1969)), *Indoeuropäische Institutionen. Wortschatz, Geschichte, Funktionen*, trans. W. Bayer, D. Hornig and K. Menke, ed. S. Zimmer, Frankfurt and New York: Campus Verlag; Paris: Editions de la Maison des Sciences de L'Homme.

Bergmann, B., Farrell, J., Feeney, D., Ker, J., Nelis, D. and Schultz, C. (2012), 'An Exciting Provocation: John F. Miller's *Apollo, Augustus and the Poets*', *Vergilius* 58: 3–20.

Berkowitz, L. (1972), 'Pollio and the Date of the Fourth *Eclogue*', *California Studies in Classical Antiquity* 5: 21–38.

Bernabé, A. (2004–7), *Poetae Epici Graeci Pars II Fasc. 1–3*, Bibliotheca Teubneriana, Munich and Leipzig: K.G. Saur.

Bernabé, A. and San Cristóbal, A. I. J. (2008), *Instructions for the Netherworld*, Leiden and Boston: Brill.

Bernstein, M. A. (1994), *Foregone Conclusions: Against Apocalyptic History*, Berkeley: University of California Press.

Betensky, A. (1979), 'The Farmer's Battle', *Ramus* 8: 108–19.

Bianchini, E. (2001), *Carmina Priapea*, Milan: BUR Rizzoli.

Biggs, T. (2014), 'A Roman Odyssey: Cultural Responses to the First Punic War from Andronicus to Augustus', PhD diss., Yale University.

Blyth, I. (2008), 'A Sort of English Georgics: Vita Sackville-West's *The Land*', *Forum for Modern Language Studies* 45: 19–31.

Boldrer, F. L. (ed.) (1996), *Iuni Moderati Columellae rei rusticae liber decimus*, Pisa: ETS.

Bone, J. D. (1982), 'On "Influence", and on Byron's and Shelley's use of *terza rima* in 1819', *Keats-Shelley Memorial Bulletin* 32: 38–48.

Bowditch, P. L. (2001), *Horace and the Gift Economy of Patronage*, Berkeley: University of California Press.

Boyle, A. J. (1986), *The Chaonian Dove: Studies in the Eclogues, Georgics, and Aeneid of Virgil*, Mnemosyne Suppl. 94, Leiden: Brill.

Boyle, A. J. (2006), *An Introduction to Roman Tragedy*, London and New York: Routledge.

Bradley, F. M. and Gilkeson, L. A. (1995), *Rodale's Garden Answers*, New York: Rodale Press.

Braund, S. (2013), 'Equity and Fairness: An Argument Against Abstract Ideas', in J. P. Sarra (ed.), *An Exploration of Fairness: Interdisciplinary Inquiries in Law, Science and the Humanities*, 17–32, Toronto: Carswell.

Braund, S. (forthcoming), *A Cultural History of Translations of Virgil: From the Twelfth Century to the Present*, Cambridge: Cambridge University Press.

Brazeau, B. (2009), *Writing a New France, 1604–1632: Empire and Early Modern French Identity*, Farnham: Ashgate.

Bremmer, J. (2014), *Initiation into the Mysteries of the Ancient World*, Berlin: De Gruyter.

Brink, C. O. (1971), *Horace on Poetry, II, The Ars Poetica*, Cambridge: Cambridge University Press.

Brown, J. (1985), *Vita's Other World: A Gardening Biography of V. Sackville-West*, Harmondsworth, Middlesex, and New York: Viking.

Buchheit, V. (1972), *Der Anspruch des Dichters in Vergils Georgika: Dichtertum und Heilsweg*, Darmstadt: Wissenschaftliche Buchgesellschaft.

Burkert, W. (1982), 'Craft versus Sect: The Problem of Orphics and Pythagoreans', in B. F. Meyer and E. P. Sanders (eds), *Jewish and Christian Self-Definition III: Self-Definition in the Graeco-Roman World*, 1–22, 183–9, London: SCM Press (reprinted in 2006, F. Graf (ed.), *Kleine Schriften III: Mystica Orphica, Pythagorica*, 191–216, Göttingen: Vandenhoeck & Ruprecht).

Burkert, W. (1987), *Ancient Mystery Cults*, Cambridge, MA: Harvard University Press.

Butter, P. (1954), *Shelley's Idols of the Cave*, Edinburgh: Edinburgh University Press.

Cairns, F. (2008), 'C. Asinius Pollio and the *Eclogues*', *Proceedings of the Cambridge Philological Society* 54: 49–79.

Cameron, A. (2011), *The Last Pagans of Rome*, Oxford: Oxford University Press.

Campeau, L. (1967), *Monumenta Novae Franciae*, vol. 1, *La première mission d'Acadie (1602–1616)*, Monumenta Historica Societatis Jesu, vol. 96, XXIII, Quebec.

Cannon, J. (2002), *The Oxford Companion to British History*, rev. edn, Oxford: Oxford University Press.

Cantrell, C. H. (1994), 'Women and Language in Susan Griffin's *Woman and Nature: The Roaring Inside Her*', *Hypatia* 9: 225–38.

Carile, P. (2000), *Le regard entravé: Littérature et anthropologie dans les premiers textes sur la Nouvelle-France*, Quebec: Editions du Septentrion.

Carroll, P. D. (1976), 'Columella the Reformer', *Latomus* 35: 783–90.

Casali, S. (2006), 'The Making of the Shield: Inspiration and Repression in the *Aeneid*', *Greece and Rome* 53: 185–204.

Cave, T. (2001), *Poétiques de la Renaissance: le modèle italien, le monde franco-bourguignon et leur héritage en France au XVIe siècle*, Geneva: Librairie Droz.

Chalker, J. (1969), *The English Georgic: A Study in the Development of a Form*, Baltimore, MD: Johns Hopkins University Press.

Chandler, C. E. (2005), *Philodemus. On Rhetoric. Books 1 and 2: Translation and Exegetical Essays*, London: Routledge.

Chevrolet, T. (2007), *L'idée de fable. Théories de la fiction poétique à la Renaissance*, Geneva: Librairie Droz.

Chew, K. (trans.) (2002), *Virgil. Georgics; translated with an introduction and notes*, Indianapolis, IN: Hackett.

Christmann, E. (1982), 'Zur antiken Georgica-Rezeption', *Würzburger Jahrbücher für die Altertumswissenschaft* 8: 57–67.

Christmann, E. (2003), 'Zum Verhältnis von Autor und Leser in der römischen Agrarliteratur. Bücher und Schriften für Herren und Sklaven', in M. Horster and C. Reitz (eds), *Antike Fachschriftsteller: Literarischer Diskurs und sozialer Kontext*, 121–52, Wiesbaden: F. Steiner.

Citroni, M. (2015), 'La vittoria e il tempio: interpretazione del proemio al III libro delle *Georgiche*', in H. C. Günther and P. Fedeli (eds), *Virgilian Studies: A Miscellany dedicated to the Memory of Mario Geymonat (26.1.1941 – 17.2.2012)*, 39–87, Nordhausen: Verlag Traugott Bautz.

Clausen, W. (ed.) (1994), *A Commentary on Virgil, Eclogues*, Oxford: Oxford University Press.

Clay, D. (2004), 'Vergil's Farewell to Education (*Catalepton* 5) and Epicurus' Letter to Pythocles', in D. Armstrong, J. Fish, P. A. Johnston and M. B. Skinner (eds), *Vergil, Philodemus, and the Augustans*, 25–36, Austin: University of Texas Press.

Clay, J. (1981), 'The Old Man in the Garden: *Geo.* 4.116–48', *Arethusa* 14: 57–65.

Clément-Tarantino, S. (2006), 'La poétique romaine comme hybridation féconde. Les leçons de la greffe (Virgile, *Géorgiques*, 2, 9–82)', *Interférences – Scribendi* 4. Available online: http://ars-scribendi.ens-lyon.fr/spip.php?article37 (accessed 2 July 2018).

Coffee, N. (2009), *The Commerce of War: Exchange and Social Order in Latin Epic*, Chicago: University of Chicago Press.

Coffee, N. (2017), *Gift and Gain: How Money Transformed Ancient Rome*, Oxford: Oxford University Press.

Cole, S. (2001), 'The Dynamics of Deification in Horace's *Odes* 1–3', in S. R. Asirvatham, C. O. Pache and J. Watrous (eds), *Between Magic and Religion: Interdisciplinary Studies in Ancient Mediterranean Religion and Society*, 67–91, Lanham, MD: Rowman & Littlefield.

Comparetti, D. (1872), *Virgilio nel medio evo*, Livorno: F. Vigo (latest English reprint, 1997, *Vergil in the Middle Ages*, trans. E. F. M. Benecke, Princeton, NJ: Princeton University Press).

Conte, G. B. (1980), *Il genere e i suoi confini: cinque studi sulla poesia di Virgilio*, Turin: Stampatori.

Conte, G. B. (1992), 'Proems in the Middle', in F. M. Dunn and T. Cole (eds), *Beginnings in Classical Literature*, YCS 29, 147–59, Cambridge: Cambridge University Press.

Conte, G. B. (2007), *The Poetry of Pathos, Studies in Virgilian Epic*, ed. S. J. Harrison, Oxford: Oxford University Press.

Coppolino, N. C. (2003), 'Poetic Ambitions: Vergilian Influence on Book 10 of Columella's *De Re Rustica*', *New England Classics Journal* 30, no. 2: 65–73.

Cornis-Pope, M. (1994), 'From Cultural Provocation to Narrative Cooperation: Innovative Uses of the Second Person in Raymond Federman's Fiction', *Style* 28, no. 3: 411–31.

Cossarini A. (1977), 'Aspetti di Virgilio in Columella', *Prometheus* 3: 225–40.

Courtney, E. (1991), *The Poems of Petronius*, Atlanta, GA: Scholars Press.

Cowan, R. (2010), 'Virtual Epic: Counterfactuals, Sideshadowing and the Poetics of Contingency in the *Punica*', in A. Augoustakis (ed.), *Brill's Companion to Silius Italicus*, 323–51, Leiden: Brill.

Cramer, R. (1998), *Vergils Weltsicht: Optimismus und Pessimismus in Vergils Georgica*, Berlin: De Gruyter.

Cummings, M. S. (2002), 'Review of Kristina Chew, *Virgil. Georgics*', *Bryn Mawr Classical Review* 2002.09.30. Available online: http://bmcr.brynmawr.edu/2002/2002-09-30.html (accessed 23 September 2018).

Daintree, D. (1990), 'The Virgil Commentary of Aelius Donatus – Black Hole or "Éminence Grise"?', *Greece and Rome* 37: 65–79.

Dallinges, L. (1964), 'Science et poésie chez Columelle', *Études de Lettres* 7: 137–54.

Danielewicz, J. (1990), 'Deixis in Greek Choral Lyric', *Quaderni urbinati di cultura classica* 34: 7–17.

Danielewicz, J. (2013), 'Vergil's *certissima signa* Reinterpreted: The Aratean LEPTE-Acrostic in *Georgics* 1', *Eos* 100: 287–95.

Davies, J. P. (2004), *Rome's Religious History: Livy, Tacitus and Ammianus on Their Gods*, Cambridge: Cambridge University Press.

Day, H. J. M. (2013), *Lucan and the Sublime: Power, Representation and Aesthetic Experience*, Cambridge: Cambridge University Press.

Day-Lewis, C. (trans.) (1940), *The Georgics of Virgil*, London: Jonathan Cape.

Day-Lewis, C. (1970), *On Translating Poetry*, Abingdon-on-Thames: The Abbey Press.

De Bruyn, F. (2005), 'Eighteenth-Century Editions of Virgil's *Georgics*: From Classical Poem to Agricultural Treatise', *Lumen* 24: 149–63.

De Jong, I. J. F. (1987), *Narrators and Focalizers: The Presentation of the Story in the Iliad*, Amsterdam: B. R. Grüner.

De Jong, I. J. F. (2014), *Narratology and Classics: A Practical Guide*, Oxford: Oxford University Press.

de la Cerda, I. L. (1647), *P. Virgilii Maronis Bucolica et Georgica*, 2nd edn, Cologne: Johann Kinckius.

DelConte, M. (2003), 'Why *You* Can't Speak: Second-Person Narration, Voice, and a New Model for Understanding Narrative', *Style* 37, no. 2: 204–19.

DelConte, M. (2013/14), 'The Influence of Narrative Tense in Second Person Narration: A Response to Joshua Parker', *Connotations* 23, no. 1: 55–62.

Della Corte, F. (1984–91), *Enciclopedia Virgiliana*, Rome: Istituto della Enciclopedia italiana.

Dench, E. (1995), *From Barbarians to New Men: Greek, Roman, and Modern Perceptions of Peoples of the Central Apennines*, Oxford: Oxford University Press.

Derrida, J. (1991), *Falschgeld. Zeit geben I*, trans. A. Knop and M. Wetzel, Munich: Fink.

Diels, H. and Kranz, W. (1951–2), *Die Fragmente der Vorsokratiker*, 6th edn, Berlin: Weidmann.

Dietz, D. B. (1995), 'Historia in the Commentary of Servius', *Transactions of the American Philological Association* 125: 61–97.

Dodds, E. R. (1960), *Euripides: 'Bacchae'*, Oxford: Oxford University Press.

Dolan, F. E. (2017), 'Compost/Composition', in H. Eklund (ed.), *Ground-Work: English Renaissance Literature and Soil Science*, 21–39, Pittsburgh: Duquesne University Press.

Doody, A. (2007), 'Virgil the Farmer? Critiques of the *Georgics* in Columella and Pliny', *Classical Philology* 102: 180–97.

Dorcey, P. F. (1992), *The Cult of Silvanus: A Study in Roman Folk Religion*, Leiden: Brill.

Drew, D. L. (1924), 'Virgil's Marble Temple: *Georgics* III.10–39', *Classical Quarterly* 18: 195–202.

Dufallo, B. (2013), *The Captor's Image: Greek Culture in Roman Ecphrasis*, Oxford: Oxford University Press.

Dumont, J. C. (2008), 'Columella and Vergil', *Vergilius* 54: 49–58.

Durling, D. L. (1935), *Georgic Tradition in English Poetry*, New York: Columbia University Press.

Ecker, G. (2008), *Giftige' Gaben. Über Tauschprozesse in der Literatur*, Munich: Fink.

Edmunds, L. (2008), 'Deixis in Ancient Greek and Latin Literature: Historical Introduction and State of the Question', *Philologia Antiqua* 1: 67–98.

Effe, B. (1977), *Dichtung und Lehre: Untersuchungen zur Typologie des antiken Lehrgedichts*, Munich: Beck.

Eklund, H. (ed.) (2017), *Ground-Work: English Renaissance Literature and Soil Science*, Pittsburgh: Duquesne University Press.

Emont, B. (2004), *Les Muses de la Nouvelle-France de Marc Lescarbot: Premier recueil de poèmes européens écrits en Amérique du nord*, Paris: L'Harmattan.

Ensslin, A. and Bell, A. (2012), '"Click = Kill": Textual *You* in Ludic Digital Fiction', *Storyworlds* 4: 49–73.

Erren, M. (1985), *P. Vergilius Maro. Georgica. Band 1. Einleitung. Praefatio. Text und Übersetzung*, Heidelberg: Winter.

Erren, M. (2003), *P. Vergilius Maro. Georgica. Band 2. Kommentar*, Heidelberg: Winter.

Everest, K. and Matthews, G. (2000), *The Poems of Shelley, Volume 2: 1817–1819*, London and New York: Routledge.

Ewald, O. M. (1990), 'Virgilian End Rhymes (*Geo.* 1.393–423)', *Harvard Studies in Classical Philology* 93: 311–13.

Fallon, P. (trans.) (2004), *The Georgics of Virgil*, Oldcastle, Co. Meath, Ireland: Gallery Press.

Farnsworth, R. (2001), *Mediating Order and Chaos: The Water-Cycle in the Complex Adaptive Systems of Romantic Culture*, Amsterdam and New York: Rodopi.

Farrell, J. (1991), *Vergil's Georgics and the Traditions of Ancient Epic: The Art of Allusion in Literary History*, New York and Oxford: Oxford University Press.

Feeney, D. C. (1991), *The Gods in Epic: Poets and Critics of the Classical Tradition*, Oxford: Oxford University Press.

Feeney, D. C. (2007), *Caesar's Calendar: Ancient Time and the Beginnings of History*, Berkeley: University of California Press.

Feeney, D. C. (2016), *Beyond Greek: The Beginnings of Latin Literature*, Cambridge, MA: Harvard University Press.

Felson, N. (ed.) (2004), *The Poetics of Deixis in Alcman, Pindar, and Other Lyric*, *Arethusa* 37, no. 3 (Special Issue).

Ferguson, J. (1970), *The Religions of the Roman Empire*, London: Thames & Hudson.

Fernandelli, M. (1996), 'Il prologo divino dell'*Eneide* (il prologo delle "Troiane" di Euripide e Aen. 1.3452)', *Lexis* 14: 99–115.

Fernbach, I. (2012), 'From Copy to Copia: Imitation and Authorship in Joachim Du Bellay's *Divers Jeux Rustiques* (1558)', in P. J. Usher and I. Fernbach (eds), *Virgilian Identities in the French Renaissance*, 93–114, Woodbridge: Boydell & Brewer.

Finley, M. I. (1973), *The Ancient Economy*, Berkeley: University of California Press.

Fitzgerald, W. (1996), 'Labor and Laborer in Latin Poetry: The Case of the *Moretum*', *Arethusa* 29: 389–418.

Flower, H. I. (1995), '*Fabulae Praetextae* in Context: When Were Plays on Contemporary Subjects Performed in Republican Rome?', *Classical Quarterly* 45: 170–90.

Fludernik, M. (1993), 'Second Person Fiction: Narrative *You* as Addressee and/or Protagonist', *Arbeiten aus Anglistik und Amerikanistik* 18, no. 2: 217–47.

Fludernik, M. (ed.) (1994a), *Second-Person Narrative*, *Style* 28, no. 3 (Special Issue).

Fludernik, M. (1994b), 'Introduction: Second-Person Narrative and Related Issues', *Style* 28, no. 3: 281–311.

Fludernik, M. (1994c), 'Second-Person Narrative as a Test Case for Narratology: The Limits of Realism', *Style* 28, no. 3: 445–82.

Fludernik, M. (1996), *Towards a Natural Narratology*, London: Routledge.

Fögen, T. (2009), *Wissen, Kommunikation und Selbstdarstellung. Zur Struktur und Charakteristik römischer Fachtexte der frühen Kaiserzeit*, Munich: Beck.

Forbiger, A. (1852), *P. Virgilii Maronis Opera*, Leipzig: Hinrichs.

Fowler, D. P. (1989), 'First Thoughts on Closure: Problems and Prospects', *Materiali e discussioni per l'analisi dei testi classici* 22: 75–122.

Fowler, D. P. (1997), 'The Virgil Commentary of Servius', in C. Martindale (ed.), *The Cambridge Companion to Virgil*, 73–8, Cambridge: Cambridge University Press.

Fowler, D. P. (2000a), 'The Didactic Plot', in M. Depew and D. Obbink (eds), *Matrices of Genre: Authors, Canons, and Society*, 205–19, Cambridge, MA: Harvard University Press.

Fowler, D. P. (2000b), 'Epic in the Middle of the Wood: Mise en Abyme in the Nisus and Euryalus Episode', in A. Sharrock and H. Morales (eds), *Intratextuality: Greek and Roman Textual Relations*, 89–113, Oxford: Oxford University Press.

Fowler, D. P. (2002), 'Masculinity under Threat? The Poetics and Politics of Inspiration in Latin Poetry', in E. Spentzou and D. P. Fowler (eds), *Cultivating the Muse: Struggles for Power and Inspiration in Classical Literature*, 141–60, Oxford: Oxford University Press.

Fowler, P. G. (1997), 'Lucretian Conclusions', in F. Dunn, D. P. Fowler and D. Roberts (eds), *Classical Closure*, 112–38, Princeton, NJ: Princeton University Press.

Freudenburg, K. (2001), *Satires of Rome: Threatening Poses from Lucilius to Juvenal*, Cambridge: Cambridge University Press.

Galasso, L. (1995), *Epistularum ex Ponto Liber II*, Florence: Le Monnier.

Gale, M. R. (1994), *Myth and Poetry in Lucretius*, Cambridge: Cambridge University Press.

Gale, M. R. (2000), *Virgil on the Nature of Things: The Georgics, Lucretius and the Didactic Tradition*, Cambridge: Cambridge University Press.

Gale, M. R. (2003), 'Poetry and the Backward Glance in Virgil's *Georgics* and *Aeneid*', *Transactions of the American Philological Association* 133: 323–52.

Gale, M. R. (2004), 'The Story of Us: A Narratological Analysis of Lucretius' *De Rerum Natura*', in M. Gale (ed.), *Latin Epic and Didactic Poetry: Genre, Tradition and Individuality*, 49–71, Swansea: Classical Press of Wales.

Gale, M. R. (2008), 'Virgil's Metamorphoses: Myth and Allusion in the *Georgics*', in K. Volk (ed.), *Oxford Readings in Classical Studies: Vergil's Georgics*, 94–127, Oxford: Oxford University Press (orig. 1995, *Proceedings of the Cambridge Philological Society* 41: 36–61).

Gale, M. R. (2013), 'Virgil's Caesar: Intertextuality and Ideology', in J. Farrell and D. P. Nelis (eds), *Augustan Poetry and the Roman Republic*, 278–96, Oxford: Oxford University Press.

Galinsky, K. (1996), *Augustan Culture: An Interpretive Introduction*, Princeton, NJ: Princeton University Press.

Genette, G. (1980), *Narrative Discourse*, trans. J. E. Lewin, Ithaca, NY: Cornell University Press (orig. 1972, *Discours du récit*, Paris: Éditions du Seuil).

Genette, G. (1982), *Figures of Literary Discourse*, trans. A. Sheridan, Oxford: Blackwell.

Geue, T. (2013), 'Princeps "avant la lettre": The Foundation of Augustus in Pre-Augustan Poetry', in M. Labate and G. Rosati (eds), *La costruzione de mito augusteo*, 49–67, Heidelberg: Winter.

Geue, T. (2018), 'Soft Hands, Hard Power: Sponging Off the Empire of Leisure (Virgil, *Georgics* 4)', *Journal of Roman Studies* 108: 115–40.

Gibson, R. K. (1998), 'Didactic Poetry as "Popular" Form: A Study of Imperatival Expressions in Latin Didactic Verse and Prose', in C. Atherton (ed.), *Form and Content in Didactic Poetry*, 67–98, Bari: Levante.

Gibson, R. K. (2003), *Ovid Ars Amatoria 3*, Cambridge and New York: Cambridge University Press.

Gigante, M. (2004), 'Vergil in the Shadow of Vesuvius', in D. Armstrong, J. Fish, P. A. Johnston and M. B. Skinner (eds), *Vergil, Philodemus, and the Augustans*, 85–99, Austin: University of Texas Press.

Gigante, M. and Capasso, M. (1989), 'Il ritorno di Virgilio a Ercolano', *SIFC* 7: 3–6.

Gildenhard, I. (2003), 'The "Annalist" Before the Annalists: Ennius and His *Annales*', in U. Eigler, U. Gotter, N. Luraghi and U. Walter (eds), *Formen römischer Geschichtsschreibung von den Anfängen bis Livius*, 93–114, Darmstadt: Wissenschaftliche Buchgesellschaft.

Giusti, E. (2018), *Carthage in Virgil's Aeneid: Staging the Enemy Under Augustus*, Cambridge: Cambridge University Press.

Glendinning, V. (1983), *Vita: The Life of V. Sackville-West*, London: Phoenix.

Goodfellow, M. S. (2015), 'Early Reception of Vergil's *Georgics*: *Protinus Italiam Concepit*', *Vergilius* 61: 43–76.

Goodman, K. (2004), *Georgic Modernity and British Romanticism: Poetry and the Mediation of History*, Cambridge: Cambridge University Press.

Goodridge, J. (1995), *Rural Life in Eighteenth-Century English Poetry*, Cambridge: Cambridge University Press.

Goodyear, F. R. D. (1972), *The Annals of Tacitus: Books 1–6*, Cambridge: Cambridge University Press.

Goodyear, F. R. D. (1977), 'The *Copa*: A Text and Commentary', *Bulletin of the Institute of Classical Studies* 24: 117–31.

Goold, G. P. (1970), 'Servius and the Helen Episode', *Harvard Studies in Classical Philology* 74: 101–68.

Gosman, M. (2001), 'Espace autre: Espace français: Le refus de la dissemblance dans "L'Histoire de la Nouvelle-France" de Marc Lescarbot', in J. Lintvelt and F. Paré (eds), *Frontières flottantes: lieu et espace dans les cultures francophones du Canada*, 33–47, Amsterdam: Rodopi.

de Gournay, M. (1620), *Eschantillons de Virgile*, Paris.

Gowers, E. (2000), 'Vegetable Love: Virgil, Columella, and Garden Poetry', *Ramus* 29: 127–48.

Gowers, E. (2011), 'Trees and Family Trees in the *Aeneid*', *Classical Antiquity* 30: 87–118.

Gowers, E. (2016), 'Under the Influence: Maecenas and Bacchus in *Georgics* 2', in P. Hardie (ed.), *Augustan Poetry and the Irrational*, 134–55, Oxford: Oxford University Press.

Gradel, I. (2002), *Emperor Worship and Roman Religion*, Oxford: Oxford University Press.

Graf, F. (1974), *Eleusis und die Orphische Dichtung: Athens in Vorhellenistischer Zeit*, Berlin and New York: De Gruyter.

Graf, F. (1985), 'Review of West (1983)', *Gnomon* 57: 585–91.

Graf, F. (2006), 'Iacchus', *Brill's New Pauly*, ed. H. Cancik and H. Schneider. Available online: http://referenceworks.brillonline.com/entries/brill-s-new-pauly/iacchus-e520740?s.num=0&s.q=iacchus (accessed 2 July 2018).

Graf, F. and Johnston, S. I. (2013), *Ritual Texts for the Afterlife: Orpheus and the Bacchic Gold Tablets*, 2nd edn, London and New York: Routledge.

Graver, B. E. (1991), 'Wordsworth's Georgic Beginnings', *Texas Studies in Literature and Language* 33: 137–59.

Griffin, M. (2003), '*De Beneficiis* and Roman Society', *Journal of Roman Studies* 93: 92–113.

Griffin, M. (2013), *Seneca on Society: A Guide to De Beneficiis*, Oxford: Oxford University Press.

Griffin, S. (1978), *Woman and Nature: The Roaring Inside Her*, New York: Harper & Row.

Grilli, A. (2002), 'Verg. *Georg.* 2,290–297', in L. Torraca (ed.), *Scritti in onore di Italo Gallo*, 351–4, Naples: Edizioni scientifiche italiane.

Grimal, P. (1984), *Les Jardins Romains*, Paris: Fayard.

Grisart, A. (1966), 'Tityre et son dieu: des identifications nouvelles', *Les Études Classiques* 34: 115–42.

Gros, P. (1993), '*stabunt et Parii lapides*: Virgile et les premiers frontons augustéens d'après *Géorgiques*, iii, v.34', in M. M. Mactoux and E. Geny (eds), *Mélanges Pierre Lévêque*, vol. 7, 155–9, Paris: Les Belles Lettres.

Gruen, E. S. (1992), *Culture and National Identity in Republican Rome*, Ithaca, NY: Cornell University Press.

Hackemann, L. F. (1940), *Servius and his Sources in the Commentary on the Georgics*, New York: Columbia University Press.

Hadot, P. (2006), *The Veil of Isis: An Essay on the History of the Idea of Nature*, trans. M. Chase, Cambridge, MA: Harvard University Press.

Hall, E. (1989), *Inventing the Barbarian: Greek Self-Definition through Tragedy*, Oxford: Oxford University Press.

Hall, E. (1993), 'Asia Unmanned: Images of Victory in Classical Athens', in J. Rich and G. Shipley (eds), *War and Society in the Greek World*, 108–33, London: Routledge.

Halliwell, S. (2012), *Between Ecstasy and Truth: Interpretations of Greek Poetics from Homer to Longinus*, Oxford: Oxford University Press.

Hardie, A. (2002), 'The *Georgics*, the Mysteries and the Muses at Rome', *Proceedings of the Cambridge Philological Society* 48: 175–208.

Hardie, P. R. (1986), *Virgil's Aeneid: Cosmos and Imperium*, Oxford: Oxford University Press.

Hardie, P. R. (1990), 'Ovid's Theban History: the first Anti-*Aeneid*?', *Classical Quarterly* 40: 224–35.

Hardie, P. R. (1997), 'Virgil and Tragedy', in C. Martindale (ed.), *The Cambridge Companion to Virgil*, 312–26, Cambridge: Cambridge University Press.

Hardie, P. R. (1998), *Virgil*, Oxford: Oxford University Press.

Hardie, P. R. (2004a), 'Don Fowler and Middles', in S. Kyriakidis and F. De Martino (eds), *Middles in Latin Poetry*, 25–6, Bari: Levante.

Hardie, P. R. (2004b), 'Ovidian Middles', in S. Kyriakidis and F. De Martino (eds), *Middles in Latin Poetry*, 151–82, Bari: Levante.

Hardie, P. R. (2004c), 'Political Education in Virgil's *Georgics*', *Studi italiani di filologia classica* 97: 83–111.

Hardie, P. R. (2007a), 'Images of the Persian Wars in Rome', in E. Bridges, E. Hall and P. J. Rhodes (eds), *Cultural Responses to the Persian Wars: Antiquity to the Third Millennium*, 127–43, Oxford: Oxford University Press.

Hardie, P. R. (2007b), 'Poets, Patrons, Rulers: the Ennian Traditions', in W. Fitzgerald and E. Gowers (eds), *Ennius Perennis: The Annals and Beyond*, 129–44, Cambridge: Cambridge University Press.

Hardie, P. R. (2008), 'Cosmology and National Epic in the *Georgics* (*Georgics* 2.458–3.48)', in K. Volk (ed.), *Oxford Readings in Classical Studies: Vergil's Georgics*, 161–82, Oxford: Oxford

University Press (orig. 1986, in *Virgil's Aeneid: Cosmos and Imperium*, 33–51, Oxford: Oxford University Press).

Hardie, P. R. (2009), *Lucretian Receptions: History, The Sublime, Knowledge*, Cambridge: Cambridge University Press.

Hardie, P. R. (ed.) (2016), *Augustan Poets and the Irrational*, Oxford: Oxford University Press.

Harrigan, P. and Wardrip-Fruin, N. (eds) (2007), *Second Person: Role-Playing and Story in Games and Playable Media*, Cambridge, MA: MIT Press.

Harrison, E. L. (1972–3), 'Why Did Venus Wear Boots? Some Reflections on *Aeneid* 1.314f.', *Proceedings of the Virgil Society* 12: 10–25.

Harrison, E. L. (1989), 'The Tragedy of Dido', *Echos Du Monde Classique / Classical Views* 33, no. 8: 1–21.

Harrison, S. J. (1990), *Oxford Readings in Vergil's Aeneid*, Oxford: Oxford University Press.

Harrison, S. J. (2004), 'Virgil's *Corycius senes* and Nicander's *Georgica*', in M. Gale (ed.), *Latin Epic and Didactic Poetry*, 109–24, Swansea: Classical Press of Wales.

Harrison, S. J. (2005), 'Vergil and the Mausoleum Augusti: *Georgics* 3.12–18', *Acta Classica* 48: 185–88.

Harrison, S. J. (2007), *Generic Enrichment in Vergil and Horace*, Oxford: Oxford University Press.

Haskell, Y. (1999), 'Work or Play? Latin "Recreational" Georgic Poetry of the Italian Renaissance', *Humanistica Lovaniensia* 48: 132–59.

Haskell, Y. (2003), *Loyola's Bees: Ideology and Industry in Jesuit Latin Didactic Poetry*, Oxford: Oxford University Press.

Heath, M. (1985), 'Hesiod's Didactic Poetry', *Classical Quarterly* 35: 245–63.

Henderson, J. (2002), 'Columella's Living Hedge: The Roman Gardening Book', *Journal of Roman Studies* 92: 110–33.

Henderson, J. (2004a), *Morals and Villas in Seneca's Letters*, Cambridge: Cambridge University Press.

Henderson, J. (2004b), *HORTVS: The Roman Book of Gardening*, London and New York: Routledge.

Henkel, J. (2014), 'Virgil Talks Techniques: Metapoetic Arboriculture in *Georgics* 2', *Vergilius* 60: 33–66.

Herman, D. (1994), 'Textual *You* and Double Deixis in Edna O'Brien's *A Pagan Place*', *Style* 28, no. 3: 378–410.

Herman, D. (2002), *Story Logic: Problems and Possibilities of Narrative*, Lincoln and London: University of Nebraska Press.

Heslin, P. (2015), *The Museum of Augustus: The Temple of Apollo in Pompeii, the Portico of Philippus in Rome, and Latin Poetry*, Los Angeles: J. Paul Getty Museum.

Heyne, C. G. (1788), *P. Virgilii Maronis Opera: varietate lectionis et perpetua adnotatione illustrata*, 4 vols, Leipzig (Lipsiae: sumptibus Caspari Fritschii).

Heyworth, S. J. (2007), *Cynthia: A Companion to the Text of Propertius*, Oxford: Oxford University Press.

Heyworth, S. J. (2015), 'Notes on the Text and Interpretation of Vergil's *Eclogues* and *Georgics*', in H.-C. Günther (ed.), *Virgilian Studies: A Miscellany Dedicated to the Memory of Mario Geymonat*, 196–249, Nordhausen: Verlag Traugott Bautz.

Hickman, M. B. and McIntyre, J. D. (2012), *Rereading the New Criticism*, Columbus: Ohio State University Press.

Hinds, S. (1998), *Allusion and Intertext: Dynamics of Appropriation in Roman Poetry*, Cambridge: Cambridge University Press.

Holler, L. (1990), 'Thinking with the Weight of the Earth: Feminist Contributions to an Epistemology of Concreteness', *Hypatia* 5: 1–23.

Hollis, A. S. (1996), 'Octavian in the Fourth *Georgic*', *Classical Quarterly* 46: 305–8.

Holzberg, N. (2004), 'Impersonating the Young Vergil: The Author of the *Catalepton* and His *libellus*', *Materiali e discussioni per l'analisi dei testi classici* 52: 29–40.

Holzberg, N. (2005), *Die Appendix Vergiliana. Pseudepigraphen im literarischen*, Tübingen: Narr.

Hopkins, D. (2007), 'The English Voices of Lucretius from Lucy Hutchinson to John Mason Good', in S. Gillespie and P. R. Hardie (eds), *The Cambridge Companion to Lucretius*, 254–73, Cambridge: Cambridge University Press.

Hopkins, M. F. and Perkins, L. (1981), 'Second-Person Point of View in Narrative', in F. N. Magill (ed.), *Critical Survey of Short Fiction*, vol. 1, 19–32, Englewood Cliffs, NJ: Salem Press.

Hordern, J. (2000), 'Notes on the Orphic Papyrus from Gurôb (P. Gurôb 1; Pack^2 2464)', *Zeitschrift für Papyrologie und Epigraphik* 129: 131–40.

Horsfall, N. (1991), 'Philippe Bruggisser: Romulus Servianus: la légende de Romulus dans les Commentaires à Virgile de Servius: mythographie et idéologie à l'époque de la dynastie théodosienne', *Classical Review* 41: 242–3.

Horsfall, N. (2000), *Virgil, Aeneid 7: A Commentary*, Leiden: Brill.

Horsfall, N. (2001a [1995]), 'The *Georgics*' in Horsfall, N. (ed.), *A Companion to the Study of Virgil: Second Revised Edition*, 63–100, Leiden: Brill.

Horsfall, N. (2001b), 'The *Moretum* Decomposed', *Classica et Mediaevalia* 52: 303–15.

Horsfall, N. (2013), *Virgil, Aeneid 6, A commentary*, 2 vols, Berlin: De Gruyter.

Horster, M. (2005), 'Was bleibt von Vergils *Georgica*? Zur Rezeption von Lehrdichtung im 2. und 3. Jh. N. Chr.', in M. Horster and and C. Reitz (eds), *Wissensvermittlung in dichterischer Gestalt*, 264–94, Stuttgart: F. Steiner.

Höschele, R. (2005), 'Moreto-Poetik: Das Moretum als intertextuelles Mischgericht', in N. Holzberg (ed.), *Die Appendix Vergiliana: Pseudepigraphen im literarischen Kontext*, 244–69, Tübingen: Gunter Narr Verlag.

Houghton, L. B. T. (2015), '*Salve, Magna Parens*: Virgil's *Laudes Italiae* in Renaissance Italy and Beyond', *International Journal of the Classical Tradition* 22, no. 2: 180–208.

Houston, P. (1990), 'How to Talk to a Hunter', in R. Ford and S. Ravenel (eds), *The Best American Short Stories 1990*, 98–104, Boston: Houghton Mifflin.

Howard, J. (2008), 'Measuring the *Aeneid* on a Human Scale' [review of Ruden], *Chronicle of Higher Education*, 16 May.

Howe, A. (2012), 'Shelley and Philosophy: On a Future State, Speculations on Metaphysics and Morals, On Life', in M. O'Neill and A. Howe (eds), and with the assistance of M. Callaghan, *The Oxford Handbook of Percy Bysshe Shelley*, 101–16, Oxford: Oxford University Press.

Hulubei, A. (1931), 'Virgile en France au XVIè siècle: Éditions, traductions, imitations', *Revue du seizième siècle* 18: 1–77.

Hunt, A. (2016), *Reviving Roman Religion: Sacred Trees in the Roman World*, Cambridge: Cambridge University Press.

Hunter, R. (1993), *The Argonautica of Apollonius: Literary Studies*, Cambridge: Cambridge University Press.

Huss, B. (2000), '*Gattung/ Gattungstheorie*', in M. Landfester (ed.), *Der Neue Pauly. Enzyklopädie der Antike*, vol. 14: *Rezeptions- und Wissenschaftsgeschichte*, 87–95, Stuttgart: Weimar.

Hutchinson, G. O. (2010), 'Deflected Addresses: Apostrophe and Space (Sophocles, Aeschines, Plautus, Cicero, Virgil and Others)', *Classical Quarterly* 60: 96–109.

Ingpen, R. and Peck, W. E. (1930), *The Complete Works of Percy Bysshe Shelley, Volume VII*, London and New York: Ernest Benn Limited and Charles Scribner's Sons.

Innes, D. C. (1979), 'Gigantomachy and Natural Philosophy', *Classical Quarterly* 29: 165–71.

Jahn, P. (1903), 'Eine Prosaquelle Vergils und ihre Umsetzung in Poesie durch den Dichter', *Hermes* 38: 244–64.

Jancovich. M. (1993), *The Cultural Politics of New Criticism*, Cambridge: Cambridge University Press.

Janko, R. (2000), *Philodemus: On Poems Book 1*, Oxford: Oxford University Press.

Jashemski, W. (1979), 'The Garden of Hercules at Pompeii (II.viii.6): The Discovery of a Commercial Flower Garden', *American Journal of Archaeology* 83: 403–11.

Jenkyns, R. (1998), *Virgil's Experience*, Oxford: Oxford University Press.

Jermyn, L. A. S. (trans.) (1947), *The Singing Farmer: A Translation of Vergil's 'Georgics'*, Oxford: Blackwell.

Johnson, K. (trans.) (2010), *The Georgics: A Poem of the Land*, London: Penguin.

Johnson, W. R. (2004), 'A Secret Garden: Geo. 4.116–48', in D. Armstrong, M. Skinner and P. Johnston (eds), *Vergil, Philodemus and the Augustans*, 75–83, Austin: University of Texas Press.

Johnston, P. A. (1977), 'Eurydice and Proserpina in the *Georgics*', *Transactions of the American Philological Association* 107: 161–72.

Johnston, P. A. (2009), 'The Mystery Cults and Vergil's *Georgics*', in G. Casadio and P. A. Johnston (eds), *Mystic Cults in Magna Graecia*, 251–73, Austin: University of Texas Press.

Johnston, P. A. (trans.) (2012), *The Aeneid of Vergil*, Norman, OK: University of Oklahoma Press.

Jones, F. L. (ed.) (1964), *The Letters of Percy Bysshe Shelley. Volume I: Shelley in England*, Oxford: Clarendon Press.

Jones, J. W. (1961), 'Allegorical Interpretation in Servius', *Classical Journal* 56: 217–26.

Jones, P. J. (2005), *Reading Rivers in Roman Literature and Culture*, Lanham, MD: Lexington Books.

Kacandes, I. (1994), 'Narrative Apostrophe: Reading, Rhetoric, Resistance in Michel Butor's *La Modification* and Julio Cortazar's "Graffiti"', *Style* 28, no. 3: 329–49.

Kacandes, I. (2001), *Talk Fiction: Literature and the Talk Explosion*, Lincoln, NE and London: University of Nebraska Press.

Kaiser, E. (1964), 'Odyssee-Szenen als Topoi', *Museum Helveticum* 21: 109–36, 197–224.

Kallendorf, C. (2012), *A Bibliography of the Early Printed Editions of Virgil, 1469–1850*, New Castle, DE: Oak Knoll Press.

Kallendorf, C. (2014), 'Renaissance Literature', in R. F. Thomas and J. M. Ziolkowski (eds), *The Virgil Encyclopedia*, 1072–4, Chichester and Malden, MA: Wiley-Blackwell.

Kaster, R. A. (1980), 'The Grammarian's Authority', *Classical Philology* 75: 216–41.

Kaster, R. A. (1988), *Guardians of Language: The Grammarian and Society in Late Antiquity*, Berkeley: University of California Press.

Kavanagh, P. (1942), *The Great Hunger*, Dublin: Cuala Press.

Keach, W. (1984), *Shelley's Style*, New York and London: Methuen.

Keegan B. (2008), *British Labouring-Class Nature Poetry, 1730–1837*, Basingstoke and New York: Palgrave Macmillan.

Keeline, T. (2013), 'Did (Servius') Vergil Nod?', *Vergilius* 59: 61–80.

Keith, A. (2008), *Propertius: Poet of Love and Leisure*, London: Duckworth.

Kennedy, D. F. (1992), '"Augustan" and "Anti-Augustan": Reflections on Terms of Reference', in A. Powell (ed.), *Roman Poetry and Propaganda in the Age of Augustus*, 26–58, London: Duckworth.

Kenney, E. J. (1984), *The Ploughman's Lunch. Moretum: A Poem Ascribed to Virgil*, Bristol: Bristol Classical Press.

Keyser, P. T. and Irby-Massie, G. L. (2008), *The Encyclopedia of Ancient Natural Scientists*, London and New York: Routledge.

Kier, H. (1933), *De laudibus vitae rusticae*, PhD diss., University of Marburg.

Kleberg, T. (1932), '*De Columella Horatii imitatore*', *Eranos* 30: 115–21.

Klingner, F. (1963), *Virgils Georgica*, Zurich: Artemis.

Klingner, F. (1967), *Virgil: Bucolica, Georgica, Aeneis*, Zurich: Artemis.

Koestermann, E. (1963), *Cornelius Tacitus Annalen. Band I, Buch 1–3*, Heidelberg: Winter.

König, J. and Whitmarsh, T. (eds) (2007), *Ordering Knowledge in the Roman Empire*, Cambridge: Cambridge University Press.

Konstan, D. (2005), 'Friendship and Patronage', in S. J. Harrison (ed.), *A Companion to Latin Literature*, 345–59, Malden, MA, and Oxford: Blackwell.

Koortbojian, M. (2013), *The Divinization of Caesar and Augustus: Precedents, Consequences, Implications*, Cambridge: Cambridge University Press.

Korenjak, M. (1995), 'Parthenope und Parthenias: Zur Sphragis der *Georgika*', *Mnemosyne* 48: 201–2.

Koster S. (1988), 'Vergils unbestellter Garten oder Columellas Berufung', in *Ille ego qui. Dichter zwischen Wort und Macht*, 83–96, Erlangen: Universitätsbibliothek Erlangen-Nürnberg.

Kouremenos, T., Parássoglou, G. M. and Tsantsanoglou, K. (2006), *The Derveni Papyrus, Edited with Introduction and Commentary*, Studi e Testi per il Corpus dei Papiri Filosofici Greci e Latini, 13, Florence: Leo S. Olschki.

Kraggerud, E. (1998), 'Virgil Announcing the *Aeneid*: On *Georgics* 3.1–48', in H.-P. Stahl (ed.), *Vergil's Aeneid: Augustan Epic and Political Context*, 1–20, London: Duckworth.

Kraggerud, E. (2017), *Vergiliana. Critical Studies on the Texts of Publius Vergilius Maro*, London and New York: Routledge.

Kronenberg, L. J. (2000), 'The Poet's Fiction: Virgil's Praise of the Farmer, Philosopher, and Poet at the End of *Georgics* 2', *Harvard Studies in Classical Philology* 100: 341–60.

Kronenberg, L. J. (2009), *Allegories of Farming from Greece and Rome: Philosophical Satire in Xenophon, Varro and Virgil*, Cambridge: Cambridge University Press.

Kruschwitz, P. (2014), 'Gallic War Songs (II): Marcus Cicero, Quintus Cicero, and Caesar's Invasion of Britain', *Philologus* 158, no. 2: 275–305.

Kyriakidis, S. (2002), '*Georgics* 4.559–566: The Vergilian Sphragis', *Kleos* 7: 275–86.

Kyriakidis, S. and De Martino, F. (eds) (2004), *Middles in Latin Poetry*, Bari: Levante.

Laird, A. (2006), *The Epic of America: An Introduction to Rafael Landívar and the Rusticatio Mexicana*, London: Bloomsbury.

Lange, C. H. (2009), *Res Publica Constituta: Actium, Apollo and the Accomplishment of the Triumviral Assignment*, Leiden: Brill.

La Penna, A. (1977), 'Senex Corycius', in *Atti del Convegno Virgiliano sul bimillenario delle Georgiche 1975*, 37–66, Naples: Istituto universitario orientale.

La Penna, A. (1995), 'Towards a History of the Poetic Catalogue of Philosophical Themes', in S. J. Harrison (ed.), *Homage to Horace*, 314–28, Oxford: Oxford University Press.

La Rocca, E. (1985), *Amazzonomachia: le sculture frontonali del tempio di Apollo Sosiano*, Rome: De Luca.

Laroche, R. and Munroe, J. (2017), *Shakespeare and Ecofeminist Theory*, London: Bloomsbury.

Leadbetter, M. (1808), *Poems*, Dublin: Keene; London: Longman and Co.

Leigh, M. (1994), 'Servius on Vergil's *Senex Corycius*: New Evidence', *Materiali e discussioni per l'analisi dei testi classici* 33: 181–95.

Lembke, J. (1990), *Looking for Eagles: Reflections of a Classical Naturalist*, New York: Lyons & Burford.

Lembke, J. (trans.) (2005), *Virgil's Georgics*, New Haven, CT: Yale University Press.

Lembke, J. (2006), *From Grass to Gardens: How to Reap Bounty from a Small Yard*, Guilford, CT: The Lyons Press.

Lentricchia, F. (1980), *After the New Criticism*, Chicago: University of Chicago Press.

Liegle, J. (1943), 'Die Tityruskloge', *Hermes* 78: 209–31.

Lightfoot, J. (2009), *A Hellenistic Collection*, Cambridge, MA: Harvard University Press.

Longo Auricchio, F. (2004), 'Philosophy's Harbor', in D. Armstrong, J. Fish, P. A. Johnston and M. B. Skinner (eds), *Vergil, Philodemus, and the Augustans*, 37–42, Austin: University of Texas Press.

Lote, G. (1991), 'La poésie didactique et la poésie satirique', in G. Lote (ed.), *Histoire du vers Français. Tome VI : Deuxième Partie: Le XVIe et les XVIIe siècles. III. Les genres poétiques; Les vers et la langue; La réforme de la déclamation dans la seconde moitié du XVIIe siècle*, 47–64, Aix-en-Provence: Presses universitaires de Provence.

Lovatt, H. (2013), *The Epic Gaze: Vision, Gender and Narrative in Ancient Epic*, Cambridge: Cambridge University Press.

Low, A. (1983), 'New Science and the Georgic Revolution in Seventeenth-Century English Literature', *English Literary Renaissance* 13, no. 3: 231–59.

Low, A. (1985), *The Georgic Revolution*, Princeton, NJ: Princeton University Press.

Lowrie, M. (1997), *Horace's Narrative Odes*, Oxford: Oxford University Press.

Lowrie, M. (2009), *Writing, Performance, and Authority in Augustan Rome*, Oxford: Oxford University Press.

Luck, G. (1973), 'Virgil and the Mystery Religions', *American Journal of Philology* 94: 147–66.

Ludwig, W. (1982), 'Neulateinische Lehrgedichte und Virgils *Georgica*', in D. H. Green, L. P. Johnson and D. Wuttke (eds), *From Wolfram and Petrarch to Goethe and Grass: Studies in Literature in Honour of Leonard Forster*, 151–80, Baden-Baden: V. Koerner.

Lundström, S. (1976), 'Der Eingang des Proömiums zum dritten Buche der Georgica', *Hermes* 104: 163–91.

Lyne, R. O. A. M. (1974), '*scilicet et tempus ueniet* . . . Virgil, *Georgics* 1.463–514', in T. Woodman and D. West (eds), *Quality and Pleasure in Latin Poetry*, 47–66, Cambridge: Cambridge University Press.

Mac Góráin, F. (2014), 'The Mixed Blessings of Bacchus in Virgil's *Georgics*', *Dictynna* 11. Available online: http://dictynna.revues.org/1069 (accessed 2 July 2018).

Mackail, J. W. (1934), *Virgil's Works: The Aeneid, Eclogues, Georgics*, New York: The Modern Library.

Mackenzie, L. (2011), *The Poetry of Place: Lyric, Landscape, and Ideology in Renaissance France*, Toronto: University of Toronto Press.

Maggiulli G. (1980), 'Il lessico non-virgiliano del X libro di Columella', *Orpheus* 1: 126–51.

Mahoney, C. (2011), 'The Temptations of Tercets', in C. Mahoney (ed.), *A Companion to Romantic Poetry*, 44–61, Malden, MA and Oxford: Wiley-Blackwell.

Maltby, R. (2005), 'Donatus and Terence in Servius and Servius Danielis', in T. Fögen (ed.), *Antike Fachtexte*, 207–20, Berlin and New York: De Gruyter.

Maltby, R. (2011), 'Servius on Stylistic Register in His Virgil Commentaries', in R. Ferri (ed.), *The Latin of Roman Lexicography*, 63–73, Pisa and Rome: Fabrizio Serra Editore.

Manuwald, G. (2011), *Roman Republican Theatre*, Cambridge: Cambridge University Press.

Manuwald, G. (ed.) (2000), *Identität und Alterität in der frührömischen Tragödie*, Würzburg: Ergon.

Martin, R. P. (2005), 'Pulp epic: the Catalogue and the Shield', in R. Hunter (ed.), *The Hesiodic Catalogue of Women: Constructions and Reconstructions*, 153–75, Cambridge: Cambridge University Press.

Martindale, C. (1993), *Redeeming the Text: Latin Poetry and the Hermeneutics of Reception*, Cambridge: Cambridge University Press.

Martindale, C. (2005), *Latin Poetry and the Judgement of Taste: An Essay in Aesthetics*, Oxford: Oxford University Press.

Martyn, J. (1746), *Publii Virgilii Maronis Georgicorum libri quatuor: The Georgicks of Virgil, with an English Translation and Notes*, 2nd edn, London: R. Reily.

Marzano, A. (2014), 'Roman Gardens and Elite Self-Representation', in K. Coleman and P. Derron (eds), *Le Jardin dans L'Antiquité*, 195–244, Geneva-Vandoeuvres: Fondation Hardt.

Mayer, R. (1983), 'Missing Persons in the *Eclogues*', *Bulletin of the Institute of Classical Studies* 30: 17–30.

Mayer, R. (2005), 'Creating a Literature of Information in Rome', in M. Horster and C. Reitz (eds), *Wissensvermittlung in dichterischer Gestalt*, 227–41, Stuttgart: F. Steiner.

McInerney, J. (1984), *Bright Lights, Big City*, New York: Vintage.

Meban, D. (2008), 'Temple Building, *Primus* Language, and the Proem to Virgil's Third *Georgic*', *Classical Philology* 103: 150–74.

Medwin, T. (1824), *Conversations of Lord Byron*, London: Henry Colburn.

Mildorf, J. (2012), 'Second-Person Narration in Literary and Conversational Storytelling', *Storyworlds* 4: 75–98.

Miles, G. B. (1975), 'Georgics 3.209–294: Amor and Civilization', *California Studies in Classical Antiquity* 8: 177–97.

Miles, G. B. (1980), *Virgil's Georgics: A New Interpretation*, Berkeley: University of California Press.

Miller, J. F. (2009), *Apollo, Augustus and the Poets*, Cambridge: Cambridge University Press.

Milnes, T. (2004), 'Centre and Circumference: Shelley's Defence of Philosophy', *European Romantic Review* 15.1: 3–22.

Milnor, K. (2005), *Gender, Domesticity, and the Age of Augustus*, Oxford: Oxford University Press.

Mittsdörffer, W. (1938), 'Virgils Georgica und Theophrast', *Philologus* 93: 449–75.

Monreal, R. (2010), *Flora Neolatina: Die Hortorum libri VI von René Rapin S. J. und die Plantarum Libri VI von Abraham Cowley. Zwei lateinische Dichtungen des 17. Jahrhunderts*, Berlin and New York: De Gruyter.

Montfort, N. (2003), *Twisty Little Passages: An Approach to Interactive Fiction*, Cambridge, MA: MIT Press.

Moore, L. (2008), 'How', in *The Collected Stories*, 577–85, London: Faber & Faber (orig. 1985, *Self-Help*, New York: Vintage).

Morgan, L. (1999), *Patterns of Redemption in Virgil's Georgics*, Cambridge: Cambridge University Press.

Morrissette, B. (1965), 'Narrative "You" in Contemporary Literature', *Comparative Literature Studies* 2, no. 1: 1–24.

Morson, G. (1994), *Narrative and Freedom: The Shadows of Time*, New Haven, CT: Yale University Press

Moul, V. (2012), 'Horatian Odes in Abraham Cowley's *Plantarum Libri Sex* (1668)', in L. B. T. Houghton and G. Manuwald (eds), *Neo-Latin Poetry in the British Isles*, 87–104, London: Bristol Classical Press.

Moul, V. (2017), 'Didactic Poetry', in V. Moul (ed.), *A Guide to Neo-Latin Literature*, 180–99, Cambridge: Cambridge University Press.

Murgia, C. E. (1975), *Prolegomena to Servius 5: The Manuscripts*, Berkeley: University of California Press.

Murray, W. M. and Petsas, P. M. (1989), *Octavian's Campsite Memorial for the Actian War*, Philadelphia: American Philosophical Society.

Myers, K. S. (2018), 'Representations of Gardens in Roman Literature', in W. F. Jashemski, M. Gleason, K. Hartswick and A. Malek (eds), *Gardens of the Roman Empire*, 258–77, Cambridge: Cambridge University Press.

Mynors, R. A. B. (1969), *P. Vergili Maronis Opera*, Oxford: Oxford University Press.

Mynors, R. A. B. (1990), *Virgil. Georgics. Edited with a Commentary*, Oxford: Oxford University Press.

Nagel, R. (2004), 'Farming Poetry: Vita Sackville-West and Virgil's *Georgics*', *Classical and Modern Literature* 24: 1–22.

Nance, K. A. (1994), 'Self-Consuming Second-Person Fiction: José Emilio Pacheco's "Tarde de agosto" ("August Afternoon")', *Style* 28, no. 3: 366–77.

Nappa, C. (2003), 'Fire and Human Error in Vergil's Second *Georgic*', *American Journal of Philology* 124: 39–56.

Nappa, C. (2005), *Reading After Actium: Vergil's Georgics, Octavian, and Rome*, Ann Arbor: University of Michigan Press.

Nauta, R. R. (2006), 'Panegyric in Virgil's *Bucolics*', in M. Fantuzzi and T. Papanghelis (eds), *Brill's Companion to Greek and Latin Pastoral*, 301–32, Leiden: Brill.

Nelis, D. P. (1992), 'Demodocus and the song of Orpheus: (Ap. Rhod. *Arg.* I, 496–511)', *Museum Helveticum* 49: 153–70.

Nelis, D. P. (2004a), 'From didactic to epic: *Georgics* 2.458–3.48', in M. Gale (ed.), *Latin Epic and Didactic Poetry: Genre, Tradition and Individuality*, 73–107, Swansea: Classical Press of Wales.

Nelis, D. P. (2004b), '*Georgics* 2.458–542: Virgil, Aratus and Empedocles', *Dictynna* 1. Available online: http://dictynna.revues.org/161 (accessed: 2 July 2018).

Nelis, D. P. (2008), 'Caesar, the Circus and the Charioteer', in J. Nelis-Clément and J.-M. Roddaz (eds), *Le cirque romain et son image*, 497–520, Bordeaux: Ausonius.

Nelis, D. P. (2013), 'Past, Present and Future in Virgil's *Georgics*', in J. Farrell and D. P. Nelis (eds), *Augustan Poetry and the Roman Republic*, 244–62, Oxford: Oxford University Press.

Nelis, D. P. and Nelis-Clément, J. (2011), 'Vergil, *Georgics* 1.1–42 and the *pompa circensis*', *Dictynna* 8.

Nelson, S. (1998), *God and the Land: The Metaphysics of Farming in Hesiod and Vergil*, Oxford: Oxford University Press.

Nicholson, A. (1991), *Lord Byron: The Complete Miscellaneous Prose*, Oxford: Oxford University Press.

Nicolson, N. (1973), *Portrait of a Marriage*, London: Weidenfeld and Nicholson.

Noè, E. (2002), *Il Progetto di Columella: profilo sociale, economico, culturale*, Como: New Press.

Noè, E. (2003), 'Gerarchie sociali e alimentazione nel *De hortis* pliniano', *Rendiconti dell'Istituto Lombardo* 137: 233–49.

Norden, E. (1916), *P. Vergilius Maro: Aeneis Buch VI*, 2nd edn, Leipzig: Teubner.

Notopoulos, J. A. (1969), *The Platonism of Shelley*, New York: Octagon Books.

Obbink, D. (1994), 'A Quotation of the Derveni Papyrus in Philodemus' *On Piety*', *Cronache Ercolanesi* 24: 111–35.

Obbink, D. (1997), 'Cosmology as Initiation vs. the Critique of Orphic Mysteries', in A. Laks and G. Most (eds), *Studies on the Derveni Papyrus*, 39–54, Oxford: Oxford University Press.

Obbink, D. (ed.) (1995), *Philodemus and Poetry: Poetic Theory and Practice in Lucretius, Philodemus, and Horace*, Oxford: Oxford University Press.

Ogilvie, R. M. (1969), *The Romans and their Gods*, London: Chatto and Windus.

O'Hogan, C. (2018), 'Irish Versions of Virgil's *Eclogues* and *Georgics*', in S. Braund and Z. M. Torlone (eds), *Virgil and his Translators*, 399–411, Oxford: Oxford University Press.

Osgood, J. (2006), *Caesar's Legacy: Civil War and the Emergence of the Roman Empire*, Cambridge: Cambridge University Press.

Otis, B. (1964), *Virgil: A Study in Civilised Poetry*, Oxford: Oxford University Press.

Pandey, N. (2013), 'Caesar's Comet, the Julian Star, and the Invention of Augustus', *Transactions of the American Philological Association* 143: 405–49.

Papillon, T. L. (1882), *P. Vergili Maronis Opera*, Oxford: Clarendon Press.

Parker, D. (1997), 'Interpreting the Comedy Tradition to the *Comedy*', in A. A. Ianucci (ed.), *Dante: Contemporary Perspectives*, 240–58, Toronto: University of Toronto Press.

Parker, J. (2011–12), 'In Their Own Words: On Writing in Second Person', *Connotations* 21, nos 2–3: 165–74.

Parker, R. (1995), 'Early Orphism', in A. Powell (ed.), *The Greek World*, 483–510, London and New York: Routledge.

Parker, R. (2011), *On Greek Religion*, Ithaca, NY, and London: Cornell University Press.

Peirano, I. (2012), *The Rhetoric of the Roman Fake: Latin Pseudepigrapha in Context*, Cambridge: Cambridge University Press.

Penwill, J. (1996), 'The Ending of Sense: Death as Closure in Lucretius Book 6', *Ramus* 25: 146–69.

Perkell, C. G. (1981), 'On the Corycian farmer of Vergil's Fourth Georgic', *Transactions of the American Philological Association* 111: 167–77.

Perkell, C. G. (1989), *The Poet's Truth: A Study of the Poet in Virgil's Georgics*, Berkeley: University of California Press.

Perutelli, A. (1980), 'L'episodio di Aristeo nelle *Georgiche*. Struttura e tecnica narrativa', *Materiali e discussioni per l'analisi dei testi classici* 4: 59–76.

Perutelli, A. (1983), *Vergili Maronis Moretum*, Pisa: Giardini.

Petersen, J. H. (2010), *Die Erzählformen: Er, Ich, Du und andere Varianten*, Berlin: Erich Schmidt.

Petropoulos, J. C. B. (1994), *Heat and Lust: Hesiod's Midsummer Festival Scene Revisited*, Lanham, MD, and London: Rowman and Littlefield.

Phelan, J. (1994), 'Self-Help for Narratee and Narrative Audience: How "I" – and "You"? – Read "How"', *Style* 28, no. 3: 350–65.

Phelan, J. (1996), *Narrative as Rhetoric: Technique, Audiences, Ethics, Ideology*, Columbus: Ohio State University Press.

Phillips, C. R. (1997), 'Cato the Elder', in M. Kiley (ed.), *Prayer from Alexander to Constantine: A Critical Anthology*, 128–32, London: Routledge.

Pieri, B. (2011), *Intacti saltus. Studi sul III libro delle Georgiche*, Bologna: Pàtron Editore.

Pioffet, M.-C. (2007), 'Gaulois et Souriquois a travers les mailles de la généalogie lescarbotienne', in P. Guillaume and L. Turgeon (eds), *Regards croisés sur le Canada et la France: Voyages et relations du XVIe Au XXe siècle*, 38–62, Paris: Édition du CTHS; Laval (Canada): Presses de l'Université Laval.

Pioffet, M.-C. and Lachance, I. (eds) (2014), *Marc Lescarbot: Poésies et opuscules sur la Nouvelle-France*, Montreal: Nota bene.

Plumwood, V. (1993), *Feminism and the Mastery of Nature*, London: Routledge.

Pobjoy, M. (1998), 'Dido on the Tragic Stage: An Invitation to the Theatre of Carthage', in M. Burden (ed.), *A Woman Scorn'd: Responses to the Dido Myth*, 41–64, London: Faber & Faber.

Polanyi, K. (1944), *The Great Transformation*, 10th edn 2013, New York: Farrar & Rinehart.

Pollard, E. A. (2009), 'Pliny's Natural History and the Flavian *Templum Pacis*: Botanical Imperialism in First-Century Rome', *Journal of World History* 20: 309–38.

Pollini, J. (1990), 'Man or God: Divine Assimilation and Imitation in the Late Republic and Early Principate', in K. A. Raaflaub and M. Toher (eds), *Between Republic and Empire: Interpretations of Augustus and his Principate*, 334–63, Berkeley and Los Angeles: University of California Press.

Pomeroy, E. W. (1982), 'Within Living Memory: Vita Sackville-West's Poems of Land and Garden', *Twentieth Century Literature* 28: 269–89.

Powell, A. (2008), *Virgil the Partisan: A Study in the Re-integration of Classics*, Swansea: Classical Press of Wales.

Power, H. (2014), 'Georgics, Reception of', in R. F. Thomas and J. M. Ziolkowski (eds), *The Virgil Encyclopedia*, 1072–4, Chichester and Malden, MA: Wiley-Blackwell.

Prag, J. R. W. (2010), 'Tyrannizing Sicily: the Despots who cried "Carthage!"', in A. Turner, K. O. Chong-Gossard and F. Vervaet (eds), *Private and Public Lies: The Discourse of Despotism and Deceit in the Graeco-Roman World*, 51–71, Leiden: Brill.

Prioux, É. (2013), 'Columelle et le *genus floridum*: images programmatiques et parodie dans le livre X du *De Re Rustica*', *Dictynna* 10: 2–25.

Pucci, J. (1998), *The Full-Knowing Reader: Allusion and the Power of the Reader in the Western Literary Tradition*, New Haven, CT: Yale University Press.

Punday, D. (2012), 'Narration, Intrigue, and Reader Positioning in Electronic Narratives', *Storyworlds* 4: 25–47.

Purcell, N. (1996), 'The Roman Garden as a Domestic Building', in I. Barton (ed.), *Roman Domestic Buildings*, 121–51, Exeter: University of Exeter Press.

Putnam, M. C. J. (1979), *Virgil's Poem of the Earth: Studies in the Georgics*, Princeton, NJ: Princeton University Press.

Putnam, M. C. J. (2008), 'Italian Virgil and the Idea of Rome', in K. Volk (ed.), *Vergil's Georgics: Oxford Readings in Classical Studies*, 138–60, Oxford: Oxford University Press. (orig. 1975, in J. Mellaart and L. L. Orlin (eds), *Janus. Essays in Ancient and Modern Studies*, 171–99, Ann Arbor: University of Michigan Press).

Pycroft, J. (1846), *Valpy's Virgil Improved. The Bucolics, Georgics, and Æneid; with Marginal References and Notes*, London: Longman, Brown, Green, and Longmans.

Quint, D. (1993), *Epic and Empire: Politics and Generic Form from Virgil to Milton*, Princeton, NJ: Princeton University Press.

Raitt, S. (1993), *Vita and Virginia: The Work and Friendship of V. Sackville-West and Virginia Woolf*, Oxford: Clarendon Press.

Rand, E. K. (1916), 'Is Donatus' Commentary on Virgil Lost?', *Classical Quarterly* 10: 158–64.

Ravinthiran, V. (2011), 'Dante and Shelley's *Terza Rima*', *Essays in Criticism* 61, no. 2: 155–72.

Reay, B. (2003), 'Some Addressees of Virgil's *Georgics* and Their Audience', *Vergilius* 49: 17–41.

Reiman, D. H. (ed.) (1986), *Shelley and His Circle, 1773–1822*, vols 7 and 8, Cambridge, MA: Harvard University Press.

Reitan, R. (2011), 'Theorizing Second-Person Narratives: A Backwater Project?', in P. Krogh Hansen, S. Iversen, H. Skov Nielsen and R. Reitan (eds), *Strange Voices in Narrative Fiction*, 147–74, Berlin and New York: De Gruyter.

Richardson, B. (1991), 'The Poetics and Politics of Second Person Narrative', *Genre* 24: 309–30.

Richardson, B. (1994), 'I Etcetera: On the Poetics and Ideology of Multipersoned Narratives', *Style* 28, no. 3: 312–28.

Richardson, B. (2006), *Unnatural Voices: Extreme Narration in Modern and Contemporary Fiction*, Columbus: Ohio State University Press.

Richter, W. (1957), *Vergil, Georgica herausgegeben und erklärt*, Munich: M. Hueber.

Riedweg, C. (1995), 'Orphisches bei Empedokles', *Antike und Abendland* 41: 34–59.

Riedweg, C. (2005), *Pythagoras: His Life, Teaching, and Influence*, trans. S. Rendall, Ithaca, NY and London: Cornell University Press.

Riggsby, A. (2007), 'Guides to the wor(l)d', in J. König and T. Whitmarsh (eds), *Ordering Knowledge in the Roman Empire*, 88–107, Cambridge: Cambridge University Press.

Rimell, V. (2015), *The Closure of Space in Roman Poetics*, Cambridge: Cambridge University Press.

Riposati, B. (1939), *M. Terenti Varronis De vita populi Romani*, Milan: Pubblicazioni dell'Università Cattolica del S. Cuore 33.

Roberts, H. (1997), *Shelley and the Chaos of History: A New Politics of Poetry*, University Park: Pennsylvania State University Press.

Roberts, M. (1989), *The Jeweled Style: Poetry and Poetics in Late Antiquity*, Ithaca, NY: Cornell University Press.

Robinson, J. C. (2006), 'The translator', in T. Morton (ed.), *The Cambridge Companion to Shelley*, 104–22, Cambridge: Cambridge University Press.

Rodgers, R. H. (2010), *Columellae Res Rustica*, Oxford: Oxford University Press.

Rodríguez, M. R. (2005), *Orfeo y el orfismo en la poesía de Empédocles: influencias y paralelismos*, Colección de Estudios, 98, Madrid: Ediciones de la Universidad Autónoma de Madrid (UAM Ediciones).

Roller, M. (2013), 'On the Intersignification of Monuments in Augustan Rome', *American Journal of Philology* 134: 119–31.

Rose, C. B. (2005), 'The Parthians in Augustan Rome', *American Journal of Archaeology* 109: 21–75.

Ross, D. O. (1975), 'The *Culex* and *Moretum* as Post-Augustan Literary Parodies', *Harvard Studies in Classical Philology* 79: 235–63.

Ross, D. O. (1987), *Virgil's Elements: Physics and Poetry in the Georgics*, Princeton, NJ: Princeton University Press.

Ruden, S. (trans.) (2008), *The Aeneid, Vergil*, New Haven and London: Yale University Press.

Rüpke, J. (2007), *Religion of the Romans*, Cambridge: Cambridge University Press.

Russo, A. (2007), *Quinto Ennio: Le Opere Minori*, Pisa: ETS.

Rutherford, R. (2008), 'Authorial rhetoric in Virgil's *Georgics*', in K. Volk (ed.), *Vergil's Georgics: Oxford Readings in Classical Studies*, 81–93, Oxford: Oxford University Press (orig. 1995, in D. Innes, H. Hine and C. Pelling (eds), *Ethics and Rhetoric: Classical Essays for Donald Russell on his Seventy-Fifth Birthday*, 19–29, Oxford: Oxford University Press).

Ryan, M.-L. (2005), 'Digital Narrative: Learning to Think With the Medium', in J. Phelan and P. Rabinowitz (eds), *A Companion to Narrative Theory*, 515–28, Malden, MA: Blackwell.

Sackville-West, V. (1919), *Heritage*, New York: George H. Doran Company.

Sackville-West, V. (1926), *The Land*, London: William Heinemann.

Saint-Denis, E. de (1971), 'Columelle, miroire de Virgile', in H. Bardon and R. Verdière (eds), *Vergiliana. Recherches sur Virgile*, 328–43, Leiden: Brill.

Salter, A. (2014), *What is Your Quest? From Adventure Games to Interactive Books*, Iowa City: University of Iowa Press.

Samuels, L. (1996), 'Introduction to *Poetry and the Problem of Beauty*', in L. Samuels (ed.), *Poetry and the Problem of Beauty*, *Modern Languages Studies* 27, no. 2: 1–7.

Sargeaunt, J. (1901), *Virgil: Georgics Book I*, Edinburgh: Blackwood.

Schäfer, T. (2013), 'Ciclo di rilievi Medinaceli', in E. La Rocca (ed.), *Augusto* (exhibition catalogue), 321–3, Milan: Electa.

Scheid, J. (2005), 'Augustus and Roman Religion: Continuity, Conservatism, and Innovation', in K. Galinsky (ed.), *The Cambridge Companion to the Age of Augustus*, 175–93, Cambridge: Cambridge University Press.

Scheidel, W. (1990), '*Agricola, colonus, cultor, rusticus*: Beobachtungen zum rechtlichen und sozialen Status der "Landwirte" in Columella's Schrift *de re rustica*', *Maia* 42: 257–65.

Schiesaro, A. (1993), 'Il destinatario discreto: funzioni didascaliche e progetto culturale nelle *Georgiche*', *Materiali e discussioni per l'analisi dei testi classici* 31: 129–47.

Schiesaro, A. (1997), 'The Boundaries of Knowledge in Virgil's *Georgics*', in T. Habinek and A. Schiesaro (eds), *The Roman Cultural Revolution*, 63–89, Cambridge: Cambridge University Press.

Schmid, W. (1983), *Vergil–Probleme*, Göppinger akademische Beiträge 120, Göppingen: Kümmerle.

Schmidt, A.-M. (1970), *La poésie scientifique en France au XVIe siècle*, Lausanne: Rencontre (reprint of original, 1938, Lausanne: Rencontre.)

Schneider, R. M. (1986), *Bunte Barbaren: Orientalenstatuen aus farbigem Marmor in der römischen Repräsentationskunst*, Worms: Wernersche Verlagsgesellschaft.

Schwindt, J. P. (2013), 'Der Sound der Macht. Zur onomatopoetischen Konstruktion des Mythos im Zeitalter des Augustus', in M. Labate and G. Rosati (eds), *La costruzione del mito augusteo*, 69–87, Heidelberg: Winter.

Seager, R. (1980), '*Neu sinas Medos equitare inultos*: Horace, the Parthians, and Augustan Foreign Policy', *Athenaeum* 58: 103–18.

Segal, C. P. (1989), *Orpheus: The Myth of the Poet*, Baltimore, MD: Johns Hopkins University Press.

Segal, C. P. (1997), *Dionysiac Poetics and Euripides' Bacchae*, Princeton, NJ: Princeton University Press.

Shaw, P. (2007), *The Sublime* (The New Critical Idiom), London: Routledge.

Shelley, P. B. (1840), *Essays, Letters from Abroad, Translations and Fragments, by Percy Bysshe Shelley. Edited by Mrs. Shelley. Volume 1*, London: Edward Moxon.

Sheridan, J. E. (1856), *Publii Virgilii Maronis Georgica. The Georgics of Publius Virgilius Maro; with references and Engl. notes*, London: Samuel J. Machen.

Shipham, F. P. (1895), *Vergil: Georgics I, II: a close translation*, London: University Tutorial Press.

Sider, D. (ed.) (1997), *The Epigrams of Philodemos: Introduction, Text, and Commentary*, New York and Oxford: Oxford University Press.

Sistakou, E. (2014), 'Dichtung und Lehre', in A. Rengakos and B. Zimmermann (eds), *Handbuch der griechischen Literatur der Antike*. Zweiter Band: *Die Literatur der klassischen und hellenistischen Zeit*, 115–40, Munich: Beck.

Skutsch, O. (1968), *Studia Enniana*, London: Athlone.

Skutsch, O. (1985), *The Annals of Q. Ennius*, Oxford: Clarendon Press.

Slater, W. J. (1969), 'Futures in Pindar', *Classical Quarterly* 19: 86–94.

Solomon, S. and Reinheimer, E. (2012), *The Intelligent Gardener: Growing Nutrient Dense Food*, Gabriola Island, BC: New Society Publishers.

Spawforth, A. J. S. (1994), 'Symbol of Unity? The Persian-Wars Tradition in the Roman Empire', in S. Hornblower (ed.), *Greek Historiography*, 233–47, Oxford: Clarendon Press.

Spawforth, A. J. S. (2012), *Greece and the Augustan Cultural Revolution*, Cambridge: Cambridge University Press.

Spencer, D. (2010), *Roman Landscape: Culture and Identity*, Cambridge: Cambridge University Press.

Spurr, M. S. (2008), 'Agriculture and the *Georgics*', in K. Volk (ed.), *Oxford Readings in Classical Studies: Vergil's Georgics*, 14–42, Oxford: Oxford University Press (orig. 1986, *Greece and Rome* 33: 164–87).

Stevens, B. (2005), 'Review of J. Lembke (trans.), *Virgil's Georgics: A New Verse Translation*', *Bryn Mawr Classical Review* 2005.08.06. Available online: http://bmcr.brynmawr.edu/2005/2005-08-06.html (accessed 23 September 2018).

Stöckinger, M. (2016), *Vergils Gaben: Materialität, Reziprozität und Poetik in den* Eklogen *und der* Aeneis, Heidelberg: Winter.

Stok, F. (2012), 'Commenting on Virgil, from Aelius Donatus to Servius', *Dead Sea Discoveries* 19: 464–84.

Tally Jr, R. T. (2012), *Spatiality* (The New Critical Idiom), London: Routledge.

Tandy, D. (1985), 'Vergil, *Georgics* 1.42: The Immanence of Octavian', *Vergilius* 31: 54–7.

Tarrant, R. J. (1992), 'Nights at the *Copa*: Observations on Language and Date', *Harvard Studies in Classical Philology* 94: 331–47.

Thibodeau, P. (2001), 'The Old Man in His Garden (Verg. *Georg.* 4.116–48)', *Materiali e discussioni per l'analisi dei testi classici* 47: 175–95.

Thibodeau, P. (2011), *Playing the Farmer: Representations of Rural Life in Vergil's Georgics*, Berkeley: University of California Press.

Thierry, É. (2001), *Marc Lescarbot (vers 1570–1641): Un homme de plume au service de la Nouvelle-France*, Paris: Champion.

Thierry, É. (2004), 'Champlain and Lescarbot: An Impossible Friendship', in R. Litalien and D. Vaugeois (eds), *Champlain: The Birth of French America*, 121–34, Montreal: McGill-Queen's University Press.

Thomas, R. F. (1982), *Lands and Peoples in Roman Poetry: The Ethnographical Tradition*, Cambridge: Cambridge Philological Society.

Thomas, R. F. (1983), 'Callimachus, the Victoria Berenices, and Roman Poetry', *Classical Quarterly* 33: 92–113 (reprinted in 2008, in K. Volk (ed.), *Oxford Readings in Classical Studies: Vergil's Georgics*, 189–224, Oxford: Oxford University Press).

Thomas, R. F. (1985), 'From Recusatio to Commitment: The Evolution of the Virgilian Programme', *Papers of the Liverpool Latin Seminar* 5: 61–73.

Thomas, R. F. (1986), 'Virgil's *Georgics* and the Art of Reference', *Harvard Studies in Classical Philology* 90: 171–98.

Thomas, R. F. (1987), 'Prose into Poetry: Tradition and Meaning in Virgil's *Georgics*', *Harvard Studies in Classical Philology* 91: 229–60 (reprinted in 2008, in K. Volk (ed.), *Oxford Readings in Classical Studies: Vergil's Georgics*, 43–80, Oxford: Oxford University Press).

Thomas, R. F. (1988), *Virgil. Georgics. Introduction, Text, and Commentary*, 2 vols, Cambridge: Cambridge University Press.

Thomas, R. F. (1992), 'The Old Man Revisited: Memory, Reference and Genre in Virg., *Geo.* 4.116–48', *Materiali e discussioni per l'analisi dei testi classici* 29: 35–70.

Thomas, R. F. (1993), 'Callimachus Back in Rome', in M. A. Harder, R. F. Regtuit and G. C. Wakker (eds), *Callimachus: Hellenistica Groningana*, vol. 1, 197–225, Groningen: Egbert Forsten.

Thomas, R. F. (1995), '*Vestigia Ruris*: Urbane Rusticity in Virgil's *Georgics*', *Harvard Studies in Classical Philology* 97: 197–214.

Thomas, R. F. (2001), 'The *Georgics* of Resistance: From Virgil to Heaney', *Vergilius* 47: 117–47.

Thomas, R. F. (2004), '"Stuck in the Middle with You": Virgilian Middles', in S. Kyriakidis and F. De Martino (eds), *Middles in Latin Poetry*, 123–50, Bari: Levante.

Thomas, R. F. (2009), *Virgil and the Augustan Reception*, Cambridge: Cambridge University Press.

Thomson, J. (1726–30), *The Seasons*, London.

Thumiger, C. (2006), 'Animal World, Animal Representation, and the "Hunting-Model": Between Literal and Figurative in Euripides' *Bacchae*', *Phoenix* 60, no. 3–4: 191–210.

Toohey, P. (1996), *Epic Lessons*, London and New York: Routledge.

Trépanier, S. (2007), 'The Didactic Plot of Lucretius, *De rerum natura* and its Empedoclean Models', in R. Sorabji and R. W. Sharples (eds), *Greek and Roman Philosophy 100 BC–200 AD*, vol. 1, 243–82, London: Institute of Classical Studies.

Trollope, A. (1999 (1864–5)), *Can You Forgive Her?*, Oxford: Oxford University Press.

Tsouna, V. (2007), *The Ethics of Philodemus*, Oxford: Oxford University Press.

Turcan, R. (2000), *The Gods of Ancient Rome*, Edinburgh: Edinburgh University Press.

Turner, P. (1959), 'Shelley and Lucretius', *Review of English Studies* 10: 269–82.

Tutrone, F. (2018), 'Granting Epicurean Wisdom at Rome: Exchange and Reciprocity in Lucretius' Didactics (*DRN* 1.921–950)', *Harvard Studies in Classical Philology* 109: 1–63.

Updike, J. (1979 (1972)), 'How to Love America and Leave it at the Same Time', in *Problems and Other Stories*, 40–6, New York: Random House (orig., *The New Yorker*, 19 August 1972).

Usener, H. (ed.) (1887), *Epicurea*, Leipzig: Teubner.

Usher, P. J. (2012), 'Du viatique à l'épique: L'epyllion américain de Marc Lescarbot', *Arborescences* 2. Available online: http://id.erudit.org/iderudit/1009270ar (accessed 2 July 2018).

Usher, P. J. (2013), *Epic Arts in Renaissance France*, Oxford: Oxford University Press.

Usher, P. J. and Fernbach, I. (eds) (2012), *Virgilian Identities in the French Renaissance*, Cambridge: Cambridge University Press.

Vernant J. P. (1983 (1965)), 'Hesiod's Myth of the Races: An Essay in Structural Analysis', in *Myth and Thought among the Greeks*, 25–52, London: Routledge (translation of French original, *Mythe et Pensée chez les Grecs*, Paris).

Verstraete, B. (2014), 'Translation Intertextualities: A Literary-Critical Comparison of Cecil Day Lewis's and Ida Gerhardt's Translations of Vergil's *Georgics* in the Light of the 20th Century's Turn to Modernity in the Translation of the Greek and Roman Classics', *Canadian Journal of Netherlandic Studies/Revue canadienne d'études néerlandaises* 35: 39–54.

Vogel, E. (2011), '"I don't know why I joke. I hurt": Pain, Humor, and Second-Person Narration in Lorrie Moore's "How to Be an Other Woman"', *Studies in American Humor*, n.s., 3, no. 24: 71–82.

Volk, K. (2002), *The Poetics of Latin Didactic: Lucretius, Vergil, Ovid, Manilius*, Oxford: Oxford University Press.

Volk, K. (2008), *Vergil's Georgics: Oxford Readings in Classical Studies*, Oxford: Oxford University Press.

Von Reeden, S. (2009), 'Economy and Trade', in G. Boys-Stones et al. (eds), *The Oxford Handbook of Hellenic Studies*, 211–25, Oxford: Oxford University Press.

von Stackelberg, K. (2009), *The Roman Garden*, London and New York: Routledge.

Wagenvoort, H. (1956), 'Virgil's Fourth Eclogue and the *sidus Julium*', in *Studies in Roman Literature, Culture and Religion*, 1–29, Leiden: Brill.

Wake, P. (2016), 'Life and Death in the Second Person: Identification, Empathy, and Antipathy in the Adventure Gamebook', *Narrative* 24: 190–210.

Warde-Fowler, W. (1911), *The Religious Experience of the Roman People*, London: Macmillan and Co.

Watkins, C. (1995), *How to Kill a Dragon: Aspects of Indo-European Poetics*, Oxford: Oxford University Press.

Watson, L. (2003), *A Commentary on Horace's Epodes*, Oxford: Oxford University Press.

Watson, S. R. (1972), *V. Sackville-West*, New York: Twayne.

Waugh Young, A. and Masom, W. F. (1895), *Vergil: Georgics Books I and II*, London: W. B. Clive.

Webb, T. (1976), *The Violet in the Crucible: Shelley and Translation*, Oxford: Oxford University Press.

Webb, T. (2002), 'The Unascended Heaven: Negatives in *Prometheus Unbound*', in D. H. Reiman and N. Fraistat (eds), *Shelley's Poetry and Prose*, 694–711, New York: Norton.

Weber, C. (2002), 'The Dionysus in Aeneas', *Classical Philology* 97: 322–43.

Weinold, H. (1959), *Die dichterischen Quellen des L. Iunius Columella in seinem Werk De re rustica*, PhD diss., University of Munich.

Weinstock S. (1971), *Divus Julius*, Oxford: Clarendon Press.

Welch, T. S. (2005), *The Elegiac Cityscape: Propertius and the Meaning of Roman Monuments*, Columbus: Ohio State University Press.

Wellek, R. (1978), 'The New Criticism: Pro and Contra', *Critical Inquiry* 4: 611–24.

Wells, R. (trans.) (1982), *Virgil. The Georgics*, Manchester: Carcanet New Press.

West, M. L. (1978), *Hesiod: Works and Days*, Oxford: Oxford University Press.

West, M. L. (1983), *The Orphic Poems*, Oxford: Oxford University Press.

Westra, H. (2015), 'Farewell to Canada: Marc Lescarbot's A-dieu à La Nouvelle-France (1607). Essay & Translation', *Numéro Cinq* (December). Available online: http://numerocinqmagazine.com/2015/12/11/farewell-to-canada-marc-lescarbots-a-dieu-a-la-nouvelle-france-1607-essay-translation-haijo-westra/ (accessed 2 July 2018).

Whitcomb, K. (2018), 'Vergil, Octavian and Erigone: Admiration and Admonition in the Proem to *Georgics* 1', *Classical Journal* 113: 411–26.

White, P. (1993), *Promised Verse: Poets in the Society of Augustan Rome*, Cambridge, MA: Harvard University Press.

Wiest, U. (1993), '"The refined, though whimsical pleasure": Die You-Erzählsituation', *Arbeiten aus Anglistik und Amerikanistik* 18, no. 1: 75–90.

Wigodsky, M. (1995), 'The Alleged Impossibility of Philosophical Poetry', in D. Obbink (ed.), *Philodemus and Poetry: Poetic Theory and Practice in Lucretius, Philodemus, and Horace*, 58–68, Oxford: Oxford University Press.

Wilkins, H. M. (1874), *The Georgics of Vergil with a running analysis, Engl. notes and index*, London: Longmans, Green, and co.

Wilkinson, L. P. (1969), *The Georgics of Virgil: A Critical Survey*, Cambridge: Cambridge University Press.

Wilkinson, L. P. (1970), 'Pindar and the Proem to the Third Georgic', in W. Wimmel (ed.), *Forschungen zur römischen Literatur, Festschrift zum 60. Geburtstag von Karl Büchner*, 286–90, Wiesbaden: F. Steiner (reprinted in 2008, in K. Volk (ed.), *Oxford Readings in Classical Studies: Vergil's Georgics*, 182–8, Oxford: Oxford University Press).

Williams, R. D. (1966–7), 'Servius, Commentator and Guide', *Proceedings of the Virgil Society* 6: 50–6.

Williams, S. (2004), *Wagner and the Romantic Hero*, Cambridge: Cambridge University Press.

Wilson, D. B. (1954), 'The Discovery of Nature in the Work of Jacques Peletier Du Mans', *Bibliothèque d'Humanisme et Renaissance* 16, no. 3: 298–311.

Wilson-Okamura, D. S. (2010), *Virgil in the Renaissance*, Cambridge: Cambridge University Press.

Winkler, J. J. (1985), *Auctor and Actor: A Narratological Reading of Apuleius's The Golden Ass*, Berkeley: University of California Press.

Wiseman, T. P. (2015), *The Roman Audience: Classical Literature as Social History*, Oxford: Oxford University Press.

Woolf, V. (1928), *Orlando*, London. L. & V.

Wright, J. R. G. (1983), 'Virgil's Pastoral Programme: Theocritus, Callimachus and *Eclogue* 1', *Proceedings of the Cambridge Philological Society* 29: 107–60.

Wu, D. (1990), *A Chronological Annotated Edition of Wordsworth's Poetry and Prose, 1785–1790*, PhD thesis, University of Oxford.

Yeats, W. B. (1961), *Essays and Introductions*, London and Basingstoke: Macmillan.

Zachos, K. (2003), 'The *tropaeum* of Augustus in Nikopolis', *Journal of Roman Archaeology* 16: 64–92.

Zachos, K. (2007), 'The Sculptures of the Altar on the Monument of Octavian Augustus at Nicopolis: A First Approach', *Nicopolis B*: 411–34.

Zanker, P. (1988), *The Power of Images in the Age of Augustus*, trans. A. Saphiro, Ann Arbor: University of Michigan Press.

Ziolkowski, J. and Putnam, M. C. J. (eds) (2008), *The Virgilian Tradition: The First Fifteen Hundred Years*, New Haven, CT: Yale University Press.

Ziolkowski, T. (1993), *Virgil and the Moderns*, Princeton, NJ: Princeton University Press.

INDEX OF PASSAGES

INDEX